Advanced Praise for *Philosophical Scaffolding for the Construction of Critical Democratic Education*

"With passion, clarity, and a few [...], Richard A. Brosio presents a bracing s[...] and contemporary educational thought. He is at on[...] yet appropriately critical of his sources: great and challenging thinkers—from Plato to Freire and beyond—who have shaped our understanding of teaching and learning. This book richly enlightens by stimulating both intellectual and moral reflection on the way we see our schools. It is a valuable resource for students of philosophy and foundations of education, critical pedagogy, the history of education, and related fields. I recommend it for anyone who seeks a broader understanding of schooling and society and is unafraid to question some of our most basic assumptions."

David Blacker, Assistant Professor,
School of Education, University of Delaware

"Building upon the insights of his *A Radical Democratic Critique of Capitalist Education*, Richard A. Brosio's marvelous discussion of important theorists and theories that have influenced education is invaluable for students and teachers. Writing in an engaging personal style that explains complex theoretical issues clearly, Brosio invites the reader to take part in historic dialogues in philosophy of education. Although he highlights influential thinkers, he never loses sight of the fact that working people have struggled against class, gender, and racial barriers to extend the blessings of democracy and education to all. He affirms the genuine progressive ideals of the Enlightenment in an analysis that is powerful and moving. Resting upon a foundation of Deweyan, existentialist, Freirean, and Marxist insights, his fair critique of postmodern and identity politics links class, gender, and race and reminds us that all identities ultimately reside within a capitalist political/economic context. He connects these to an ecological awareness of Mother Earth. This is an exceptional and vital work that will provoke strong and passionate reactions—as it should. It forces us to rethink many of our cherished notions about education and society."

John Marciano,
State University of New York, College at Cortland

Philosophical Scaffolding for the Construction of Critical Democratic Education

Studies in the
Postmodern Theory of Education

Joe L. Kincheloe and Shirley R. Steinberg
General Editors

Vol. 75

PETER LANG
New York • Washington, D.C./Baltimore • Boston • Bern
Frankfurt am Main • Berlin • Brussels • Vienna • Oxford

Richard A. Brosio

Philosophical Scaffolding for the Construction of Critical Democratic Education

PETER LANG
New York • Washington, D.C./Baltimore • Boston • Bern
Frankfurt am Main • Berlin • Brussels • Vienna • Oxford

Library of Congress Cataloging-in-Publication Data

Brosio, Richard A.
Philosophical scaffolding for the construction of critical
democratic education / Richard A. Brosio.
p. cm. — (Counterpoints; vol. 75)
Includes bibliographical references and index.
1. Education—Philosophy. 2. Critical theory. 3. Critical pedagogy.
4. Postmodernism and education. 5. Progressive education. I. Title.
II. Series: Counterpoints (New York, N.Y.); vol. 75.
LB14.7.B76 370.11′5—dc21 98-30632
ISBN 0-8204-3939-8
ISSN 1058-1634

Die Deutsche Bibliothek-CIP-Einheitsaufnahme

Brosio, Richard A.:
Philosophical scaffolding for the construction of critical
democratic education / Richard A. Brosio.
–New York; Washington, D.C./Baltimore; Boston; Bern;
Frankfurt am Main; Berlin; Brussels; Vienna; Oxford: Lang.
(Counterpoints; Vol. 75)
ISBN 0-8204-3939-8

Cover photograph by David K. Francis
Cover design by Nona Reuter

The paper in this book meets the guidelines for permanence and durability
of the Committee on Production Guidelines for Book Longevity
of the Council of Library Resources.

© 2000 Peter Lang Publishing, Inc., New York

Printed in the United States of America

Dedication

To all the education students I have had the good fortune to interact with as they shared my interest in the kind of philosophy that is translatable into liberatory, sober, and responsible plans for action in schools and society. This book is also dedicated to future students and teachers who may find the arguments in it useful for the construction of an authentic democracy and the education-schooling necessary to support it.

Acknowledgments

Martha (née Risberg) Brosio's love, support, intelligence, editorial and technical abilities, hard work, humor, and charm were indispensable to the construction of this work! My friend and comrade, John Marciano's knowledge and wisdom about the issues in this book—including pedagogical considerations—were invaluable. He worked on the scaffold from the beginning of the job. My social foundations of education student Stacy Archer Allen provided helpful and necessary advice from the perspective of a future teacher. Rebecca Martusewicz helped me work through the crucially important chapter seven, especially with regard to feminist philosophy. Professor Emeritus G. Max Wingo was my philosophy of education teacher at the University of Michigan and the director of my doctoral studies. His work and person have always influenced me; our correspondence about this book was especially helpful and pleasurable. Joe Kincheloe and Shirley Steinberg invited me to write this book. They encouraged me to construct the work according to my ideas and my long experience as a philosophy of education teacher-scholar. Chris Myers, the managing director, was supportive throughout this project. He, the production manager Lisa Dillon, and others at Peter Lang contributed to making my experience as an author an enriching one. *Grazie a tutti!*

Table of Contents

Preface

Philosophical Scaffolding for the Construction of Critical Democratic Education may seem daunting to some, but if it is read and studied carefully you will find it understandable. You can enrich your understanding of my work by discussing what has been studied with others. It is my intention to provide a philosophy of education book that is meaningful to those who are interested in education for democratic empowerment, social justice, respect for diversity, and the possibilities for a more "caring" school and society. My book is designed as an invitation to a holistic educational experience for the reader. You are encouraged to read through the entire work including the endnotes and the afterword. It may be approached in a different way by those individuals or members of a course of study who have criteria that suggests another strategy. I offer you my book in the belief that philosophy and philosophy of education are too important to be *done* solely by subject matter specialists. In a society that thinks of itself as democratic, philosophy and philosophy of education must be engaged in by the whole citizenry.

I make an honest attempt to use gender neutral language throughout this book. Various ways are used to accomplish this important task, e.g., using the feminine or masculine to represent us all, recognizing both genders through the use of her/his, s/he, etc., or employing the Latin term *sic* in order to indicate that a word or usage is incorrect. *Sic* appears in certain direct quotes when the quoted writer is not sensitive to gender fairness.

I offer many direct quotes as part of a cognitive map with signposts and directions for the reader to use for further study. Mike Rose wrote about his good teachers and what their courses provided him: "It was a time during which I absorbed an awful lot of information: long lists of titles, images from impressionist painters . . . snippets of philosophy, and names that read . . . [e.g.,] Goethe, Nietzsche, Kierkegaard. Now this . . . [may not yet be] the stuff of deep understanding. But it was an introduction . . . a Baedeker [guidebook for travelers] to a vocabulary of ideas. . . . With hindsight I realize how layered and important that knowledge was."[1]

Philosophical Scaffolding for the Construction of Critical Democratic Education goes significantly beyond snippets. It can serve as a Baedeker in the sense of Rose's expression. The copious use of direct quotes and the supportive endnotes is not an exercise in name-dropping. They are included so the reader can deal with the various contributors' arguments in their own words. Philosophical discourse is characterized and even driven by argumentation. The reader can benefit from experiencing some representative arguments that have developed around certain key, historical, philosophical issues about schools, education, and society. In lieu of including various excerpts from philosophers' work at chapters' or book's end, their voices are integrated into the narrative of my arguments and theses. The careful reader can easily discern what my positions (in the broadest sense) are on the philosophical issues dealing with education. Far from being a pedantic exercise, the generous stitching of references throughout the book is intended as a heuristic tool to encourage the reader to inquire deeper, more holistically, and further.

You are advised to read carefully so that new words/terms do not unduly prevent you from understanding the gist of what has been written. Considering these novelties within sentence, paragraph, and page contexts will be helpful. I suggest that you consult a good dictionary while studying this work. The glossary featured at this book's end is intended to be of further assistance. The special words/terms which are used are not intended as in-house jargon but as valuable tools for those who wish to better understand philosophical discourse as it affects education, and to facilitate your ability to join the conversation.

The **Suggested Tasks for the Reader** that are found throughout the text are included as a form of study guide and/or possible assessment design. The reader's written or verbal responses to these tasks should not preclude addressing self-constructed tasks. The tasks that are included are designed to elicit various responses from a wide range of readers, ones that they construct from their own readings and interpretations of the philosophical discourses. Although they are open-ended instead of "correct answer" oriented, one's interpretative responses should demonstrate some knowledge of what has been presented in the various chapters. This does not mean that the responses should be in agreement with the various thinkers represented.

The leitmotif of *Philosophical Scaffolding for the Construction of Critical Democratic Education* is the need for broad participation in deciding which kinds of epistemologies, meanings, and interpretations are more justifiable than others, especially with reference to the construction of schools and societies that are more democratic and equitable. Which kinds of knowledge claims can be made that have the possibility of being seriously considered in a very diverse society and world? John Dewey asked: What is warranted for us to assert without relying on faith-based transcendental certainties? He argued that given the human tools at our disposal, the quest for certainty has been a futile one. Bertrand Russell argued: We must not be paralyzed into inactivity just because we cannot be absolutely certain that we are correct and/or right.

Note

1   Mike Rose, *Lives on the Boundary* (New York: Penguin Books, 1989), 36.

Chapter One

Introduction: Blueprint, Scaffolding, and Main Construction

Prologue

The ideas quoted in this opening have influenced my thinking. Their inclusion serves to set the tone for this work. I never knew Mills personally; Entwistle has been a valued colleague; Wingo was my doctoral studies mentor at the University of Michigan. His work provides much of the scaffolding for this book.

C. Wright Mills made an important distinction between a *model* and a *theory.* "A *model* is a more or less systematic inventory of the elements to which we must pay attention if we are to understand something. It is not true or false; it is useful and adequate to varying degrees. A *theory,* in contrast, is a statement which can be proved true or false, about the causal weight and the relations of the elements of the model."[1]

Harold Entwistle forwarded the following thesis: "The job of theory is to evoke judgement rather than rote obedience. The application of theory to practice means bringing critical intelligence to bear on practical tasks rather than merely implementing good advice. . . . That is, some initiative is required from the practitioner in discovering the pertinence of theory to his or her own practical situation."[2] Entwistle went on to make an analogy between what theory can do for educational practice and the role of liberal education vis-à-vis life itself. In Entwistle's view, "the point of a liberal education is not that one arrives at a [particular] destination but that one travels with a different point of view. . . . In [R.S.] Peters' sense, a liberal education transforms one's perception of what the problems are, what opportunities are offered by life, what new interests might enrich one's daily experiences. . . . Theory of education . . . does not provide [merely] knowledge and skills which are applicable to a given practical situation: it provides [instead] new perspective such that one confronts educational problems and opportunities from a different point of view. Educational theory can provide a liberal education, such that the teachers' reflection on practice becomes intelligent, morally sensitive, capable of making finer conceptual distinctions, and more subtle. . . . The justification for educational theory is the same as the justification for liberal education itself. The teacher reflecting upon teaching equipped with more subtle educational theory, is much like the liberally educated citizen reflecting upon public affairs."[3]

My philosophy of education teacher and mentor argued that, during comparatively settled times, teachers have not been highly motivated to question accepted ideas and practices; speculative activity is often frowned upon by the community. Such conditions can help make a teacher's life rather comfortable—but dull. It is apparent to many, if not most people, that our society is faced by many disagreements about numerous issues and beliefs. As a result, theory becomes important not only for the educational reformer, but also for those who wish to conserve and even roll back what change has brought about. In fact, "whether we think of ourselves as liberal or conservative, radical or regressive, we cannot escape in these times the necessity of attending to our basic ideas. The luxury of operating our schools on the basis of ideas 'everybody knows are right' is gone, provided that it ever . . . existed. . . . A certain lag between theory and practice is . . . present in any period. Today's question, however, is not so much the relation of certain practices to an accepted body of theory; it is rather what practices and what theories are to be accepted. Thus in unsettled times, at least, the theory of education becomes controversial and dialectical. In this sense, it becomes philosophical."[4] I maintain, along with Wingo, that although it may seem strange to expect educators to be philosophers, can we afford to have them be anything else? Philosophy and philosophy of education are too important to be thought about and "done" by only the few, especially during these times which feature the inability or refusal of many people to agree with the orthodoxies of others. In the absence of agreed-upon orthodoxies and grand narratives—and in societies that claim to be democratic—*doing* philosophy with regard to society and school becomes the responsibility of all citizens and educators, not just those who make a living in this field of study.

I

I begin this intellectual work by considering how our near and remote ancestors tried and often succeeded in making sense of their worlds. This central, continuing, human endeavor provides us with the advantage of belonging to a heritage consisting of various attempts to understand ourselves within physical, social, intellectual, and spiritual contexts. Our search for understanding, or love of wisdom, is often called philosophy, although this great endeavor is not limited to philosophy—and certainly not to philosophers' formal work. Standing on the shoulders of those who came before us is beneficial; however, it is still necessary for each of us to construct our own operative understanding of ourselves as well as the world in which we live. We change ourselves and our world as we think and act upon our hypotheses: The things we endeavor to understand and solve are affected by our individual and/or collective interventionist labors. Such labor profoundly affects us all. You are invited to examine and reflect upon your own foundational or ultimate beliefs and value system. You are encouraged to think about their sources, development, and the potential and actual action consequences. The accent is on your educational philosophy, because this book is mainly intended for those who seek to deepen and broaden their understanding of teaching and learning, as well as for the many who are interested in the broader idea of education.

You are invited to consider the thesis that the ancient classical Greeks invented philosophy in the West because they had a need for and confidence in constructing an explanatory model that would assist them in making sense of their personal and social lives. My reference to Greece and the West does not reflect a bias; there is no doubt that indigenous people in the "Americas," Africans, Chinese, Indians, original Australians et al.[5] also "did philosophy." My life and intellectual experiences in the West and its civilization(s) makes it natural to express myself within its framework. Many Europeans and those who left Europe to settle around the world tend to exaggerate the "glory that was Greece." Edith Hamilton's writing represents well the point I seek to make.

> Before Greece all religion was magical. . . . It was [hu]mankind's sole defense against fearful powers. . . . A magical universe was so terrifying because it was [perceived of as] so irrational, and therefore . . . incalculable. There was no [belief in a] dependable relation . . . between cause and effect. It . . . [can] readily be seen what it did to the human intellect to live in such an atmosphere. . . . Fear is of all the emotions the most brutalizing . . . In one little country the terror was banished. The Greeks . . . changed a world that was full of fear into . . . [one] of beauty. . . . We know . . . that in Homer men [the contemporary critique of the ancient Greeks' failure to include women is warranted] are free and fearless. There are no fearful powers to be propitiated . . . very human like gods [and goddesses] inhabit a . . . delightful heaven. . . . The universe has become rational. . . . "All things were in confusion until Mind

came and set them in order." That mind was Greek [in the West], and the first exponent of it we know about was Homer. . . . [His] universe is quite rational . . . well ordered and very well lit. When night comes . . . the gods go to sleep. There are no mysterious doings. . . . The stamp of Greek genius is everywhere on his two epics [the *Iliad* and the *Odyssey*], in the banishment of the ugly . . . frightful and . . . senseless; in the courage and undaunted spirit with which the heroes faced any opponent. . . . [However, Homer's] gods . . . could not continue long to be adequate. . . . They were unable to satisfy people who were thinking soberly of right and wrong, who were using their critical powers to speculate about the universe. . . . [The Greeks] began to ask for a loftier Zeus . . . one who cared for all, not only, as in the *Iliad*, for the great and powerful. So in a passage . . . [from] the *Odyssey* he has become the protector of the poor and helpless. . . . The peasant-poet Hesiod . . . placed justice in Olympus as Zeus' companion: "Fishes and beast and fowls . . . devour one another. But to men [sic] Zeus has given justice. Beside Zeus . . ., Justice has her seat."[6]

The history of the West and elsewhere features the development of claims and rights that move from the few to the many. Western Civilization is characterized by insistencies and struggles aimed at the inclusion of the poor, workers, various nationalities and races, women, children, the handicapped et al. who had not benefited previously from memberships in the philosophical, political, economic, cultural, and educational contexts of their societies. We know that the ancient Greeks did not include women, "barbarians," slaves, or foreigners as citizens of the polis. Today, the idea of democracy is characterized by the formal inclusion of one and all under the protection of the law and its government. This unsteady march toward inclusion was neither inevitable nor peaceful. Some postmodernist critiques argued that the whole of Western Civilization represents little more than hypocrisy and injustice because of so-called universal claims made by a select few for their own advantage—from the ancient Greeks to the present.[7] This book represents a more generous, although still critical, reading of Western Civilization.

My generosity of interpretation is dependent on the analysis of ancient Greek life provided by scholars such as Ellen Meiksins Wood. I draw from her work in order to understand that the potential and reality for what contemporary rationalists and democrats favor can be found in the ancient polis called Athens. The connection between widespread rational capacities and abilities, and the struggle for bona fide democracy, social justice, and respect for authentic diversity among human beings are highlighted in this book. Wood argued that it was within the Greek polis, especially Athens, where free labor was invented. Free laborers toiled in a world where much of the work was done by slaves. In Wood's view many political and cultural developments which occurred in Athens were affected by conflicts between peasant-democrats and those who sought to keep power and riches for the "well-born." She pointed out that "nowhere [up to that time] . . . was the . . . division between appropriating and producing classes [rulers and workers], a tension . . . between citizens who had an interest in restoring an aristocratic monopoly of political status and those who . . . [resisted] it, a division between citizens for whom the state would serve as a means of appropriation and those for whom it served as a protection from exploitation [as distinct as in Athens]. . . . This opposition is nowhere more visible than in the classics of Greek philosophy[:] . . . the division between rulers and producers is the fundamental principle of Plato's philosophy, not just his political thought but his epistemology [or, theory of knowledge]."[8]

Joel Spring reinforced Wood's claim that the ancient Greeks argued about who possessed—and who did not possess—the cognitive abilities necessary for citizenship and self-government. Those who believed that intellectual ability was not widespread in the population expected that those who were neither bright, nor educable, should serve those who allegedly were. Spring reminded us of the "myth of the metals," through which Socrates argued that people were mixtures of gold, silver, and brass. "Those most fit to rule were [said to be] composed primarily of gold and therefore were the most precious. The guardian soldiers were composed primarily of silver, while farmers [peasants] and workers were composed of iron and brass. . . . If people believe . . . [this myth], then they believe a person's place in society is the result of inherent qualities. . . . One could argue that intelligence tests served the same function in the early twentieth century. . . . People might . . . accept their lowly place in society because of a low score . . . . Socrates argues that gold parents will tend to beget gold children . . . [and so on]. However, Socrates maintains . . . [also that] some children of gold parents will be born brass, and some children of brass parents will be gold. When this occurs, children who are unlike their parents are to be placed in their proper social class. As stated in [Plato's] . . . Republic, an important role of the educational system is the determination [i.e., selecting and sorting] of the mixture of metals within each child. . . . There should be a determination of who should be placed among the farmers and workers and who should be educated [for political and economic power]."[9] Wood confirmed Spring's critique of intellectual and political stratification favored by some Athenian philosophers. It is important in the classic arguments of this polis and time that we in the West have sought to clarify our own positions. Western philosophy can be characterized as playing with cards dealt to those of us who came after Socrates, Plato, and Aristotle. In Wood's view, the division of labor between rulers and producers is what the idea of justice is based on in the *Republic*. This division is central to Plato's epistemology. The cognitive ability to recognize and understand what is essential, universal, most real and true is assigned to the gold metalists; the common folk are portrayed as those who can understand only appearances and particulars. This head-hand divide continues to shape the harmful educational stratification in the West.[10]

The question of who should have political rights, as well as the justification for it, has been raised and fought over throughout our history. The expansion of citizen's rights and greater inclusion has been among the most important and progressive human achievements. It is well to remember Wood's insistence on civic status, especially in view of the current attacks on citizens' rights in the effort to make everyone live by market outcomes alone. "The civic status of the Athenian citizen was a valuable asset which had direct economic implications. Political equality not only coexisted with but substantially modified socio-economic inequality, and democracy was more substantive than [merely] 'formal'. . . . Citizenship had profound consequences for peasants and craftsmen; and . . . a change in the . . . [legal] status of slaves . . . and, women would have transformed the society entirely."[11]

The critique of ancient classical Greek thought is not intended to minimize its importance.[12] A description of this intellectual and social achievement follows. It may be an exaggeration to claim, as Edith Hamilton did, that "in a world where the irrational had played the chief role . . . [the Greeks] came forward as the protagonists of the mind."[13] Their ancient but extant achievement provides the necessary starting point for our philosophical scaffolding as well as the blueprint guiding the main construction. I have chosen a book published in 1957, one of a kind that used to be called a classic in its field, because it assists in portraying a succinct, fair, and honorific account of the remarkable foundational contributions made by the ancient Greeks. One could easily criticize C.M. Bowra's celebratory account through deconstructing the text by way of multiple readings that enjoy the advantage of retrospect; however, it is important to learn about the intellectual glory that was Greece in order to begin the philosophical scaffolding for the construction of critical democratic education. I shall be as critical and iconoclastic as need be during the course of this book.

Bowra addressed the place of reason in Greek thought by pointing out how in the preclassical, i.e., archaic, period the Greeks expressed their most significant and profound beliefs via poetry—reinforced by sculpture and painting. By the sixth century B.C., the desire to understand things more precisely and completely led to the development of rational discourse and to attempts to establish principles and rule-governed explanations of human and social phenomena. They wanted to move beyond the whims of mythological gods as explanations for the complexities, dangers, and possibilities facing them. Bertrand Russell said, "philosophy, as distinct from theology, began in Greece in the sixth century . . .; [furthermore, philosophy can] teach how to live without certainty, and yet without being paralyzed by hesitation."[14] Bowra informed us that developments in Greek social, economic, and political life fostered this new spirit of inquiry into the visible world; it assumed three forms: mathematics, philosophy, and natural science. Like mathematics, philosophy was an attempt to find realities behind phenomena and/or appearances. The Greek inquirers wished to learn about the origin and nature of things. Bowra offers us this insight:

> In their desire to find some universal principle[s], they assumed as religious thinkers did, the existence of a cosmic order. . . . Even if they could not finally unravel what laws governed phenomena, they could at least claim that such laws existed. . . . The first glimmerings of . . . [natural laws] were . . . derived from [assumed] divine laws. . . . These branches of inquiry all presuppose that it is both possible and proper for man [sic] to discover the truth about the nature of things. . . . Solon [Athenian lawmaker] . . . follows a[n] ascending scale from utter ignorance to reasonable expectation. . . . [Human beings] may of course make mistakes . . . but [we] do not work in utter ignorance. . . . [Although] men cannot hope for certainty, they can make good surmises.[15]

These Greeks did not claim omniscience, which was reserved for the deities. They developed confidence that revelation could be assisted by and/or replaced by a pursuit of truth through rational inquiry. The old view was superseded by the conviction that we could find truth for ourselves.

It is important to realize that Greek philosophers tried to understand the world as a whole. It will become apparent later in this work that such a view is currently seriously attacked by some postmodernist thinkers. We are in debt to our intellectual ancestors for establishing certain central and perennial philosophical concerns, such as the distinctions between one and many, knowledge and opinion, reality and appearance, being and not-being, form and matter, universals and particulars, etc. Bowra tells us, "in making such distinctions the Greeks tried to solve the discord between the infinite multiplicity and variety of phenomena and the need for some permanent reality behind them. . . . The strength of Greek philosophy lies . . . in its assumption that there is no problem which cannot be solved by hard and careful thought. It assumes that words are instruments of thought."[16] Greek geographers and historians chose prose rather than poetry to communicate their findings, in part because they were convinced that it better suited the necessary qualities of detachment, tenacious labor, and the ability to sift evidence that characterized secular inquiry. The historian Thucydides was concerned with human action rather than supernatural forces.

Although Greek science and philosophy began as allies of religion, certain issues and inquiries made the incompatibilities between secular thought and religious revelation obvious. This occurred again in Europe during the fourteenth century, A.D., when the reappearance of Greek reason proved to be incompatible with certain religious claims to knowledge and truth. The conflict between science and religion was complemented by another; between science and philosophy. Greek science depended upon the human senses; the philosophers did not trust the senses as a sure basis for knowledge. This great cleavage lives on in our history. Thomas Aquinas tried to create a synthesis/harmony between the claims of reason and faith in the thirteenth century, A.D. Plato attempted to find a solution to the tensions between science and philosophy during the fourth century, B.C. Considering the great importance of Greek philosophy and its giant figure, Plato, it is worth reading Bowra on the suggested Platonic cure:

> Reality for him consists of ideal Forms, which are at once logical universals [timeless and applicable everywhere], capable of being understood, and particulars [imperfect representations of these Forms]. To establish his Forms he appealed . . . to religion, and argued that we know them through recollection from a former existence. This might mean . . . that our knowledge of them is innate . . . [moreover,] it is not derived from the senses. Though this impressive system removed [for some] doubts about the possibility of knowledge, it dealt a cruel blow to science. For it meant that observation and experiment gave . . . [way] to *a priori* reasoning. Plato . . . was so possessed by the notion that the universe is rational that he thought it possible to dictate its structure from his own conception of . . . how the creator ought to have made it. In his search for certainty he failed to allow that on many matters we can hope for no more than a reasonable opinion and that this may be more valuable than any dogmatic assertion.[17]

We will look carefully at the quest for certainty in chapter two.

Bowra recognized the greatness of Plato, as anyone who takes the history of ideas seriously surely must. It is plausible to argue that Plato's answers given to queries about the nature of reality and knowledge have played on the central stage longer than any others. These answers have won the greatest historical agreement although this theory has been under assault during the last two hundred years, especially in these postmodernist times. Aristotle's encyclopedic labor aimed at synthesizing the whole of knowledge as it was during his life and made great contributions to metaphysics, logic, biology, ethics, and politics. Bowra suggests that "through this double [Plato and Aristotle] achievement the fourth century has a place of high honour in the history of human thought . . . neither in Athens nor elsewhere in Greece did these . . . [achievements] fully compensate for what had been lost."[18] What had been lost was the earlier openness between the human mind and material phenomena; there is the condemnation of democracy by Socrates, Plato, and Aristotle—a condemnation of common persons as laborers, i.e., in their brass roles. Even the very limited democracy of Periclean Athens was rejected, i.e., its fundamental assumption that its citizens could be trusted to decide on the factors and circumstances that affected their lives. Superstition and rule by the powerful again engulfed the Greek world.[19]

Still the Greek achievement, epitomized by the myth of Prometheus (who allegedly stole fire from the gods for human benefit but was punished by the deities), continues to teach us about the arts of life and helps us free ourselves from confusion and ignorance. The Greeks were aware of their humble beginnings; many of them saw this as a summons—a possibility at least—to grasp for unrealized potentials and accomplishments. Human beings were seen as creatures in which intelligence and emotions work together to develop *aretê* (virtue, goodness, the quality of good citizenship) from inborn capacities, as far as possible. During the fifth century, B.C., this development was seen as operating in the sociopolitical context—the polis—which is a much different arena than the contemporary market, characterized by a race for material rewards.[20] People were considered social beings who, through political interaction with others in the polis, might rise above the animals and one's mere potential; this vision prevailed instead of one that portrayed men and women as being alone in the wilderness. Some religionists view the city as unholy, making it necessary to go off on one's own to find identity and/or salvation.

The unique achievement of the classical Greeks was their recognition that although they were humans rather than gods, they were content and proud of their placement. The Greeks, at their secular best, sought to find their own excellence. By the fourth century, B.C., the notion of human beings able to almost reach beyond human placement began to give way to the construction of barriers between human beings on the ground and the increasingly rarefied, detached, but self-contained, realm of the transcendental. Bowra explains, by making the transcendental realm and its deities completely separate from the lived experiences of ordinary human beings, the earlier attempt to emulate the (formerly) familiar and anthropomorphic deities became impossible. "In different ways the great thinkers helped break up the universe in which the Greeks had enjoyed [formerly] the illumination of a lower order of things by a higher [one] and had felt that there was . . . hope of transcending their . . . limitations in some unforeseen direction. It emphasized that the ordinary . . . [person] must rely on his own experience . . . . Instead of reinforcing and extending the . . . [range] of human activities, the new speculations confined them to a man-centered world and destroyed the consciousness of a superior dimension which had given a special splendour to the [classical] Greek vision of experience."[21]

The *tension* between limitations and the potential to break beyond them provided the progressive dynamism of classical Greece. Educators and citizens struggle with the problems and possibilities of human volition (or agency) as it bumps up against limitations and structure. Perhaps the Greeks were among the first to help us understand that it is the *struggle* to rise above our fears, limitations, temptations, fatigue, lack of imagination, and unethical tendencies that is most important and admirable. Consider the following passage from Nikos Kazantzakis (1885–1957), a Greek writer born in Crete. He was writing to his honorary grandfather, the great painter called El Greco (1541–1614), also a Greek from Crete. Kazantzakis' words represent well the tension which Bowra and I write about. This *creative tension* did not entirely expire during the Greek fourth century, B.C.

> Our Center, grandfather, the center which swept the visible world into its whirl and fought to elevate it to the upper level of valor and responsibility, was the battle with God. Which God? The fierce summit of man's [sic] soul, the summit which we are ceaselessly about to attain and which ceaselessly jumps to its feet and climbs still higher. . . . That is why the whole of our lives was an ascent grandfather. . . . We set out with many fellow strugglers, many ideas. . . . But as we ascended and as the summit shifted and became more remote, fellow strugglers, ideas, and hopes kept bidding us farewell. . . . They were neither willing nor able to mount higher. We remained alone. . . . We were swayed neither by arrogance nor by the naive certainty that one day the summit would stand still and we would reach it; nor yet, even if we should reach it, by the belief that there on high we would find happiness, salvation, and paradise. We ascended because the very act of ascending, for us, was happiness, salvation, and paradise.[22]

Think about how this passage epitomized the sense of *tension* and *struggle* that characterized the classical Greeks. They realized that human beings were both individuals and members of societies which featured certain histories. The possible relevance of these ideas for professional educators—and active citizens—can be answered only by the readers themselves. For those who are reading this book together, it would be easy enough to engage in conversation based upon multiple readings and interpretations of the text.

II

The interpretation of the classical Greek experience in this book portrays our forebears as having the need, and for a time, the confidence to make sense of their world and their roles in it. It could be plausibly argued that need and confidence helped these ancient people move haltingly and imperfectly to a form of limited participatory democracy in some of their city-states. Democracy, art, architecture, theater, and even the anthropomorphic Greek religions served to place human beings near the center of things. The considered importance of, and reliance on, reason, are keys to understanding the Greeks' confidence in human beings, our central roles, and especially the ability to see things holistically, as well as in terms of the common good. Although the classical Greeks failed to develop a political vision and practice that would allow unity among themselves, the belief that a big picture existed and could be understood persisted throughout Western Civilization. A persistent theme in Western history has been the belief in the possibility of, and the need for, a constructive process aimed at articulating a notion of the common good. Judeo-Christian religious traditions have contributed to the Greek project of holistic thinking and *pro bono publico* initiatives. Much of this belief came together in the Roman Empire and lived on in the synthesis called Christianity, as it was shaped in part by its progenitor, Judaism.

I think it is warranted to assert that, in spite of grave failures along the way, there has been a historical attempt in Western Civilization to make people at home in their social and physical worlds. These difficult-to-achieve accomplishments were used to further the opportunity for human beings to live more dignified lives—through the expansion and deepening of certain rights and safeguards. I do not suggest a teleological development, only to indicate certain actions that sought to construct spaces in which people could live more humanely. I remind the reader that I make no claim that the "West is best." I merely want to suggest that the struggle for human dignity (in terms of recognized worth) has been carried on by some of those who have come to live in the West—either because of birth, or as willing/unwilling migrants and/or emigrants. These continuous struggles for dignity can be characterized roughly by the following land-marks: (1) Religious dignity through the belief in interfering, mostly be-neficent, and anthropomorphic deities. (2) Philosophical dignity via Greek rationalism that insisted on the central place of human beings and their intellectual prowess, an understandable cosmos/universe, Promethean audacity, and the possibility for using this reason and orderliness to con-struct (albeit imperfect) democracies. (3) Political dignity as epitomized by self-government in the polis, Roman republic, Renaissance city-states, the curbing of the monarchies, the rise of constitutional government, and the eruptions of democracy beginning in the late eighteenth century and in-creasingly afterward. (4) The basic and continuing struggle for economic dignity, often stated in terms of citizen and political rights, accentuated in the late-eighteenth, nineteenth, and twentieth centuries by labor and vari-ous socialist movements whose members insisted that citizens' political rights and dignity were inextricably related to socioeconomic justice. (5) A recognition that the inner life is of great importance and organically re-lated to social life; citizens and workers must be able to enjoy the psycho-logical well-being that is essential to human dignity.

It bears repeating that the continuing struggle to achieve human dig-nity and justice has not been linear; there have been regressions, tan-gents, uneven developments, and threats posed by various barbarisms, including the historical repressive reaction by most ruling elites. This dan-gerous situation has not been solved in our time. The struggle must con-tinue although we can see ourselves as part of a long and worthwhile effort. Albert Camus captured the essence of my point in the following passage from his novel, *The Plague*.

> Dr. Rieux resolved to compile . . . [a] chronicle, so that he should not be one of those who hold their peace but should bear witness in favor of those plague-stricken people; so that some memorial of the injustice and outrage done them might endure; and to state . . . simply what we learn in a time of pestilence: that there are more things to admire in men [and women] than to despise. None the less, he knew that the tale he had to tell could not be one of final victory. It could be only the record of what had to be done, and what assuredly would have to be done again in the never ending fight against terror and its relentless onslaughts, despite their personal afflictions, by all those who, while unable to be saints but refusing to bow down to pestilence, strive their utmost to be healers. . . . Rieux . . . knew what those jubilant crowds did not know . . . that the plague bacillus never dies . . .; it can lie dormant for years . . . and that perhaps the day would come when . . . it would rouse up its rats again and send them forth to die in a happy city.[23]

III

What I have presented so far can help the reader to consider some perennial intellectual/epistemological dichotomies: (1) certainty-uncertainty; (2) universal-particular; (3) revelation, intuition, mysticism-reason, especially of the secular kind; (4) deductive-inductive; (5) and a dichotomy along a continuum of optimism and pessimism with regard to knowing and the human condition. I have mentioned that I am not implying that dichotomous either/or thinking is necessary or advisable. Those who have been and currently are involved in the struggle for human dignity and justice, according to their own interpretations of these terms, are positioned roughly along these continua. We are situated along an epistemological continuum or axis that is anchored at one end by the certainty claimed by revelatory religion and/or idealist philosophy, to realism, pragmatism, existentialism, poststructuralism, constructivism, postmodernism, cynicism, and perhaps nihilism on the other end. These issues are crucially related to the current explosive educational and political debates concerning what it might mean for us to venture *from* the putative security of hoped-for certainty (often interpreted by our so-called elites and even "betters") *to* the problematic situation characterized by *all* persons participating in the construction of educational/political/social/cultural meanings, preferences, and proposed actions. Progressing toward participatory democracy can hopefully increase the chance for social justice and respect for bona fide diversity and human worth.

The reader is invited to organize her/his thoughts/beliefs/intellectual positions around the intersecting continua in figure 1.

This intellectual work can assist you as you begin to think more systematically and enter into discussions about your preliminary construction of an educational philosophy. For example, the constructor may decide upon a defensible, authoritarian position should s/he believe that absolut-

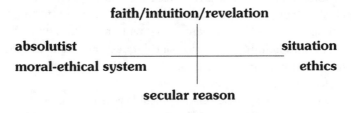

Figure 1

ist knowledge is possible; or, a more uncertain and/or democratic position may be chosen because of the positioning taken within the intersecting continua. Discussion can move easily to initial choices concerning philosophies of education, e.g., essentialism, progressivism, existentialism, etc.[24] Such a discussion will most likely be preliminary at this point because some readers may lack information about philosophies of education. The knowledgeable teacher and the students can use these preliminary discussions as opportunities for introductory ideas that can be studied in depth later in this book and/or course of study. The student is well advised to think and read about various theories concerning the "nature" of our genus and species, i.e., the "nature" of man-woman. These considerations are central to where one is situated on figure 1. Such considerations will be revisited throughout this book.[25]

I have learned that high school, undergraduate, and graduate students come to discussions such as I have proposed in relation to figure 1 with some information and/or fairly well-thought-out views. Students are not "empty vessels" to be filled when it comes to ideas about human nature and our place in the world. I wrote in the introduction to an experimental high school philosophy class during the 1960s, "Through careful critical examination we are trying to evaluate the information and beliefs we have about the universe . . . and the world of human affairs. . . . This . . . understanding can provide a . . . framework in which the ordinary person can place [her] his own, more limited conception of the . . . world. . . . Through such an examination and evaluation we may . . . better assess our ideals and aspirations, as well as to understand . . . why we accept them, or whether we ought to do so."[26]

Suggested Task for the Reader
During these times, characterized in part by the seeming inability of many people to adhere to orthodox and/or absolutist positions with regard to ethical/moral problems, how does a teacher-citizen ground her/his educational philosophy and practice so that it is personally meaningful as well as publicly defensible? Prepare a brief written position with which to guide your contribution to discussion of this question. Walter Lippmann's *A Preface to Morals* (Boston: Beacon Press, 1929), passim, can be used as a tool for laboring at this task.

The *doing* of this specific philosophical task is of central importance to chapter one. John Dewey explained, that from ancient times to the present, human beings have constructed meanings and explanations for themselves in the face of what was and is problematic. This introductory chapter does *not* present philosophy as a finished contemporary product. Readers are encouraged to familiarize themselves with important conversations in the historical discourse called philosophy. The focus is on the construction of one's own blueprints, scaffolding, and building. Teachers and ordinary citizen-workers in a democracy must understand the need to think philosophically in order to deal with the problems and possibilities of intellectual, professional, and overall civic life. This imperative should become increasingly clear to the reader as s/he reads and studies on.

IV

In this section the reader is presented with some ideas about philosophy of education and how it can be congruent with the kind of philosophy being praised in this chapter. It is quite a stretch to go from classical Greece and other historical philosophical references to philosophy of education in the twentieth century. The careful reader—especially when s/he discusses the chapter with others—can make certain connections between then and now, and philosophy and philosophy of education. My sense of philosophy of education is that it should be a broad and deep analysis into schooling-education and how it relates to the larger societies of which they are a part. Max Black wrote the following which has guided my own work in philosophy and education since first reading it in a book written by my teacher. "'All serious discussion of educational problems, no matter how specific, soon lead to consideration of educational *aims*, and becomes a conversation about the good life, the nature of man [woman], the varieties of experience. But these are the perennial themes of philosophical investigation. It might be a hard thing to expect educators to be philosophers, but can they be anything else?'"[27] Black's and Wingo's conception of educational philosophy has influenced my own conception of the discourse and field. The first time I articulated the material presented in section IV was in an article published in 1996.[28] What I offer for your consideration is not intended to be definitive or official. It is in keeping with the thesis of this book; good philosophy of education serves the interests of those who favor education and a society characterized by broad, democratic empowerment, social justice, and respect for bona fide diversity. For a brief history of philosophy of education as a field of study in the United States, see the appendix at the end of the chapter.

I present my views on philosophy of education *within* the context of the social foundations of education. The social foundations are most commonly thought of as philosophy/history/sociology of education. Foundations inquiry is characterized by the *interpretive*, *normative*, and *critical* perspectives on education. Michael Apple presented us with the following insight:

> "The most important things . . . we can know about man is what he takes for granted, and the most elemental and important facts about a society are those that are . . . generally regarded as settled." That is, to . . . understand, the activity of men and women of a specific historical period, one must start out by questioning what to them is unquestionable. As Marx would say, one does not accept the . . . participants' own commonsense appraisals of their . . . activities (though these are important . . .); rather, the investigators must *situate* these activities in a larger arena. . . . In fact, if one were to point to one of the most neglected areas of educational scholarship, it would be . . . the critical study of the relationship between ideologies and educational thought and practice, the study of . . . seemingly commonsense assumptions that guide our overly technically minded field. Such critical scholarship would lay bare the political, social, ethical, and economic interests and commitments that are uncritically accepted as "the way life really is" in our day-to-day life as educators.[29]

Foundational and philosophy of education inquiry must address the knowledge, signs, symbols, curriculum, and pedagogy that are taken for granted in our schools. We must figure out how this "taken for grantedness" assists some students, and may block the progress of others. Apple questioned the relation between education and power by arguing that schools help reproduce the social and economic stratification of the larger capitalist-dominated society through the use of a neutral process of instruction and reward. The cultural capital, or advantages, of the middle classes and rich are presented as natural and as though all students have access to it. "Just as our dominant economic institutions are structured so that those who inherit or already have economic capital do better, so too does cultural capital act in the same way . . . [because it] is unequally distributed . . . and this is dependent . . . on the division of labor and power in the society. 'By selecting for such properties [as "good taste," particular types of prior knowledge, and language usage], schools serve to reproduce the distribution of power within the society.'"[30]

Educators must come to grips with underlying problems such as reproduction of the present societal and school stratification. Teacher education must make it more possible for undergrads as well as practicing teachers to analyze, understand, and be committed to democracy, equity, diversity, a moral economy, and a sociopolitical system in which it is comparatively safe more often than not to act altruistically. Our educators must be encouraged to be in touch with the caring and nurturing aspects of their character. They must be offered the commensurate and necessary opportunities to develop their theoretical powers. The relationships between intellect and feeling have been studied throughout history. Many of those who have commented formally upon what they learned have supported positions that call for a balance between the two, there may not be a stark dichotomy between intellect and feeling. Current educational literature is rich in considerations of this historical discussion. I do not see affect and intellect as necessarily dichotomous. This education must be "radical" in the sense of being able to get to the roots of things, in addition to striving to see phenomena holistically. Perhaps,

> most important of all, teachers must see themselves as workers who are part of the vast majority of citizens . . . who are . . . [also] classed workers. . . . This class-consciousness must be . . . part of the complexity that makes up other . . . [identities] such as race, ethnicity . . . and gender. It is as class-conscious workers that teachers should enter into broad umbrella-coalitions with *other class-conscious workers*. This strategy will provide the best chance to alter the conflicting imperatives [of capitalism and democracy upon the schools] in favor of [the latter]. . . . Public K–12 schools can become sites where the democratic imperative prevails [but] only when synchronized action takes place in schools and elsewhere and especially in the capitalist-dominated economy and . . . [national government].[31]

Suggested Task for the Reader

It has been argued that the Kindergarten through grade 12 (K–12) public schools in the United States historically have been subject to the incompatible imperatives of the capitalist economy and of democracy—conceived of in its broad sense. The capitalist imperative is said to demand competent, but not necessarily critical workers, whereas democracy requires critical, broadly educated (rather than just trained), and culturally enriched citizen-workers, persons who have the ability to analyze the socioeconomic and political systems in which they live. Explain how a K–12 teacher might find it difficult to satisfy both imperatives. It might be useful to focus on the difficulties posed by the need for teachers to select and sort their students according to so-called objective criteria which historically arranges students along an A–F continuum, and being committed to educating all of the students for mastery of what is considered to be of crucial importance to successful democratic citizen empowerment. Does democracy require rank ordering, or is it the economy that places the pressure on teachers to do so?

Maxine Greene claimed that it is "important for teacher education to stimulate critique—not solely of the constructs used to interpret and direct the educational process itself, but of the [academic] discipline or the subject matters. Without such critique, the disciplines are likely to be used for domination, for *fixing* the vision of young people on the reality others have named."[32] Greene asserted that "what has so long been treated as unquestionable must be questioned from a human vantage point and on the ground of shared ethical concerns. Teacher educators must ask themselves whether this kind of questioning can occur in teachers' colleges and schools."[33] She is not naive enough to think that teacher education can change the social order without the help of allies. She refers to Albert Camus's character called Tarrou (in *The Plague*): "'There are pestilences, and there are victims . . . and it is up to us not to join forces with pestilences.'"[34] Although life is characterized by great complexities that surely defy simplistic portrayals of right or wrong, it is possible to recognize rather clear-cut sides in certain conflicts. Camus used the metaphor of the plague to represent the social-ethical crisis that threatened to overcome Europe, especially during the 1930s.

William Leiss et al. have written about how good teachers must combat cynicism. They define cynicism as a way of thinking that identifies truth with what exists; focusing on the parts rather than the whole; refusing to consider alternatives to established (constructed) reality; interpreting reason as the mere manipulation of so-called facts; and failing "to judge established conditions in the light of . . . existing possibilities for . . . [overcoming] these conditions."[35] Marcuse spoke of "negative thinking" and he viewed it as central to critical thinking itself. Negation seeks to counter the tendency to accept the given/"what is"/so-called established facts as the whole of reality. "Negative thinking" seeks to undermine self-contentment and what is called common sense. Critical thinking and/or theory insist that we *judge* the so-called facts, acceptable practices, and institutions of any constructed society *by* the possibilities for their replacement. Critical theory insists that we endeavor to understand the historical causes that have made possible a particular status quo. Marcuse was a professor of philosophy. His writing and teaching practice are useful to our consideration of educational philosophy, as well as its relevance for teacher education—and K–12 teaching. Marcuse's work can remind us that teaching and learning need not always reinforce dominant social relations or reproductive schooling practices. In agreement with the material presented in this chapter, Leiss et al. tell us Marcuse believed that "in its origins and intentions knowledge (in the strictest sense:

philosophy) was highly subversive of . . . established values and institutions."[36] This subversion is neither capricious nor arbitrary. It is an activity that is necessary if we are to shape our existence in accordance with our rational capacities. For Marcuse, knowledge is inextricably part of the human attempt to create free and rational lives.[37]

One does not have to be an advocate of critical theory in order to do philosophy of education well. Many other philosophical discourses concerned with school and society are also committed to viewing inquiry as subversive of any unjust, nonrational status quo that is unable to withstand public scrutiny. In 1929 John Dewey wrote in *The Quest for Certainty* that, although various theories of knowledge (epistemology) differ from one another, their adherents share a good deal in common. In Dewey's view, Western philosophies such as idealism, realism, and their variations subscribe to the notion that reality is antecedent to the search for it, i.e., inquiry is mainly about getting right with what is, or established reality. He argued that scientific inquiry demonstrates that a belief in the inherent properties of the real is a survival of an old metaphysics; to know "reality" means that the inquirer changes what is studied as a result of inquiry itself. It is best to read Dewey's own words as he argues against the old metaphysics.

> The . . . difference between the attitude which accepts the objects of perception, use and enjoyment as final . . . and that which takes them as starting points for reflection and investigation . . . marks a revolution in the . . . spirit of life, in the entire attitude taken toward whatever is found in existence. When the things which exist around us . . . are regarded as interrogations for which an answer must be sought . . . nature as it already exists ceases to be something which must be accepted and submitted to . . . just as it is. It is now something to be modified, to be intentionally controlled. It is material to act upon so as to transform it into new objects which better answer our needs. Nature [and society] as it exists at any particular time is a challenge, rather than a completion.[38]

Dewey, like Marcuse, suggested that we can and should refuse to accept a punishing physical "reality" and/or unjust social one. We must and can transform it through rational, solidaristic, human effort.

Dewey's intellectual radicalism went beyond his place in the liberal political contexts of his time. He maintained that the most important job for philosophers is to "search out and disclose obstructions; to criticize habits of mind; to focus reflection upon needs congruous with present life; to interpret the conclusions of science with respect to their consequences for our beliefs about purposes and values in all phases of life. . . . [Because] the development of a system of thought capable of giving this service is a difficult undertaking; it can proceed only slowly and through cooperative effort."[39] The young Dewey saw science as a method of public inquiry and decision making that was a necessary alternative to arbitrariness, obscurantism, superstition, and other flawed processes. As he matured, he began to broaden his idea of scientific inquiry to include the many people who neither work in laboratories nor believe that exact knowledge can be had about human beings and our society in the same way that quasi-certainty may be had about non-human phenomena. The mature Dewey moved beyond this "positivism" of his youth and pointed out that "the moral prophets had always been artists. . . . All poetry and art set . . . standards by which to compare the everyday existence that surrounds us against the criterion which speaks of potential. What a society . . . will desire or think to be good, will . . . be taught by . . . poets, who communicate most deeply about what experience *should* be. Art has been the means of keeping alive the sense of purpose that outruns evidence and of meanings which rise above banal habits."[40] Dewey had always known that the scientific method permits only a pursuit of comparative meaning, rather than achieving the exact knowledge of the immutable. He wrote in 1948, "the borderline between what is called hypotheses in science and what is called speculation (usually in a tone of disparagement) in philosophy is thin and shadowy at the time of initiation of new movements—those placed in contrast with 'technical application . . .' such as take place . . . after a new and revolutionary outlook has managed to win acceptance."[41] Chapter four will provide further analysis of Dewey's important contributions to education for democratic empowerment.

In an effort to continue the presentation of ideas about philosophy of education that are congruent with the kind of philosophy being honored in this chapter, I will turn to various editorial introductions I have written between 1989–96 in the published proceeding of the Ohio Valley Philosophy of Education Society. I draw from this editorial-scholarly writing as a sample of work that can support the philosophical scaffolding for the construction of critical democratic education. If you are not familiar with philosophy of education discourse, you should not be concerned if questions arise that may require discussion in order to answer them. The same is true with regard to words, concepts, and ideas that may be unfamiliar. The reader is best served by a holistic contextual approach to studying what is to be presented. Further reading, reflection on it, making connections with what is already known well, and discussion among readers will help in the effort to make what follows meaningful. Come and look into the window that reveals some of what contemporary philosophers of education talk about, as well as some examples of how it can be done. The following is mostly paraphrasing from the editorial introductions I have written, whose original purpose was assisting the readers of the proceedings—called *Philosophical Studies in Education*—to have a critical overview of the various published papers that comprise the proceedings. The names of the various authors are not included in my critical overview; one can refer to the published proceedings for this information.

For the 1989 publication I emphasized that philosophy of education must obviously attempt to connect theory to the problems and possibilities of education and schooling. In fact, the field must serve its own professorial members, doctoral candidates, potential professional (preservice) teachers, practicing educational professionals, and ordinary citizens. (See the last paragraph in the appendix at chapter's end for an amplification of the first four points in the preceding sentence.) Scholarly competence is necessary. This accomplishment must be relevant to great issues confronting educators and citizens in the institutional school, the broader educational communities, and the larger society itself. This means that philosophers of education must address themselves to questions of fairness and justice for the old and new persons/groups who have been labeled as minorities and/or marginal. Serious attempts to understand the lived experiences of those who have only recently "found their voices" is of crucial importance to the work we do as teachers, scholars, and citizens. Our field's historical focus on epistemology has allowed us to make a strong case for a pedagogy that does not treat students as containers to be filled up with school knowledge dispensed by teachers. Seeing and treating the student as capable of proactive behavior—one who already knows a good deal about many things even before coming to school—allows us to practice a pedagogy that values many different people who, and groups which, comprise our heterogeneous society. Such an epistemology, pedagogy, and liberatory curriculum are central to forwarding the project of social class, racial/ethnic, gender, and sexual-orientation justice. Philosophers of education have helped clarify the difficult problems inherent to pluralism and tolerance for those marginalized as "other." In the absence of agreed upon universals, does it follow that each and everything is as worthy of support as everything else? Must we construct plausible and warranted criteria to help us choose among competing claims—even though we cannot be certain? Diversity for its own sake may not be warranted after one critically examines her/his core values, and the beliefs and practices of others. This examination may be especially important in these times when increasingly large numbers of people worldwide are bombarded by advertising and products, in a manner that suggests consumer choices are tantamount to reflective citizen choices about politics, justice, and other more important issues than new-and-improved gadgets in all their diverse and various forms.

To live without certainty and yet not be paralyzed by hesitation or inaction has never been easy. The recent past has featured powerful reactionary forces throughout the world that have contested fiercely the positions of brave people who have not insisted on being in possession of absolute truth. There have occurred many quests for certainty as our lives have been buffeted by forces that make it difficult to know old signposts and maps. In the United States we have experienced a seemingly orchestrated call for a return to the so-called basics in schooling; a restoration of an essentialist curriculum; the replacement of heuristic pedagogy by authoritarian didactics; the enlistment of our youth into the service of business and industry through a renewed emphasis on various forms of reproductive vocationalism; the restructuring of schooling for leadership roles to the daughters and sons of the affluent and powerful; and the attempted abandonment of public schooling as a place where the harshness of the market has been somewhat alleviated for more than a few students, many who have learned how to become critical citizens with skills to make the promise of democracy, social justice, and respect for bona fide diversity possible. It is not yet decided whether a return to the unhappy quest for certainty will be successful, or if those who realize the injustice of establishing an orthodoxy based on alleged certainties for one and all will prevail. We shall all play roles in determining whether it is possible to live with uncertainty, hypotheses, warranted assertibility, and abundant choices, while still being committed to constructing a common public place where differences need not be considered handicaps. Can education and politics that respect our considerably varied views be successful in ultimately developing a socioeconomic and cultural space in which persons can become more human, and where it will be safer to act altruistically?

In the 1991 editorial introduction to *Philosophical Studies in Education,* I emphasized that contributors to the proceedings insisted that our field be committed to concerns of teachers and laypersons. Philosophers of education were not cautioned to assume that we are working in universally applicable frameworks. We must realize that understanding is an outcome of activities, rather than the grasping of timeless realities. As I argued earlier in this chapter, inquirers alter that which is studied, as well as ourselves. We conduct inquiry in a complex cultural life that is interactive and dialogic. Classed, raced, and gendered actors create knowledge as we interact and attempt to understand our world, and sometimes, change it.

The attempt by some philosophers of education to establish a value-free method of inquiry has been judged to have been a failure. The attempt by British philosophers of education et al. to develop an "objective" point of reference has been criticized by those who are convinced that education must be analyzed within the specific contexts in which they occur. The persistence of social class, racial, ethnic, gender, national, religious, and other differences make it difficult, if not impossible, to establish convincing value-free methods of inquiry. This does not mean that human intelligence is incapable of understanding complex issues concerning school and/or society. Certain values can be evaluated as being better than others. But, this must be accomplished by convincing argumentation within the hurly-burly of lived experience.

An example of this kind of argument appears in the 1991 proceedings. An insightful, easily understood, and ethically grounded argument favoring equal opportunities in our school and society is effective in countering the recent calls for retreat from promises made for social, racial, and gender justice in the United States. Drawing on the work of philosopher John Rawls, this particular contributor reminds us that in all too many cases reward and/or punishment is experienced by students and adults because of genetic inheritance, socioeconomic conditions, luck, and systematic bias and discrimination. Even after one becomes aware of the uneven playing field, concerned people must decide to act in order to alter this lack of fairness and justice. Rawls challenges us to see the possible connections between equal opportunities and more roughly equal outcomes! Otherwise, we must reconsider our egalitarian rhetoric.

Another contributing philosopher of education provides an analysis of how the metaphor of vision-as-knowledge has dominated Western epistemology. Plato is blamed for arguing that true knowledge, based on clear vision, is about "out there" universal things. This model has permitted historically powerful men and groups of them to dominate others—including women. The spectators were unequally able to perceive and understand the objectivity and truth represented in the universal concepts. A metaphor of voice is suggested as a replacement for one of vision, because the former implies that knowledge emerges out of conversations among a large representation of discussants. Democracy is favored over the antidemocracy of Plato. The voice epistemological metaphor is recommended for education that is democratically empowering, committed to social justice, and based on diverse speakers. Paulo Freire helped us understand that conversations among many people lead to an emerging developmental way of knowing that is central to real participatory democracy. Some multiculturalists have insisted that members of various minority groups seem to learn best within pedagogy based on the voice metaphor.

Other philosophers of education expressed support of pluralism and varied voices in the 1991 proceedings. In a paper arguing that it is defensible to teach *about* religions in schools—as contrasted to proselytizing for a particular religion—the author insists that students should be able to learn about more and varied religious viewpoints, beyond the so-called "major" ones. Educators are urged to discuss religious viewpoints in a community-like atmosphere characterized by civility; this condition helps make it possible for discussants to enter into a covenant of respect for each others' differences. This achievement can make possible the attainment of some forms of unity based on freely articulated self-definitions rather than on coercion. Many other contributors to this proceedings addressed the problem of how to arrive at some consensus on important issues of school and society while insuring that agreement was freely achieved.

One interesting point of view expressed in 1991 claimed that good teachers must reconceptualize teaching as interactive collegial participation, a process in which the student gradually assumes a greater participatory role. The student viewed as initially part of the audience at a performance gradually comes on the stage to join the play/discourse. This teacher-as-performer model can be used to invite the student audience into the conversations that they must master in order to have voice in a plural democratic society. There must be room for all on the stage during the last act of the play.

The 1993 proceedings included some of the following ideas in philosophy of education. The presidential address forwarded the thesis that what has been called gossip was demeaned because it was used to describe women's talk. The society's president argued that in male-dominated Western culture, certain kinds of talk were categorized as less valid and important. It kept women and other subaltern people quiet. Gossip was categorized as outside of public discourse by male power in order to deprive women of citizen rights. Feminists argued that gossip is a counter-discourse that should be recognized in an expanded public sphere. When powerful men talk about their work and concerns, it is not called gossip. The historical dichotomy that kept most women in the private sphere (raising children, laboring in the kitchen, etc.) while reserving the public sphere to men (bourgeois and citizen) was analyzed and deconstructed by the philosopher of education who gave the presidential address. In the editorial introduction to these proceedings, I added that critical theorists such as Herbert Marcuse strengthen the thesis of the presidential address by asserting that without fantasy, philosophy remains in the grip of an unrationalized and possibly unjust past and present. Fantasy as another counterdiscourse frees imagination to take us beyond the given, the so-called real, or, the "what is." The naming of things that are absent in the present situation helps break the spell of things that are in place. Both feminist thought and critical theory have opened up spaces in which oppositionalist and reformist persons, ideas, and groups can maneuver. The contemporary emphasis on viewing social class, race/ethnicity, and gender (as well as sexual orientation) identities as importantly interactive provides opportunities for broad-based coalitions aimed at advancing social class, racial, gender, and sexual justice.

The keynote address published in the 1993 proceedings dealt with the challenge posed by multicultural realities in terms of whether we are capable of living together safely and justly in a world of differences. This contribution included expanding the concept of multiculturalism to the formerly colonized areas in the Caribbean and Latin America. The reader was presented with literature that may not have been known to her/him previously. For example, Wilson Harris's *The Palace of the Peacock* encourages us to take seriously the oppressed people's myths as statements against colonial domination. Giving voice to such viewpoints is similar to a reconsideration of gossip and fantasy as honorable discourses. The keynote address urged teachers and students to engage in the rewritings of the so-called official accounts of reality and value that have been presented by those with power—at the expense of those without it.

Another contributor to the 1993 proceedings made a case for social foundations of education, and especially philosophy of education, to be among the vanguard in the analyses of the social conditions of schooling. These discourses have much to offer the study of pluralism and multicultural education. Interpretive, normative, and critical skills are of the greatest importance to those of us who seek to understand how to balance the wonderful differences among us with the need for some democratically constructed agreements on common purposes and actions. We are reminded by a following contribution that because of our personal and local situatedness, it is difficult to see things holistically. Localized positionality and everyday activities occur within a context of "chaos." All too many philosophers in the past have tried to deny this condition and have constructed safe, but false, big-picture explanations in order to ameliorate their fears. Ernest Hemingway's short story, "A Clean Well-Lighted Place," provides a good analysis of actions taken by one who is afraid of chaos; in this case the dark. We should not be hesitant to use our own critically reflected upon autobiographies in order to establish our embeddedness or, view from somewhere, so that reaching out and making common cause with progressive allies is more possible.

Another fine contribution explained how quantum physicists have taught us that what we observe is not nature itself, but only nature as exposed by our method of inquiry. The observer is dependent on her/his position in time and space. Quantum, unlike Newtonian, physics compels us to consider our cognitive/epistemological/theoretical assumptions in limited terms. Newtonian physicists may have shrouded their assumptions from their own critical evaluation by assuming the assumptions were objective and universally applicable.

The next contributor gave us a bit more. The argument was made that master narratives are not objectively or universally true; they are constructed by those with power to impose their views on others. These master, or official, stories are often seen as merely myths, misrepresentations, lies, and oppressive to some critics, especially those who may suffer personally as a result of the living conditions prevailing because of these controlling narratives. An example presented was the myth of market logic as related to arguments for abandoning public schools. So-called free-market models have been used to push rival ideas to the margins. The free-market model and discourse must be critiqued so that they no longer appear as part of the very nature of things, i.e., a natural law. This constructed myth should stand revealed as a partisan political view that favors certain people while ignoring and/or punishing others. We are encouraged by yet another contributing philosopher of education to work toward democratically constructed "universals," albeit ones that will need continuous reconstruction. Although to be human is to err, it may still be possible to argue that a secular basis for democratically developed ethics and morality is a realistic and necessary task. Warranted assertibility is not truth; it is superior to "everyone's opinion is as good as any other."

Let us continue to look through the window provided by paraphrasings from the editorial introductions, this time from 1994. The conference theme from which these proceedings derived was called "Globalism, Postmodernism, the Politics of Identity, and the Problems-possibilities for Democratic/educational Coalitions." The call for papers made it clear that the Ohio Valley Philosophy of Education Society wanted to include as many and varied papers as possible. It was specifically stated in the call for submissions that "proposals concerning diversity, multi-culturalism, community, social class, feminist . . . issues, as well as democracy . . . would all fit under the general umbrella theme." I served as president of the Society in 1994. My presidential address was commented on by a colleague, Kevin McDonough. I wrote the rest of the editorial introduction, "Perennial Problems of Philosophy and Education Played Upon an End of the Millennium Post_____ Landscape." You are to decide which kind of "post" best describes these times—some would say, "postmodernism."

The first paper in the 1994 proceedings spoke to the postmodernist critique of modernist/Enlightenment traditions. Its author worried that such critique destroys the possibility of understanding the world we inhabit. Such cognitive failure makes progressive politics in school and society meaningless or impossible. The contributor expressed concern about how an emancipatory discourse and action based on the recognition and valuing of human differences could develop also the necessary experiences of commonality and unity. In the end, this writer turned to "social dreaming" and "bridges of faith" as ways to activate differentiated people's potential for engaging in a politics of common cause, an activity that might support a pedagogy for democratic empowerment, social justice, and respect for bona fide diversity. I raised the editorial caution that relying on spirituality and faith may be incongruous with the radical, democratic, secular tradition that has importantly driven the broad-based struggles for democracy we have experienced in the modern West. It is well known that reliance on spirituality and faith can result in internecine warfare and obscurantism, as well as the mixture of faith and reason exemplified by struggles led by Mohandas Gandhi and/or Martin Luther King.

It is well for philosophers of education to keep in mind the problem articulated by the playwright Bertolt Brecht as he tells of the physicist and astronomer Galileo and his assistant who is a monk. The monk worries aloud about the possible consequences concerning Galileo's "discovery" that ours is a heliocentric universe. The monk realizes that a change from the comforting belief that the earth is the center of the universe will unsettle the lives of ordinary people who labor so hard within a context they have tried to interpret as reasonable and safe. "They have been told that God relies on them and that the pageant of the world has been written around them. . . . How could they take it, were I to tell them that they are on a lump of stone ceaselessly spinning in empty space, circling a second-rate star?"[42] A philosopher and/or philosopher of education might retort: "How can you *not* tell them that such is a possibility."

Speaking of a scientific view of the world and its events, it is logical to turn next to contemporary technology and the problems as well as possibilities it represents. One of the best contributions to the 1994 proceedings analyzes how the hegemony exercised by capitalists, their allies in the governments, and other institutions such as the schools is often experienced as part of technology instead of direct political pressure. For example, the technology of computerized instruction and tests often serves to continue the polarization of achievement along social class lines. In fact, technology, including in the schools, can conceal the goals and interests of the ruling elites and their agents. This self-interest can be, and often is, built into the design and workings of various machines even before they are assigned to specific tasks. So much for the arguments promoting technology's neutrality. As the contemporary K–12 public schools are susceptible to ever more aggressive attempts by reactionaries to reduce schooling to a mostly reproductive (of existing power, wealth, access, privilege relations) function—including programs to encourage students to enroll in "tech prep" vocational tracks—the philosophical analysis of the partisan nature of educational technology becomes especially relevant. Educators, who are inundated by offers of technological solutions to the seemingly intractable teaching and learning problems caused by asymmetrical power relations in our society and schools, can benefit from studying this fine contribution to the 1994 proceedings. This is important when considering the drive to make school kids "computer literate" in the absence of becoming "critically literate." We must position ourselves on the side of the perennial philosophical quest for understanding, especially in radically altered socioeconomic and political global systems featuring fantastic electronic media developments.

From the analysis of technology and the continuing, vocational reproductive function of schooling, the next contributor argued that it would be easier to accept the vocationalization of our public school system if there were good jobs with generous benefits available at the time of graduation. The contributor thinks that the agents of those with the greatest economic and political power have used the alleged lack of adequate schooling-training as the main cause of unemployment in the U.S. economy. As a result, one must keep her/his eyes on the capitalist market in order to understand the social and school crisis. Perhaps the central problem is the rationalization of labor (building intelligence into the machine and/or process) as well as the exportation of all too many jobs abroad to societies where workers are virtually unprotected by organized labor and their governments. Despite the rhetorical cry for higher level skills in the work force, the deskilling of blue, white, and pink collar workers has proceeded along with the global expansion of capitalism.

The next contributor argued that teachers-as-intellectuals must be especially aware of power relations that affect school and society. Teachers can and must move beyond the role of clerical workers. Drawing on Paulo Freire's work, this philosopher of education insisted that teachers examine the causes of injustice so that it can be understood and overcome. This could clear spaces in which to construct a more just school and society. This paper included a call for the transformation of teacher preparation programs so that they may become "sites for social transformation." My response to this noble call to action argued that such transformation is dependent upon educators being able to obtain massive support from allies outside of their workplace. Such profound change will take a long time to achieve. Those in power would and do fight fiercely to preserve the system that works for them.

The 1994 proceedings included a panel discussion of the movie, "Forrest Gump." Perhaps this is an indication that philosophers of education are interested in popular culture. Popular cultural forms are ubiquitous as they are driven by commercial imperatives. They have saturated most of the spaces in which we live. Our educational analyses and projects must take popular culture into consideration, otherwise charges of irrelevancy could be made. Philosophers of education can and must help bring rigor and stability to the burgeoning field called cultural studies.

Let us conclude our brief encounter with work done in 1994 by philosophers of education with Kevin McDonough's comments on my presidential address.

[Brosio] argues that democratic politics and education can and should develop political and educational practices and institutions that privilege our common identities as citizens and workers, rather than our ethnic, cultural, sexual or other particularistic identities. . . . I would like to highlight three central themes in Richard's argument and then . . . indicate one direction his analysis might lead us. First, Richard articulates a wide ranging critique of recent postmodern themes in social, political and educational thought. The thread which ties his multi-faceted critique together is the notion that the postmodernist intellectuals have neglected to theorize the relation between the cultural issues that preoccupy them and underlying economic and social class factors; consequently, postmodernists have failed to seriously challenge the prodigious power of global capitalism. The point is not, of course, that we should ignore the cultural issues that postmodernists have brought to the forefront of social, and educational, discourse. Rather, Brosio argues that we need to examine and attempt to understand more adequately the relationship between such issues and bigger, underlying economic forces. This theme is important because it forces us to consider that many postmodernist intellectual concerns provide a feeble response to real educational problems such as the "savage" economic inequalities characterizing modern capitalist society and schools. . . . [The reference here is . . . to Jonathan Kozol's *Savage Inequalities*, New York: Harper Perennial, 1991.] Richard's second central theme develops a critique of what he takes to be post-modernism's political expression—the politics of identity. For Brosio, the politics of identity as it is currently constituted—theoretically by postmodernist intellectuals and concretely in the political arena of capitalist, democratic societies—is a futile response to capitalism's corrosive influence of established forms of communal identity. At the same time, he understands the potential for the best possible expression of a politics of identity in terms of the need for a robust resistance to capitalist hegemony. The argument here is not that economic causes underlying cultural, gender, sexual or other forms of inequality are genuine while psychological or spiritual ones are false. Rather, the argument is that economic causes are primary, and we need explanatory frameworks that recognize this in order to be able to understand and construct political practices and institutions that will enable subaltern people to actually exercise their capacity to construct and express their particular identities in meaningful ways. Richard's analysis here encourages us to remember that claims by subaltern groups and individuals for recognition are often responses—conscious or unconscious—to deteriorating material conditions under conditions of modern, global capitalism, rather than to real or perceived psychological insults. Thus, he suggests the appropriate response on the part of a democratic society that values and encourages the vibrant expression of plural identities may not be the mere inclusion of multiple "voices" in a discourse dominated by the unchallenged hegemony of capitalism, but rather the radical transformation of capitalism itself. The third and most fundamental theme develops Richard's argument for broad "rainbow coalitions" focused around common citizen-worker identities. He argues that such coalitions are both possible and necessary in order to achieve the sort of political agency required for democratic, anti-capitalist political and social transformation that enables the celebration and recognition of pluralistic group and individual identities. According to Brosio, the category of citizen-worker (where work is defined broadly to include unpaid labor as well as non-traditional forms of "work", such as the very process of cultural identity formation that characterizes human action) is primary because it represents the necessary platform for resisting the capitalist forces that make the process of constructing meaningful expressions of cultural, gender, sexual, etc. identity impossible, or at least very difficult, for dispossessed people. Importantly, the construction of common modes of identity around the categories of citizen and worker are not meant to subvert local cultural, gender or other communal identities. Rather, Brosio emphasizes that the construction of common citizen-worker identities is necessary for permitting our more basic identities to flourish. Having summarized, too briefly, the main features of Brosio's far-reaching essay, it is nevertheless illuminating to consider where his analysis might lead us. Richard's argument for broad political and educational coalitions points toward—but does not answer—at least two important educational questions. First, what actual groups and individuals might constitute such coalitions in contemporary democratic political contexts? Second, what motivational sources might exist, and be developed, to enable diverse groups and individuals to coalesce into broader coalitions? . . . The points [suggested] in the preceding paragraph are not intended as a refutation or even a criticism of Richard's argument for broad, democratic coalitions. It merely highlights the point that such coalitions will not automatically form once people discover and/or construct the common social interests that underlie their diverse identity claims. People who find they share common interests as workers and citizens may and will continue to ask why shared, perhaps even universalistic, considerations of social class should take precedence over particularistic considerations of race, ethnicity, gender when these come into conflict in particular cases? Moreover, educators will wonder why they should privilege considerations of social class over other considerations. These questions are beyond the scope of Brosio's essay because they address issues of ethical justification that he is not concerned with in the present context. Nevertheless, they are questions that must be addressed and answered before we can get on with the task of creating a just social and political order that allows and encourages the toleration and meaningful celebration of differences. I would argue that Richard Brosio's . . . presidential address is important and valuable for educators not only because it forces us to re-examine the important role that socio-economic class plays in democratic politics and education, but because it provokes us to examine the complex dynamics that must underlie our understanding of, and justification for, a politics and education for the common good in democratic societies.[43]

Perhaps the reader can better understand what philosophy of education conversations are like after considering Professor McDonough's supportive but critical response to my work.

Finally, we will consider the proceedings from the 1995 annual meeting of the Ohio Valley Philosophy of Education Society. My editorial introduction was called, "'On the Edge': Warranted Desperation, With a Bit of Class." I pointed out that although there are varied themes and even formats of presentation in the 1995 meeting and its published proceedings, there are topics, concerns, and arguments that are related to one another. These similarities may very well characterize, to some extent, where many philosophers of education "are at" during these times—especially in North America. The works represented in the 1995 proceeding represent the problems and intellectual/structural problems as well as perceived possibilities during these last years of the second millennium.

In the editorial response to the 1995 presidential address I draw from Russell Jacoby's work. He stated that in these times not only is the personal life considered (by some) a part of politics—in terms of engagement in struggles to advance one's or a group's goal—but everything is considered political by those lacking the ability to make fine and necessary distinctions. The failure to distinguish among various public and/or private actions results in the unfortunate position characterized by the following: If everything is political, then no action assumes more significance than any other. "Reinterpreting pop[ular] culture becomes as political as running for office, organizing labor unions, or working on the local school board. The upshot is the politicization of self, language, and knowledge—the immediate domain of the academic. . . . The focus on interpersonal encounter, however, shifts attention away from [arguably] more important issues, such as the structures of racism or economic injustice."[44] I use Jacoby to critique the views of some postmodernist thinkers.

The philosopher of education who gave the invited address speaks to Jacoby's point. This address included arguments explaining how feminists are correct to avoid concentrating on "grand issues," because not everyone agrees what these are. There are many sites on which to struggle for social and education justice. This contributor reminded us that we must realize that gender is also classed and raced. All too often, spokespersons for feminist concerns do so from privileged social-class and white positions, whereas solidarity with others who occupy subaltern positions in the ranked order of U.S. society is of utmost importance if significant change is to occur. This address supports my position concerning the central importance of citizen and worker as identities around which to build progressive coalitions of classed, raced, and gendered people.

Another contribution to the 1995 proceedings explained the gendered nature of teachers' work, historically and in the United States, as well as in Europe. The public elementary schools featured "moral education" aimed at keeping working-class students in place. The children of the rich and powerful were educated for eventual leadership. Because of the stereotypes about women concerning their emotive side rather than rational/intellectual capacities, the nineteenth and early-twentieth century featured poorly paid women teachers whose task it was to prepare the working class for its eventual role in the stratified capitalist economy, with proper loyalties to the class State. This paper explained that the education of teachers has not been as academically effective as necessary, in part, because teacher preparation programs too often are designed to service the job and credentials market, rather than the imperative of democracy and its need for broadly educated, critical citizens.

I will examine the final contribution to the 1995 proceedings and bring this section of chapter one to a close. This provocative contribution serves us well as a bridge to the 1995 Ohio Valley Philosophy of Education

Society meeting which called for papers specifying "how the climate of downsizing, rightsizing, retrenchment . . . is affecting philosophers of education." I remind you that the published papers, i.e., *Philosophical Studies in Education*, are made available after the annual meetings.

The following passage is quoted from the 1995 proceeding's editorial introduction as I comment on David Blacker's paper, "Saints, Sinners, Selves: Into Pedagogy's Outer Zone."

Blacker begins by telling us . . . that poverty, marginalization, and other forms of social injustice do not, in most cases, give rise to a noble sufferer who is then prompted to act solidaristically and altruistically. He compares the conditions in the Nazi death camps with some facets of situations within more than a few inner cities in this country. Blacker makes a poignant and powerful case for how people who have been under siege as well as subject to violations of their bodies and spirits tend to act: actions which many more fortunate people condemn out of ignorance—if not malice. The author is not afraid to argue that the architects of the new economic world order are importantly responsible for creating the conditions wherein too many human beings have been declared superfluous. Zeroing in, Blacker makes clear that ghetto oppression has led to concentration camps before; moreover, these camps became sites for annihilation! Blacker makes palpably clear how many of the inner city youths' actions are sensible within the frames of reference they have been structurally bound within. The severity of the problems that David describes makes the conventional, self-serving, mean-spirited Rightist explanation of the alleged reasons for ghetto dwellers' behaviors seem like part of the problem. His assessment of the damage done to ghetto youth does not serve to strengthen United Statesian liberal explanations and/or policies either. Courageously, Blacker argues that some of the ghetto youth have been so severely damaged that pedagogy in the "normal" sense is inadequate to the task. He insists that K–12 teachers must become political activists in order to have a chance to help solve the human-created problems of economic superfluousness, racism, and forms of malign neglect—as well as malign actions within the free-fire zones of our urban centers. The advocates of better "classroom management" and "harmless innovation" appear to be either fools or knaves when juxtaposed beside David's searing analysis. A sample of Blacker's work which can serve as an inviting coming-attraction reads as follows: "The often slow-moving violence of capitalism and of institutionalized racism does more than cause pain, sadness, and anger. It peels the skin off of live selves, exposing them naked and raw to one another and to a barbed wire world. These selves are forced to contest one another in an almost Hobbesian state of nature, a beeper and uzi-toting war of all against all." . . . Blacker explains how those with power have created a serviceable other, as well as the structural conditions that force the other(s) to fulfill the denigrative stereotype intrinsic to the original construction of this s/he who can be used, abused, and cast outside the protections enjoyed by those who are more fortunate—and often complicitous. Blacker would have us face up to Dewey's challenge that it is irrational to value something, e.g., progressive/humane/equitable education, while refusing to value means that are necessary to make such goals possible and concrete. Let us hear the last words from Professor Blacker himself while noticing his emphasis on structure and especially its meaning during the end of the second millennium when so many insist that there is no structure, no totalizing logic, and no capitalism. "As the stresses and strains of late capitalism proceed apace, as, for example, the school population is further polarized into hirable and economically superfluous unhirable 'extra people,' and as public institutions across the board are drained and then abandoned by an ever-more untethered transnational corporate capitalism, this feature of teaching [the teacher as necessarily a political activist] will only become more pronounced. And as structural conditions deteriorate for large segments of the school-age populations, as 'savage inequalities' widen, teaching in any meaningful sense—as opposed to, say, warehousing or surveillance—increasingly demands politicization, even radical rethinking of what it might mean to teach and learn under conditions so dehumanizing as to place ever more teachers and students 'on the edge.'"[45]

Conclusion

Chapter one provides an imperfect blueprint and some scaffolding in preparation for the main construction project. I have deliberately refrained from writing an orthodox introduction that would have been characterized by a neatly packaged presentation of philosophy of education. This invitation into serious philosophical discourse—especially about education—is intended to whet your appetite with regard to the rest of the book. It is my experience that a learner's interest is enlisted best when her/his serious concerns are addressed. As one becomes involved in relevant and difficult intellectual labor the incentive to learn about special tools increases. By way of example, there is evidence that indicates the ineffectiveness of trying to teach students how to diagram sentences grammatically when they see little or no need to express themselves differently from their current practice. Learning more words and where to place them, as well as in the correct tense, become relevant as the need or desire to express oneself about increasingly complex thoughts and actions increases. This development may also be related to the discovery of an audience for one's verbal and/or written expression. Let us involve ourselves in serious concerns about the human condition, especially as it relates to education, and learn about some tools of the trade as we become aware of them and their potential usefulness.

The challenge to the reader is to think about what publicly defensible alternatives one could espouse in place of education for democratic empowerment, social justice, and respect for bona fide diversity. We must make clear what these alternatives might mean within the complexities of our experience. Consider what education for your alternatives would mean.

If you do support what I favor, how would you go about defending democracy, social justice, and diversity in the possible absence of cognitive certainty, objectivity, and/or *terra firma* upon which to stand; i.e., how would one justify the favored trio over other societal and school goals if not through alleged access to what is universally correct and good?

I will argue throughout this work that there exists a secular tradition in the West and elsewhere that allows—and even demands—that the favored trio must be sought after by those who see reality as complex, uncertain, and in need of human interference and ultimate shaping. Many of the intellectual workers featured in this book believe that reality is not objective data. It is neither external to the knower nor is it unaffected by the attempts of human beings to describe and, yes, master it—if only imperfectly and temporarily. Some of these contributors have maintained that reality is in fact shaped by human action. "The activist character of human beings is best represented by labor, the activity through which . . . [we] shape the social-physical realities around . . . [us], and in the process change . . . [our]selves."[46] Many writers and/or activists featured in this book agree that theory can and must construct a plausible interpretation of social—including educational—conditions in order to go forward toward change and improvement. The theory-builders must believe that understanding phenomena deeply and broadly is possible, and that reconstruction can and should occur as an outcome of understanding. In a word, praxis is possible. Reconstruction does not just occur; it is made possible by purposive actors. Democratic actors who insist on social justice and respect for diversity must view themselves as subjects, rather than objects to be hammered upon by powers seemingly beyond their control and/or understanding.

Contributor Antonio Gramsci provides us with important ideas about how mass intellectual advancement can occur so that most, if not all, people will be capable of "self-rule," which is what democracy means. He maintains that those who had been shut-out of formal education in the past could respond to the power of invitation based on viewing learning as hard labor. Those who have done difficult jobs already know what hard work is. If studying is portrayed as related to physical labor those who were once excluded from formal schooling opportunities might have more confidence in their abilities to do mental labor. Such a portrayal would help demystify the world of schooling; i.e., all students could see that learning was not a form of magic or tricks that were possessed only by the well-to-do people. Gramsci portrayed studying as comprised of skills that were learnable even by those who had formerly been excluded. This achievement was thought possible in spite of their obvious handicaps with regard to leisure, tradition, and cultural capital (school readiness).

For Gramsci—as well as for John Dewey and Paulo Freire—the possibility for the intellectual development of nearly everyone exists because the learner is not just passive, but is active and knowledgeable about many things, even if the school curriculum does not include them. Ordinary people's everyday experiences often contradict the official knowledge and view of the world imposed on them by powerful persons and institutions. Gramsci knew that everyone has a culture, even if ideas about it may not be fully developed. The learner is not an empty vessel to be filled, nor is s/he a blank sheet to be written upon. Education must begin with what the students already know as well as what may trouble them. Gramsci "begins not from the point of view of the teacher [although he believed that instruction was of great importance] but from the learner, and he emphasizes that the learning process is a movement toward self-knowledge. Education is not a matter of handing out 'encyclopedic knowledge' but of developing and disciplining the awareness which the learner already possesses."[47]

The ability to learn is related to the ability to do and to be a participatory democrat—*homo faber* cannot be separated from *homo sapiens*. My use of these Latin words includes both genders. Each of us has a picture of the world and a somewhat conscious sense of moral conduct. It is possible to develop a new, better, and larger democratic group of intellectuals. Education at its best consists of the critical elaboration of the intellectual ability and activity possessed by everyone in varying degrees. The keystone to Gramsci's democratic "bias" is articulated:

> Differences among people's competencies, intelligence, interests, and accomplishments do not disappear but are negotiated and understood in new ways 'between: leaders and led . . . mental and manual labour . . . politics and society . . . philosophy and science.' Gramsci never stresses differences in invidiously comparative terms; rather, he arranges them within a structured division of labor that is based on the foundation of skills possessed by nearly every human being. 'The question is not whether a division of labor is necessary but which . . . [one] . . . and for which reasons . . . .' Relations among persons who vary a good deal in . . . their abilities . . . must be mediated with the good of all as the goal.[48]

This belief in the widespread distribution of intelligence and potential among us allowed Gramsci and other democrats to insist on participatory democracy based on social justice and human diversity. Democracy does not mean merely that an unskilled worker can become skilled and/or a "professional." It means that every citizen can govern; that educational experiences are widely available in order to develop necessary critical citizen skills and meaningful empowerment. Gramsci's educational project consists of helping us understand things as they are, while at the same time laying the foundation for things as they might be.

Mike Rose's *Lives on the Boundary* described well the kind of teacher and education that flows logically from the philosophical and political underpinnings held by Gramsci and others who subscribe to a democratic "bias." Rose understood that because of social injustices according to class, race, gender, and other criteria, students are very differently equipped to "do school." His experiences as a rookie teacher in East Los Angeles made him aware that it is the whole child who is at risk in a society that fails to promote the overall welfare of each and every human being. Rose's democratic "bias" became radical because he sought, like Gramsci et al., to get to the root causes for poor school performance, political uninvolvement, poverty, crime, etc. He taught kids who could not easily master the narrow cognitive tasks so often required by school "experts," those who fail to understand why their demands are unfair. His writing assignments were designed to allow students to draw on their own experiences and knowledge. Rose explained that the official English curriculum he was supposed to use was mostly geared to grammatical analyses and subskills. This made it difficult for the exploration of the far more important communication of information, narrative construction and "shaping what we see and feel and believe into written language . . . Writing and reading [in schools] are such private acts that we forget how fundamentally [in the last analysis] social they are."[49]

In spite of its shortcomings, Rose was convinced that the U.S. K–12 public school system is a remarkable institutional achievement. This public system provides schooling for virtually all youngsters, including those who are poor, minorities, and those labeled as differently abled. Now we must make certain that every student who is included under the big tent of the K–12 public schools is educated for critical citizenship and empowerment. The school experience must help prepare its students to become involved in making the praiseworthy, official rhetoric of this country a reality instead of just words. Teachers, administrators, parents, ordinary citizens—as well as students—must struggle to undo the reproductive function of schooling. Rose asked us to be mindful of how the everyday conditions of life in the United States lay bare the weakness, and even misrepresentation, of claims that our society is a level playing field from which an authentic meritocracy can arise. He asked us to "consider not only the economic and political barriers . . . [students] face, but . . . that judgments about their ability are made at a very young age, and those judgments, accurate or not, affect the curriculum they receive, their place in the school, the way they're defined institutionally. . . . Meanwhile the children gradually internalize the definition the school delivers to them."[50]

Educators and citizens can and should use the power of invitation in order to welcome those who have been discriminated against and suffer from injustice. This invitation must not be viewed as a summons to disinvite students who have *not* been historically marginalized. In Rose's words: "The more I . . . understand . . . education, the more I've come to believe in the power of invitation. Programs like the Teacher Corps— and many others that [were] developed through these [1960s] years— generated possibilities for all kinds of people who had traditionally been excluded from the schools."[51] It is well known that the political, economic, social, cultural, and educational reaction against real and/or perceived gains made by those who were formerly excluded has sought to discredit progressive government intervention into the inequitable distribution of power, access, privilege, and outcomes in both school and society. I have argued throughout this chapter that radical democrats who are interested in promoting social justice as well as respect for bona fide diversity in this vast land must be fortified by, if not entirely dependent upon, certain philosophical assumptions and convictions. This is also true with regard to educational philosophy. If one does not believe that intelligence is widespread throughout various populations or, that in the absence of certainty some beliefs and courses of action are still better than others, it is difficult to see how one could hold to democratic principles. I began my introductory chapter with the classical Greeks' achievements. I have held that a belief in widespread human ability to understand and act upon the world is essential to democratic politics and education. I have pointed out that there exist traditions in philosophy of education that support the democratic "bias" of which the philosopher (and educational philosopher) John Dewey spoke. You are invited to wrestle intellectually with what you have read so far. You must critically appropriate what has been presented and decide if it makes sense to you; if not, why not? Although discussion need not occur in a formal classroom setting, it is warranted to assume that discussion about this chapter is one of the very best ways to clarify your own positions.

Appendix

For those readers who want to learn more about philosophy of education as a field of study in the United States, you are invited to consider this necessarily brief historical description of it. The National Society for the Study of Education has published three volumes on philosophy of education: *The Forty-first Yearbook: Part I, Philosophies of Education,* copyright 1942; *The Fifty-fourth Yearbook: Modern Philosophies of Education,* copyright 1955; and *The Eightieth Yearbook: Part I, Philosophy and Education,* published 1981. The editor for the Society of the first two is Nelson B. Henry. John S. Brubacher, chairman of the Society's Committee on Philosophies of Education, is responsible for the direction taken in the 1942 and 1955 volumes. The editor for the Society in 1981 was Kenneth J. Rehage. Brubacher's successor as chairman of the Society's Committee on Philosophy and Education is Jonas F. Soltis. Soltis is also *called* the editor in the 1981 volume. You can also learn about philosophy of education by consulting *Philosophy of Education* which consists of the publication of scholarly papers and responses that occur at the annual Philosophy of Education Society of the United States. There are various regional societies, e.g., the Ohio Valley Philosophy of Education Society (PES), the Midwest (PES), Southeast (PES), etc. The first of these regional societies' publications is *Philosophical Studies in Education.* These publications, along with the quarterly journal, *Educational Theory,* will allow the interested reader to enter the discourses constructed by philosophers of education in the United States, North America, and beyond. The internet is a system where philosophers of education can be found for purposes of information and dialogue.

I will take a brief look at the philosophical ideas concerning education that have been articulated in the three yearbooks as well as in the commentary on them. The Forty-first Yearbook states that philosophy helps determine what kind of knowledge is best suited to various educational goals. It also points out that because the 1940s were characterized as "muddled times," philosophy of education became especially useful to educators with regard to the possible relations between ends and means. This volume features serious disagreements concerning what problems in philosophy of education were most important. Five main schools of thought were selected for comparison: pragmatism, realism, idealism, Aristotelianism, and scholasticism or Catholicism. This is in keeping with the isms approach to philosophy and philosophy of education. Content endnote number 24 speaks to the isms approach to philosophy of education.

The editors of the Forty-first and Fifty-fourth Yearbooks said they offer students of educational theory and practice access to "authoritative" views on key issues with respect to educational goals and procedures. Brubacher sought to identify some of the principal philosophical issues underlying education in the Fifty-fourth Yearbook. Some of the issues are rudderless education; worry about standards erosion; uncertainty about what democratic education means; decline of authority; and whether schools are becoming too secular. It is obvious that these concerns are ones indicating the strength of conservative voices during the mid-1950s.

In spring 1956 the *Harvard Educational Review,* vol. 256, no. 2 devoted a whole issue to philosophy of education. The contributors to this journal were responding to two articles that appeared in the October 27, 1955 issue of *The Journal of Philosophy*, vol. 52, no. 22. More specifically, these articles are by: Harry S. Broudy, "How Philosophical Can Philosophy of Education Be?", pp. 612–22; and Kingsley Price, "Is A Philosophy of Education Necessary?", pp. 622–33. The *Harvard Educational Review* is rich in terms of philosophy of education discourse and argument. Because philosophy does not change as rapidly as science and technology, it may still be worth studying the conversations of these students of philosophy and education in 1955–56. One example is William Frankena's assertion that philosophy of education consists classically of: *speculation* about the universe as whole and our place in it; *normative* criteria for action; and critical *analytical* evaluations of assumptions and methods, as well as careful attempts to define terms such as "real," "true," "good," "rigor," etc. Frankena argued that the normative function is most important for philosophy of education. Educators must have help as they attempt to make good decisions about what should or should not be done. Theories about the ends and compatible means of educational activity represent the normative and ethical service philosophers of education can and must provide.

A special issue of the *Teachers College Record*, vol. 81, no 2 (Winter 1979), provided a context for understanding the *Eightieth Yearbook* which appeared in 1981. Jonas Soltis wrote in the *Yearbook* that the main purpose of that volume was to acquaint readers with how philosophy of education had changed since 1955, as well as how philosophy and education could be connected. Soltis was speaking about how philosophy of education had followed trends that were occurring in the parent discipline during the years between 1955 and 1981. The movement was away from system building and isms and toward the careful examination of important educational issues by those who saw themselves as philosophers *interested* in education rather than philosophers *of* education. There was an attempt to use philosophy to help educators think more critically about what they were doing. This reflected the growing specialization in academe generally. Soltis hoped that the trends in philosophy of education during the period between the *Yearbooks* would facilitate a congruence between what philosophers of education could do, and what educators expected of them and the field.

Some argued that the *Eightieth Yearbook* represented a victory for narrow academic specialization and philosophical analysis, at the expense of a more holistic, big-picture approach. Many of these arguments for and against this victory in philosophy of education can be studied in: the symposium on the *Eightieth Yearbook* in the *Harvard Educational Review*, vol. 51, no. 3 (August 1981), and the special issue devoted to the *Yearbook* in *Educational Theory*, vol. 31, no. 1 (Winter 1981). David Nyberg explained, in *Educational Theory*, that the *Yearbook* reflects the state of Anglo-American philosophy at that time. One could add that this state was caused in part, by a kind of political quiescence in old, rich, and comparatively settled societies. The voices of those who were not so settled or affluent were not heard in this philosophical state of affairs.

Suggested Task for the Reader
Readers/students are encouraged to think about how analyzing specific issues, rather than looking critically at a whole system—whether societal or school—tends to favor the status quo. Discussion could focus on whether it should be surprising that philosophy, including philosophy of education, would be strongly affected by the political, economic, and cultural characteristics of the societies of which philosophers are a part.

A source that might be helpful to enrich this discussion is Isaiah Berlin's, *The Hedgehog and the Fox: An Essay on Tolstoy's View of History* (New York: Simon & Schuster, Inc., 1953). Berlin argued that the fox knows many things, but the hedgehog knows one big thing. Berlin and Soltis seem to prefer the fox's knowledge in part, because they distrust unifying, centralizing, totalistic grand or master narratives. Students can explore some of the reasons these narratives are feared and criticized by many contemporary thinkers, especially postmodernists. On the other hand, readers might consider also Harry Broudy's argument that, "the layman [sic] is incurably metaphysical, and if the philosophy of education ignores or merely makes fun of this need, it will be satisfied from non-philosophical sources." In Chapter II, "Between the Yearbooks" in the *Eightieth Yearbook*, p. 27, Broudy argues, perhaps in support of the hedgehog, that wholeness of view and internal consistency are necessary. The *Eightieth Yearbook* does not provide either to his satisfaction.

Let us consider some other critical reactions to the controversial *Eightieth Yearbook*. Barbara Arnstine is disturbed because "the thrust . . . [of the *Yearbook* is] toward the abstract problems of educational research

. . . [Moreover, there] is the absence of any serious attempt to deal with the social, economic, and political context in which educational research and practice function." *Educational Theory* (Winter 1981), p. 20. A more biting criticism of the *Yearbook* is provided by Foster McMurray. He argued that what the contributors to the *Yearbook* do, mostly, "is to inform others about philosophic ideas and analytic patterns which they happen to like and which, they think, ought to be better known by educators, or actually, by persons at large. [These] educational philosophers function as partisan pleaders for favorite materials from contemporary philosophy." Ibid., p. 88. McMurray suggested that this kind of philosophy of education is the result of these writers' belief that "educational doctrines are a function of other and more fundamental ideas about more universal human concerns. The real meat, they think, lies elsewhere than in theory of education; it [allegedly] lies in the exciting . . . higher status stuff from philosophy, political theory, and social consciousness. . . . It is a way of thinking that is not only responsible for the failure of educational philosophers to offer leadership in educational theory; it is also a product of bad reasoning, or of failure to understand the nature of that which is called 'philosophy of.'" Ibid., p. 89. McMurray's arguments are indicative of disagreements among philosophers of education. Those who do not understand the value of this kind of disputation should never have power over those who do, and who must continue their valuable activities. Soltis might respond to McMurray that philosophy and education are "natural allies."

The *Harvard Educational Review* published a symposium response to the *Eightieth Yearbook* in 1981. Consider a critique provided by C.A. Bowers. Drawing on sociology of education, Bowers urged philosophers of education to address the problems and possibilities inherent to a perspective that sees the world as humanly and historically constructed, therefore amenable to progressive *reconstruction*. He asked that philosophers of education help students and teachers understand better "what is the relationship between political power and the language codes of different [social] classes . . . [and speech communities]. What are the metaphors of legitimization that give one speech community power over other . . . [ones]? What happens to the students' ability to exercise communicative competence . . . when the school transmits the culture . . . of [some adults'] taken-for-granted knowledge?" *Harvard Educational Review* (August 1981), pp. 429–30. It is right to be reminded that even "expert" knowledge and/or speech is never politically or valuatively neutral. In the absence of deity-derived certainties, educators must make decisions among complex alternatives. These alternatives often seem like competing goods, rather than clear choices between good and bad. Broudy would concur. He has suggested that philosophers of education must explain and defend the need for rational discussion, as well as freedom to inquire. He preferred these things over operating from a position of "fixed faith" that may not be credible and/or convincing to others.

In conclusion, let us consider a persuasive, commonsense argument for those who value philosophy of education as central to teacher education. In 1982, George Kizer had the following to say in his presidential address before the Midwest Philosophy of Education Society:

> As philosophers of education, I believe that we have four primary audiences to serve: (1) ourselves; (2) our doctoral candidates . . . ; (3) potential teachers, administrators, and other educational professionals who are in preservice preparation programs; and (4) practicing professionals who now serve in our schools and who are seeking . . . professional growth and development. . . . The evidence is that our performance in serving the needs of the first two of our audiences is excellent. . . . If we cannot, however, improve our performance and communicate with professional educators in our other two audiences, I fear that support for our programs and services will be diminished with the ultimate consequence of undercutting our performance with our first two audiences. George A. Kizer, *Midwest Philosophy of Education Proceedings*, eds., Michael Smith and Jack Williams (Milwaukee, WI: Midwest Philosophy of Education Society, 1983), 93.

Kizer was aware that professional K–12 educators can come to appreciate the relevance of certain philosophical insights and analyses that go beyond their present immediate concerns. He believed that philosophy of education must increase its power of invitation for those who may need it. Kizer is convinced that philosophy of education must be committed to something: "if not to democracy, then to some form of social arrangement that our intelligence convinces us is superior." Ibid., 97. Kizer judged the *Eightieth Yearbook* to be mostly an apology for increased specialization and fragmentation of educational philosophy. He recommended the further development of social philosophy and greater attention to our primary audiences. Kizer would probably approve of Tony W. Johnson's *Discipleship or Pilgrimage? The Educator's Quest for Philosophy* (Albany, NY: State University of New York Press, 1995) because of Johnson's insistence that philosophers of education reconstruct the field according to the problems and possibilities within the K–12 schools. Johnson was sharply critical of philosophers of education for trying to make the field just one more university guild while refusing to take responsibility for their most important constituents, K–12 students and educators. The first chapter provides a historical account that explains philosophy of education as a field of study. At the end of the chapter he makes common cause with Dewey by insisting the field must become philosophy *as* education.

Notes

1   C. Wright Mills, *The Marxists* (New York: A Delta Book, 1962), 36.

2   Harold Entwistle, "The Relationship Between Educational Theory and Practice: A New Look," in *Philosophy of Education: Introductory Readings*, eds. William Hare and John P. Portelli (Calgary, Alberta, Canada: Detselig Enterprises Ltd., 1988), 27.

3   Ibid., 29–30.

4   G. Max Wingo, *Philosophies of Education: An Introduction* (Lexington, Mass.: D.C. Heath and Company, 1974), 7.

5   See, Timothy Reagan, *Non-Western Educational Traditions: Alternative Approaches to Educational Thought and Practice* (Mahwah, N.J.: Lawrence Earlbaum Associates, Inc., 1996), for a window into non-Western educational thought and practice.

6   Edith Hamilton, *The Greek Way to Western Civilization* (New York: Mentor Books, 1930), 210–13.

7   The term, postmodern, is a complex one. With regard to chronology, it refers to what has and is occurring *after* modernism. For those who are not familiar with such periodizing terms, be patient as you read on. Careful reading of this book, as well as of other references, will help you understand the term postmodern. Chapter eight of this book will specifically consider certain postmodernist ideas.

8   Ellen Meiksins Wood, *Democracy Against Capitalism: Renewing Historical Materialism* (Cambridge, U.K.: Cambridge University Press, 1995), 190–91.

9   Joel Spring, *Wheels in the Head: Educational Philosophies of Authority, Freedom, and Culture from Socrates to Paulo Freire* (New York: McGraw-Hill, 1994), 7.

10 For an informative analysis and critique of these characteristics of antidemocratic Greek philosophy, see: John Dewey, *Reconstruction in Philosophy*, enlarged edition (1948) with a new introduction by the author (Boston: Beacon Press, 1920), introduction and chapter one "Changing Conceptions of Philosophy"; John Dewey, *The Quest for Certainty* (New York: G.P. Putnam's Sons, 1929), chapters one "Escape From Peril," two, "Philosophy's Search for the Immutable," and three "Conflict of Authorities."

11 Wood, *Democracy Against Capitalism*, 202.

12 Harvey J. Kaye articulated the notion of critique without complete renunciation. He said that we engage in a "critical appropriation of the 'traditions of Western Civilization' and their rearticulation in the narratives we . . . develop." *The Powers of the Past* (Minneapolis: University of Minnesota Press, 1991), 164. Kaye wrote:

"'Western culture' is a product of a complex history of adaptation . . . [and] innovation . . . resulting both from the interactions among 'Western' peoples . . . and from those with non-Western peoples by way of exploration, exchange, theft, conflict . . . and migration (elected and coerced)." p. 166.

13   Hamilton, *The Greek Way*, 10–11.

14   Bertrand Russell, *A History of Western Philosophy* (New York: Simon and Schuster, 1945), xiv.

15   C.M. Bowra, *The Greek Experience* (New York: A Mentor Book, 1957), 180–81.

16   Ibid., 186–87.

17   Ibid., 197.

18   Ibid., 202.

19   Gilbert Murray explained that the political failure of the Greeks, the destruction of the city-state and democracy as well as their falling under the control of others, helped cause a loss of hope in the world. They were thrown back upon their own souls, "upon the pursuit of personal holiness . . . emotions, mysteries and revelations . . . and the comparative neglect of the transitory and imperfect world for the sake of some dream-world far off, which shall . . . [be] without sin or corruption, the same yesterday, today, and forever." *Five Stages of Greek Religion* (Garden City: Doubleday Anchor Books, 1955), 4. Murray reminded us that "the best seed-ground for superstition is a society in which the fortunes of men [and women] seem to bear practically no relation to their merits and efforts." p. 127.

20   For a standard examination of classical Greek political thought, see Ernest Barker, *The Political Thought of Plato and Aristotle* (New York: Dover Publications, Inc., 1959), passim, but especially the epilogue.

21   Bowra, *The Greek Experience*, 209.

22   Nikos Kazantzakis, *Report to Greco* (New York: Bantam Books, Inc., 1961), 477–78.

23   Albert Camus, *The Plague* (New York: The Modern Library, 1947), 278.

24   It may be helpful at this point to provide a brief description of what some of the philosophical isms are. Ideaism (usually referred to as idealism) is characterized by a belief that reality is unchanging; its adherents hold that consciousness is prior to, and in some ways responsible for, the world in which we live. Idealism has served as philosophical justification for educational essentialism. Essentialism is based on the belief that there are certain essentials or basics that must be taught to every student. Epistemologically the essentialists claim to be certain about what they consider to be essential because they believe that this curriculum is supported by the idealist belief in a reality that is unchanging as well as knowable by educated human beings. Educational essentialists have also depended on philo-

sophical realism because its adherents hold that reality is objective, independent of the knower (although knowable), constructed of forms and matter, and based on natural laws; human beings can know and rely on this physical but orderly universe without knowing the ultimate cause for its existence. As the power and prestige of science grew during the modern period, many educational essentialists switched from philosophical idealism to its near relative, realism. Another ism that is relied on by those educators who desire certainty is Thomism, or Perennialism. These educators seek to base their curriculum and pedagogy on a hoped-for certainty based on the synthesis of reason and faith. The great medieval synthesis constructed by Thomas Aquinas in the late thirteenth century is the terra firma for these educators. Perennialists and Thomists share the idea of the proactive student with philosophical pragmatists and their educational counterparts, called progressives or instrumentalists. Pragmatists view reality as the result of the interaction between human praxis and the physical social world. Pragmatists and their educational counterparts do not think that absolute certainty can be had. An instrumental, experimental concept of reality can be grasped by intelligent human beings who learn to use the scientific method. The ideas of John Dewey and those who were influenced by his work comprise the rationale for pedagogy drawn from philosophical pragmatism. Philosophical existentialism is characterized by a view that human beings can know neither the physical, social, personal worlds objectively nor completely. Existentialists are unconvinced that the pragmatist reliance on the scientific method can result in the kind of instrumental knowledge claimed. The existentialist educator stresses the difficulty and absurdity caused by human beings' desire to know where we are in space and time because the universe in their view is opaque as well as "indifferent" to the human demand for meaning. Education for existentialists consists of helping students to make personal—and I hope—(secular) ethical choices, while realizing that cognitive power is seriously limited. This "aside" is not presented as definitive. It is offered as one more tool that you can use. There are many sources that describe and explain the various isms; a good place to look is among the various social foundations of education textbooks. One of the best sources, one that features breadth, depth, and intelligent interpretation, is G. Max Wingo's *Philosophies of Education: An Introduction* (Lexington, Mass.: D.C. Heath and Company, 1974). This classic philosophy of education book provides the reader with an analysis of how philosophical positions are represented by various educational philosophies, curricula, and pedagogy. This analysis is done in a sociopolitical context. For another useful source on the isms approach to philosophy of education, see Howard A. Ozman and Samuel M. Craver, *Philosophical Foundations of Education*, 5th ed. (Columbus, Ohio: Merrill, an imprint of Prentice Hall, 1995), passim. See also the appendix to this chapter.

25   A useful and readable book for learning about and discussing various ideas concerning our "nature" is Leslie Stevenson's *Seven Theories of Human Nature* (New York and Oxford: Oxford University Press, 1974).

26   Richard Brosio, unpublished work on an experimental philosophy course for high school students from around the San Diego Unified School District, 1968.

27   Wingo, *Philosophies of Education: An Introduction,* 22. The passage can be found in its original place also: Max Black, "A Note on 'Philosophy of Education,'" *Harvard Educational Review* 26, vol. 2 (Spring 1956): 155.

28   Richard A. Brosio, "The Battle For Social Foundations of Education: A Report From the Middletown Front," *Vitae Scholasticae* 12, no. 2 (Fall 1993,* but published in 1996): 9–88. See Alan H. Jones' introduction, 3–7, and his afterword, 89–90.

29   Michael W. Apple, *Ideology and Curriculum* (London: Routledge & Kegan Paul, 1979), 13–14.

30   Ibid., 33.

31   Richard A. Brosio, *A Radical Democratic Critique of Capitalist Education* (New York: Peter Lang Publishing, Inc., 1994), 325–26.

32   Maxine Greene, "Challenging Mystification: Educational Foundations in Dark Times," *Educational Studies* 7, no. 1 (Spring 1976): 16.

33   Ibid., 22.

34   Ibid., 27.

35   William Leiss, John Ober, and Erica Sherover, "Marcuse as Teacher," in *The Critical Spirit: Essays in Honor of Herbert Marcuse,* ed. Kurt H. Wolfe and Barrington Moore, Jr. (Boston: Beacon Press, 1967), 422.

36   Ibid., 424.

37   For further analysis of Herbert Marcuse's work, see Richard A. Brosio, *The Frankfurt School: An Analysis of the Contradictions and Crises of Liberal Capitalist Societies* (Muncie, Ind.: Ball State Monograph Number Twenty-nine, 1980).

38   Dewey, *The Quest for Certainty,* 100.

39   Ibid., 313.

40   Richard A. Brosio, *The Relationship of Dewey's Pedagogy to His Concept of Community,* The University of Michigan Social Foundations of Education Monograph Series, Number 4 (Ann Arbor, Mich.: Malloy Lithoprinting, Inc., 1972), 69.

41   Dewey, *Reconstruction in Philosophy,* xvii. From the new introduction written in 1948.

42   Bertolt Brecht, *Galileo* (New York: Grove Press, 1966), 83.

43   Richard Brosio with Kevin McDonough, "Perennial Problems of Philosophy and Education Played Upon an End of the Millennium Post_____ Landscape," *Philosophical Studies in Education,* Proceedings of the Annual 1994 Meeting of The Ohio Valley Philosophy of Education Society. Terre Haute, Ind.: Ohio Valley Philosophy of Education Society, 1994, xv–xviii.

44   Russell Jacoby, "America's Professoriate: Politicized, Yet Apolitical," *The Chronicle of Education* 42, no. 31 (April 12, 1996): B-2.

45   Richard Brosio, "'On The Edge': Warranted Desperation, With A Bit of Class," *Philosophical Studies in Education*, Proceedings of the Annual 1995 Meeting of The Ohio Valley Philosophy of Education Society. Terre Haute, Ind.: Ohio Valley Philosophy of Education Society, 1995, xxiii–xxv.

46   Brosio, *A Radical Democratic Critique of Capitalist Education*, 449.

47   David Forgacs, ed., *An Antonio Gramsci Reader: Selected Writings, 1916–1935* (New York: Shocken Books, 1988), 54.

48   Brosio, *A Radical Democratic Critique of Capitalist Education*, 454.

49   Mike Rose, *Lives on the Boundary* (New York: Penguin Books, 1989), 109.

50   Ibid., 128.

51   Ibid., 132.

Chapter Two

The Unsuccessful Quest for Certainty: From Classical Greece to Postmodernist, New World (dis)Order

Introduction

In chapter one, philosophers wrestled with the question of epistemological certainty-uncertainty and with human consequences involved in the various answers. It was argued that philosophical studies, at their best, are involved with and highly relevant to concrete human concerns—including educational ones. In this chapter I shall consider further why and how human beings have been involved in the quest for certainty. Section I of this chapter is organized around Bertrand Russell's chronological account of Western philosophy's quest for certainty, including important contributions by John Dewey and G. Max Wingo—plus some of my interpretations. I encourage you to relate the material to your own philosophy-educational philosophy project. I hope this chapter will help the readers to consider the possible outcomes for their teaching practice. References to perennialist education are offered for this purpose.

Section II of this chapter suggests certain other educational outcomes related to the quest for certainty. The reader is treated to an argument that philosophical certainty, especially in its idealist form, has served to underpin educational essentialism. Wingo's *Philosophies of Education: An Introduction* serves as a rich resource with which to clarify the connections among philosophical idealism, educational essentialism, and political conservatism. It is argued that this triad still represents the dominant framework of K–12 schooling in the United States. The conflict between the dominant way of conducting the schools and the most im-

portant protest against it, namely progressivism, is described and analyzed in chapter four.

The conclusion takes us beyond the quest for certainty versus its philosophically pragmatic, educationally progressive, and politically liberal opponent in order to consider briefly the ideas of those who trust neither the
quest for certainty nor the "scientific method" to keep us safe in the
darkness of uncertainty. Existentialist and postmodernist thought ven-
tures beyond "a clean well-lighted place" and bravely—or foolishly—confronts the darkness and its goblins. Existentialist philosophy is dealt with
again in chapter five. Postmodernist philosophy is featured once more in
the last chapter.

I

During November 1968 I was working at a high school and wrote the
following for my sophomore humanities classes—what follows is paraphrased. Mid-twentieth century is a time of hiatus. In the Western world
it is often difficult to ascertain what the real issues and trends consist of.
The shape of things to come is highly uncertain. We are living in one of
the great watershed periods of history. The birth of a new era is spotted
with acrimony and even blood. The old era is not perfectly definable.
There are certain dominant characteristics that constitute it. One of these
has been the quest for certainty. This quest was conducted, for the most
part, by nonempirical, deductive, and various transcendental religious
methods that were driven by the need to have hoped-for order prevail
over the messiness of everyday life. The putative certainty that was achieved
by philosophers and religionists was shrouded by obscurantism and
esotericism, i.e., beyond ordinary knowledge or understanding. It was
made to appear that only an elite could understand the timelessness and
universality of the "real" which allegedly lay behind the seeming chaos of
popular perception. The masses of people desired certainty as much as
did their masters. They endured a position of inferiority with regard to
their "betters." Those who assumed the status of epistemological superiority also claimed the authority to govern the secular and spiritual lives of
"ordinary" people. Education was mainly restricted to the few. The brightest
and perhaps most cooperative members of the masses were often co-
opted into the elite ruling system. Because of the lack of meaningful public education, it was difficult for members of the subaltern classes to construct an outside point of view that would have made possible a critique
of the status quo, as well as its being overcome and replaced by a more
just order.

Let us fast-forward to 1996, when I wrote the following: "Part of [Joel] Spring's book [*Wheels in the Head: Educational Philosophies of Authority, Freedom, and Culture from Socrates to Paulo Freire* (New York: McGraw-Hill, 1994)] is about 'Education and the Authoritarian State' and 'Educational Problems in a Democratic State.' These two chapters set the . . . tone for the book. . . . Spring reminds us that 'in The Republic only rulers know the good. For Socrates, the ideal state is ruled by philosopher-kings who are selected because they are [allegedly] born with intellectual abilities that can be educated to know the good [in no uncertain terms]. . . . Any state [or organized religion?] that claims only the rulers have access to the truth provides a justification for totalitarianism [or at least, authoritarianism].'"[1] The insistence on having exact knowledge that makes certainty possible has changed in terms of words; the melody, however, has remained rather constant. Those who continue the attempt to convince others of their access to certainty have been remarkably successful even in these times. The 1960s was a time when many people in the West seemed to have rejected such a stratified, elite-mass dichotomy. It may not be surprising that authoritarianism flourished for many reasons in the schools, one of which was the belief among some educators that they had access to certainty and/or *the* truth.

The philosopher of education, Jim Garrison, wrote about this quest for certainty and some educational results.

Learning is a process of growth and change. Some learning, such as learning through self-initiated inquiry, caused Plato special problems in the dialogue called the *Meno*. There he set out the *Meno* paradox: It is impossible to learn anything through inquiry. Why? Because either you already know the thing sought . . . or you have no knowledge whatsoever and therefore would never recognize it. This paradox . . . does not allow for coming to know. Plato took it very seriously. . . . He asserted a theory of recollection. This theory presumed that before birth everyone caught a brief glimpse of what he called the immutable and eternal Forms. For him learning just meant recollecting the Forms. . . . For Plato all knowledge is of the . . . abstract . . . eternally fixed Forms. All the rest is just opinions about things in the empirical world of space and time copied from the Forms. Plato placed a supreme harmonizing principle—the Good—above the Forms. . . . "[T]he Good" not only guarantees that reality is rational, it also assured that reality is an aesthetic and moral order. For Plato, indubitable knowledge of the Forms (and above all "the Good") is the source of timeless wisdom. Through a variety of expressions, the metaphysic of Plato's supernaturalism [and idealism] exercises an immense influence on Western thought.[2]

The following is drawn from a handout given to my philosophy of education students at the teachers college where I work. It was constructed in 1974 and is called, "The Philosophic Base of Essentialism." I believe it serves to clarify and relate Garrison's passage to the analysis before you. Paraphrased:

> If one is to be an educational essentialist s/he must have some anchor attached to what is considered essential. Historically, the great Platonic schema of ideas has been considered the most appropriate anchor. For our purposes, the central Platonic insight is that there is a universal unchanging order of things—and it is knowable to human beings when they use their reason. Plato argued that there were universal Forms, and that what we experience through the senses only shares imperfectly in the characteristics of the universal Forms. Our empirical knowledge deals with death, decay, and seeming irrationalism; if our intellect is properly developed, then we can perceive/understand the majestic orderliness of the universals. What we teach our young can be considered essential, unchanging, and universally applicable because the curriculum is based on our accumulated rational knowledge concerning the Forms. The curriculum is anchored to terra firma. This terra firma for the essentialist is the belief that we live in a cosmos in which natural, universal, immutable, predictable, knowable, and benign laws are dominant. There is a real difference between philosophical idealism and realism; Plato and Aristotle have important differences of opinion, namely in terms of the static versus developmental. Hegel's nineteenth-century system reads differently from the Greeks; what these philosophers (and others) have in common is a belief that the universe is a cosmos. The world we inhabit did not just happen; in fact, it was pre-planned and derivative of the idea of a supernatural mind/spirit. The essentialist curriculum allows us to know the work of the divine mind as it translates itself into the cosmos in which we live. The Christian idea of a personal interfering God—a concept which is one with the earlier Jewish one—strengthens the schema of Plato and the whole idealist—and realist—schema. For many centuries it was thought that science would undermine the belief in certainty, terra firma, and universals which have been described; *misunderstood science* has become a new bedrock of "certainty" for many—including contemporary essentialists. Misunderstood science is seen neither as being hypothetical in nature, nor based on the premise that the inquirer is changed by her inquiring into the nature of physical and social phenomena, which in turn are importantly affected by the method of inquiry. Bertrand Russell wrote: To teach how to live without certainty, and yet without being paralyzed by hesitation, is perhaps the chief thing that philosophy, in our age, can still do for those who study it.[3] John Dewey offered the following insight that supports Russell's passage: "Indulge for a moment in an imaginative flight. Suppose that men [and women] had been systematically educated in the belief that existence of values can cease to be accidental [even though not anchored by transcendental certainties, but instead] directed by the best available [human] knowledge. Suppose also men [and women] had been systematically educated to believe that the important thing is not to get themselves personally right in relation to the antecedent author and guarantor of these values, but to form their judgments and carry on their activity on the basis of public, objective and shared consequences. Imagine these things and then imagine what the present [1929] situation might be."[4]

Imagine what the present situation would be as you read Dewey from a contemporary perspective. Return to Russell and his *A History of Western Philosophy*, as we seek to better understand the historic quest for certainty. This book served me well as a teacher of secondary, social studies students during the 1960s and it remains a useful tool for providing an intelligible portrayal of significant ideas in Western, intellectual history.

Russell's view, as well as Dewey's, is that the quest for certainty has been a project that resulted in the establishment of elite political, social, economic, and intellectual-education power. The fear of chaos and the irrational is understandable, yet there can and should be middle ground between adherence to false certainties on the one hand, and capitulation to radical relativism on the other. Russell argued that since the Reformation, the argument about who the legitimate and/or true authority figures and sources are have exploded into the mainstream of Western intellectual life. His view is that liberalism has been an intellectual tradition committed to finding safe ground between authority and anarchy. Whether or not Russell's liberalism is capable of securing a "social order not based on irrational dogma and insuring stability without involving more restraints than are necessary for the preservation of community"[5] remains to be seen. Russell's middle-ground liberalism is based on epistemology: "All *definite* knowledge . . . belongs to science; all dogma as to what surpasses definite knowledge belongs to theology. But between theology and science there is a No Man's Land, exposed to attack from both sides . . . [namely] philosophy."[6]

Consider the organizing principles of Russell's book and how it relates to our own project. One must always critically appropriate what is learned; my nuanced differences with Russell have affected how I present what follows. We are presented with a stark historical dichotomy: philosophers have been divided into those who sought to tighten social bonds and their counterparts who wished to loosen them. The "disciplinarians" have used alleged certainty and dogma to empower their claims. The "libertarians" have relied mainly on scientific, utilitarian, rationalistic, and nondogmatic philosophy for their arguments and proposed policies. Russell admitted the obvious need for social cohesion and order, but he warns of the dangers caused by too much discipline and uncritical reverence for tradition. Russell views liberalism as representing the middle point between these contested positions. A citizen-educator's view of "human nature" would affect the choice made with regard to the continuum.

Russell's philosophy was greatly influenced by the certainty, lucidity, and timelessness of mathematics, his later work as a popularizer of the West's philosophical history was based on respect for empirical investigation.[7] His technical philosophy represents a quest for certainty through the understanding of mathematics. He thought that, "those who have experienced the intoxicating delight of the sudden understanding that mathematics gives . . . the Pythagorean view will seem . . . natural even if untrue. It might seem that the empirical philosopher is the slave of . . . material but that the pure mathematician, like the musician, is a free creator of . . . ordered beauty."[8] The mature Russell condemned Pythagoras and his influence on Plato, as the latter sought semireligious certainty, in part, through mathematics. Russell correctly saw Plato as antidemocratic. A priori reasoning and faith have also served as bulwarks of organized religion in the West.

It is in our interest to discern what is timeless and universally unchanging, because individuals and societies can build on this solid ground in order to make the world safe for value. That which is presumably or actually unchanging provides justification for values that are not subject to situational and/or relative interpretations. According to Wingo: "It has been said that the real purpose of philosophical idealism [with Platonic antecedents] is to make the world safe for value."[9] In part II of this chapter, the conservative must support an epistemology that assures him that "our judgments can be true, . . . certainty of truth is possible, and that some objective and trustworthy criterion for truth exists."[10] It should be apparent that the quest for certainty has been driven by legitimate human needs; educators are and/or should be concerned with the soundness of their epistemological claims. The need for certainty is not the same thing as being able to have it. This widespread historical need for certainty has been dramatized by Manuel Komroff. "The theme and philosophy of [Dostoyevsky's novel] The Brothers Karamazov occupied . . . [the author] for many years. In a letter to a friend he writes: 'The chief problem dealt with throughout this particular work is the . . . one which has, my whole life long, tormented my conscious and subconscious being: The question of the existence of God.' What if God does not exist? Then for Dostoyevsky the world is nothing but a 'vaudeville of devils' and 'all things are lawful' even crime."[11] Let us hear from one who appears in Ivan Karamazov's nightmare: "'Everyone who recognizes the truth [allegedly that human beings created God in their own image because of the need for certainty and salvation] now may legitimately order his life as he pleases. . . . In that sense, "all things are lawful" for him . . . [because] the new man may . . . become the man-god. . . . Promoted to his new position, he may lightheartedly overstep all the barriers of the old morality. . . . Where I stand will become the foremost place. . . . "All things are lawful" and that's the end of it.'"[12] Plato could tolerate neither the flux nor the impermanence of the lived world; he would have been an interested reader of Dostoyevsky's novel. Aristotle argued that nothing in the material world was exempt from change and decay. He too constructed a more sophisticated defense of permanence amidst change. For Aristotle, universals exist not in the abstract, or transcendentally, but in particular things. The form of a thing is its essence, formless matter or things are merely potential. Potential and change are guided by teleology or drawn toward preordained ends or goals. A deity, or First Cause, is responsible for guided change and improvement. This First Cause was considered to be pure thought by Aristotle. It was eternal and unmovable. It was separate from physical/sensate things but responsible for their "evolution."

The rise of various forms of religious fundamentalism around the world during the last years of this century and millennium are examples of a renewed quest for certainty. Many so-called fundamentalists have used their declared certainty and correctness to drive their energetic participation in politics and even armed insurrection. Russell explains further, the failure of the classical Greeks to solve their political and intellectual problems led to the Hellenistic period that was characterized by withdrawal from public life as many people sought solace in the private life as well as various versions of salvation-promising religions. He argued that "the psychological preparation for the other-worldliness of Christianity begins in the Hellenistic period, and is connected to the eclipse of the City State. . . . [The philosophers] no longer asked: how can men create a good State? They asked instead: how can men [and women] be virtuous in a wicked world, or happy in a world of suffering?"[13]

Russell explained that the first great period of Catholic thought in the West was dominated by Augustine whose mentor was Plato. The second period features Thomas Aquinas backed by Aristotle. During this second period, from the fifth century A.D. to the Renaissance, philosophy was used to defend the faith. It employed reason to argue against those who did not accept the validity of Christian revelation. From Augustine's fifth-century attempt to harmonize Platonism with Genesis, to the twelfth-century's Scholastic[14] beginnings (based in part on the rediscovery of Aristotle's work), and especially to the thirteenth-century Medieval Synthesis of Aquinas which also relied on Aristotle, Catholic intellectuals sought to have Greek philosophy strengthen the faith, especially as it was argued that both philosophy and religion allowed the achievement of certainty. For Aquinas, the role of reason/philosophy is to make deductions from first principles that are established by faith. What we learn from sense data serves to solidify our belief in what religious sources have already portrayed. Reason serves to link the natural and supernatural universes. An example of Aquinian thought is the catechism book from which I learned about Catholicism that features the following in the second lesson: "Can we know by our natural reason that there is a God? We can know by our natural reason . . . for it tells us that the world we see about us could have been made only by a self-existing Being, all-wise and almighty. Can we know God in any other way than by our natural reason? . . . We can also know Him from supernatural revelation—that is, from the truths, found in Sacred Scripture or Tradition, which God Himself has revealed to us."[15] It was never doubted that if reason and faith clashed, then the former must get in line with what the latter reveals.

Thomas Aquinas agreed with Aristotle that the universe is orderly and rational. For Thomas, the guarantee of that order could only be the reason and order in God's mind that was reflected in the lived world and that was comprehensible to human reason. So, the world, or cosmos, is knowable by human reason and is connected through logical probability with the supernatural, which must be accepted in faith. Let us consider some of the educational implications of Aristotelian and Aquinian thought. The following is drawn from Wingo's chapter on "The Protest of Perennial Philosophy" as well as from my experience with this material in the classroom. Those who are called perennialists can be categorized as Aristotelians (rational humanists), or Thomists (neoscholastics); the former emphasizes secular sources, the later is indebted to the religious tradition beginning with Thomas Aquinas.

For the perennialists, education must help people realize the nature that is inherent in them. They have insisted that the ultimate goals of education are universal; they are not subject to time or circumstance. This can be asserted because perennialists believe that all human beings have roughly the same basic nature. The goal of education is to make a developed human being. Because Aristotelians and Thomists assume the existence of a particular human nature, they can define the art of teaching as encouraging the exercise of the person's own powers in a way that this volitional potential is developed and perfected. It is assumed that all persons desire to know; at first this is just a potentiality that must be developed. Some cause must serve to help the student move from potentiality to increasing degrees of actuality. Education, as opposed to training, is the process that serves to move our students to actuality. The art of teaching can be defined as helping to convert the natural powers of reason from potentiality to actuality. The Thomist perennialists hold that the primary cause that makes this possible is God. Human beings can learn on our own through discovery and/or by virtue of instruction. The teacher acts similarly to a physician when the latter assists in healing, through cooperation with human nature. The teacher and the physician are secondary causes. Teachers do not fill the student's empty tank with bodies of knowledge. Instead, in the perennialists' view, the self-activity of the learner is the principal cause of learning.

For perennialist educators, the curriculum consists mainly of the liberal arts, which are derived from the trivium: grammar, rhetoric, and dialectic; and the quadrivium: arithmetic, geometry, astronomy, and music; or, as they say: reading, writing, and reckoning! This curriculum is thought to be best suited for releasing mere potential; it must be studied by all students. The liberal arts curriculum is the material on which the students' unfolding intellectual competence feasts. Perennialists insist that students read the great books, or canon of Western Civilization—they are not satisfied with secondary sources. These so-called great books were not initially decided upon democratically. Great conflicts surround the question of who should help decide what constitutes the canon today. Indeed, there are some who insist there can be no, single canon. There is some agreement among canonists that limiting any canon to the West alone is no longer warranted. For those who have asked: "What of those who cannot master such a curriculum?," the following response has been given by perennialists: "Presumably, once the school has done as much for a student as it can, to the limits of his [her] own potentialities, its obligation ceases. . . . [For example,] unemployment may be a social [economic] problem of great importance . . . but in [the perennialists'] view, it is hardly an educational problem."[16] You may feel the need to challenge the perennialists' answer, especially as a result of what we know about teaching-learning, the *social* role of public schools in this century, and the effects that the inequitable distribution of school readiness and cultural capital have on student success. Perhaps the perennialists' dismissal of unemployment as an educational problem would be more justified were they to commit themselves effectively to constructing a moral economy in which unemployment and even meaningless or exploitative labor were overcome for everyone.

My own reading of perennialist education sees their dependence on certainty/absolutes as problematic, as is their antidemocratic orientation. As an antidote to the "filling station" conception of teaching-learning that features the student as an empty vessel, and the increasingly vocational direction taken by many educators in response to economic and political pressures—the perennialists may look a good deal better. As Wingo explained, perennialists hold that the purpose of education is to develop the students' intellectual virtues, and because these virtues are similar for all persons, the educator's strategy must never be constructed around accidental human differences. All persons are potentially rational; every student is entitled to the kind of education that is committed to the development of our "supremely human qualities." In a phrase: the goal of education is to "make" the wo/man. The goal should never be to make the person into merely an economic tool or uncritical servant of the State. Training is not the same as education! For a brilliant perennialist analysis and condemnation of education that is bastardized through excessively narrow vocational training for jobs that society may not value, see Robert Hutchins, *The Higher Learning in America*. Here is an example of the Hutchins' bull's-eye sarcasm: "Turning professional schools into vocational schools degrades universities and does not elevate the professions. . . . My contention is that the tricks of the trade cannot be learned in a university, and that if they can be they should not be. They cannot . . . because they get out of date and new tricks take their place, because the teachers get out of date and cannot keep up with current tricks, and because tricks can be learned only in the actual situation in which they can be employed."[17]

My response to perennialism is: If only we had the epistemological ability to grasp out-there reality with certainty; and, if only our society were a just, somewhat egalitarian one wherein each student came to school ready to learn a (more democratically constructed) canon, or multiple canons, that took seriously what each student already knows and cares about, then we might all be perennialists. Mortimer Adler would argue that perennialist education can answer my "if onlys." He and his Paideia Group have published a number of books that seek to explain how perennialism can be translated into successful educational practice. The word paideia signifies the Greek word for the upbringing of the child; it has come to be used also as the Latin term "humanitas" that signifies general learning which should be had by every person. Adler addresses the following educational topics in *The Paideia Proposal*: democracy and education; the same objective for all; the same course of study for all; individual differences; the preparation of teachers; earning a living and living well; and the future of our free institutions. For those who doubt the perennialist arguments, Adler wrote the following: "Those who think the proposed course of study cannot be successfully followed by all children fail to realize that the children . . . have never had their minds challenged by requirements such as these. It is natural for children to rise to meet higher expectations. . . . They will respond when their minds are challenged by teachers able to give . . . different types of instruction . . . and who are themselves vitally interested in what they are teaching."[18]

The perennialist emphasis on our common humanity is praiseworthy as well as highly relevant to education for democratic empowerment. Their insistence that "we can know things as they really are, that is, in their essential natures; and thus . . . demonstrate the possibility of objective truth,"[19] provides an important scaffold for democracy, in part because such objectivity provides criteria with which to distinguish between good and bad. My decision to include perennialism in this chapter—namely in the nondemocratic camp—is caused by my uneasiness with their claim to know things in starkly objective and certain terms. This claim is based on the philosophical principle of independence, which asserts that objects that are known exist independently of the human mind. Whether or not this principle is true is an empirical question, one that has not been answered to everyone's satisfaction. Constructivists hold that to know is to "interfere" with what is being studied; to change it; as well as changing ourselves in the process. Interference need not mean hands-on; in fact, the telescopic study of outer space is a form of interference—especially when the viewers are academically and experientially prepared to interpret the data they see and measure. Because ordinary people have not been involved in philosophical discourse, it has been possible for certain powerful people to claim that they and their allies know what the truth is. They have punished all too many others who do not agree with the proclaimed certainty. In this sense, I do not consider perennialism as an adequate scaffold for the kind of democracy I favor.

II

The most important philosophies affecting U.S. schooling, which are representative of the historical quest for certainty, are idealism and realism. These philosophical traditions have provided the main scaffolding for educational essentialism. Drawing on Wingo's work, I argue that these philosophical traditions and educational practices are logically and historically allied with socioeconomic conservatism in this country. My strategy here is one developed in the classroom as I attempted to make Wingo's central thesis clear to students in teacher education. Discussion among the readers of this section can serve to make the concepts meaningful to students of teaching and learning. You are invited to critically appropriate the concepts and arguments as I did when first introduced to them in Wingo's classroom. When I first took a class with him, his ideas were in lecture notes form. In classic professorial fashion his books, *The Philosophy of American Education* and the second edition called, *Philosophies of Education: An Introduction*, were developed from the courses he gave at the University of Michigan's College of Education.

The central thesis I learned from Wingo is that "the purposes the American school have generally served are those of preserving and transmitting the so-called essentials of Western culture and acting as a conserving [allegedly] civilizing force in society. This conception of purpose is reflected . . . in the way . . . schools are organized, the kind of curricula established, and the teaching methods employed."[20] Wingo refers to Michael Katz's *Class, Bureaucracy, and Schools: The Illusion of Educational Change in America* to drive his point home; that the structure constructed and used to enact conservative education policy has been school bureaucracy. A functional relationship is said to exist between purpose and organization.[21] My interpretation of Wingo's central thesis while working as a secondary, social studies teacher in the 1960s can be summed up as follows: "As I became involved in the daily attempts at school reform, it became apparent to me that there was a need for a cogent, theoretical overview. It was out of this need that Dewey's work became important to me. I had first become acquainted with Dewey's philosophy in 1962 while studying with Professor Wingo. Dewey's explanation of the danger involved with Western man's [sic] quest for certainty became a useful analytic tool for me. It seemed . . . that if there is no truth that is antecedent to the search for it, then the . . . essentialist and authoritarian posture of school policy makers could be criticized by the . . . social use of the scientific method."[22]

This section provides a description of what I consider to be the essentialistic, authoritarian, and conservative tradition in U.S. schooling. Wingo and I agree that "conservative modes of education, both in . . . theory and . . . practice . . . are in a position of very strong dominance."[23] I have argued that although educational essentialism, philosophical idealism and/or realism, as well as socioeconomic/political conservatism have been subject to intellectual critique and political opposition, this trio remains hegemonic with regard to our K–12 public schools. I invite you to think of this hegemonic trio as a Spanish galleon that has undergone serious damage from repeated attacks (by Errol Flynn, the swashbuckling movie actor, and his cinematic pirates). The galleon is listing, its sails in tatter but still afloat. The protesters are not yet aboard the vessel. As you read what follows, think systematically and imaginatively about your experiences in schools in order to determine whether the trio is still hegemonic and/or afloat.

Begin by using figure 1 as a way to visually conceptualize the explanation that follows; an explanation which is necessarily general and big-picture rather than one that space does not allow.

Figure 1 offers a possible conceptualization for understanding what I argue is the dominant triad in United States K–12 public schools, namely educational essentialism, philosophical idealism (and/or realism, neo-realism), and sociopolitical conservatism. Philosophical idealism—in some sense a secularized version of generic Judeo-Christian thought—provides an omega creator and the understandable/rational/orderly cosmos in which ethical parameters cordon off unacceptable, unethical behavior. All of this rests on a reassuring terra firma, solid ground, for human beings. I use the term omega in the sense of its being the last, or ultimate, letter in the Greek alphabet. Perhaps the first letter, alpha, could serve as well. Some Western religions use the idea of from alpha to omega to symbolize the deity's power. The historic curriculum is thought to be essential and basic because it is an explanatory tool or microcosm of the created cosmos. The traditional report card—along with failing grades—is justified because it is linked to a curriculum that is in turn integrally part of "reality." Many of the educational philosophy-isms that are based on various forms of cognitive/epistemological certainty adhere, *mutatis mutandis*, to figure 1. I explain below how this conceptualization allows/demands a rather didactic teaching methodology.

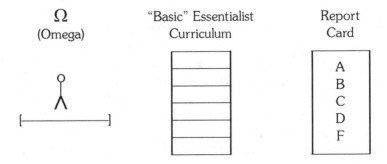

Ω
(Omega)

"Basic" Essentialist
Curriculum

Report
Card

A
B
C
D
F

Figure 1

Those philosophers, religionists, and educators who have been involved in the quest for certainty in the West have agreed that the world and universe in which we live did not just happen. Human beings are thought to exist in a cosmos, a world and universe regarded as orderly and harmonious. Although idealist and realist philosophers rarely talk about an anthropomorphic personal deity, they do posit the existence of an omega figure or watchmaker deity (even if unknowable) who created the cosmos according to a deliberate and mostly rational plan. In biblical religion and idealist philosophical terms, in the beginning was the word and/or the idea. The creation and lived reality have resulted from the *priority of consciousness* that is central to idealist philosophy. The religious word implies, if not demands, that the world we inhabit did not just become what it is in an aimless way. The human race is seen as, in some way, part of this creation-according-to-plan. The philosophical and religious traditions of the West being considered view the essence of humanity as spirit and intellect. Men and women inhabit a cosmos that is orderly as well as knowable—to some extent. There exist boundaries beyond which we must not venture. These boundaries indicate the limits of lawful and good behavior—to go beyond means crime and sin. The ground on which we stand is terra firma that enables us to know where we are in space and time.

This view has been challenged by the success of theoretical and applied science. The work of Copernicus, Galileo, Darwin, Marx, Freud, et al. have challenged the idealist and religious views of humanity and the world. The world has been demoted to one of several that revolve around the star we call the sun. The uniqueness of created human beings is challenged by arguments that we have evolved from lower forms of life. It is suggested that lurking beneath our spiritual and intellectual personas lies an irrational libidinally driven person. Marx's challenge is to recognize, confront, and overcome systematic social-class injustice that is inherent to capitalism-as-a-system. The powers that be seek to camouflage this injustice. Marx argued that social-class consciousness and struggle can be successful. These challenges have made the saying, "God is in heaven and all is right with the world," suspect to many Westerners, especially since the advent of modernity and even more so (*a fortiori*) in these postmodernist times.

The relationship between what has been explained so far in reference to the first part of figure 1 to its second part can be understood by focusing on why educational essentialists claim that their curricular choices are essential and/or basic. One is tempted to ask those who insist that we "go back to basics" to explain how they can know what they favor is basic or essential. The model being discussed permits its advocates to answer the question posed. For them, various subject areas within their essentialist curriculum are essential to understanding the cosmos, which has been constructed by an interventionist deity—with us in mind. The historical curriculum represents the rational understanding of a cosmos that results from the priority of consciousness or, as some religionists believe, in the beginning was the word. The word represents a preconceived plan of what was to be or created. It would be helpful to refer back to "The Philosophic Base of Essentialism" in part I of this chapter to better understand what is being offered in the following explanation. There have been and continue to be arguments about the specificities of this essential curriculum. The conservative domination of this discourse has made John Wild's view quite definitive for many. Wingo introduces the passage from Wild as follows:

> The conservative's basic conception of the curriculum may be summarized by saying that from the beginning of school to the end the curriculum is an ordered series of subject matters drawn from the total heritage and designed to be transmitted to all who attend school. [Wild articulates it in this way.] "There is certainly a basic core of knowledge that every human person ought to know in order to live a genuinely human life as a member of the world community, of his [sic] own nation, and of the family. This should be studied by every student and should be presented at levels of increasing complexity and discipline throughout the entire curriculum. First of all, (a) the student should learn to use the basic instruments of knowledge, especially his own language. In order to understand it more clearly and objectively, he should gain some knowledge of at least one foreign language as well. In addition, he should be taught the essentials of humane logic and elementary mathematics. Then (b), he should become acquainted with the methods of physics, chemistry, and biology and the basic facts so far revealed by these sciences. In the third place (c), he should study history and the sciences of man. Then (d), he should gain some familiarity with the great classics of his own and of world literature and art. Finally (e), in the later stages of this basic training, he should be introduced to philosophy and to those basic problems which arise from the attempt to integrate knowledge and practice. Here he should be shown that the world we inhabit is not pure chaos but possesses some stable structure on which certain moral principles at least may be solidly grounded. Of course there should be room for the choice of additional, peripheral subjects to train exceptional capacities, to realize special interests, and to prepare for the professions. But this central core, based on the nature of our human world, should be given to everyone."[24]

Many conservatives have added computer literacy to their "basics." Perhaps this should not be surprising when conservatives, similar to many other people, have come to view schooling as importantly, if not exclusively, vocational. Even the passage by Wild can be interpreted as vocational in the sense that white, middle-class, and wealthy students enjoy a cultural advantage over many others because these so-called basics represent the cultural storehouse of those who have and continue to exercise hegemony over United States society. All too many students lack the cultural capital to compete with those who have it because cultural capital is related to the possession of capital itself, i.e., various monetary factors.

Turn to the third part of figure 1. This part of the discussion is especially gratifying to me because I questioned the report cards we were given in K–12 schools while still a student. I always wondered how the arbitrariness of the letter grades were related to certain numbers, e.g., A = 100–92, and so forth until we arrived at the dreaded F number—actually called an E at that time. As early as elementary school I remember asking: "Ninety-two percent of what? Who decided? Why was an E or F marked at 65? Who decided on the books we used?" I might have said curriculum, but did not know this term in elementary school. Had I asked my teachers, instead of myself and a few trusted pals, perhaps they would have written this part of chapter two for me, or at least referred me to various educational philosophers. Perhaps! Would it have made sense to me in the 1940s and 1950s if the teachers had answered with: "Ninety-two percent of the second grade piece of the essential curriculum, that is essential and basic because it represents a description and explanation of the cosmos and people that omega has created?" It may very well have made sense, in part because the nuns who were my catechism teachers had already prepared me for this kind of argument, by way of the *New Baltimore Catechism.* My public school teachers could have avoided trouble by relying on the idealist or even realist/neorealist conception of primary cause and/or watchmaker mover instead of coming right out and mentioning God. Had they done so, there would not have occurred any criticism from our working-class parents during that time. When I began to read philosophy, and especially idealism, realism, and Thomism, it became apparent to me that rationalist philosophers who quest for certainty are close relatives of the religionist who desire the same assurance. I have little doubt that Miss Jenkins, one of my elementary teachers, and Sister Superior were quite close with regard to the issues discussed in this analysis. An F meant that you did not understand enough about the curriculum which was a microcosm of what had been created; you could get it if you tried; and failure was almost like being damned. Our religious instructors had an advantage over our public school worthies because they *did* invoke the threat of damnation more than a few times. Neither of these faculties refrained from corporal punishment; albeit, "For our own good." This kind of punishment is not completely absent from schools even today.

Suggested Task for the Reader

After having read the description and analysis of figure 1, return to the figure itself and erase the omega from the drawing. Address this question: What is logically and likely to happen to the constructed/created cosmos, human beings, terra firma, boundaries, the essential curriculum, and the A to F report card in the wake of omega's removal or demise? What could essentialists-conservatives put in its place?

Focus your attention further on a specific explanation of philosophical idealism's links with educational essentialism and conservatism. Conservatives and essentialists need an authoritative basis for their political and educational projects, and Wingo proposes that they have found it in idealism. It may be that not *every* conservative-essentialist is consciously aware of this debt; however, s/he finds comfort in believing that,

> there is more to the nature of reality . . . human nature and destiny than has been or ever will be revealed by the scientific approach. Many . . . [idealist academicians] believe that the road to complete cultural dissolution is paved with positivism, ethical relativism, and psychological behaviorism that have been fostered by science—and . . . by much of . . . [contemporary] philosophy. It is natural, therefore, that persons with this attitude should continue to hold with philosophic ideas that stress the transcendent character of human selfhood, the objectivity of truth . . . and the fundamental regularity . . . of the cosmos. To them it is only in a world . . . portrayed by idealism that the human drama has meaning, and only in this kind of world that the highest aspirations of man [sic] can have any chance of being realized. . . . [Therefore, it is not surprising that] idealism is still influential in affecting the perceptions of many people in the field of education.[25]

Although there are variations in philosophical idealism, consider what Wingo called absolute idealism, a version he attributed to the philosopher Georg Hegel (1770–1831). "The metaphysical meaning of *idealism* has little to do with the ordinary meaning of the word. Instead, its philosophical usage relates to a *theory which holds that the most important element in the nature of reality is mind or spirit*."[26] For idealists, the basic proposition is the irreducible fact of individual thought: the philosopher René Descartes' (1596–1650) famous expression—*cogito ergo sum* (I think, therefore I am). Absolute idealism holds that reality is one unified whole. This reality that we know is a concrete manifestation of the Absolute Mind (omega) as it develops levels of self-realization. As Wingo explained in chapter four, "Philosophy and Educational Essentialism," what we call history is, in the idealists' view, the absolute's march toward self-realization; it is not the history of daily chaos and/or meaningless events. According to Hegel, "every event has a purpose because it is part of a vast logical system, and every event, no matter how inconsequential it may appear, has meaning because it is part of this vast process [and whole] whose innermost character is regularity and . . . order."[27]

This conception of reality is congruent in many ways with views held by Western religionists. The idealist, essentialist, conservative educator is convinced that there is a way to know the difference between good and evil. A vision of the good life for us is possible. Schooling-education need only follow this vision. Wingo made clear how the conservative tradition coincides with philosophical idealism. "The conservative tells us that our ideas and actions should always be judged in the light of tradition, which is another way of saying that our ideas are worthy *if they are in harmony with the accumulated wisdom of all the generations.* The idealist tells us that the test for the truth of an idea is *its coherence with the body of existing and accepted truth.* . . . [T]his body of . . . truth can be nothing else but the wisdom of our ancestors about which social conservatives say so much. It seems clear therefore . . . that the responsibility of the school must be to transmit the essential portions of this . . . tradition to all . . . [students]."[28]

Science became more powerful during the last two centuries in the West; it had a profound effect on philosophy. In the early-twentieth century, neorealism entered the philosophic stage in the United States and its supporters argued that there exists a world of things, events, and relations among them. These phenomena are independent of any knower. This represents a break from idealist epistemology. This reality principle is compatible with common sense and some forms of scientific inquiry. The neorealists argued further that what is known can be grasped *as it is in itself.* The naturalism of neorealism meant that the cosmos exists per se, making unnecessary the quest for a supernatural creator. Inquiry's task is to discover the natural laws that govern the cosmos, i.e., to discover what is already in place. As the thoughtful reader can see, neorealists provided a different kind of certainty than what organized religion and/or idealist philosophy promised. The neorealist knowing subject is still a spectator with regard to what is real; this epistemic subject allegedly has access to bedrock and certainty. In a sense, neorealism circumvented the search for the watchmaker deity who some believed built this complex cosmic machine in the first place, settling instead for a science-influenced philosophic description of the natural terra firma that provided a new basis for certainty. Misunderstood science allowed conservatives and essentialists to find a new source of certainty. Not all scientists or philosophers who take science seriously subscribe to a spectator theory of knowledge. Dewey, Marx, et al. view the knowing subject as necessarily changing her/him/self and what is studied during the process of inquiry.

The switch by conservatives and essentialists to a scientific description of the cosmos made possible the belief that universal laws governing human behavior could be uncovered so that education could become scientific. Behaviorist psychology, epitomized by the work of B.F. Skinner, represents such a quest for certainty. You are invited to further explore the possible connections between twentieth-century behaviorism in education and elsewhere and a particular kind of scientific view of reality—including human beings. Wingo asked us to consider the following: "[The essentialism] . . . that developed originally out of prescientific conceptions of human nature, now finds itself attempting to combine the humanism of the older conservatism with the behaviorism of the scientific realists. In this respect, at least, essentialism is a house divided."[29] Wingo did not write about the rise of fundamentalist religion in the United States and elsewhere; had he done so, it is probable his analysis would have included the fierce attack on scientific inquiry mounted by many conservative fundamentalists. It seems that many people who subscribe to the inerrancy of the Bible, or other alleged sources of certainty, wish to restrict the logic of hypothetical science to the nonhuman world of things, e.g., consumer goods, weaponry, etc. In the end, conservatives and essentialists must insist that objective truth exists along with trustworthy ways for people to know what it is. They are compelled to subscribe to an essential curriculum that must be taught to all who come to school. The essentialness of this curriculum is thought to be grounded in the bedrock of certainty.

The conservative essentialist teacher is to be academically strong, i.e., one who knows the essentialist curriculum well. This person must also have a certain kind of character and moral disposition. Remember that the conservative is concerned with making the world safe for her/his kind of value and morality. This tradition sees the school's function as one of preserving and refining that which already exists. One would think that fairness would dictate that this position be analyzed with regard to who benefits most from the educational and social status quo. The public school may find it difficult to establish a single moral code for everyone because this society is heterogeneous. The conservative essentialist view of the teacher as the active transmitter of the basic curriculum to the rather passive student is problematic because of socio-psychological knowledge of human beings' volition and proactivism, even in infancy. The student as an empty vessel to be filled by the expert and moral teacher, with pieces of the basic curriculum, has been criticized and opposed by more than a few people in the United States and elsewhere. Critics have vociferously challenged the basis on which conservative essentialists decide what is basic and/or essential.

The public schools have historically assigned very poor and failing grades to many students. Most of these unsuccessful students were and are members of classes, races, and ethnic groups that lacked power, wealth, access, and prestige in United States society. If the essentialist curriculum they were forced to master is not essential at all, but only the construction of powerful people who sought to maintain their sociopolitical, economic, and educational advantages over others, then it is not surprising that many subaltern people have cried foul. This raises the question of official knowledge and who decides on what it is, i.e., whose words and whose knowledge get to become essential and official?[30] Wingo articulated well, the most important problem for educational essentialism: "On the one hand, there is the essentialist's insistence on a common core of essential subjects; on the other hand, there is the brute fact that people differ greatly in their ability to learn abstract material. Since nobody at present knows how to alter significantly [and safely] the genetic equipment of individuals and thus narrow the range in learning ability, and since essentialism is unwilling to make any significant compromise in the thesis of a common core, the schools are full of . . . low achievers together with . . . 'nonachievers.'"[31] Perhaps cognitive ability is more complex than any essentialist curriculum can ever accommodate. There are many kinds of intelligences and abilities that are seldom or ever taken into consideration in the reproductive schools of this country and elsewhere.

The interested reader can benefit from further study of what conservativism means historically and presently. There is voluminous literature on this subject. The conservative tradition in the West has had a less optimistic view of the common person's intellectual and political abilities than is the case for liberals and radicals. Conservatives have claimed that various kinds of elites are necessary in order to keep the subaltern people responsible and on the straight and narrow. The political right(s) in the West have distrusted democracy—especially of a participatory kind that brings power to bear on the dominant economic system (currently capitalism), and on establishment political, social, and educational institutions. It is argued in this text that perennialist, idealist, neorealist, and various organized religions' epistemologies, as well as metaphysics and ontology, support elitist and authoritarian political, economic, and educational systems. Following Wingo, educational essentialists have been conservative in their politics, as well as reliant on philosophies/world views/religions that claim to be able to authoritatively arrive at certainty about how the cosmos works and how human beings should live their lives.

Suggested Task for the Reader

The quest for certainty has been central to religion, philosophy, and education—for understandable reasons. One of the reasons is because human beings are afraid of the darkness of uncertainty. Most of us are frightened by the prospect of death. If there is a human need to act justly, then there must be some way to decide between right and wrong among various competing goods. Many religionists have relied on interventionist, supernatural deities for knowledge of certainty. Philosophers have argued that there are universal truths that can be known by certain human beings through the use of reason, i.e., without reliance on revelation and/or pure faith. How does a citizen-teacher decide on his/her need for certainty, the attainment of it, or relying instead on intelligent trial-and-error methods for grounding her/his life and teaching practice? How do we decide on which epistemological tools to employ in our attempts to ground our ethics on solid ground? What are some possible relationships between reason and faith in reference to this quest? Why have faith and reason been so difficult to hold in tandem since the Medieval Synthesis constructed by Thomas Aquinas et al. during the thirteenth century A.D.? Perhaps figure 2 will assist you in thinking about whether certainty or doubt are the best foundations for authoritarian or a democratic school and society. Note that authoritarian is not intended as a pejorative term,

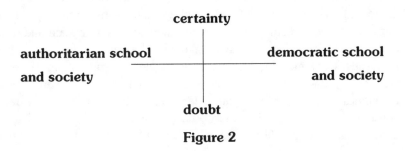

Figure 2

because if one is in the possession of certainty s/he is entitled—even compelled—to share it with others. For example, more than a few Christians claim that they are obliged to bring the "good news" to others.

The student is invited to think about where s/he is positioned on this representation.

Conclusion

The conclusion of this chapter is intentionally brief; in a sense it is offered as a contextualization of what has been offered already. It is constructed in order to provide a vantage point for what follows in this book. The rest of the chapters present ideas and philosophies that I have judged to be among the most promising scaffolding for critical democratic education. All of these ideas and philosophies are characterized by the refusal to engage in a quest for certainty. For the most part, the thinkers represented in chapters three through eight are secularists. Those religionists who are included have also refused the quest for certainty. If people are not able to discover what the truth is in order to guide their actions—including the practice of formal schooling—then several alternatives suggest themselves. These secularists conclude that the quest for certainty is always a most unhappy one; human beings were thought cognitively incapable of perceiving certainty or the ultimate good, even if such a thing existed. It was recognized by these secular thinkers and actors that a human-constructed certainty that was portrayed as universal and/or deity-given allowed certain persons/groups to assume great and dangerous power over others either politically, socially, economically, or educationally.

Some thinkers who have abandoned the quest for certainty have given into extreme moral relativism, amoralism, immoralism, cynicism, solipsism, and other forms of publicly, irresponsible ideas/actions. The ideas presented in the rest of this volume tell a different story. These thinkers have labored to construct a rational, secular, publicly accountable system of human ethics that is based, for the most part, on broadly inclusive democratic participation. If human beings cannot know the truth, all is not lost, for we can come to understand how to better educate and govern, if not do so perfectly. Many existentialist thinkers do not fit into what I have just explained. My interpretation of the existentialists included in chapter five allow them to qualify. The great nemeses of educational essentialism's philosophical scaffolding and political support have been educational progressivism, philosophical pragmatism, and political liberalism. This tradition will be dealt with in chapter four. I wrote: "The will

of the people . . . can be informed by reflection on experience; a respect for a modicum of factualness (which can be altered by more study);
and by 'the use of imagination in constructing theory . . ., the constant
search for alternatives, [and] the cooperation of many in diverse fields to
build a coherent framework.' In spite of the need for modesty in making
explanatory claims, it is imperative to keep at the difficult task of trying to
understand the world in which we live, as well as our neighbors in the
global village. The real danger in our historical period may not be the
unwarranted claims of those who use the scientific method (writ large) but
the sinister manipulation by power elites who encourage a reversion to
solipsism, absurd relativism, and unhealthy nostalgia, irrationalism, obscurantism, and claims of religious inerrancy."[32]

Postmodernist thought is a complex phenomenon which I will address
in the last chapter. Suffice it to say that, like many existentialists, more
than a few postmodernist thinkers do not look favorably on the social use
of the scientific method as an adequate way to deal with the complexities
of human life in a post-quest-for-certainty era. Postmodernists have criticized not only religious quests for certainty but also what they consider to
be their secular substitutes. These critics argue that human beings are
incapable of constructing any authentic explanatory grand narrative that
assists in situating us in space and time. For instance, they attack the
Enlightenment tradition and its child, Marxism, for attempting to substitute secular certainty for the earlier attempt by organized religionists.[33]
Allow me to provide a taste of postmodernist dissatisfaction with modernity and especially the Marxist explanatory model.

> Madan Sarup tells us that "for [Jean-François] Lyotard . . . the postmodern
> condition is one in which the *grands récits* [grand, big-picture narratives con-
> cerning the human condition] of modernity—the dialectic of spirit [from Hegel],
> the emancipation of the worker . . . the classless society—have all lost credibil-
> ity." These master narratives speak of human attempts to find our identity, fulfill-
> ment and justice in the conquest of nature. The Marxist grand récit presents the
> story of the workers' struggle to establish a realm of freedom and plenitude . . . .
> But Lyotard's fear is that Marxism seeks only to create a homogeneous society
> which, in the end, can only rely on coercion. Better, then, to live within the
> "plurality" of the buy-and-sell culture of postmodernism during this period of late
> capitalism.[34]

Bertrand Russell argued that modernism meant the decline of organized religion's authority and the rise of science. Postmodernists and existentialists asked whether criteria for decision-making must necessarily be
limited to these two sources. One of the central issues faced by modern-

ists, following the collapse of Aquinas's medieval synthesis comprising of faith and reason in tandem, is: "Who should decide on the important issues facing human beings?" Walter Lippmann articulated the difficulties faced in the modern period—a period that may be evolving into one called postmodernism.

> For the modern man [sic] who has ceased to believe, without ceasing to be credu-lous, hangs . . . between heaven and earth, and is at rest nowhere. There is no theory of the meaning and value of events which he is compelled to accept, but he is . . . compelled to accept the events. There is no moral authority to which he must turn . . . but there is coercion in opinions, fashions and fads. There is for him no inevitable purpose in the universe, but there are elaborate necessities, physical, political, economic. He does not feel himself to be an actor in a great and dramatic destiny, but he is subject to the massive powers of our civilization, forced to adopt their pace. . . . He can believe what he chooses about this civilization. He cannot, however, escape the compulsion of modern events. They compel his body and senses as ruthlessly as ever did king or priest. They do not compel his mind. They have all the force of natural events, but not their majesty, all the tyrannical powers of ancient institutions, but none of their moral certainty. Events are there, and they overpower him. But they do not convince him that they have that dignity which inheres in that which is [allegedly] necessary and in the nature of things. . . . In the new order the compulsions are painful and, as it were, accidental, unnecessary, wanton, and full of mockery. The modern man does not make peace with them. . . . [Instead] he has replaced natural piety with a grudging endurance of a series of unsanctified compulsions. . . . He is conquered but unconvinced.[35]

I encourage the reader to carefully read this classic passage from Lippmann, for it is crucial to the work of citizen-educators as we continue to face a crisis of legitimacy vis-à-vis our public institutions—including the schools. I submit that a close reading and discussion of the passage could serve as a useful preface to the endless talk about school discipline—especially its alleged absence. This is the case because Lippmann describes a historical crisis in authority. The need to convince rather than conquer may help to develop more student and parental respect and trust for schools and teachers.

The modern era in history has been characterized by unprecedented increases of power available to human beings. This increase in great con-centrations of power: economic, technological, political, military, etc. has continued relentlessly during the twentieth century, unaffected by what some consider to be the beginning of a postmodernist era. Russell argued that: "To frame a philosophy capable of coping with men intoxicated with the prospect of almost unlimited power and also the apathy of the power-less is the most pressing task of our time. Though many still . . . believe in human equality and theoretical democracy, the imagination of modern people is deeply affected by the . . . social organization suggested [and/or caused] by the organization of industry . . . which is essentially undemocratic. On the one hand there are the captains of industry [powerful capitalists with support from the governments of their countries], and on the other the mass of workers. This disruption of democracy from within is not yet acknowledged by ordinary citizens in democratic countries, but it has been a preoccupation of most philosophers from Hegel onwards."[36] Citizen-educators must be keenly aware of this discrepancy between official reality and what the facts reveal. Karl Marx worried that "all that is solid melts into air." Lippmann complemented Marx's concern in the following passage: "The acids of modernity are so powerful that they do not tolerate a crystallization of ideas which will serve as a new orthodoxy into which men [sic] can retreat. So the modern world [*mutatis mutandis*, the postmodern one] is haunted by a realization, which it becomes . . . less easy to ignore, that it is impossible to reconstruct an enduring orthodoxy . . . [as well as seemingly] impossible [thus far] to live well without the satisfactions which [the certainty of] an orthodoxy would provide."[37]

Notes

1   Richard A. Brosio, "Essay Review of Joel Spring's *Wheels in the Head: Educational Philosophies of Authority, Freedom, and Culture from Socrates to Paulo Freire*," *Educational Studies* 27, no. 3 (Fall 1996): 273.

2   Jim Garrison, *Dewey and Eros: Wisdom and Desire in the Art of Teaching* (New York and London: Teachers College Press, 1997), 5–6.

3   Bertrand Russell, *A History of Western Philosophy* (New York: Simon and Schuster, 1945), xiv.

4   John Dewey, *The Quest for Certainty* (New York: G.P. Putnam's Sons, 1929), 47.

5   Russell, *History of Western Philosophy*, xxiii.

6   Ibid., xiii.

7   See Stuart Hampshire, "Russell's Paradox," *The New York Review of Books* 39, no. 14 (August 13, 1992): 7–10, for a brief analysis of Russell's transition from technical to popular philosophy.

8   Russell, *History of Western Philosophy*, 33.

9   G. Max Wingo, *Philosophies of Education: An Introduction* (Lexington, Mass.: D.C. Heath and Company, 1974), 109.

10 Ibid., 88.

11 Manuel Komroff, "Introduction," to *The Brothers Karamazov*, Fyodor Dostoyevsky (New York: Signet Books, 1957), xiii.

12 Dostoyevsky, *The Brothers Karamazov*, 589.

13 Russell, *History of Western Philosophy*, 229–30.

14 Scholasticism as a philosophical school was characterized by (1) existing within the boundaries of Roman Catholic Church teaching and orthodoxy, (2) Aristotle's replacement of Plato as the most important Greek philosopher but within Catholic orthodoxy; (3) use of dialectic and syllogistic reasoning, (4) an argumentative philosophical style rather than mystical, and (5) a realization that Aristotle disagreed with Plato on the question of universals. Scholasticism was marked by a new intellectual confidence and a willingness to exercise reason vigorously until it bumped-up against orthodoxy and dogma. This should not be considered the same as scientific inquiry based on the empirical and concrete.

15 Rev. Michael A. McGuire, *The New Baltimore Catechism and Mass*, no. 2, Official Revised Edition (New York: Benziger Brothers, Inc., 1941), 18. The following sources may help you understand the ideas of Aquinas and their continuing influence: (1) Gordon Leff, *Medieval Thought: St. Augustine to Ockham*

(Baltimore: Penguin Books, 1958), (2) Joseph Peiper, *Guide to Thomas Aquinas* (Notre Dame, Ind.: University of Notre Dame Press, 1962), (3) Wingo, *Philosophies of Education*, chapter eight, "The Protest of Perennial Philosophy," and (4) Russell, *History of Western Philosophy*, Book Two: Catholic Philosophy.

16   Wingo, *Philosophies of Education: An Introduction*, 258.

17   Robert Maynard Hutchins, *The Higher Learning in America* (New Haven and London: Yale University Press, 1936), 47. Perennialists, and Hutchins, are critical of Dewey and progressive education because the latter criticized the quest for certainty. This will become clear in chapter four.

18   Mortimer Adler, *The Paideia Proposal: An Educational Manifesto* (New York: Collier Books Macmillan Publishing Company, 1982), 35. See Adler's *Paideia Problems and Possibilities: A Consideration of Questions Raised by the Paideia Proposal* (New York: Collier Books Macmillan Publishing, 1983).

19   Wingo, *Philosophies of Education: An Introduction*, 274.

20   Ibid., 25.

21   Katz's historical analysis was published in New York by Praeger in 1971 with an expanded edition published in 1975. Katz's famous indictment of U.S. schools is that, from their inception in the nineteenth century, schools have been free, compulsory, bureaucratic, and racist. Wingo's social philosophical analysis complements Katz's work and Katz's work complements Wingo's analysis.

22   Richard A. Brosio, *The Relationship of Dewey's Pedagogy to His Concept of Community*, The University of Michigan Social Foundations of Education Monograph Series, No. 4 (Ann Arbor, Mich.: Malloy Lithoprinting, Inc., 1972), 1.

23   Wingo, *Philosophies of Education: An Introduction*, 135.

24   Ibid., 56–7.

25   Ibid., 94.

26   Richard H. Popkin and Avrum Stroll, *Philosophy Made Simple* (Garden City, NY: Made Simple Books, Inc., 1956), 87.

27   Wingo, *Philosophies of Education: An Introduction*, 98. The reader would benefit from consulting Frederick Copleston, *History of Philosophy, Volume 7, Modern Philosophy, Part I, Fichte to Hegel* (Garden City, N.Y.: Image Books, 1963), passim, for a more complete understanding of post-Kantian idealism after the work of Immanuel Kant (1724–1804).

28   Wingo, *Philosophies of Education: An Introduction*, 109.

29   Ibid., 127.

30   See Michael W. Apple, *Official Knowledge: Democratic Education in a Conservative Age* (New York & London: Routledge, 1993) and Donaldo Macedo, *Literacies of Power: What Americans Are Not Allowed to Know* (Boulder: Westview Press, 1994), for useful analyses of these questions.

31   Wingo, *Philosophies of Education: An Introduction*, 74.

32   Richard A. Brosio, "Essay Review of Abraham Edel, *Relating Humanities and Social Thought: Science, Ideology and Value,* volume 4," *Educational Studies* 22, no. 4 (Winter 1991): 477–78.

33   For a lucid analysis of the shift from religions to secular sources for bedrock, meaning, and justification, see Carl L. Becker, *The Heavenly City of the Eighteenth-Century Philosophers* (New Haven: Yale University Press, 1932), passim.

34   Richard A. Brosio, *A Radical Democratic Critique of Capitalist Education* (New York: Peter Lang Publishing, Inc., 1994), 552.

35   Walter Lippmann, *A Preface to Morals* (Boston: Beacon Press, 1929), 9–10.

36   Russell, *History of Western Philosophy*, 729.

37   Lippmann, *Preface to Morals*, 19–20.

Chapter Three

Various Reds: Marx, Historical Materialism, Critical Theory, and the Openness of History

Introduction

The thinkers and their ideas presented in this chapter may seem misplaced, due to the identification of Marxist thought with the former Soviet system and current socialist systems that have been declared repressive by our leaders and mainstream media. However, my assessment is that the ideas presented here are central to the critical democratic traditions of Western Civilization—as well as elsewhere. Democratic Marxist thought does not lead to the vast "Gulag Archipelago" system of prisons in the former Soviet Union. The end of the Cold War will, perhaps, permit interested people to reconsider the meaning of the ideas and traditions offered in this chapter as central to critical democracy, as well as to the education necessary to achieve it. Sidney Hook wrote the following about Marx:

> He chose his vocation [philosopher, economist, revolutionary] on the basis of what he believed to be true about the nature of society and the process necessary to change it. His watchword was struggle. . . . He tended to judge people only in the light of their possible use[fullness] in the political battles of the movement, which he regarded as linked with the continuing struggle for human liberation from antiquity to the present [he lived from 1818–1883]. Marx . . . glorified Prometheus as the "foremost saint and martyr in the philosophical calendar." . . . Marx was a man who lived by his ideas [and was] . . . incorruptible. . . . [He] had a passionate sense of social injustice which burns fiercely in everything he wrote. . . . Marx had no pride of race or nationality. He considered himself a European . . . [and] was a great admirer of the Greek tragic poets, of Dante,

Shakespeare, and Balzac. He was a radical democrat who had no respect for the
will of unenlightened majorities, a fierce individualist who would become . . .
[enraged] at the notion of party discipline or of loyalty to anything but his own
creative insights. He would have been an intellectual firebrand in any society,
including the socialist Utopia of his fantasy. It was characteristic that he concluded
his introduction to *Capital* [published in 1867] with a line from Dante: "Follow
your own course, and let people talk."[1]

As we shall see in Section I of this chapter, democratic Marxist thought
is part of the secular development in Western Civilization that places
human beings and their welfare at the center of social analysis. As a living
intellectual tradition owing much to the Enlightenment of the eighteenth
century, its adherents believe that human reason represented the spark
for human action that could free us from ignorance, superstition, and
injustice. This belief should be important to educators because it connects
understanding to the possibility for action and improvement. Human agency
and responsibility lay at the heart of Marxist philosophy; this did not
mean the erroneous belief that we can do whatever we like. It was Marx's
view, as a historical materialist, that although human beings make their
own histories, we do so neither under conditions of our choosing nor just
as we like. This position is highly relevant to contemporary political, economic, and educational discourse because it provides a commonsense
middle ground between extremist claims, that the individual is wholly responsible for her/his fate, and environment is totally dominant. Marxist
thought portrays human struggle that is necessary because the world we
live in is neither an Eden nor an unchangeable hell; rather, history is seen
as open! However, there are no guaranteed outcomes; there can be no
certainty. Again we learn of an intellectual tradition which asserts that we
must not be paralyzed by inaction just because it is impossible to achieve
certainty—a tradition that is dependent on a secularly unprovable hope.

As human beings who are embedded in the material conditions of
everyday life think about their circumstances and attempt to change social and physical realities which they find unjust or intolerable, they change
themselves as a result of their collective struggle. This constructivist view
of epistemology and human action has important ramifications for participatory democracy as well as educational preparation for it. This is the
case because, unlike the spectator theory of knowledge, constructivists
believe that human action helps construct the world and that we are
changed in the process. Men and women are not powerless with regard
to understanding the world. Human reason and theory can be translated
into practice so that the social and physical worlds can be made better

places for us. Marxist constructivists argued that the dominant elites and classes have power, but they do not have access to certainty with which to justify their rule over subaltern people. Their power is based on conquest. It is not part of the very nature of things. Because some people have constructed a particular status quo, others (e.g., the working class) can have the understanding, power, and motive to change it.

Marxist thought has also helped us understand that democracy cannot be restricted to politics because economic realities are of central importance to political systems as well as to our daily lives. The term, social class, represents the Marxist understanding of our complex relationships to the socioeconomic system in which we live. For example, the proletariat is said to have only labor power to trade, where the capitalist class owns the means of production. It was Marx's contention that the proletariat suffered from the capitalist attempt to commodify everything and everyone. The organized working class was able to realize eventually that its liberation from economic exploitation and political impotence required the development of liberatory theory, collective action, and the overcoming of capitalism-as-a-system. He thought that capitalism should be replaced by a moral economy that was answerable to human needs, as well as compatible with a *de facto* participatory democracy. The democratic Marxists never thought that schooling alone could enable subaltern people to recognize the chains that bound them, in part, because most socioeconomic and political systems have constructed formal schooling according to reproductive criteria that serve to maintain social class and other (e.g., racial and gender) advantages. We shall consider further this reproductive possibility and its consequences for formal schooling subsequently.

The first section of this chapter focuses on Marx's idea of historical materialism, in Section II it focuses on the ideas of Antonio Gramsci. His analysis owes an acknowledged debt to Marx; his historical conditions were different in important way(s) from Marx's. His response to his lived experiences provides another rich lode of critical democratic thought. Gramsci claimed that intelligence is widespread; intellectual ability among subaltern people makes democracy possible. Section III features the ideas of the Frankfurt School thinkers, especially their views on critical theory.[2] Members of the Frankfurt School had varied experiences in the early to middle twentieth century that were different from Marx's and Gramsci's. Their work is not homogeneous, although they shared some underlying assumptions, and their debt to Marx is great. Yet they were not familiar with Gramsci's work until after World War II. Gramsci's main work was done while he was imprisoned in Fascist Italy and was not widely known until the fall of Fascism. Section IV provides a broad brush look at what critical pedagogy might look like, though there is no attempt to provide a how-to recipe.

I

In our attempt to understand Marx's idea of historical materialism, let us begin with reference to sociology of knowledge, i.e., the supposition that there are relationships between human thought and the social contexts in which this occurs. Marx helped sociologists of knowledge understand that human consciousness is determined by our social being. Some have misunderstood Marx to have claimed that the superstructure of ideas merely reflects the material substructure in a crudely mechanistic fashion. In fact, Marx's dialectical approach to the complex relationships between super- and substructure is understood in terms of human activity, labor, in its broadest sense. The social relations brought about by labor activity are central to Marx's understanding of the embeddedness of human thought in material and social contexts. Peter Berger and Thomas Luckmann wrote: "The sociology of knowledge understands human reality as socially constructed. . . . Since the constitution of reality has . . . been a central problem of philosophy, this understanding has certain philosophical implications. . . . Sociology takes its place in the company of sciences that deal with man [sic] *as* man . . . [i.e.,] a humanistic discipline. . . . Sociology must be carried on in a continuous conversation with both history and philosophy or lose its proper object of inquiry. This object is society as part of a human world, made by men, inhabited by men, and, in turn, making men [as they seek to transform the social and material furniture of their existence], in an ongoing historical process."[3]

This is not the place to examine Marx's debt to Georg Hegel (1770–1831), the idealist philosopher, although it seems that Marx valued his senior colleague's work. Marx thought he had critically transformed Hegel's philosophy of history by turning it right side up; attributing causality to our interaction with the material world, rather than to the idealist conception of priority of consciousness. In *The Economic and Philosophical Manuscripts* of 1844, Marx achieved an economic/materialist interpretation of Hegelian idealism that resulted in an explanation of human alienation that depended on our social relations with one another, replacing an earlier concept of self-alienation. As Robert Tucker explained, for Marx: "Only man [sic] . . . can be this alien power over man. . . . This relation . . . takes practical shape as . . . [one] between the alienated worker and . . . the capitalist. In this way the inner conflict of alienated man with himself became, in Marx's mind, a social conflict between 'labour' and 'capital,' and . . . the class-divided society. Self-alienation was projected as a social phenomenon."[4] Alienation is concretely situated in the sociologically and historically definable material world of economic and material relations. Alienated labor was called wage labor by Marx; people work in order to live. "Thus does the Marxism of the *Manifesto* [1848] evolve directly out of the Marxism of the manuscripts of 1844. A system concerned itself with the generic human self in its hostile relations with itself turns into one that . . . [is explainable by] a dualized [unjust] society."[5] The cure for alienation is no longer to be found in the mind alone but in the social relations characteristic of undemocratic, unjust capitalism. In philosophical terms, materialism refers to a belief that matter-in-motion is the fundamental "constituent" of the universe. Rather, philosophical idealism holds that ideas constitute the most basic reality. Marx opposed the crude materialism of his time because it failed to consider the human construction of meaning, ideas, and history in relationship to material realities. Marx insisted that people learn about the world by concretely acting on it, rather than contemplating a supposed reality that is independent of the search for it. You are invited to reflect on this paragraph with the following as a possible guide. Marx took the perennial philosophical problem of human alienation and placed it into the material world of capitalist socioeconomic and political relations. This feat allowed him and us to historicize and politicize our understanding of alienation as well as empowering us to do something about it.

I will inquire further into what the "new materialism" means. First of all, it has nothing to do with purely material, mechanical, or physiological phenomena; instead, it refers to Marx's belief that we are productive mentally as well as materially. He argued that we cannot think or even live without producing the material necessities for human existence. The "new materialism" is historical materialism, i.e., a way of thinking that takes the practical lives of human beings as the foundation of our ideas. Hegel and other idealists stress human consciousness rather than real life that consciousness reflects, as the primary datum.[6] The idealists stand accused of erroneously believing that human thought is in perfect correspondence with reality that is "out there." It is clear that much of our consciousness has been "false consciousness," mainly because it failed to acknowledge the human creation of both intellectual, and to some extent, material reality. The Hegelian idealists held that ideas and their consciousness of them must be in keeping with the unfolding of spirit as the motor force of history.

Marx's "new materialism" depends on the soundness and convincing-ness of the following ideas. He argued that the external world is the *ma-terialization* of historical human labor. What he called the "sensuous world" around us is the product of our labor. The old materialism failed to grasp this fact. Marx explained that the reality we "apprehend" through our senses and cognition should be viewed as the objectification of hu-man activity—not as a given to be studied and grasped as natural or su-pernaturally provided. Marx criticized the old materialist, Ludwig Feuerbach (1804–72), by pointing out that the latter could not even study the sen-sory world, altered and constructed by humans, without the assistance of his spectacles! Marx's "new materialism" is "dialectical" because it views historical development in a nature constructed by humans, i.e., human agency results in alterations of our environment. This changed context affects us.

I will borrow from Tucker once more in order to nail down the crucial difference between Marx's "new materialism" and the idealism of Hegel et al. Marx admitted his debt to Hegel in terms of their common under-standing that reality must be understood subjectively, i.e., the roles played by the creative subjects of the historical process. However, the two posi-tions "differ in that Hegelian idealism construes the world-creating activ-ity as mental production, an . . . activity of abstract thought, whereas Marxian materialism construes it as human activity of material produc-tion."[7] Erich Fromm may countersink the nail with his explanation that "Marx's 'materialistic' or 'economic' interpretation of history . . . mean[s] that the real and total man [sic], the '. . . living individuals'—not [just] the ideas produced . . . are the subject matter of history. Marx's interpreta-tion of history could be called . . . anthropological. . . . It is the under-standing . . . based on the fact that men are 'the authors and actors of their history.'"[8]

The alert reader can readily understand that if Marx's philosophy is credible, then one's approach to social and material structures that we encounter as volitional actors/agents on a daily basis need not be viewed as universal or unalterable. Social and school realities can and should be seen as the work of certain actors. Other actors can and perhaps should change them. It is also apparent that those who insist on certainty and a supernatural explanation of reality would be opposed to the implications of Marx's "new" or historical materialism. During this period of political, social, and economic reaction, some seek to convince us that poverty as well as massive school failure represent a certain inevitability and natural-ness. Marx would not agree. Racism, unemployment, social injustice, school tracking, homophobia, misogyny, etc. can be seen by the alert teacher and/or layperson as practices that can be historically explained and collectively overcome.

According to Marx, the humanly constructed world in which we live has all too often been experienced as alien as well as an obstacle to progress and justice due to the division of labor under capitalism. The wage-laborer is forced, although not by law, into a relationship with capital and capitalists that leads to her/his commodification, exploitation, and dehumanization. The division of alienated humans against themselves becomes for Marx the division of social class against social class, i.e., laborer vs. capitalist. Class consciousness and class conflict emerge from the division of labor—a division that favors the capitalist owners and bosses. Marx believed that serious study, reflection, and ultimately thoughtful, experimental action could empower human beings to struggle collectively against people, procedures, and institutions that oppress them. Here we see the possibility for a collective unbound Prometheus. C. Wright Mills wrote of how Marx's workers finally free themselves from the animal world as they create conditions which are really human. The so-called objective external forces that have "hitherto dominated history will . . . pass under the control of men [sic] themselves. . . . It is humanity's leap from the realm of necessity into the realm of freedom."[9] Although this leap occurs in the context of a remaining but altered structure, it is a leap nevertheless!

Some educators, among others, have been taught to believe that there is little or no opportunity for human initiative in the Marxian scheme of things. The erroneous determinist reading of Marx and some Marxists has caused more than a few educational theorists to declare that Marxist thought is either irrelevant or harmful to the construction of education for democratic empowerment, social justice, and respect for bona fide diversity. My interpretation of the various Reds' work that I admire causes me to disagree with these theorists.[10] For example, although Marx argues that the dominant ideas of any particular society are the ones held by those who control the means of production and the command posts in the socioeconomic status quo, he asserts that these ideas are not the only ones. In fact, "every . . . society carries its own negation . . . the inner contradiction which finds its most striking expression in class struggle. . . . Thus the dominant ideas are always permeated by other, rebellious ones . . . so that class struggle is fought not only as an economic but also as a political and intellectual [see our schools] battle."[11] The evidence of such struggles conducted by those with antidominant ideas about schools and education is both clear and overwhelming. During periods of serious social disagreement, the schools become contested sites, especially in countries that are characterized by compulsory schooling. I have analyzed this contestation in a chapter called "The Janus-faced Public Schools in the United States." The thesis is that the K–12 public school is caught in the cross-hairs of the incompatible conflicting imperatives of capitalism and democracy. The first imperative insists that the schools produce willing, competent, and loyal workers; the second one calls for critical education in order to prepare the citizen-worker for the task of analyzing and understanding the economic system itself. Such understanding is central to empowering action committed to socioeconomic, political, and cultural change.[12]

For Marx, the instruments of labor, e.g., tools, machines, etc., are part of the forces of production; however the workers "with their technical and social experience, their needs and insights, the degree of their organization and consciousness, are more important. . . . It is not . . . [new technology] that creates revolutionary ideas which will grip the new class [proletariat] and make it . . . revolutionary."[13] Professional teachers are not paid to be revolutionaries. Very few see their roles this way. Nevertheless if one views democracy, social justice, and respect for diversity as goals and conditions requiring struggle, then Marx is a rich source of support. Teachers who hope and believe that students are volitional and proactive, in spite of vast differences in their abilities to "play school," should have philosophical, as well as psychological, bases on which to rest their optimism. Marx, John Dewey, et al. have held that human beings, through their thoughts and actions, are "circumstance changers"; we have accomplished profound and progressive revolutionary transformations throughout history. People have relied on the ideas that are rooted in social reality and have invented language as a primary tool with which to humanistically rearrange/refashion the furniture of human existence. Must we tolerate the human constructed ghettos of the late-twentieth century, when it is obvious that those who are confined in them suffer unnecessarily? The thinkers and actors featured in the work before you have answered the question with a resounding, NO!

During the last years of the twentieth century and in the second millennium it is important to articulate well the human condition, one which features both human freedom and necessary restraining and/or stabilizing structural limitations. Common sense tells us that we are free to take on and able to accomplish many things. This same common sense alerts us to human and societal limitations. All too often those with privilege and power have punished those who are less fortunate by charging that the "losers" must have chosen their lot. Those born into privilege and power because of social class, racial, ethnic, gender, and/or sexual orientation advantages have seldom understood well or admitted (when and if they did) the head start they enjoyed. All too many subaltern people have been bamboozled into believing that their poor situations are entirely due to their own shortcomings. For many people, schooling-education has served to keep them unaware of the real power relations in their schools and societies. The Marx offered here belongs to a long tradition of subversive educators who seek to call things by their correct names. These subversives have argued that power and privilege that cannot withstand critical interrogation directed at the foundations of such advantages do not deserve to stand.

Suggested Task for the Reader

Teachers are attracted to a belief that their students can get beyond their limitations as a result of good teaching and supportive schooling. Many teachers seem uncomfortable with analyses that suggest important structural boundaries to human agency. This discomfort does not preclude their seeing through the most flagrant Horatio Alger, pull-yourself-up-by-your-own-bootstraps stories. The specter of a completely determined Skinnerian person seems to cause hesitation with regard to abandoning Horatio. You are invited to develop a middle position between "bootstrapism" and environmental determinism by taking the following assertion by Marx seriously. We make our own histories, not under circumstances chosen by ourselves but, in contexts inherited from the past and/or constructed by others. This idea provides space for teachers to construct middle ethical positions that may be warranted to assert to those who may have initially believed the Horatio Alger myth, or were convinced that Skinner's position is accurate. Students are volitional; however, they do bump up against various barriers, limits, and structures.

Marx criticized the economists who came before him, especially the so-called classical, political economists who argued that the capitalist system represented universally valid characteristics and the best that history had to offer. This argument is also made by contemporary neoliberal, procapitalist economists. Marx criticized the economists who were apologists for capitalism partly because they likened so-called economic laws to the laws of physics and chemistry. Marx and many Marxists argued that because of the development of human productive power, both social conditions and the putative laws governing them also changed. As Marx made clear, "'History does nothing, it "possesses no immense wealth," it "wages no battles." It is *man* [sic], real living man, that does all that, . . . who possesses and fights; "history" is not a person apart, using man as means for his own particular aims; history is *nothing but* the activity of man pursuing his [individual and/or collective] aims.'"[14] History is full of accidents and probabilities; purposive human action—activity based on theoretical insight—can and does make a difference.

History is not a lifeless collection of facts in Marx's view, but rather the masses and classes in motion as they transform reality and shape history. He was aware, e.g., of the role played by the black masses in the American South during the nineteenth century. He celebrated the role of the Parisian masses in 1870–71 as they built a self-governing democracy, known as the Paris Commune. Marx described this revolutionary democratic struggle as their having "stormed the heavens"—forming a government consisting of freely associated workers. Philosophical existentialists and phenomenologists have always been attracted to Marx's description of earth-bound human beings who can, nevertheless, "storm the heavens" and steal fire from the gods and goddesses. Raya Dunayevskaya wrote, "in . . . his struggle with Hegel's . . . [idealism], Marx . . . pointed to how different the problems could be when actual corporeal Man [sic], standing on firm . . . earth, inhaling and exhaling all natural forces, becomes 'subject,' and . . . philosophy . . . has Man at its center."[15] She has pointed out that Marx constructed a new unity composed of economics, philosophy, and revolution. He believed that human beings could think and act rationally and that there was an innate feeling of hope in us. Marx argued that it is people who work out the meaning of philosophy by liberating themselves. Twentieth-century liberation theology is not entirely dissimilar to Marx on this point. He contended that capitalism and its attendant class stratification hinder the development of innate human talent and potential.

Dunayevskaya called historical materialism a "new continent of thought," in part because Marx broke with bourgeois society, capitalist economics, and philosophical idealism. She argued convincingly that Marx began considering and "listening to new voices from below," e.g., the Silesian weavers (in Central Europe) during their uprising of 1844. He considered this struggle as an early example of proletarian class struggle against oppression. As Fischer pointed out, for Marx, "revolutionary practice changes circumstances and . . . [human beings]. It sees . . . [us] not only as the object [anvil] of history but also its subject [hammer]: he [she] is . . . capable, by subjective activity, of . . . changing existing circumstances. It is in the recognition of this constant interaction between man and his works, between social 'laws of nature' and the nature of man as being capable of changing the circumstances . . . around him, between production relations which tend to conserve what has already been achieved and material and intellectual productive forces which press . . . forward, that we find the quintessence and culmination of historical materialism."[16] Marx knew that the "old materialists" had not realized that education allows us to actively and subjectively change the so-called real world. In his trenchant style, Marx reminded his philosophical opponents that the educators must be educated about the "new materialism," what his successors have named, historical materialism.[17]

II

We turn our attention in this section to Antonio Gramsci (born 1891 in Sardinia; died 1937 in Rome after a long period of incarceration in Fascist prisons), who was both theorist and political activist. His intellectual accomplishments must be understood in the historical context of the political struggles to which he was committed. He may not be well known to many readers of this book, but there is a rich literature (in many languages, including English) on Gramsci's work. It is possible to go beyond the work before you in order to learn more about this important radical democrat's contributions. His place in this chapter has been earned by his special insights into education, as central to the construction of liberatory theory as well as a collective action capable of implementing it. Like Marx, Gramsci held that knowing is not just a passive reflection on a reality which is unaffected by cognition, but is the beginning of a process that can alter so-called reality. In keeping with Marx, Gramsci also held that human action was bound by certain social and physical structures. Gramsci's own involvement in political struggle epitomized his teachings about how ordinary people could use their intelligences to understand and/or fashion a plan, then act in order to struggle for a better life.

Gramsci's originality as a democratic Marxist lies in his recognition that the oppressive powers that be in any society do not maintain their power over others merely by the threat and/or use of physical force. Gramsci argued that: "The bourgeois [capitalist] civilization that controlled the workers and other subaltern classes could do so because its leaders [imperfectly] controlled the very definitions of what was considered real, commonsensical, good, and so forth. Bourgeois hegemony meant that a social class could rule a highly developed society without the flagrant or regular use of naked force. . . . Control of the economic apparatus was in bourgeois, or capitalist hands . . . however, hegemony is more than economic control. Gramsci has taught us that hegemony consists of a group or class creating a state of affairs in which their leadership and privileged positions seem natural. It consists too of ways of living, thinking, speaking, habits, hopes, fears, and underlying assumptions."[18]

Gramsci sought to understand how the rulers accomplished the establishment and maintenance of their hegemony. This understanding is relevant for us, especially in the "developed" societies which feature some forms of democratic government as well as capitalist economies, because if class domination is still a factor, its domination is secured for the most part on a daily basis through hegemonic strategies—including formal schooling—rather than by the use of prisons and/or armed might. If there are ideological blinders on all too many people in a given society, then those who have the power to construct the main features of what is considered official knowledge and even common sense will seldom have to rely on physical force. The police often use direct force on poor people, people of color, and/or others considered to be "underclass." There has occurred a dramatic growth of the United States prison population, an increase that is disproportionately black. Hegemony is contested by subaltern people. As we rely more and more on the media as well as on official channels like government and school to name our lived realities, it becomes increasingly possible for hegemonists to continue their dominance as a result of their control over the cultural signs and meanings around which we organize our lives. Direct repression by "security forces" is the iron fist underneath the hegemonic glove. This occurs when indirect control becomes ineffective. The "advanced" capitalist societies of this period have not featured control over the workplace alone. They are characterized by what Henri Le Febevre has called, "the colonization of everyday life."[19]

Herbert Marcuse argued that advanced industrial societies are constructed in a way that allows certain differences *in* the parameters of capitalist priorities. There exists meaningful pluralism, diversity, and choice as well as other freedoms celebrated in these societies. Unfortunately it becomes increasingly difficult to get outside of the nondemocratically constructed, one-dimensional society in order to assess its overall rationality and/or irrationality. Marcuse defines what Gramsci was so prescient in first realizing, namely that contemporary industrial (or postindustrial) societies appear to be successful in containing social change that would represent the building of different institutions and practices. He argued, in agreement with Gramsci, that just because many people have come to accept the one-dimensional society does not alter its irrationality and injustices. Some people suffer from "false consciousness," the inability to escape from Plato's cave. In Marcuse's words, the one-dimensional society "shapes the entire universe of discourse and action, intellectual, and material culture. In the medium of technology, culture, politics, and economy merge into an omnipresent system that swallows up or repulses all alternatives."[20] Referring more specifically to the United States and education, Donaldo Macedo argued that: "It is all right to have an opinion as long as . . . [it] coincides with the dominant ideology."[21] He charged that both major parties in the United States subscribe to the same basic ideology and world views. Peter McLaren has asked whether teachers and other cultural workers have access to, and/or know how to use, a language that enables substantive critique of the givens that are shored up by the two dominant parties; givens that are portrayed as the be-all and end-all of genuine democratic choice.

Suggested Task for the Reader

As you reflect critically on your schooling experience, what are some examples of instruction that may have consciously or inadvertently provided versions of hegemonic, official reality that made it difficult to think beyond these givens? How were teachers, curricula, texts, other learning materials, classmates, etc. possibly ensembles of hegemonic beliefs and practices that served (perhaps unwittingly) to support a socioeconomic, political, cultural, and education system (i.e., status quo) that may not have served the legitimate interests and needs of all its citizens? Some critics have used the term "propaganda of integration" in order to describe a one-dimensional society where the dominant forces have been able to build a hegemony that is so effective that outright lies are not needed in order to protect against possible opposition. Reflect on questions you may never have thought of asking because your knowledge and attitudes rested squarely in hegemonic "common sense" or conventional wisdom. Who and what were absent from the "all things considered" format of discussions, characteristics of societies that are formally democratic and capitalistic as well as featuring classed, raced, and gendered actors? In societies where a particular status quo has existed for a long period of time, how can subversive thoughts be co-opted into the system so that they never become translated into meaningful action aimed at structural change? Is there any need for outright censorship in a society where official versions of literacy do not include the education and training in order to read Gramsci et al.? What is not considered in a putatively "all things considered" infotainment culture?

How does Gramsci help us escape from the one-dimensional society and its hegemonic colonization of life? Can his work assist educators as we attempt to break the reproductive function of schooling? Does he suggest ways through which the class-stratified society can be significantly altered? Although he does not provide packaged formulas, the alert citizen-educator can find powerful ideas in Gramsci's work that can be used to confront present structural impediments that make it difficult or impossible to carry out the belief that ordinary people can learn to govern themselves, as well as construct a moral economy—one based on the recognition that work must be educative, life-enhancing, and congruent with our human and civil rights. Like Marx, Gramsci held that human knowledge could never be certain. He, like his German forebear, was convinced that our individual/collective problem-solving abilities allowed us to improve living conditions for everyone—not just the elite. Although Gramsci recognized the effectiveness of the hegemony constructed—and kept in good repair—by the powers that be in a capitalist society, he had faith that intelligence was widespread enough to make radical democracy possible. Gramsci grasped the little recognized fact that all human beings are educable! Educability was not the ability and right of the rich and powerful alone. Gramsci's own experience as a wretchedly poor person taught him how difficult liberatory, educational achievement is to accomplish. Yet he knew it could be done.

Gramsci was interested in educating intellectuals from the working class so that they could provide leadership and help others through the hegemony exercised by the capitalist class and their agents. He wished to build a revolutionary, working-class party comprised of men and women who could *deconstruct* the hegemony (based on material conditions and physical coercion) of the ruling class, and reconstruct an idea of a new and democratic polity with a moral economy based on social justice. In spite of the difficult odds in Italy during his time, he maintained that insight, theory, organization, combativeness, bravery, and coalition-building would allow subaltern people to change their lives for the better. Gramsci valued the formal school system in his country. Still, he criticized the exclusion of working-class students from it.[22]

Gramsci knew that studying was hard work. He realized that the working-class youngsters of his time were already engaged in concentrated physical labor. Gramsci reasoned that if continuities between mental and physical labor were pointed out, then working-class students could develop confidence in doing school work. Such a realization would serve to demystify academic work, as well as the hegemonic insistence that only the wellborn could engage in mental labor. Gramsci presented studying as using skills that all people had, ones that were improvable, and that there was no stark difference between intelligences used to solve very different problems. In his view, the possibilities for intellectual achievement for subaltern people exist because "the 'pupil' is never a passive recipient of what is 'taught' and because of the contradiction which exists between the [widely held, uncritical] conception of the world . . . [initially held by] the masses and their daily practical activities [i.e., reality contradicts the hegemonically constructed view carried by all too many workers and other poorly schooled persons]."[23]

Gramsci began with the assumption that everyone has a culture, although sometimes only in a crude and undisciplined way. He held that all persons are intellectuals in the sense that we all operate in various contexts that are comprised of ideas and representations of how things become, how they are, as well as how they could/should become. The hegemonists of his time (and ours) fought to devalue the intellectual capital of those they wished to keep in subaltern conditions. One example of how this is done is through the use of "official knowledge" by educators who collaborate with those more powerful than they in order to deliberately or unwittingly disregard and/or disrespect the things that subaltern students already know.

Gramsci began from the perspective of the student, while recognizing the crucial importance of good teaching. In good, antiessentialist fashion, he saw the learning process as a movement toward self-knowledge and an understanding of our social and physical worlds. In Gramsci's view, education is not a matter of handing out prepackaged school commodities to know-nothing students, instead it is a process of helping to develop and discipline abilities the learner had. Belief in various levels of intelligences, competencies, aptitudes, and interests is central to education and to possibilities for democracy. Gramsci's views on hierarchical realities based on individual differences are of great importance to our education for democratic empowerment. He believed that every human activity contained some form of intellectual exercise; our doing and our knowing cannot be separated. Each of us thinks philosophically and artistically; we all participate in forming certain conceptions of reality and what must be done. He believed that almost everyone has a conscious idea of moral conduct, and that this idea leads to criticizing what is unjust, as well as to efforts aimed at change.

Gramsci's belief in the abilities of ordinary people is central to his insistence that education's main objective should be self-governance in a just society. He realized that people have different skills and interests—or as we say in these times, are "differently abled"; his interpretation of these conditions provides resources for those who wish to consider differences as plusses rather than minuses. He maintained that differences among people's abilities, intelligences, interests, and accomplishments cannot be disregarded, but they can and must be negotiated and understood in new ways. Gramsci did not stress differences in invidiously comparative terms; he would have us arrange them in structured divisions of labor that are based on a recognition that we are all potentially capable. Divisions of labor are fine and necessary; however, they must be based on human enhancement criteria—ones which do not punish or exclude. Gramsci insisted that relationships among variously abled people must be negotiated with the good of all as the primary goal. Gramsci, like Marx, knew that, by definition, democracy could not mean only that an unskilled worker could be trained to become a skilled one. Gramsci wrote, "'It must mean that every "citizen" can "govern" and that society places him [her] . . . in a general condition [through formal and informal schooling] to achieve this.'"[24] Gramsci believed that democracy means rule by the people. It did not mean only that an unskilled worker could become skilled, hence more useful to capitalist bosses and be somewhat better paid. Gramsci knew that every revolution was preceded by great intellectual activity. He concluded that during his place and time, the working class must become conscious of itself—as a class—in the socioeconomic, political, cultural, and educational realities in which it lived. He hoped that this achievement could lead to a comprehensive world view with resultant political strategy.

Gramsci realized workers must learn to think and act as successors to the ruling classes which oppressed them. He gave much attention to the place of education in the making of a radical democratic and socialist counterhegemony, with overcoming the capital's regime as the ultimate goal. Gramsci demonstrated his awareness of education's importance by including on the masthead of a journal he edited: "Instruct yourselves because we shall need our intelligence. Agitate because we shall need all our enthusiasm. Organise yourselves because we shall need all of our power." Gramsci's slogan captures his philosophical belief that so-called ordinary people can think well, act in solidarity, and achieve a more just society.

III

Gramsci believed that democratic Marxism represented the most recent (early twentieth century) synthesis of what was best in the Western tradition. His goal was to further develop what he thought this tradition's best actors had been aiming for: the free social person described by Marx, whose ancestry went back to the best Greek and Judeo-Christian thought. Gramsci was convinced that a profound twentieth-century revolution was needed in order to realize the best of the West's historical promise. This realization would come to fruition in large part by the abolition of social class divisions based on inequities of wealth and power—divisions that prevent us from becoming human beings in the richest and most complete sense of the term. Gramsci provided a bridge from Marx to critical theory. This intellectual tradition has been referred to as the Frankfurt School because of its adherents' memberships in The Institute of Social Research in Frankfurt, Germany. Some of the Frankfurt colleagues are Max Horkheimer, Herbert Marcuse, Theodor Adorno, Erich Fromm, Walter Benjamin, Leo Lowenthal, Franz Neuman, Friedrich Pollock, and Jurgen Habermas.[25] I offer the following introductory passage to invite the reader into critical theory, via my reading of Marcuse.

> Marcuse's term, one-dimensional, became famous after his book *One-Dimensional Man* was published in 1964. Central to a one-dimensional society is capitalist hegemony that is based on monopoly capitalism's power to control production, distribution, and the formulation of desire for commodities itself. Although this class-stratified society is non-democratic, it has delivered a plethora of consumer goods to people in Western society. Marcuse asserts that such a society is both democratic and unfree. The contemporary status quo is totalitarian by virtue of its economic organization: the range of choices in the merchandise mart of consumer capitalism may be great, but this is not as crucial as what can, or cannot, be chosen. The atomizing power of monopoly/consumer capitalism creates a marketable mass man [sic] who is told by the advertising media what he needs. The problem is that in a one-dimensional society, dominated by a capitalist agenda, man develops a distorted second nature that ties him to the commodity market; moreover, it is in this realm of consumption where gratification is to occur. The rhetoric of individualism is a subterfuge for the imposition of patterns which feature collective imitation. The consumers of the one-dimensional society are, in fact, well-dressed, manipulated objects in a non-democratically administered whole. Marcuse and his neo-Marxist colleagues of the Frankfurt School have formulated a way that allows the critic to get outside of any status quo in order to analyze and evaluate the whole. For Hegel, Marx, and Marcuse, a rational man is one who tests human activity by a standard of truth that goes beyond the status quo.[26]

Suggested Task for the Reader
Explore the possible meaning and/or accuracy of the concept: democratic and unfree. If Marcuse and other critical theorists are accurate in their description and critique of a society where what people desire is in

part determined by a sophisticated, massive, and nearly total culture of advertisement, what does this tell us about human volition and freedom? What does freedom mean for youngsters and adults if choices are exercised mostly in the supermarkets and shopping malls of contemporary capitalist societies? If the situation is as dire as critical theorists suggest, how does one move beyond this "one-dimensional" society in order to develop a more rational criteria of what our authentic needs are—or should be? Can we teach ourselves and our students how to criticize the descriptive "is," in the name of the normative "ought"? If so, can the "ought" be found as a result of a quest for certainty, revelation, or inerrant texts, or must it be constructed democratically without guarantees and in the human condition? Is the utopian vision of human freedom, beyond exploitative and numbing work, one that can and should be transformed into an achievable goal?

Let us turn our attention to the Frankfurt School's relationship to the Enlightenment tradition, the tensions in this tradition, and to Habermas's reliance on democratic, public discourse to ameliorate, if not solve, these tensions. You should be alert to the educational ramifications of what follows. Section III draws on various scholarly sources, especially David Ingram, *Critical Theory and Philosophy* (1990); Robert E. Young, *A Critical Theory of Education: Habermas and Our Children's Future* (1990); Philip Wexler, editor, *Critical Theory Now* (1991); and Richard Brosio, *The Frankfurt School: An Analysis of the Contradictions and Crises of Liberal Capitalist Societies* (1980). We begin with the Enlightenment tradition which took hold in France and elsewhere in Europe, based on Isaac Newton's scientific explanation of how our universe works. The thought was that if reason, physics, mathematics, and science could help us understand the heavens, then human intellect could further our understanding of social realities on earth. The reliance on secular reason began to take hold in certain parts of Europe as early as the Renaissance, driven in part by the rediscovery of the classical Greek contributions to human understanding of social and physical phenomena. Secular reason challenged and sometimes replaced religious explanations and justifications. Some Europeans (including colonial subjects living in North America) endeavored to justify their ideas and actions by claiming support from universal principles characterized by consistency as well as utilitarian results. This development helped promote an emphasis on more individual responsibility with regard to deciding between rights and wrongs. These changes contributed to demands for democratic rights for some of the people. If people could understand their social and physical worlds, and if such understanding banished supernatural causes in favor of natural and secular, explicable ones, then human beings can construct their own worlds—based on understanding and action. So far, so good. What if the concept of reason is itself a construct, i.e., with no validity whatsoever? What if reason itself is ideological, no more worthy of use in solving human problems than the dependence on revelation, faith, and mystery that the proponents of reason accused the religionists of erroneously standing on?

Critical theorists focused on the developing crisis of dependence on reason—reason that had been used for both good and evil purposes. They realized that the Enlightenment's championing of reason included a dichotomy that threatened its stability. They worried about how "objectivist" science could be guided by "subjectivist" moral claims. The efficacy of reason-become-physical science seemed much greater than reason-as-philosophy and more reliable than social science. The problem of enlightenment through secular reason was highlighted by the French philosopher and mathematician, René Descartes (1596–1650), when he articulated the difficulty of preserving a belief in human volition and autonomy in a universe that was increasingly described by mathematics and science as mechanistic and deterministic. This tension between freedom and determinism characterized the Enlightenment tradition. It continues to challenge Western philosophers such as Immanuel Kant (1724–1804), Georg Hegel, Marx, and the critical theorists of Frankfurt. The crisis of rationality featured philosophical/speculative rationalists and their claims against those rationalists who were turning to, and relying increasingly on, empirical considerations. Reason alone was no longer seen as adequate to support an empirical science that brought great power to some Western countries and to the capitalist economic system which took hold in England in the early eighteenth century.

The German philosopher Hegel (1770–1831) argued that a reconciliation between freedom and determinism—or between human volition/agency and structure which can be described by the growing power of physical, and to some extent, social science—can be achieved by the human mastery of nature and the society in which we live. He insisted that human beings impose their identities on the structures of the world we inhabit; this is accomplished by "assimilating" recalcitrant structure through the use of technology and science. When free, rational agency is understood and practiced in the concreteness of everyday life, it is possible for human beings to reconcile human subjectivity (freedom) with natural objectivity (determinism). This is a precursor to Marx's challenge to philosophers to go beyond trying to describe "reality" and instead endeavor to change it! The Italian philosopher and jurist, Giambattista Vico (1668–1744), argued that human beings had constructed the social world; other people—contemporary ones—could reconstruct what had been put into place. David Ingram pointed out: "Factually, scientific knowledge of causal necessity enables the [knowing] subject to gain mastery over nature, thereby [knowing] achieving [some] freedom from nature. Causal necessity without freedom . . . would be meaningless just as a free floating mind would be. For it is only by freely intervening in our world that we 'constitute' it as orderly, thereby enabling the 'discovery' of lawful patterns."[27]

Marx admired Hegel, but the former was convinced that the moral thrust of Enlightenment reason, one which celebrated democracy, community, equity, and justice, could not be easily reconciled with the acquisitive individualism resulting from the other face of Enlightenment reason; that self-preservation and self-aggrandizement followed logically from a universe described by hard-nosed science which had no place for deities or secularly grounded axiological foundations. Marx argued that any realistic reconciliation must result from revolutionary politics, not just philosophy. By the middle-nineteenth century, enlightenment began to look more like capitalism with its highly stratified and antidemocratic class-stratification and centers of private power. Marx's philosophical conception of historically grounded reason was based on the emergence of a mass-action politics aimed at bringing justice to those who had been oppressed by the dangerous side of Enlightenment reason. Marx and critical theory continued to hold that knowledge could emancipate if it were used as an historically grounded guide to action. Neither Marx nor the Frankfurt School claimed that historically grounded and human constructed knowledge, based on reason, was infallible. There was an insistence that the many, rather than the Platonic few, could become enlightened through reason in order to make their conditions more supportive of people's attempt to become more human. For the critical theorists, "reality had to be judged by the 'tribunal of reason': a version of reason which was thought to exist in the historical process . . . [They] attempted to avoid the . . . trap of having to choose between the concept of immutable transcendental thought on the one hand and crude relativism on the other. For the Frankfurt [School] . . . , what is true and rational are the societal forces in history that foster social change in the direction of a free and rational community."[28] We shall see how critical theory addressed other versions of the Enlightenment's theory-practice problem, one based on the alleged incompatibility between volitional men and women and our lives in physical and social realities that comprise structural barriers to our agency and specifically our roles as moral decision-makers.

Continue to examine critical theory's relationship to the Enlightenment tradition as we consider the following: How do human beings find reliable norms of justice and well-being in the messiness of everyday social life which is embedded in material conditions? It was apparent to the critical theorists that conventional wisdom, false consciousness, propaganda, ideology, and hegemony exercised by the rich and powerful often obscured critical clear-sightedness. Some critics of critical theory argue that the Frankfurt School philosophers were elitist because of their lack of confidence in ordinary people to see through the blinders fit on them through reproductionist schooling, advertising, government pronouncements, and other forms of official knowledge. Critical theorists argued that knowledge of how things are will not enable us to grasp how things should be. They struggled with how best to balance knowledge as mere description and as critique. This has important ramifications for contemporary teacher education and practice, for example, should the emphasis for both education and practice be on mastering the what is, or should it include the ability to critique current realities through the construction of criteria that speaks of what could/should be? Should teacher education be based on an apprenticeship model, or a critical model based on theoretical and holistic views of how things are supposed to be? How do professional teachers decide among various competing and conflicting claims in their theoretically empowered practice? If these teachers are firmly convinced that they are on solid ground, how do they convince students, parents, citizens et al. that they are more correct than their critics and opponents? The Frankfurt School's position was that philosophy's role is relegated to "salvaging relative truths from the wreckage of false ultimates."[29]

The critical theorists responded to the historical events of their time, roughly the first half of the twentieth century. They analyzed reason as scientific knowledge and technology from the perspective of moral enlightenment. This project was closely connected to their sophisticated critique of capitalism. They were forced to deal with the inability of Marx's proletariat to make a democratic, anticapitalist revolution. There were many reasons for this failure, including government repression of the working class. The Frankfurt School sought to discern the complex psychological reasons why subaltern people refused to leave Plato's cave, "choosing" instead to remain oppressed. Marcuse and some of his colleagues looked to Sigmund Freud's work in order to better understand the psychological reasons for the lack of enlightenment among those who were not served well by the capitalist system, the procapitalist central governments, and the overall system's use of social class, ethnicity, race, and/or gender identities to keep workers divided. The critical theorists were made pessimistic by their findings of continued working class passivity and deference to authority in their native Germany. The increasingly effective use of mass culture to divert people's attention from their best interests continued to cause pessimism among Marcuse and his colleagues even after some of them had emigrated to the United States in order to escape the Hitler terror and the ensuing holocaust against the European Jews.

The terrible events of World War II tempted the Frankfurt School colleagues to doubt the possibilities for the Enlightenment's humane realization. Some feared that the dichotomy within the Enlightenment, e.g., philosophy and science, freedom and necessity was unresolvable. They seemed ready to admit that capitalism and tyrannical government were not just distortions of the Enlightenment, but integral to it. I have argued against their position in chapter twelve of *A Radical Democratic Critique of Capitalist Education*, "The Challenge of Postmodernism to the Enlightenment and Its Democratic Legacy."

The critical theorists' pessimism was reinforced by social scientist Max Weber (1864–1920), who argued that if our values are to be judged mostly by the consequences resulting from committing them to action, then we are still in a subjectivist and morally relativistic position. Weber and critical theorists were neither confident that our values could be solidly based, nor that our alleged needs, those which propelled us into action, were autonomously developed, i.e., they very well may have been arbitrarily given from within the mostly nondemocratic culture. Weber wrote of modern society as an "iron cage" in which all too many people live their whole lives without any attempt to justify their actions, and/or inaction, before the tribunal of historical reason. This caged person toiled ceaselessly and consumed insatiably in a capitalist system that seemed to promise greater gratification at the cost of increasingly greater denial. Because the gratification followed the logic of consumer society's "hidden persuader," the satisfaction was not genuine, i.e., it was meretricious. One had to return to jobs that were not satisfying, based on denial and self-repression, in order to earn enough money to go back for more addictive, consumer, false satisfaction. I am reminded of The Rolling Stones' rock song hit, "I Can't Get No Satisfaction." The search for moral autonomy is replaced by the twin deities of capitalism: the blind necessities of work and buying consumption. How was one to get out of Weber's "iron cage"?

If reason is laid bare to reveal that it is a mere subjective illusion, i.e., another myth, and if science is just another narrative, then how do we get to bedrock? In response to this question Ingram wrote: "Ultimately the rational subject celebrated by liberalism [and United States schools] is neither individual nor free. In the parameters of formal rationality, the only value capable of motivating action is self-preservation. . . . Thus the enlightened bourgeois society is fragmented into isolated, egotistic bearers of property rights who, ironically, lack any *substantive* properties that might imbue their personalities with a sense of moral purpose. What identities they do possess are shaped by the collective forces that surround them—publicity being the most important."[30] For Weber and some critical theorists, formal reason becomes instrumental calculation, namely, a tool for self-aggrandizement; therefore, the rationalization of society is incompatible with moral autonomy and justice. The tensions of the Enlightenment were not resolved or resolvable. The pessimists feared that dystopia would dominate the future. Reason became a tool in the service of oppression and domination. As enlightenment counters older dogma and prejudice, it results in the enslavement of imagination and the regimentation of our social lives.

In fairness to critical theory, it must be said that most of its adherents continued to see small cracks in the monolithic dystopia, i.e., a bad place. They encouraged us to look into our aesthetic imaginations in order to refuse to succumb to the one-dimensional, totally administered, unfree, iron cage of modern society. They still held to their earlier conviction and hope that action informed by carefully constructed theory could help combat un-freedom, at least on certain chosen sites. In spite of this, perhaps the Frankfurt colleagues were too pessimistic! Ingram thinks that although our society is characterized by much of what critical theory claimed, there are many moral, individual, communitarian, democratic, and equitable examples of the Enlightenment tradition in our society.

I turn my attention to the work of Jurgen Habermas in order to learn how the youngest (born 1929) of the marquee critical theorists attempted to escape from the dead end of the Enlightenment described. It is important to note that although Marcuse and Habermas looked to outsiders and outcasts, and some intellectuals to replace the proletariat as a revolutionary force, the conservative restoration since around 1970 has made talk of anticapitalist democratic revolution seem fanciful at best and irresponsible at worst. Perhaps, because of the unlikely prospect for a more direct revolutionary change, Habermas would have us escape the iron cage through the development of better discourse. Robert E. Young argued, "it is only in the creation of a public realm of discourse, open to all, in which citizens come together to pursue their common rather than private interests . . . that the reconstructed life-world can be studied and critically evaluated in a way that frees . . . [us] from its reifying [to mistakenly consider an idea a concrete thing] power. . . . Habermas believes that this kind of discourse is inherent in the nature of speech itself. . . . [In fact, for Habermas] the post-Enlightenment creation of public discourse . . . was one of the most progressive and hopeful developments of our time."[31] This emphasis on discourse and its potential for freedom and justice is welcome by many serious, and certainly critical, educators. Habermas's concept, "life-world," refers to how we subjectively experience, comprehend, and interpret our world. The life-world is said to be constructed through communicative action. The family and public components of life-world can and must be made responsible to participatory democrats as we make good and serious talk that has the potential for liberatory action. It is in discourse that the kind of reason favored by critical theorists is to be developed. Such discourse, if occurring in the population (as opposed to only an elite), would serve to solve the dichotomies in the troubled Enlightenment tradition discussed earlier in this chapter. Habermas held that discourses are engaged in when certain issues need clarification and/or resolution.

Educators can play important roles in helping to develop the kind of discourse and discussions that Habermas favored. It is difficult to achieve what Habermas would have us do, i.e., the difficulty is caused in part by the uneven power relations that exist in which we converse. Habermas would have the discussants be mutually open to one another, an openness based on considering other discussants neither as opposites nor objects but instead as partners with things in common. As a result of critically questioning and answering one another in noncoercive conditions, certain understandings and agreements can arise. As opposed to monologue and talking "at" or "down to" another, the discourse favored by Habermas and other critical theorists emphasized mutual openness and even vulnerability, reminiscent of Martin Buber's hope that we treat one another as "thou(s)" rather than manipulated "it(s)." Critical theory insists that we force the established way people speak to reveal what is hidden and/or omitted. Such an accomplishment is crucial to critical education. One can easily recall conversations had, or formal presentations heard, which are less than satisfying because of what is taken for granted. Educators must be especially aware of such "sins of omission."[32] Young explains how Habermas's ideas on discourse were expressed in formal schooling terms: "'The goal of [education] lies in the establishment of a communication structure [in the classroom] which makes the acquisition of a capacity for free and open discussion . . . possible.'"[33]

I must emphasize that Habermas considered ordinary speech (talk that is materially grounded and articulated by classed, raced, and gendered speakers) as anticipatory of an "ideal" speech situation that enables the achievement of reconciliation, justice, autonomy, and solidarity. His concept of a "communicative ethic" advocated an expansion of participatory democracy which questioned the fairness and/or injustice of social institutions and processes. This ethic is committed to broad inclusion of participants as well as action outcomes. Habermas believed we must keep talking and acting in order to get better, not "right." This concept is called "fallibilism," knowledge is likely to be revised as we know more and as conditions change. Contrary to relativism, fallibilism maintains that we can make assertions that claim to be *provisionally* true or "universally" valid.

The discourse favored by critical theory is based on a historical community of discussants using their intelligence in order to practice a nonspecialized version of the scientific method—a method described further in Deweyan and progressive educational terms in chapter four. As Ingram wrote, "the conditions underlying the possibility of objective knowledge . . . include the maintenance of free and undistorted communication. Ultimately they imply [demand] a democratic society free of social [and economic] inequality and domination."[34] Habermas would have face-to-face discussants imagine a third person in the conversation, namely a "generalizable other" who represents the interests of the larger society. This version of the scientific method is based on the necessity to translate ideas into action in order to extract meaning from the complexity of our lives. Involvement in such broad and noncoercive discourse and ultimate action is the best way to achieve the intersubjective agreement favored by Habermas. "Objective reality" is the outcome of historical, solidaristic intersubjective agreement constructed by ordinary persons. Habermas seems to hope that if all persons who ever lived achieved profound knowledge of themselves and their world, then they would come to some broad agreement on the issues most central to their lives. He has continued to believe that the Enlightenment project was on the right track, and that the distortion of it is mostly due to capitalism. Habermas argued that truth can only be conceived of as an ideal consensus among free and rational people who face one another as equal discussants in open public discourse. The knowledge that results from such discussion is liberatory for those who participate. Critical theorists believe that discourse conducted under favorable conditions can construct a "universal" perspective, but not a transcendental one.

Critical theorists recognize that all too many people use language in ways that make what they desire nearly impossible to achieve; they understand well that asymmetrical power relations make authentic discourse difficult, if not impossible. Discourse must reveal complex motives as well as hidden advantages enjoyed by some of the discussants. Equitable compromises must follow from uncoerced broad participation—including discussion of the great discrepancies in power, income, wealth, privilege, and access among participants. Perhaps ethically alert teachers can help prepare youngsters to understand and practice such potentially liberatory discourse. However, merely having a voice is not the same as discussing why voice is a necessary but not sufficient condition for the kind of communication aimed at substantive change favored here. In our society there are competing voices. The power behind these utterances is not even close to being equal, and most talk does not occur in contexts that approximate ideal speech conditions, let alone achieve the ideal. One important weakness in contemporary talk is the lack of attention to the possibility for a general public good as a preferred outcome. Habermas believed that Jean Jacques Rousseau's (1712–78) concept of the "general will" (a *pro bono publico* concept) is not already out there, but must be constructed by the discussants.

In keeping with Rousseau's concept of participatory democracy, critical theory insists that each and every one of us must have a say over the things that affect our lives. Discussants must be convincingly invited to the roundtable of democratic talk. They must be convinced that there is nothing to fear. Good teachers can help prepare their students to demand such democratic speech conditions, ones which make possible unconstrained consensuses. I use Ingram to nail down Habermas's communication ethic. Its aim "is to bring about conditions of rational participatory democracy, in which existing needs can be critically assessed and transformed. For only by publicly discussing our needs can we begin to assess their impact on the lives of others . . . [and their] rationality, or compatibility with the general interests of all involved. . . . People [who] . . . enter into democratic discussions . . . are accountable to others for what they say and do, they must always be prepared to justify—through giving reasons in argumentation—the beliefs underlying their conduct."[35] The practice of communication ethic can help us achieve justice and solidarity, in part because intersubjective communication can help us realize that we have much in common. As the poet John Donne wrote: "Do not ask for whom the bell tolls, it tolls for thee."

In keeping with what I wrote in chapter three, I must emphasize that Marx, Gramsci, and the critical theorists all insist that the construction of a "more just" society depends on hammering out what "more just" means through the application of sound theory to transformative action—in history and materiality. Through good talk we can share our imaginations concerning where we can and must go. The democratic imaginary must be "made real" in the same way that a blueprint is translated into a building. Historical struggle is necessary in order to think clearly about "what should be," and even more necessary with regard to changing "what is" into "what ought to be."

The reader is invited to think about how the discourse conditions favored here can be accomplished in a society where all too many are subaltern to others in complex ways, e.g., in terms of social class, race, ethnicity, gender, sexual preference, and/or differently abled. Salvatore D'Urso has argued that "'where there are marked inequalities in the distribution of power, the full exercise of the method of intelligence depends solely on the goodwill of those in superior position. Hence a preliminary condition of deliberation may frequently be the organization and exercise of force to effect a redistribution of social power.'"[36] You are invited to think further about how socioeconomic and cultural conditions must be changed concomitantly as discourse becomes more like what Habermas has described and advocated; talk alone is unlikely to construct a society and school that are more democratic, socially just, and respectful of diversity.

IV

Robert E. Young wrote that "from the beginning of the period when the ideas of the Enlightenment began to find their way into the revolutionary (organizational) processes which gave us modern democratic states such as the USA and France, the importance of public education, or rather the education of a public as a basic means for the organization of enlightenment was recognized."[37] In Young's view, schools are places where hope exists that things can be made better than they are. Although this characteristic may exist among educators of all kinds, this section focuses on critical theorists and their versions of education that take the students beyond the present givens of a status quo that is not necessarily all that it can/should be. Klaus Mollenhauer tried to apply Habermas's ideas to education. He defines emancipatory education as "'the freeing of the subject [i.e., students] . . . from conditions which limit their rationality and the social actions connected with it.'"[38] Timothy Luke argued that:

critical theory must adopt the goal [once again] of guiding human actions to realize greater emancipation and enlightenment in . . . [their] lives. . . . By refining
people's thinking abilities and moral sensibilities, critical theorists should hope to
equip individuals with a new consciousness of what must be done and how to do
it. This consciousness might help them determine what their best interests should
be besides gauging how far they must move away from currently held beliefs that
embody elements of domination and exploitation. By helping people come to
such realizations, critical theory could advance the process of human emancipation by lessening the victimization that people impose on themselves from within
or that is forced on them from without.[39]

Whether teachers who are critical theorists face the fact of exploitation
in the various workplaces, the injustices experienced by people because
of race/ethnicity, gender, and/or sexual preference, or even the mislead-
ing hyperreal media-driven society characteristic of the United States and
elsewhere during the last years of the twentieth century, it is clear that
these educators must strive to develop their intellectual insights in order
to analyze deeply as well as to help sketch holistic pictures for their students. I refer to Marcuse's view of the intellectual's role-as-teacher in societies that are both capitalist and formally democratic, specifically, the
following controversial part of his position. Marcuse's seemingly undemocratic view was based on a conviction that powerful forces and institutions could and do keep people in variations of Plato's cave. Liberation
would mean subversion of the conventional wisdom, ideology, and hegemony characteristic of any particular historical time. Spontaneous action
which is not the outcome of careful empirical and theoretical study, would
most likely lead to a spontaneity serving to strengthen the forces that
imprison our thoughts and actions. The critical pedagogue should consider the following argument: "In a class system, some have greater access to knowledge than others; therefore, it is [perhaps] inevitable that in
the short-run those who know something should teach others who are
not yet aware. Marcuse was convinced that those who are educated [about
the asymmetrical relations of power, wealth, access, and privilege] have a
commitment to use their knowledge to help . . . [others] realize the necessity for constructing a democratic community. All authentic education
is political education, 'and in a class society, political education is unthinkable without leadership, [that is] educated and tested in the theory
and practice of radical opposition.'"[40] Proceed from this view of how
educators should be, to a general discussion of critical pedagogy as it has
been articulated by some of those who currently write about it—and perhaps even practice it.

Section IV concludes with broad brush strokes that are intended to
motivate the reader to think about what critical pedagogy might look like.

I invite the reader to study beyond this section by consulting some of the sources that are provided. What you are about to read is intended neither as definitive, nor as a how-to recipe. The methodologies we use in our practice must be derived from our own carefully considered positions on educational philosophy. It must be realized that the individual is to be viewed as inextricably part of her/his society. David Purpel wrote that although there is no agreement on what critical pedagogy is, some practitioners of it, e.g., Barry Kanpol, emphasized "critical examination (personally, communally, and historically) of the conditions that contribute to oppression, with particular reference to . . . race, class, and gender. The context of this . . . [examination] is a deeply-held vision of a community of freedom and justice for all and a strong commitment to engage in the struggle for individual dignity and the liberation of all peoples."[41] Kanpol's pedagogic emphasis includes how students use language, what they appreciate and why, their levels of personal and social awareness, their abilities and desire to explore, and their performances as serious critics. Other teachers can and must construct their own strategies for their particular subject areas, grade levels, and specific overall teaching-learning conditions in order to practice in keeping with an appreciation of critical theory.

Peter McLaren contributed to our understanding of critical theory-pedagogy. He offered a number of suggestions with regard to what should be presently emphasized. You can translate McLaren's ideas into your developing intellectual and professional framework, so that theoretically informed practice can result. We are encouraged, as critical theorists-pedagogues, to always consider the historical specificity of our ideas so that we avoid making false universal claims. Critical pedagogy must deal with specific, local, and *concrete* issues while still being committed to recognizing the larger context. The Frankfurt School philosophers insisted that at the heart of critical theory was its recognition that people could organize their lives and societies in order to provide basic human needs; Marcuse even spoke of happiness—although not of the type advertised in the media of "advanced" capitalist countries. Such a recognition could empower teachers to argue convincingly against those who maintain that physical and social infrastructures have little or nothing to do with the probabilities for student and/or adult success.

McLaren reminded us that educators must continue to focus on how intelligence has been unfairly defined, with serious consequences that disempower and discredit all too many subaltern people. Critical educators must continue to lay bare the connections between this destructive definition of intelligence—and the supposed lack of it—in our schools to

the asymmetrical relations of power, privilege, wealth, and access in society. In keeping with critical theory's Marxist orientation, McLaren emphasized the need to keep in mind our complex relations to the capitalist-
dominated political economy; with special emphasis on social class and
its relevance to school achievement and/or failure. Critical educators must
also consider the relevance of race/ethnicity, gender, and sexual orientation to social class—as well as to how complex identities help define the
likelihood of school and socioeconomic success.[42] McLaren was correct
to stress the changing nature of capitalism-as-a-system, while reminding
us of its continuities. In the spirit of the Frankfurt School, he advised
critical educators to realize the postmodernist explosion of signs, signals,
and images that tend to make opaque the real relations of power and
privilege in late capitalism. We must endeavor to understand, represent,
and portray the complexities that are characteristic of societies that are
both capitalist and, at least, formally democratic. Marx, Gramsci, the Frankfurt School, et al. have provided important explanatory analyses of the
status quo of their historical times. We can and must do no less.

Although McLaren stressed the importance of discourse and communicative democracy, he recognized the relationships among speech, writing, political economy, politics, and action. He encouraged critical educators to help students understand that they can develop from self-interest
to concern for public affairs, as well as solidarity with the most oppressed
among us and elsewhere. He wrote, "the struggle over education is fundamentally linked to struggles in the larger theater of social [economic] and
political life. The struggle that occupies . . . us as school activists and
educational researchers should entertain global and local perspectives in
terms of the way in which capitalist relations and the international division
of labor are produced and reproduced. While I am . . . sympathetic to
attempts to reform school practices at the level of policy, curriculum, and
classroom pedagogy, such attempts need to be realized and acted on
from the overall perspective of the struggle against capitalist social
relations."[43]

Had Marx lived in a society that featured long-term and inclusive schooling, perhaps he would have become an educational philosopher, having
realized that for many students, schools are their places of work. Gramsci
wrote specifically about the schools in Italy, whereas the Frankfurt School
did not devote much of their critical analyses to formal schooling. It is
fitting and important that so many critical theoreticians take education-
schooling very seriously. Those who I admire most realize that all too
many educators claim that they are critical thinkers, without taking seri-

ously what the tradition of critical theory has to offer. Critical Theorists ask what an educator is being critical about? This is a crucial factor. In many cases, educators, as well as others, seem to be using their critical skills in order to rearrange the deck chairs on the Titanic. Too many teacher education programs are rendered ineffectual by featuring uncritical "classroom management and, mostly, harmless innovations." McLaren pointed out that Paulo Freire (see chapter six) worried about the domestication of critical pedagogy as it is practiced without consideration to the need for social critique and revolutionary agendas.[44] Critical pedagogy is not simply student-directed learning. This was known by John Dewey as he criticized his supposed followers in *Experience and Education* (1938) for misunderstanding his philosophy of education.

McLaren's *Life in Schools* provided a very helpful introduction to critical pedagogy. Part three of this readable book is called "Critical Pedagogy: An Overview"; it explained the emergence of this pedagogy and a discussion of major concepts. The reader learns that critical pedagogy goes beyond explanations of oppression in schools and society, and beyond mere analysis of imposition on subaltern people; there is an emphasis on resistance, overcoming, and hope. The work of Henry Giroux is also central to interpreting critical theory as a discourse of possibility in addition to serious problems to be faced. His central role is apparent to anyone who reads his extensive scholarly and pedagogical production. Critical pedagogy allows educators to deal specifically with the results of societal power as it penetrates—albeit in mediated and resisted ways—into the warp and woof of school life. An awareness of what the central actors, featured in this chapter, opposed and favored allows one to fashion a pedagogy of resistance and hope. There is an accompanying rich literature available that provides the teacher with many helpful ideas about how to conduct one's critical pedagogical practice. I offer the following as an example from *Life in Schools*: "Critical educational theorists argue that teachers must understand the role that schooling plays in joining knowledge and power, in order to use that role for the development of critical and active citizens. The traditional view of classroom instruction and learning as a neutral process antiseptically removed from the concepts of power, politics, history, and context can no longer be endorsed."[45] Critical pedagogy seeks to develop a public language that will allow previously silent voices to be heard in key discussions and decision-making concerning education-schooling.

Critical theory can help educators, students, parents, and ordinary citizens understand how the connections between power and knowledge play themselves out in schools. Good theory helps us to understand the specifics of how school curricula is often presented as objective, neutral, and technical, whereas critical investigation can reveal various curricula's usefulness in reproducing various advantages and disadvantages students experience in schools. Certain discourses become dominant in schools, making it possible for some things to be said and studied, and others overlooked. McLaren reminded us that participation in various curricula is induction into particular kinds of lives; historically, some students have been groomed for lives of privilege and leadership, while others are prepared for subaltern roles. David Livingstone also argued that although classed, raced, and gendered actors in school and society have significantly lost confidence in many established institutions characteristic of advanced capitalist societies, including schools, they have not been able to change progressively these institutions' structural and/or systemic characteristics. Livingstone thought that this failure is due in large part to the inability of subaltern people to develop "cultural power" with which to contest the dominant official language and processes which characterize schools and other institutions that serve them rather poorly. He argued that critical pedagogues and other progressive cultural workers must learn how to help students see beyond the commonsense notions that are supportive of hegemony in their society and communities, so that these notions can be contested in terms of students', parents', and others' reflected on concrete experiences. Reflection upon one's own experiences makes possible critical evaluation of alleged common sense and or official knowledge.

Critical pedagogy is committed to empowering subordinate people, in part, through understanding the social construction of reality. If more educators accepted this as one of the most important goals, it is possible that much could be accomplished given the talent and imagination among current professional teachers. Currently all too many capable and well-intentioned teachers experience frustration as their attempts to help their students bump up against structural barriers. It must be pointed out that cultural hegemony—a state in which many people accept the views of the powers that be as reality itself and good for subaltern people—is fortified historically by economic, political, and police-military power. Perhaps some teachers would become critical pedagogues if they did not fear punitive retaliation. Livingstone and other critical pedagogues insist that collective action must follow from understanding, and I agree; the bravery needed to translate ideas into practice is understandably difficult to achieve. It has been my view that teacher education must address itself seriously to the need for bravery if professional teachers are going to be successful at translating their good and progressive ideas into practice. This view necessitates an analysis of how progressive coalitions are to be constructed in the United States and elsewhere. Such an analysis is beyond the province of this work. The reader can refer to the endnote for some ideas concerning coalitions and their construction.[46]

In agreement with Livingstone and the contributors to his book, I believe that critical pedagogy must be judged in terms of whether it succeeds in enlisting the support of those taught. As Marx argued, people must ultimately free themselves, as history is open and it is possible to understand one's and others' concrete situations; collective action is possible. Gramsci argued convincingly that the working class could and must develop intellectuals from its own ranks. Professional educators and other intellectuals from outside a particular subaltern group would not need to serve as bringers of the truth to their poor, benighted clients. Contemporary professional teachers are educational workers themselves. They could be seen as "organic intellectuals" of and for those who are not the main beneficiaries of this society. Livingstone is correct to call for dialogue among all those who seek to transform a social order that is not constructed for the good of all, one that can be fundamentally improved. In the absence of revealed truth or other forms of certainty, public dialogue is the best epistemological strategy to be employed. Livingstone realized how difficult it has been and continues to be to understand and then transform a powerful educational and societal status quo. "There is no 'quick fix,' no clear road from the discomfort felt by so many today to liberatory social change. The briefest engagement should be sufficient to convince . . . [us] that deeper practical understanding . . . of the complex layers of ideological forms . . . [and] of the material bases of group conflict and co-operation, as they limit both local and wider efforts at progressive social change in advanced capitalism, is urgently needed. . . . The historical project of critical pedagogy persists; to expose the dynamics of cultural power and to enable popular engagement in creating alternative futures."[47]

In keeping with the themes and arguments presented throughout this chapter, the importance of historical materialism, critical theory, and the openness of history—while recognizing that human agency does bump up against structural limits—the conclusion of section four touches on critical pedagogy for vocational-technical education and for methods instruction. The Marxist insistence on the importance of the working class and its potential to free itself from its subaltern status is still relevant, especially when one reconsiders the many who are still in the working class, although not all as blue collar workers. Gramsci was especially insistent that intelligence is widespread throughout populations. It can be developed so that intellectual work can be done at all levels of labor. Richard Lakes wrote a compelling argument for how critical pedagogy can allow vocational-technical educators to transform their practice into one that prepares students for critical citizenship in addition to quality work potential. This argument is in keeping with the historic attempt to bridge the gap between humanist and scientific reason at least since the Enlightenment period. Lakes insisted that critical pedagogues feature an analysis of careers and occupations because students who will become citizen-workers must understand the economic, political, and social histories of labor in all its complex relations with power, problems, and possibilities. Lakes, Joe Kincheloe, et al. believe that vocational-technical learning contexts are important sites for analysis and championing democratic work practices. Marx, Gramsci, and the Frankfurt School would agree, so would John Dewey as will be shown in chapter four. Lakes wrote, "critical pedagogues reject vocational-technical curricula that deprives occupational study of sociocultural significance."[48]

Lakes thought that critical education for work can empower teachers to rethink the relationship between school and the socioeconomic system, one which has historically tracked all too many sons and daughters of the working class, racial/ethnic minorities, and others into slots and training for labor that those who had choices, avoided and looked down on. Lakes hoped that critical education for work will allow students to see through the historic attempt to use schools to reproduce (albeit imperfectly) our stratified society. He favored using critical pedagogy to empower students as they learn about collective experiences of workers who sought and achieved better economic, political, social, and educative conditions. Our K–12 public schools can and must be places where students learn about solidarity and activism among workers. Students must come to realize that they, as future workers of various types, must not lose their citizenship rights just because they enter workplaces dominated by capitalist realities and/or assumptions.[49]

Susan Adler and Jesse Goodman wrote about critical pedagogy's fear of classroom teachers becoming deskilled, i.e., reduced to carrying out the plans of so-called experts, bureaucrats, politicians, and others who have power over K–12 teachers. The authors constructed a compelling argument for teachers to insist on and become primarily responsible for their practice, rather than be used as tools for various powers that be.

The following passage represents their position well. "Traditional methods courses have emphasized the development of specific skills such as planning lessons, managing basal programs, and disciplining children, which [allegedly] represents competent or effective teaching. A 'critical methods course' would strive to prepare teachers with analytic and reflective abilities, teachers who would not accept 'unthinking submergence in the social reality that prevails.' Teacher educators would work to counter the 'deskilling' of teachers."[50]

Suggested Task for the Reader

I invite the reader to consider the following. If Marxist thought was and is correct that the schools in capitalist societies are neither autonomous nor powerful enough to resist—let alone overcome—the capitalist imperative on them, i.e., to produce competent workers who lack adequate critical citizen skills, then how can teachers look on the possibilities for overcoming the reproductionist role played by our schools? How can teachers translate their educational philosophies into action when the powers that be may not really want education for democratic empowerment, social justice, and respect for bona fide diversity? If schooling reproduces the asymmetrical realities of power, access, wealth, and privilege in the United States and elsewhere, then should professional education students, their professors, and practicing teachers begin serious discussions concerning appropriate strategies for overcoming this injustice? What would some of these strategies look like? If they discover that these strategies are not successful, are there other ways to continue the struggle for critical and empowering education outside the role of professional teacher? Are there possibilities for citizen-teacher-workers to pursue strategies that link intramural issues to those in the larger society? The reader may want to think about the possibility that Marx and the democratic Marxists are too pessimistic with regard to the school's efficacy as a progressive interventionist agency in the lives of students.

Conclusion

The last **Suggested Task** provides an opportunity for the reader to pull together the central arguments and main ideas presented in this chapter. One could best respond to the task(s) as a result of reviewing chapter 3 and coming to one's own conclusions. I have attempted to bring the following points to the reader's attention. (1) There is a tradition of democratic Marxist thought that is relevant for those who are interested in making the school and society more democratic, socially just, and responsive to the wonderful variety of the human family. (2) Marx himself would have been a rebel in the societies which claimed to be Marxist. (3) Marxist thought is central to the secular development of Western civilization that places human beings at the center of social analysis. (4) Marxist thought, as an heir of the Enlightenment, is based on the belief that reason and action can educate and enable us to better our lives. (5) It is possible and necessary to act even though human beings cannot be absolutely certain about outcomes or even strategies. (6) We are volitional beings although there are material and structural barriers. (7) Democracy must go beyond the political, i.e., the socioeconomic must also be constructed by participatory democrats—ones who are educated for critical citizenship. (8) Capitalism and the attendant social-class system are incompatible with bona fide democracy. (9) The K–12 public school in the United States has been a site of contestation between democratic anti-reproductionists and their foes. (10) The work of Gramsci, the critical theory of the Frankfurt School, and educational critical theorists have addressed some problems and possibilities for democratic empowerment that Marx himself did not articulate. Section IV dealt specifically with contemporary educational theorists as they present their views on critical pedagogy.

Notes

1   Sidney Hook, *Marx and the Marxists: The Ambiguous Legacy* (New York: D. Van Nostrand Company, Inc., 1955), 47–48.

2   See the following sources for descriptions and analyses of critical theory: (1) Martin Jay, *The Dialectical Imagination: A History of the Frankfurt School and the Institute of Social Research 1923–1950* (Boston: Little, Brown and Company, 1973), passim for a definitive study of the School and its members' work; (2) Richard A. Brosio, *The Frankfurt School: An Analysis of the Contradictions and Crises of Liberal Capitalist Societies* (Muncie, Ind.: Ball State Monograph Number Twenty-nine, 1980); (3) David Held, *Introduction to Critical Theory: Horkheimer to Habermas* (Berkeley and Los Angeles: University of California Press, 1981); and my review of Held's book (along with Henry Giroux's, *Ideology, Culture, and the Process of Schooling*) in *Educational Studies* 13, nos. 3/4 (Fall/Winter 1982): 422–429.

3   Peter L. Berger and Thomas Luckmann, *The Social Construction of Reality: A Treatise in the Sociology of Knowledge* (Garden City, N.Y.: Doubleday & Company, Inc., 1966), 189.

4   Robert C. Tucker, *Philosophy and Myth in Karl Marx* (Cambridge, U.K.: Cambridge University Press, 1961), 175.

5   Ibid., 176. For an explanation of the continuity between the young Marx of 1844 and the mature Marx of *Das Kapital* (1867) and afterward, see, Richard Brosio, "One Marx and the Centrality of the Historical Actor(s)," *Educational Theory* 35, no. 1 (Winter 1985): 73–83. For a volume that includes prefaces to the *Manifesto* originally aimed at various language groups, see, Karl Marx and Frederick Engels, *Manifesto of the Communist Party* (Moscow: Progress Publishers, 1952), passim. Raya Dunayevskaya reminds us that Marx, in the *Manifesto*, did not forget the individual actor, e.g., "'The free development of each is the condition for the free development of all.' . . . Its *theory* of . . . history [did not] depart for a single instance from actual live battles." *Philosophy and Revolution* (New York: Dell Publishing Co., Inc., 1973), 60.

6   See, Richard A. Brosio, essay review of Joel Spring's "*Wheels in the Head: Educational Philosophies of Authority, Freedom, and Culture from Socrates to Paulo Freire,*" *Educational Studies* 27, no. 3 (Fall 1996): 272–82. My account of Marx's critique of idealist philosophy suggests the following: The idealists think of history as the development of consciousness—mainly philosophers' consciousness. There is no consideration of the physical and social changes that produce such development. "'Instead of treating . . . real relations . . . [the idealist] takes the distorted expression of these in ideology to be the real substance of history, and thus produces only "phrases about phrases."'", 280.

7   Tucker, *Philosophy and Myth in Marx*, 183.

8   Erich Fromm, *Marx's Concept of Man* (New York: Fredrick Ungar Publishing Company, 1961), 13.

9   C. Wright Mills, *The Marxists* (New York: Dell Publishing Co., Inc., 1962), 78.

10   See, Richard A. Brosio, "Teaching and Learning for Democratic Empowerment: A Critical Evaluation," *Educational Theory* 40, no. 1 (Winter 1990): 69–81. This analysis is critical of exaggerated views of human agency which have, in part, resulted from the misunderstanding of Marx's alleged determinism, hence lack of human volition. Certain motivationalist theorists have been overly optimistic about what can be accomplished in schools. They should take more seriously the structural limitations that Marx correctly featured in his more realistic claims for human agency.

11   Ernst Fischer, *How to Read Marx* (New York: Monthly Review Press, 1996), 97.

12   Richard A. Brosio, *A Radical Democratic Critique of Capitalist Education* (New York: Peter Lang Publishing, Inc., 1994), chapter 1.

13   Fischer, *How to Read Marx*, 92.

14   Ibid., 95.

15   Dunayevskaya, *Philosophy and Revolution*, 58.

16   Fischer, *How to Read Marx*, 99.

17   Stanley Aronowitz wrote an important critique of Marxist historical materialism in *The Crisis in Historical Materialism: Class, Politics and Culture in Marxist Theory*, 2nd ed. 1990 (Minneapolis: University of Minnesota Press, 1981). At the heart of the critique is Aronowitz's worry that the proletariat, or working class, has never represented a privileged position with regard to being the main actor for democratic revolution. Marxism is criticized for attributing causality to economic factors. We are asked to consider cultural categories and identities in terms of actors who are not only classed, but gendered, and raced as well. Aronowitz argued: "Today historical materialism is obliged to enter a dialogue with other tendencies that claim theoretical and political validity. It can no longer subsume all competing world views under the rubric of 'bourgeois' to which it counterposes its own, proletarian world view; it must face ecological, nationalist and feminist world-views, each of which has its own competing camps and whose unity, as is the case of Marxism, is in doubt" p. xix. I have wrestled with Aronowitz's critique and concluded, that the centrality of work and worker can still be most important to one's identity, if we reconstruct the meaning of labor to all kinds of efforts central to human life as we struggle in a world which is not necessarily made with us in mind. Gendered and raced persons must and do work. In addition to the unavoidability of work, each person is forced into some kind of relationship with governments at all levels. I conclude that worker-citizen is the best axis around which to organize liberatory human struggle against oppression. This concept provides for a large enough umbrella to include the actors who Aronowitz considers excluded by the original Marxist insistence on proletariat-worker as central to history, exploitation, and hopeful liberation. For those who may be interested in

further discussion of social class and agency, we turn to a concept of class that supports my broad interpretation of work and worker. Geoffrey de Ste. Croix argued that class is "the collective social expression of the fact of exploitation . . . (By 'exploitation') I mean the appropriation of part of the labor of others. . . . And a class . . . is a group of persons . . . identified by their position in the whole social production . . . according to their relationship (primarily in terms of the degree of *control*) to the conditions . . . [i.e.,] the means and labor of production . . . and to other classes. The individuals constituting a given class may or may not be wholly or partly conscious of their own identity and common interests as a class, and they may not [yet] feel antagonism toward other classes. . . . Class *conflict* . . . is essentially the fundamental relationship between classes, involving *exploitation* and resistance to it, but not *necessarily* either class consciousness or collective activity in common, political or otherwise." Source: "Class in Marx's Concept of History," *Monthly Review* 36, no. 10 (March 1985): 27–28. You can readily understand that more than a few people currently live as exploited workers, if the essence of exploitation is the "*appropriation of a surplus from the primary producer.*" This brief discussion is not meant to stop further inquiry. The aim is to encourage you to think and talk, individually and/or among others, more deeply and broadly about what work means in these times.

18   Richard A. Brosio, "Essay on Antonio Gramsci," in *Thinkers of the 20th Century: A Biographical, Bibliographical and Critical Dictionary*, eds., Elizabeth Held et al. (Detroit: Gale Research Company, 1983), 222.

19   See Le Febevre's, *Everyday Life in the Modern World* (London: Allen Lane The Penguin Press, 1971), passim. See also chapter six, "The Consequences of the Capitalist Imperative on Everyday Life," Brosio, *A Radical Democratic Critique of Capitalist Education*.

20   Herbert Marcuse, *One-Dimensional Man: Studies in the Ideology of Advanced Industrial Society* (Boston: Beacon Press, 1964), passim.

21   Donaldo Macedo, *Literacies of Power: What Americans Are Not Allowed to Know* (Boulder, San Francisco, Oxford: Westview Press, 1994), 50.

22   Harold Entwistle analyzed this Gramscian endorsement of the Italian schools during the latter's lifetime. Entwistle wrote: "There is no doubt that Gramsci was primarily concerned with radical sociopolitical change and his work ought to be especially relevant for radicals committed to counter-hegemonic educational activity. . . . But paradoxically, Gramsci's prescriptions for curriculum and teaching method are essentially conservative." *Antonio Gramsci: Conservative Schooling for Radical Politics* (London: Routledge & Kegan Paul, 1972), 2. Gramsci's endorsement resulted from his belief that the Italian elementary school was based on sound principles, a humanistic curriculum, an emphasis on instruction, hard work, and to a goal of genuine intellectual development. He believed that learning about the "facts" of the social and physical worlds was a necessary precondition if one were to grow intellectually, as well as to become a radical, counter-hegemonist activist as an adult. Gramsci was convinced that the purpose of authority need not be conservative. He opposed the abandonment of the child to mere sponta-

neity. Entwistle explained that Gramsci viewed education as a lifelong endeavor. "From this comprehensive life perspective, what looks like a conservative theory of schooling is not supportive of the existing hegemony but, on the contrary, is a necessary preparation for the education of working-class intellectuals, for the creation of a new humanism and, hence is a precondition for the exercise of working-class hegemony" pp. 109–10. For a fuller analysis of Entwistle's thesis, see Brosio, *A Radical Democratic Critique of Capitalist Education*, pp. 446–59.

23   Anne Showstack Sassoon, "The People, Intellectuals and Specialised Knowledge," *Boundary 2, A Journal of Postmodern Literature and Culture—A Special Issue: The Legacy of Antonio Gramsci* 14, no. 3 (Spring 1986): 161.

24   Quintin Hoare and Geoffrey Nowell Smith, eds. and trans., *Selections From the Prison Notebooks of Antonio Gramsci* (New York: International Publishers, 1971), 40. This quote is of Gramsci's own work, not the editors.

25   See, Jay's *The Dialectical Imagination* for a comprehensive and penetrating intellectual history of the School's work.

26   Richard A. Brosio, "Essay on Herbert Marcuse," in *Thinkers of the 20th Century*, 362–63.

27   David Ingram, *Critical Theory and Philosophy* (New York: Paragon House, 1990), 14.

28   Brosio, *The Frankfurt School*, 6–7.

29   Max Horkheimer, *Eclipse of Reason* (New York: The Seabury Press, 1947), 183.

30   Ingram, *Critical Theory and Philosophy*, 64.

31   Robert E. Young, *A Critical Theory of Education: Habermas and Our Children's Future* (New York: Teachers College Press, 1990), 30. For a critical analysis of Young's book—one that exemplifies how philosophers of education carefully assess each other's work—see, Ladd Holt and Frank Margonis, "Critical Theory of a Conservative Stamp," *Educational Theory* 42, vol. 2 (Spring 1992): 231–50.

32   For an insightful explanation of what language and discourse reveal and obscure, see, Marcuse, *One-Dimensional Man*, chapter four, "The Closing of the Universe of Discourse." This chapter is conceptually rich although daunting in its complexity. The following is representative of Marcuse's argument, in relation to our concerns: the present "authoritarian ritualization of discourse . . . leaves no time and no space for a discussion which would project disruptive alternatives. This language no longer lends itself to 'discourse' at all. . . . The closed language does not demonstrate and explain—it communicates decision, dictum, command. . . . It establishes unquestionable rights and wrongs . . . [It] pass[es] judgement in a 'prejudged form'" p. 101. Marcuse explained how one-dimensional language uses hypnotic nouns, over and over again, as well as frozen predicates that limit what can be expressed about these subjects. This development can be discussed

and analyzed with students through using examples of everyday commercial, political, and other "official knowledge" language. Marcuse speaks to the Orwellian dimensions of this dangerous development.

33   Young, *A Critical Theory of Education*, 59.

34   Ingram, *Critical Theory and Philosophy*, 113.

35   Ibid., 147.

36   Salvatore D'Urso, "An Evaluation of Dewey's 'Social Intelligence,'" *Educational Theory* 28, no. 2 (Spring 1978): 129.

37   Young, *A Critical Theory of Education*, 41.

38   Ibid., 58.

39   Timothy W. Luke, "Towering Hyperreality: Critical Theory Confronts Informational Society," in *Critical Theory Now*, ed. Philip Wexler (London: The Falmer Press, 1991), 21–22.

40   Brosio, *The Frankfurt School*, 37.

41   David E. Purpel, "Essay Review of Barry Kanpol's, *Critical Pedagogy: An Introduction*," *Educational Studies* 26, no. 3 (Fall 1995): 221.

42   McLaren stresses the importance for critical educators to stress a politics of the redistribution of economic resources (a historic social class demand), as well as a politics of recognition, affirmation, and respect for difference (a demand made by those who claim to suffer from racial/ethnic, gender, and sexual orientation injustices). For a supportive argument of McLaren's point, see Richard A. Brosio, "The Complexly Constructed Citizen-Worker: Her/His Centrality to the Struggle for Radical Democratic Politics and Education," *Journal of Thought* 32, no. 3 (Fall 1997): 9–26. See the section called "Complexly Constructed Identities, With A Little Help From Nancy Fraser," 15–20.

43   Peter McLaren, "Critical Pedagogy and Globalization: Thirty Years After Che [Guevara]," unpublished paper given at the University of California at Los Angeles in October 1997, and at the National Association of Multicultural Education convention in Albuquerque, N. Mex. in October 1997.

44   For a succinct articulation and defense of the kind of critical thinking favored by McLaren and me, see Peter L. McLaren's "Foreword: Critical Thinking as a Political Project," in Kerry S. Walters, ed., *Re-Thinking Reason: New Perspectives in Critical Thinking* (Albany: State University of New York Press, 1994), ix–xv.

45   Peter McLaren, *Life in Schools: An Introduction to Critical Pedagogy in the Foundations of Education*, 2nd ed. (New York & London: Longman, 1994), 168. For an informative analysis of the relationships between education and power, see Michael W. Apple, *Education and Power* (Boston and London: Routledge & Kegan Paul, 1982). For a social foundations of education textbook constructed in the spirit of critical theory and pedagogy, see Alan R. Sadovnik, Peter W. Cookson,

and Susan F. Semel, *Exploring Education: An Introduction to the Foundations of Education* (Boston: Allyn and Bacon, 1994). Another valuable source from which to learn about critical theory and pedagogy is Henry A. Giroux's "Citizenship, Public Philosophy, and the Struggle for Democracy," *Educational Theory* 37, no. 2 (Spring 1987): 103–120, and his, *Schooling and the Struggle for Public Life: Critical Pedagogy in the Modern Age* (Minneapolis: University of Minnesota Press, 1988), passim.

46   For an extensive analysis of this problem, see Richard Brosio, "Globalism, Postmodernism, the Politics of Identity and the Need for Broad Democratic Political/Educational Coalitions," *Philosophical Studies in Education* (Terre Haute, Ind.: Ohio Valley Philosophy of Education Society, 1994), 1–48.

47   David W. Livingstone & Contributors, *Critical Pedagogy and Cultural Power* (South Hadley, Mass.: Bergin & Garvey Publishers, Inc., 1987), 12.

48   Richard D. Lakes, "Critical Pedagogy for Vocational-Technical Educators: Some Considerations," *Journal of Studies in Technical Careers* 13, no. 4 (1991): 304.

49   Richard D. Lakes, ed., *Critical Education for Work: Multidisciplinary Approaches* (Norwood, New Jersey: Ablex Publishing Corporation, 1994), 3. For another fine analysis of critical pedagogy for vocational education, see Joe L. Kincheloe, *Toil and Trouble: Good Work, Smart Workers, and the Integration of Academic and Vocational Education* (New York: Peter Lang Publishing, Inc., 1995), passim. Kincheloe's view of critical theory is compatible with many currents of postmodernist thought.

50   Susan Adler and Jesse Goodman, "Critical Theory as a Foundation for Methods Courses," *Journal of Teacher Education* 37, no. 4 (July-August 1986): 4. Also see, Richard A. Brosio, "The Continuing Correspondence Between Political Economy and Schooling: Telling the News," *Journal of Thought* 33, no. 3 (Fall 1998): 85–105 for an analysis of recent attempts to reintroduce a potentially reproductive vocational curriculum that may threaten the critical pedagogy favored in this chapter.

Chapter Four

Saved by a Method: Science, Dewey, the Progressive Protest— And a Whiff of Reconstruction

Introduction

My colleague, Salvatore D'Urso, has argued that John Dewey's educational theory and suggested practices could provide a nondeterministic Marxism with the educational ingredients it lacks. In D'Urso's view, although Marxist analysis of the relationships between schooling and capitalism insists that we reconsider the overall objectives and rationales for schooling, it does not address the problems and possibilities of everyday school life. Marxist analysis provides little with regard to possible interventionist strategies aimed at deconstructing reproductive schooling outcomes. To quote from D'Urso: "Dewey's work may appropriately fulfill classical Marxism's missing theory of education in view of importantly similar or correlative [so related that each implies or complements the other] philosophical foundations."[1] "If Marx needs Dewey's democratic educational theory and its pedagogical practices, it can be argued that Dewey and Deweyans would be helped considerably by Marx's central insight concerning the discontinuation of capitalist domination as the sine qua non of genuine democracy."[2] Marx did not develop a theory of education or schooling to the complex degree accomplished by Dewey. This was the case, in part, because Marx was convinced that a school system could only be a tool (albeit imperfect) of the dominant classes. Dewey believed that schooling could be a vehicle for the gradual improvement of society and persons. As stated in the last chapter, various Reds after Marx have come to believe that although capitalism is very powerful, the forces of democracy do contest capital on many sites—including the schools.

Marx's own conception of knowledge features the combining of theoretical and practical activities; "Marx's operationalism would appear . . . to
demand a theory of education that stressed the . . . dynamic interrelat-
edness of knowing and doing."[3] Operationalism means that the knower
does things to what is being studied; both the knower and known are
changed. This idea is central to Dewey's educational philosophy and
practice.

In order to make the bridge between chapters three and four stronger,
I draw upon various scholarly sources that serve to demonstrate correlative philosophical foundations shared by Marx and Dewey. Both philosophers owe a great debt to the work of Georg Hegel (1770–1831); although they critiqued and went beyond Hegelian idealism. I begin by
drawing from the work of Sidney Hook, a student of Dewey and philosopher in his own right, who wrote that for Marx "a theory was a guide to
action; practice, the specific activities which had to be carried out to test
the theory. Practice (Praxis) was . . . much wider than *practicality*. It
was selective behavior. Its character was . . . given . . . by the skills
and . . . living traditions . . . which man [sic] brings to whatever he
sees and does. . . . Marx's theory of the Praxis could explain . . .
how knowledge could give power. For Marx knowledge gives power by
virtue of the activities it sets up in transforming things in behalf of social
needs."[4] Marx's ideas suggest a kinship with pragmatist philosophy as
articulated by Charles Sanders Peirce (1839–1914) and Dewey. In an
effort to conclude the bridge between the last chapter and what is about
to unfold in this one, I offer the following from my mentor, G. Max Wingo.

> To Dewey and other pragmatists, the office of thinking is one of clearing up the
> dubious and making the situation assured—of passing from doubt to belief, in
> Peirce's terms. Thinking is like any tool or natural energy that may be used to
> clear up the indeterminate. . . . Thinking is . . . reorganizing and reconstruct-
> ing experience in a world of space and time. The problematic always lies where
> the unpredictable and the stable intersect, and in this sense every act, idea, and
> existence is an experiment. Those whose wish it is to act wisely, and have their
> actions guided by intelligence, must be cognizant of the nature of the world, for
> those who do not understand how to use nature to advantage will be continually
> at its mercy. . . . Inquiry is the method of intelligence, and in the estimation of
> Peirce and Dewey, the method of intelligence is the general method of sci-
> ence. . . . In the preface to the first edition of *How We Think*, Dewey wrote:
> "This scientific attitude of mind might conceivably be . . . irrelevant to teaching
> children and youth. But this book . . . represents the conviction that such is not
> the case; that the native and unspoiled attitude of childhood, marked by ardent
> curiosity, fertile imagination, and love of experimental inquiry, is near, very near,
> to the attitude of the scientific mind."[5]

Although Dewey did not accept class struggle as the agency for needed and even radical transformation of society and schools, he did understand well the need for constant reconstruction of practices, processes, institutions, and of status quos themselves. He believed that if intelligent reconstruction did not occur, then revolution would be likely. Dewey argued: "it is too easy to utter commonplaces about the superiority of constructive action to destructive [ones]. . . . The professed conservative and classicist of tradition seeks too cheap a victory over the rebel. For the rebel is not self-generated. In the beginning no one is a revolutionary just for the fun of it. . . . If conditions do not permit renewal to take place continuously it will take place explosively. The cost of revolution must be charged up to those who have taken for their aims, custom instead of its readjustment. The only ones who have a right to criticize 'radicals' . . . are those who put as much effort into reconstruction as the rebels are putting into destruction."[6] Hook pointed out that for a long time Dewey was convinced that an expanding capitalist economy would allow liberal and progressive reforms to ameliorate capitalism's worst injustices. By the late 1920s, *before* the Great Depression, Dewey had accepted the basic diagnosis of the socialists with regard to required reconstruction. Hook argued that Dewey arrived at this conclusion by using the scientific method: a process that committed him to supporting fundamental change rather than tinkering with the parts of an unjust socioeconomic system.

I

Dewey sought to convince his contemporaries that the historical quest for certainty had been a mistake. The emergence of experimental science was demonstrating effectively that the physical world could be understood and benefited from through the intelligent use of inductive and hypothetical methods based on observation. It was widely recognized during Dewey's long life that great power could be had by harnessing the scientific method and applying it to rearranging the physical world. The achievements of industrial capitalism were evident throughout the nineteenth and early twentieth centuries in the West and elsewhere. The refusal by many of Dewey's contemporaries to apply the scientific method to personal, social, and moral issues was of great concern to him and other pragmatists and progressives. Dewey rejected the dualism inherent in Western philosophy because he saw human beings as part of the social and physical worlds. He sought to help develop a unified method for problem solving, one that would get beyond religious and/or speculative philosophical as-

sertions of certainty and truth with regard to dealing with human problems. He rejected the religious and philosophical claims based on transcendent guarantees of truth and rightness, arguing instead that knowledge could emerge only from the application of the scientific method to
problematic situations.

It is important to keep in mind that Dewey was writing as a public
philosopher, one who realized that even if certain religionists and/or speculative philosophers had managed to know the "truth" or "truths," this
achievement was confined only to those who followed them. Dewey understood that the United States was becoming a multicultural society very
rapidly. It is well to remember that, at least since the Protestant Reformation of the sixteenth century, Western Christendom had been divided.
Europe had been divided religiously between east and west long before
the Reformation. Jews were religiously distinct—although not without differences among themselves—from the Christian majority in Europe and
North America. Native peoples in the "New World" were also religiously
distinct from the conquering Europeans.

During the industrial revolution in the United States, many Europeans
came to this country from southern and eastern Europe, areas that were
predominantly Catholic and/or Orthodox. The first great influx of Catho-
lics to the United States came from Ireland as a result of widespread
famine in the middle of the nineteenth century. The immigrants who
came to the industrial cities were divided religiously, ethnically, linguisti-
cally and were stratified by social class. The migrants from the former
Confederacy made the northern cities racially mixed as well. The presence of native peoples, i.e., American Indians, added to the heterogeneity
of the population. Immigrants from East Asia came to the United States
during Dewey's life. There also occurred a fairly steady emigration from
the Caribbean islands. Mexican-Americans were in what is now called the
United States for a very long time. The indigenous people of the South-
west were there before the Spaniards arrived, and certainly before Mexico's
independence from Spain in the early nineteenth century. Last, but not
least, all of these people were gendered!

Dewey's public and educational philosophy was aimed at establishing
a widely accepted method with which to solve societal problems in a
country where enduring orthodoxies could be enforced only by proselytizing or force. People in the United States and throughout the West no
longer perceived things in a unified or homogeneous way; there occurred
many disagreements about good, bad, and reality itself. The sociologist,
Karl Mannheim, argued that every "fact" about the social world was subject to interpretation based on one's social class position. Dewey was

keenly aware of the breakdown of common meaning and values during his lifetime. In *Art As Experience* (1934) he argued that the incoherence that characterized the fine arts was a manifestation of a more basic lack of consensus with regard to many important things. In his view, greater coherence and integration in the fine arts depended on the construction of a method with which to sort out what the disagreements were. Dewey was convinced that without a common frame of reference—one that needed to be democratically constructed—it would be difficult, if not impossible, to solve public problems.[7] This realization and worry does not mean that there was a totalitarian wolf in sheep's clothing; although some existentialists and many contemporary postmodernist thinkers have accused Dewey of seeking to impose a new certainty on a heterogeneous population—this time through the use of a method. Both existentialists and postmodernists are critical of the Deweyan attempt at establishing common references and unified inquiry models. The critics claim that such attempts suffer from refusing to deal with the real stuff of material and human phenomena that is characterized by contingency, chance, and randomness. It is impossible to understand these fully or harness them for human benefit.

Dewey argued that, although certain unique difficulties arose when the scientific method was applied to individual and social concerns, this was the case because of strongly held moral, ethical, religious, and philosophical convictions. Dealing with material phenomena does not pose the same difficulty. Dewey insisted that wise decisions concerning human affairs must acknowledge that inquiry deals with what can be observed, studied, and changed. This is similar to inquiry about the physical world. There are no absolute guidelines when we seek to solve problematic situations about inanimate phenomena, or in our most personal and/or citizen-worker lives.

When Isaac Newton (1642–1727) demonstrated that mathematics allowed us to understand the universe of his time better, other thinkers who were more interested in socioeconomic, political, and educational questions concluded that they could understand the origins, workings, problems, and possibilities of their own societies. One could argue that Newton's accomplishments with regard to the physical structure of the universe led to attempts to secularly understand French society, and what is more, how to change it! The historian Crane Brinton wrote: The eighteenth-century intellectuals and reformers in France, sometimes called *philosophes,* "seized on Newton's rules of reason and on his scientific discoveries [published in *Principia,* 1687]. . . . In the principle of gravitation, Newton had disclosed the natural force that held the universe to-

gether; he made the universe make sense. The eighteenth century believed that other Newtons would find comparable laws governing and
explaining all phases of human experience. The *philosophes* pictured
themselves as the Newtons of statecraft, justice, and economics who would
reduce the most intricate institutions to formulas as neat as . . . [Newton's]
mathematical laws."[8] Dewey's view of science had gone far beyond
Principia and the *philosophes*; his scientific method was also intended
to provide his contemporaries a unified method of inquiry.

Dewey wrote early in the twentieth century that there had never been
a time in history when human relationships—their rights, duties, opportunities, and imperatives—required the tireless and systematic attention of
the method of intelligence as they did in 1908. I shall consider further
and specifically the Deweyan method of intelligence, also known as the
scientific method and the "complete act of thought," later in this chapter.
Dewey urged his contemporaries to consider that although they believed
their personal and social actions were anchored to a universally valid outside point of reference, tradition, or dogma—connections that they hoped
ensured their correctness—serious reflection would not support such a
position. The complexity and messiness of everyday life overwhelm the
so-called inerrant signposts, rendering them mostly inadequate for the
task. It becomes apparent for those who use the scientific method that
signposts, guidelines, and compasses must be constructed from in human
experience itself. He reminds us that all too many people accept guidelines and goals provided and/or imposed by putative and sometimes self-
appointed authorities. Failure to follow would be labeled as rebellion. Historically the majority of people accepted goals that they could not resist
anyway. "Because of lack of education and . . . economic stress they for
the most part do just what they have to do. In the absence of the possibility of real choice, such a thing as reflection on the purposes and the
attempt to frame a general theory of ends [i.e., goals] and of the good
would seem to be . . . luxuries."[9] I think that although the end of the
twentieth century features more freedom for more people—at least in
some societies—the attempts to control others continue through the use
of sophisticated means as well as by claiming somewhat different authority claims.[10]

Dewey was not alone in asserting that reflective morality (or reflective
teaching practice) cannot occur unless we seriously inquire into the purposes that should direct our conduct. Moral choice assumes the existence
of alternatives among choices—often ones that represent competing goods
rather than obvious good or bad choices. During the historical periods
called modernity and postmodernity in the West and elsewhere, the acids

of change have forced many people to discard old certainties because they were, and are, judged to be irrelevant to current problems and possibilities. When this occurs, when habitual behavior and orthodox signposts of belief no longer serve people well, the only alternative to "caprice and random action" is reflection as it becomes possible through the social use of the scientific method.[11] Dewey reminded us that historically, all too many parents and teachers ordered youngsters around based on a presumption that power and privilege should be paramount. "Obedience is often procured by the use of rewards and penalties . . . by what in moral theory have come to be called 'sanctions'. . . . Morality becomes servile. . . . It is difficult for a person in a place of authoritative [political] power to avoid supposing what he wants is right as long as he has power to enforce his demand. . . . The history of the struggle for political liberty is largely a record of attempt[s] to get free from oppressions which were exercised in the name of law and authority, but which in effect identified loyalty with enslavement. . . . 'Morality' gets reduced to carrying out orders."[12]

Once Newton's book, *Principia,* was published in 1687, it is not surprising that the French stormed the Bastille in 1789 and began the French Revolution in earnest—a Revolution that was constructed in their minds before a shot was fired. Once it was believed that the physical world and universe could be understood, people were encouraged and emboldened to understand the "physics" of the political and socioeconomic world as well as to change it. The royalty and aristocracy were no longer thought to have been chosen by deity after a century of controlled inquiry into the foundations of the Old Regime in France. The Great Revolution in France was not restricted to its country of origin after 1789. The American Revolution, which occurred at the end of the eighteenth century, also resulted in part from a revolution in how people thought about authority and their moral responsibilities to it. Dewey insisted that people should come to see for themselves what is being done and why. We must be sensitive to the connections between causes and effects, means and ends, anticipation and results. Approval and/or disapproval must be subjected to rigorous inquiry. The inquiry referred to here and throughout this book is based on human beings' historical attempts to use intelligence in order to deconstruct and overcome injustice and to replace it with participatory democracy, social justice, and respect for diversity. All of this in a society that makes caring for one another more possible.

Dewey knew that moral theory which is based on the realities of the human condition could not ensure easy or error-free decision-making. In his words, "it would not make the moral life as simple as wending one's way along a well-lighted boulevard. All action is an invasion of the future, of the unknown."[13] Uncertainty would still prevail. Basing moral decisions on a concern for facts could at least locate the necessary and effective resources with which to decide intelligently. Dewey insisted that intelligence and the action that resulted from it help us to decide between what is "merely desirable" and what is carefully assessed to be worthy of being desired. This method of intelligence and reflective morality allows us to clarify our own personal conflicts by placing them in larger and historical contexts in order to encourage systematic thinking in terms of possible alternatives. A new table of commandments is not and cannot be offered by Dewey. The answers cannot be as definite as the good questions asked. For Dewey, the method can only make personal choice more intelligent. But it cannot replace the need for ultimate personal decision and responsibility. He warned that "the student who expects more from moral theory will be disappointed. . . . The attempt to set up ready-made conclusions contradicts the very nature of reflective morality."[14]

So far in this chapter there are some similarities between the kind of Marxist thought presented in chapter three and Dewey's work. Section I presented an explanation of Dewey's need to construct a method that could be used to solve public problems—as well as personal ones—in a society that was rapidly becoming more heterogeneous in many important ways. Dewey was one of the prominent philosophers and public intellectuals who sought to use the scientific method in public ways in order to decide among competing claims and counterclaims. It was his intention to convince his contemporaries that the application of experimental science, as inquiry, should not be restricted to the physical or nonhuman world. It was and is the social, human, and personal use of the method of intelligence that caused great discomfort, opposition, and anger by those who wished to maintain their reliance on and allegiance to allegedly inerrant, transcendental, and sacred signposts with which to guide their actions and resolve disputes. Dewey argued that there could be no enduring orthodoxies in the modern world except among rather small groups, although even in these cases it appeared difficult for the believers to extend their orthodox beliefs beyond their own comparatively small group. History has demonstrated that the use of coercion was thought necessary for convincing and/or conversion in all too many instances.

In the next section we shall consider the complete act of thought, also known as the scientific method, as it was developed by Dewey and other American pragmatist philosophers, especially Peirce. Some schools and teachers in the United States were to play crucial roles in stressing the importance of scientific inquiry so that their students could become competent in this powerful method. Specifically, this competence could assist them throughout their lives as they empowered themselves as citizens and workers and became critically involved in political, economic, social, and cultural affairs.

II

Our focus will be on Dewey's progressive, pragmatist, and liberal interpretation of the scientific method, what it meant, implied, and perhaps logically compelled its adherents to do. Chapter two shows the dominant triad in our K–12 public schools consists of: (1) educational essentialism, (2) philosophical idealism (and/or realism, neorealism), and (3) sociopolitical conservatism. The great protest against this dominant tradition of schooling in the United States features: (1) educational progressivism, (2) philosophical pragmatism, and (3) sociopolitical liberalism. Dewey is the key figure in this protest movement, one which featured the scientific method broadly conceived as the methodology thought of as central to democratically empowering educational philosophy and practice, and for democratic politics in the society at-large. Dewey's work, enriched by some of those who understood and admired his ideas, provides an integrated view of our original place or displacement in the universe, the need and ability to make ourselves more at home, the key roles of work and education required to alter our physical and social conditions, and how our educated intelligence and labor could lead to the possibilities for meaningful lives in a democratic community.

Dewey's view of the human condition in the universe was one that compelled us to make ourselves at home because the universe is benignly indifferent to our hopes, fears, and purposes. This is not the view subscribed to by the essentialists, idealists, and conservatives. In the next chapter, I examine how existentialist philosophical positions embrace a view which is somewhat similar to Dewey's with regard to human beings in a universe in which we are far from knowledgeable about how and why we are here. The existentialists are not convinced that we can be "saved by a method." In Dewey's view, human beings have been faced historically by problems that interfere with comparatively comfortable habitual/customary behavior. When this occurs, men and women have responded in many and varied ways. Dewey's view is that effective responses were based on what we call the scientific method. The problematic or indeterminate situation calls not for magic, superstition, or acquiescence, but for action based on the method of intelligence. For Dewey, reflective thought in the face of the problematic was a "dress rehearsal" for future action. Action is postponed so that plans for action can be evaluated in terms of relevant data, and probable consequences. "Our reflective thought processes enable us to choose among possible alternatives and adopt as a course of action the plan that promises best to change the problematic and indeterminate situation. Ultimately we must act if the situation is to be altered, and if our plan works out we can know that it was adequate for the situation."[15]

Dewey believed that every complete act of thought consisted of the following steps. (1) A problematic situation confronts us, one which makes it impossible to continue to act habitually; therefore, we must begin to think reflectively, i.e., to place the problematic into the broadest and deepest context possible. (2) We must recognize the problematic for what it is, allowing a structuring of it in a manner that focuses on the impediments to be overcome. This step can be called: Statement of the Problem. In some cases people do not realize they have a problem and/or, if they do, their proposed solutions are widely and even humorously off the mark. We can all think of instances in our own lives when proposed solutions seem almost laughable as they were enacted. (3) Ideas as dress rehearsals for action are hypothetically formulated. The plans for action must follow the most accurate problem statement. This must be done in the concreteness of everyday life. The hypothesis is formed in terms of theoretical construction which is grounded in experience and the problematic. (4) The hypothesis is worked on so that it is optimum in its possible, probable, and desired outcomes that result from implementation. (5) The hypothesis is enacted and the character of the problematic is changed. If the plans for action have been wisely and realistically formulated, then the consequences produced are the ones anticipated; the hypothesis is warranted—it has "paid off." The complete act of thought has occurred, although it will have to be performed throughout our lives, in part because the world we live in is not an "extension of our nursery." Dewey's view was that the universe is, at best, indifferent to our purposes. In a Darwinian sense, we face a dangerous world of competition. Dewey did not celebrate market Darwinism. He proposed the social use of the scientific method as a way to rise above the dog-eat-dog condition that plagued all too many throughout history. Dewey was convinced that Darwin's work placed human beings solidly in the natural order; our attempts to make sense of this world and our lives would have to follow the path of science by our dealing with the objects and methods of inquiry originating in the natural world of our lived experiences. Dewey and the pragmatists argued that experience does not allow us to claim the discovery of certainties or universals with which to guide our actions.

I will pursue this pragmatic philosophy way of thinking a bit further. Peirce argued that any idea we might have of something could only be our grasp of its sensible consequences. To know is to change relationships, to reveal connections between cause and effect, or antecedents and consequences. If there are no consequences, there can be neither an object of knowledge nor any meaning. To become educated is to be engaged in placing the problematic, in terms of everyday occurrence, in a complex cause-and-effect or means-ends continuum. Pragmatist philosophers would have us think: If H represents a concept, then the meaning of H, according to the pragmatic rule, is whatever consequences result from putting H into action. No consequences, no meaning! As we know, many of our ideas, others', and historical ones are not able to be translated into action. Peirce insisted that pragmatic philosophy could teach us that most metaphysical and theological propositions are simply meaningless, although not necessarily untrue. Pragmatism does not make truth claims. Its secular empiricism insists that meaningfulness and *warranted assertibility* are all that we can claim in the human condition. The method of science in the natural world cannot make truth claims; this is the case because of science's hypothetical and tentative nature. Future experience and experimentation can always disprove what has been established. For Dewey and Peirce, although not so much for the pragmatist William James (1842–1910), truth belongs to the realm of faith. Wingo wrote that propositions for the existence of a deity or deities cannot be settled because it is impossible to gather evidence in support or refutation. Fallibilism is the philosophical doctrine that states: No statement can be accepted as true beyond all probable doubt. This doctrine is offered as a cousin of the pragmatic rule.

Let us consider the following example provided by Wingo:

> If we consider the proposition "Pixies abound in the fifth dimension," and examine this statement in the light of the pragmatic rule, we find that neither of the operations provided by the rule can be applied. If we put the statement in the hypothetical form that the rule requires and say, "If pixies abound in the fifth dimension, then what conceivable consequences follow?" we are constrained to answer that there are no operations possible that would provide any observable consequences. Therefore, the conclusion must be that this statement is meaningless and any debate about whether it is true or false is idle. . . . The statement about the pixies is a . . . proper English sentence . . . but it does not meet the requirements of the pragmatic rule because it is impossible to conceive of any operations that yield any observable consequences.[16]

Peirce's views on the nature of meaning influenced Dewey. Operationalism and the emphasis on the consequences of action were, in part, responsible for the latter's insistence on the relations between doing and
learning. One of the famous progressive education slogans was: We learn
by doing.

According to Wingo, the influence of the pragmatic rule on Dewey's
ideas about education read as follows. First, if a concept is to be meaningful for a student, s/he must translate the hypothesis into action. The
curriculum must therefore be restructured. For Dewey, the child's needs
should constitute the curriculum; or the curriculum is constructed in keeping with the child's "problems." Dewey stated it: "Abandon the notion of
subject-matter as something fixed and ready-made . . . outside the child's
experience; cease thinking of the child's experience as also something
hard and fast; see it [instead] as something . . . embryonic . . . [and
developing]; and we realize that the child and the curriculum are simply
two limits which define a single process. Just as two points define a
straight line, so the present standpoint of the child and the facts . . . of
studies [academic disciplines] define instruction. It is continuous reconstruction, moving from the child's present experience out into that represented by . . . [the disciplines] that we call studies."[17] The object of knowledge is in the consequences that result from action taken. To know is to
do something to the problematic. Changing both what is to be known, as
well as the knower. These ideas necessitate the organization of schooling
around a curriculum that consists of "active enterprises."

The pragmatic rule is useful as a starting place for implementing the
scientific method. I have written, the reconstruction of mere happening
or occurrence into experience *is* education for Dewey. A person's behavior is intelligent when proposed actions are seen with regard to possible
and anticipated consequences. "A technical definition of Deweyan education might well be that reconstruction of experience which adds to the
meaning of what is undergone and which increases one's ability to direct
the course of subsequent events. Experience, intelligence, and education
are to be understood as comparative mastery over problematic situations."[18]
Good education is based on the reflective consideration of unavoidable
and constant happenings which characterize our lives, i.e., reflection that
helps make inevitable occurrences and/or changed conditions beneficial
to s/he who must undergo them. Dewey argued that we must place what
is undergone into a broader, deeper, and historically longer course of
events, connecting what is already apparent or known to what is not. All
too many people simply undergo and are buffeted by occurrences; this

rudderless journey is plagued by accidents, catastrophic ones in some cases. By placing undergone happenings into a cause-effect continuum, catastrophe can more easily be avoided. Careful hypothesis construction and related action are our only existential human tools with which to partially direct the course of future events. This method must be learned in school so that children, teenagers, and adults can individually and socially influence the courses of our lives, instead of succumbing to whatever a benignly indifferent universe confronts us with. As we shall learn in chapter five, existentialist thinkers see human intelligence as somewhat different from the method being described here.

III

It is necessary at this point to provide an explanation of how Dewey's scientific method is central to his ideas of democracy and community. The "complete act of thought" concludes with committing our hypothesis to action and evaluating whether the problem originally faced is solved. If it has been solved, then the person or group can move from doubt and perplexity to some form of harmonious, unified, and determinate conditions—if not to belief. The terminal evaluation is not just subjective or personal. It is objective and *public*. Remember that we have learned that pragmatic philosophy and experimental science do not speak of truth. Dewey advocated using the term *warranted assertibility* to indicate a successful terminal resolution to the problematic. He agreed with Peirce that "truth" is "the opinion which is fated [likely?] to be ultimately agreed to by all who investigate."[19] The method of controlled inquiry saves us from ignorance, reliance on imagined or false absolutes, and from the worst kind of moral relativity that results from giving into abject ignorance.

The following task is placed at this point in the text in order to help guide your reading of what follows it. This strategy is similar to handing out an essay exam long before it would be due, if this were a class or unit in philosophy of education.

Suggested Task for the Reader

Statement
Dewey described a method of inquiry and action that would empower ordinary students, workers, and citizens to know enough about themselves and the conditions of their lives to help ensure possibilities for progressive individual and social growth. The absence of a democratic

community during Dewey's life made the implementation of his method
difficult.

Tasks

    A. Explain Dewey's concept of a democratic community and how it
was central to his educational and social project.

    B. Explain how Dewey's pedagogy was organically related to his con-
cept of democratic community. Be sure to touch on his concept of
"experience" as well.

    C. Analyze how the scientific method, when applied to educational,
socioeconomic, and political problems, can lead to insistences on
reform, as well as reconstruction of institutions, and practices which
are unable to stand the pressure of inquiry.

    D. Extrapolate into the present and write creatively about your own
postscript on the continuing concern for democracy and community as necessary contexts for good education.

Following from the guidelines within the tasks, let us begin our inquiry
into Dewey's concept of community. What Dewey admired about life (for
some) in America before the industrial revolution and capitalism is what
he considered the possibilities for individual identities resulting from participation in shared concerns and work. Associational relations had often
been face-to-face. This kind of community could be democratic in a participatory way similar to Athenian democracy that featured interaction in
comparatively small groups. Dewey was convinced that a socially mature
self could develop best in contexts that permitted interaction as well as
concern for others and the common good. Dewey believed that his contemporaries should recognize the importance of developing individuals
who were citizen-workers; persons who were societally aware, civic-minded,
culturally aware, and politically empowered in ways that made it possible
to maintain their citizen rights when entering paid labor sites. For Dewey,
work must be educative, meaningful, nonexploitative, and an extension
of our central human roles as meaning-makers. He realized that the regime of capitalism made this difficult if not impossible to achieve.

    Community implies a society based on practices, customs, and institu-
tions that deserve respect and allegiance at the deepest intellectual and
emotional levels. This is in contrast to market societies based on conve-
nience, contractual obligations, and ultimately the cash (or credit) nexus.
The rough equality Dewey favored was one that recognizes and respects

what is distinctive and unique in each of us. Dewey knew that the great revolutionary triad: liberty, equality, and fraternity/sorority were only slogans when divorced from the rich matrix of communal life. Dewey asserted that in order for community to arise and function well, there must be values prized in common. Without them, people become too separate, being connected to one another mostly by market mechanisms and the often nondemocratic pressures of the class-State.[20]

Perhaps the core of Dewey's concept of community can be explained as follows: There can be little communication if there is an absence of any commonly perceived reality. In *Democracy and Education* (1916) Dewey reminded us that there exists more than mere verbal similarities among the words common, communication, and community. He argued that in order for us to understand one another, there must be various ways to communicate individual and personal interpretations of experiences so that they can be understood and appreciated by more than a few others. This is certainly not a disguised ploy that really intends to support "English only" initiatives, narrowly constructed canons, and "family values" based on white, heterosexual, Dick and Jane families which certain conservative spokespersons champion in these times. When authentic communication occurs, objects acquire representative signs that permit meaning and interpretation to be shared and managed publicly.

Authentic communication is vital to education for democratic empowerment as well as for bona fide democracy in society. Perceptions of occurrences and experiences cannot easily be communicated directly and/or accurately from one person to another; one can be assisted through the use of various forms of common language, common signs, and symbols. If democracy requires the freedom for all people to use the scientific method in order to solve our most pressing problems, this means access to relevant data, the liberty to translate hypothesis into action, and the right to publish or verbally communicate results. If there is no community of shared meaning, and some form of common language, then the published results will fall on uncomprehending eyes and ears on a virtual Babel-like plaza. Without such communication, an individual all too often suffers alone, unable to understand that many ills have empirical and social origins. Dewey insisted that everyone needed and deserved education that enabled her/him to see in daily tasks all there is in terms of human and social significance.

Dewey's assessment of his time was that arbitrariness and coercion were the usual ways of settling disputes. Were he alive today, he certainly would recognize that these two forms are still with us. Some of the forces that prevented the development of the kind of democratic community for schools and society during Dewey's lifetime were, in his mind, the following: the unanswerability to public and democratic needs and wishes by private power centers, especially corporations; governments that are more answerable to capitalism and the logic of profit than to the democratic logic of human rights; class stratification, misinformation, and, especially, the failure to democratize both the scientific method and the technology that resulted from it. I argued in *The Relationship of Dewey's Pedagogy to His Concept of Community* (1972) that the United States had not become a democratic community in the years after Dewey's death in 1952. I continue to hold to this belief.

As Dewey has taught us, there can be no bona fide democracy without community because democracy is a form of associative life—rather than merely having elections. Democracy is, for Dewey, the idea of community life itself. Dewey's idea of community went beyond association alone; he insisted that community life must be civically moral. Dewey wrote that "a moral principle . . . is not a command to act or . . . [refrain from] acting in a given way: *it is a tool for analyzing a special situation*, the right or wrong being determined by the situation in its entirety, and not by the rule as such."[21] For Dewey, democracy is more than a form of government because it must be developed in the rich matrix of community where citizen-workers are able to continue transforming occurrences into experiences, and constructed stories of intrapersonal meaning. If democracy means free and enriching communion, then we must be able to participate in, and have some influence on, that which affects our lives. It has been said that for Dewey "all those who are affected by social [understood broadly, e.g., the political, economic, and school systems] institutions must have a share in producing and managing them."[22]

In specific reference to the **Suggested Task for the Reader** included at the beginning of section III, the following is offered. The progressive social use of the scientific method requires at least rough agreement with regard to what the common problems are and which hypotheses are likely to be most effective, which actions are best, and some criteria with which to decide on the varying degrees of resulting success or failure. Community makes shared effort more possible which is of central importance for democratic planning and execution. There exists an integrative wholeness to Dewey's thinking: The use of the scientific method may result in evil and crime. He insisted that there must be public checks—this could be accomplished in a participatory democracy consisting of mutual understanding and shared effort—in a word, a democratic community based on human definitions of morality and educational opportunities for one and all in order to prepare students for participation. The conversion of raw occurrences into experience can be accomplished optimally in the matrix of a democratically constructed and answerable community. Only in a democratic community resembling Dewey's societal and educational vision would tolerance be in evidence enough to maintain tentativeness with regard to inquiry that was aimed at solving difficult problems, especially those that necessitated long periods of time and effort. Next we shall turn our attention to how Dewey's pedagogy is organically related to his concepts of community and democracy.

Pedagogy means the art or science of teaching. The word is not confined to instruction in the institutional school. Dewey's pedagogy, educational philosophy, concept of community, and ideas of participatory democracy are organically related. In Dewey's mind, his favored pedagogy could work in optimum fashion when following from a certain philosophy of education, as well as in community and democracy. They are inextricably related. He realized that during his lifetime, United States society was neither the kind of community he thought necessary, nor a democracy. This is an important reason why he agreed to go to the University of Chicago in the late nineteenth century in order to have a place to practice his pedagogy in a small community that was organized around democratic principles.[23] At the center of Dewey's pragmatist philosophy is his concept of experience; it is logical that at the heart of the School's pedagogy lay the unit of instruction Dewey called "enterprise." This kind of "enterprise" is not to be confused with the common use of the word as interchangeable, if not synonymous, with business. As Wingo noted, the "enterprise" was of longer duration than a lesson. "When planned properly it has the inherent unity of organization, and it involves generally the union of thought and action. An enterprise involves some goal or end that those involved . . . wish to attain. To attain this goal, certain strategies and plans must be made that promise to bring about the desired consummation. These plans must then be implemented by appropriate actions and judged for their adequacy by the way they work out."[24] The construction undertaken by the students would be both mental and physical; it would not consist of passive absorption of what was being taught.

Students of the Dewey School were encouraged to place their own, home-oriented experiences into larger contexts. They were assisted by their teachers in the construction of plans for action that allowed them to shape the realities in which they lived. The pedagogy that was practiced moved from what the students previously understood, or recently mastered, to that which was not yet comprehended, a process that was continuously challenging. The teachers sought to develop a small community in the School because they believed common assaults on the problematic were often most effective. It was realized that problem solvers need freedom of movement in educational community settings for purposes of exploration, experimentation, and application. The scientific method requires freedom in order to engage in it. The importance of community was that it balanced freedom with the idea of commonality and public. As Dewey wrote: "Everything that exists in so far as it is known and knowable is in interaction with other things."[25] Societies that feature great unevenness in terms of power, wealth, access, and privilege do not qualify as the democratic communities Dewey favored. Social class, racial/ethnic, gender, and sexual orientation injustices make it difficult or impossible to conduct free inquiry in contexts of community understandings. Mayhew and Edwards wrote, "the development of intelligence and knowledge has historically been a cooperative matter, and culture in its broadest sense has been a collective creation. The individual must be able to engage in a free give and take in order to be part of this collective creation; so education could prepare the youth for . . . future social life only when the school was itself a cooperative society on a small scale."[26]

For Dewey, community is best achieved by people communicating common aspirations with reference to goals. The free use of the scientific method is considered the best way to work out these problems and aspirations. When people work cooperatively to solve problems which they perceive in roughly the same way, an important part of Dewey's concept of community is operative. Later in this book we shall learn that many postmodernist thinkers believe Dewey and the Deweyans were naive with regard to the supposed ease with which commonality could be achieved. Existentialist thinkers share in this criticism. Various Reds are critical of Dewey's liberalism and pragmatism, in part, because they have concluded that Dewey did not take social class differences seriously enough.

The Dewey School experiences of the students were constructed under the teachers' guidance which encouraged the conscious following of historical human experiences. At the beginning of human history, people and groups were thought to have employed the scientific method, but rather unconsciously for the most part. The School community, comprised of participatory democrats, would employ the method at a very conscious level of awareness. Hook warned that the conscious use of the method and its widespread use could not occur in a society where a group, class, party, or religious institution exercises a monopoly of power. In his words: "The widest use of organized intelligence is possible . . . only in a truly democratic society."[27]

In specific reference to the **Suggested Task for the Reader** stated previously in section III, Dewey argued that the scientific method "contagiously diffused" could be employed best where the norms of inquiry were widely accepted and its self-corrective procedures well understood. Only a democratic community is characterized by enough persons who possess the necessary tolerance for the tentativeness of authentic inquiry. This fact raises a difficult question: How can the inquiry method of Dewey's pedagogy flourish as a way of solving problems and settling disputes? How can it be *the* method on which democracy and community rest when the scientific method requires a supportive democratic community in the first place? These questions have troubled many students of Dewey's work including me, for as Salvatore D'Urso reminded us, democratic procedures have worked best historically when the issues to be decided on do not involve interests for which people would rather fight than compromise or surrender. When minorities can easily and regularly become new majorities, then democracy and the method of intelligence are more likely to flourish. The use of reason and deliberation for conflict resolution depend in large part on the prior existence of favorable conditions. It follows that "'where there are marked inequalities in the distribution of power the full exercise of the methods of intelligence depend solely on the goodwill of those in superior positions. Hence a preliminary condition of deliberation may frequently be the . . . redistribution of power.'"[28]

The scientific method demands fidelity to whatever the consequences of planned action indicates. The students of the Dewey School were learning some of these lessons by employing the scientific method. They were not just taught *about* democracy and inquiry, they engaged in both—and about problems that were important. The curriculum and pedagogy provided for opportunities to demonstrate that, if a concept is to have meaning for an individual, then s/he must put it to work. However, the School was a planned and protected environment.

For Dewey, community and democracy represented the civilized alternative to chaos, namely, dangerous disorder caused by natural and/or human indifference and arbitrariness. The democratic use of the scientific method in community was intended to serve as the methodological solution to the stark choices caused by the inability to believe that I, we, and others have a direct pipeline to certainty, one whose alleged epistemological certainty could be used to guide action. The lack of certainty must neither paralyze action nor result in human beings believing that any belief or action is as good as any other. The dangers of cynicism or uncontrollable moral relativism have been discussed earlier in this book. It remains a continuing theme. The scientific method was offered to provide a reasonable and effective middle ground to which all could subscribe. The Dewey School and other Deweyan, progressive educators attempted to educate democrats so that democracy could be possible. For Dewey, democracy is a moral concept, a practice that is used on an everyday basis. Democracy is all of one piece, the alternative is immoral authoritarianism and arbitrariness. Dewey, like Marx, refused to agree with those who sought to make history behind our backs!

The individual and the individual-in-a-group have a right to make experience meaningful; we as workers have the right to create what is both socially useful and aesthetic. Inquirers of all kinds have the right to probe into the unknown and the participatory democrat has the right to associate, plan, and act in solidarity in order to rearrange the furniture of our socioeconomic, political, cultural, and educational existences. Just as Dewey's pedagogy needed a special Laboratory School in order to break free of the educational essentialism of that time, so do contemporary Deweyans require a radically transformed school and society in which to learn the method of experimental science. The success and fame of the Laboratory School never caused Dewey to think that such a singular and unique success was a solution to the problems that originally caused him to develop the School in the first place. If Deweyan pedagogy required a special school, then such a school is dependent on a particular kind of democratic community in which to flourish. An authentic Dewey School could not be tolerated in the bestial regimes that have despoiled much of the twentieth-century landscape. Dewey's educational philosophy and pedagogy did not become implemented to a significant degree in the public school system in the United States because the democratic community which his educational ideas presupposes and, in part depends on, existed neither during Dewey's lifetime nor now. This is *not* to claim that Dewey's work failed to have important and significant impact here and abroad. United States schools and society have been answerable to both the contradictory and incompatible imperatives of democracy and capitalism. Dewey was aware of the difficulties this fact presented for his attempted reforms and his work which strengthened the first imperative. Perhaps the reader can now more easily accomplish the **Suggested Task** set forth at the beginning of this section.

IV

Consider briefly the historical "progressive protest" in society and schools. This protest occurred in the late nineteenth and early twentieth centuries. Wingo wrote: "Progressivism in education developed as a protest movement against essentialism and its domination of American education. The protest . . . against the conservative tradition in education was part of a larger liberal reform movement. . . . Progressive education, as a historic reality, was a movement of vast and untidy proportions. It was eclectic in its origins . . . and self-contradictory on numerous theoretical points. The thing the progressives had in common . . . was a profound distaste for the traditional school and for many aspects of the society that supported . . . [it]."[29] For a classic but critically challenged book on progressivism, see Lawrence Cremin's, *The Transformation of the School*. He argued, "progressive education began as part of a vast humanitarian effort to apply the promise of American life—the ideal of government by, of, and for the people—to the puzzling new urban-industrial civilization that came into being. . . . The word *progressive* provides the clue to what it really was: the educational phase of American Progressivism writ large."[30] Wingo agreed and stated that the progressive protest, driven by liberals and their ideas, represents an attempt to reconstruct the "ideals of moral equality and individual worth" in the revolutionary developments of the capitalist political economy.[31]

Liberal progressive reform was influenced by the Enlightenment belief that improvement of the human condition could be achieved through widespread, intelligent reform of both society and the schools. It was the liberals who had been the motor behind the drive to construct and support the free public school system in the United States. These nineteenth- and twentieth-century reformers believed that only an educated people could be free. The school system soon was challenged by the profound consequences caused by urbanization, industrialization, immigration, and other related developments serving to transform the United States into the leading capitalist nation. Some of the reform responses to the challenge made by liberal progressives follow: (1) moving the school's focus to the kinds of problems and possibilities faced by a heterogeneous mass of students; (2) changing the school's authoritarian culture to a somewhat more democratic one; (3) abandoning a curriculum and pedagogy that were out of sync with the principles of experimental science, democracy, and interactive community; (4) broadening the school's program to include concern with health, vocation, and the quality of the students' famil-

ial and community lives; (5) insisting on equity and excellence for all the
various kinds of students being served; and (6) as the reformer Jane
Addam's wrote, "'the good must be extended to all of society before it
can be held by any one person or . . . class.'"[32]

Dewey's *My Pedagogic Creed* (1897) exemplified the progressive educational protest as well as the proposed reforms being considered here.
Wingo believed that Dewey "never departed significantly" from what he
articulated in 1897. John McDermott wrote:

> "My Pedagogical Creed" contains, in seminal form, most of his subsequent judge-
> ments about matters educational. His stress on the individual as social, the school
> as a community, and the necessity of integrating discipline with needs and poten-
> tialities of the children constitute major themes in . . . [Dewey's later works
> also]. Dewey also attempts to sketch the necessary relationship among feeling,
> thought, and action, while opposing both dull academic formalism and sentimen-
> talism. Perhaps the most trenchant remark in his "Creed" is Dewey's comment
> "education must be conceived as a continuing reconstruction of experience; that
> the process and the goal of education are one and the same thing." Learning for
> Dewey is . . . a process, yielding its rewards enroute and from time to time
> consummating in an insight, a breakthrough, or even a mastery of a discipline or
> an area of study. Attention to detail and rigor of method are not separated in
> Dewey's . . . view from the joy and celebration that accompanies the process of
> learning.[33]

Dewey's Creed is composed of five articles intended to convey the
basics of his education theory. The first one is: "What Education Is," and
each article is followed by the words, "I believe that." Dewey maintained
that the education process was both psychological and social; the former
provides the basis of all education, the child's instincts and powers. This
sociological factor allows the educator to understand the child's psychological agency in terms of its social equivalence, as well as to construct a
learning context for the student. Because exact prediction of the future is
impossible, the teacher concentrates on helping the child gain control of
her/himself in order to be somewhat prepared for the problematic future.
The second article concerns "What the School Is." Dewey believed that
"'the school is primarily a social institution. . . . The school is . . .
that form of community life in which all . . . [social] agencies are concentrated that will be most effective in bringing the child to share in the
inherited resources of the [human] race, and to use his [her] own powers
for social ends. . . . [Furthermore] education . . . is a process of living
and not a preparation for future living.'"[34] The school is considered a
form of community life, one with moral dimensions, e.g., developing a
sense of responsibility for oneself and to the community.

The next article is "The Subject-Matter of Education," which should consist of the progressive reconstruction of the child's experience rather than a premature introduction of the student to specialized subject matters, such as reading, writing, arithmetic, etc. The historic subject matters are important as means; however, they are not the ends of the educational process. The fourth article is "The Nature of Method," and here Dewey connects methods to the developmental stage of the child's interest and abilities. Methodology is dependent on the child's readiness, abilities, and needs. In his words: "'Only through the continual and sympathetic observation of childhood's interests can the adult enter into the child's life and see what . . . [s/he] is ready for, and on what material it could work . . . [best].'"[35] The fifth and last article is "The School and Social Progress": in Dewey's words, "'I believe that education is the fundamental method of social progress and reform.'"[36] Dewey believed that the best means for social reconstruction are educational, because this allows the learner to act on the basis of social consciousness. In fact, he was convinced that this approach is sensitive to both individual and social factors, e.g., an ideal Deweyan school would reconcile personal and institutional ideals and goals. "'Through education society can formulate its own purposes, can organize its own means and resources, and thus shape itself with definiteness and economy in the direction in which it wishes to move.'"[37]

What did this liberal progressive protest and reform accomplish? This is a complex question whose answers depend on one's educational and political points of view. Wingo warned us to avoid extreme assessments of liberal progressive accomplishments. Some conservatives and essentialists have blamed many of our social and school problems on liberals and progressives. Some adherents of progressive/pragmatist educational philosophy seem to think that almost every improvement in public education is due to their ideas and work. Wingo's careful evaluation of the liberal progressive impact includes six points, although he does not favor monocausal explanations. He makes clear that the causes of cultural and educational change are complex and Dewey's experimentalism did not drive reform by itself. "The really foundational elements in Dewey's educational philosophy never received widespread testing [even] in the progressive movement."[38] My own studies have caused me to write the following which supports Wingo's assessment: The hypothesis advanced is that Dewey's educational philosophy and pedagogy were not able to be implemented to a significant extent in the American public school system because the Deweyan concept of a democratic community, which his educational ideas presupposed, was not a reality. I developed this argument further in my monograph, *The Relationship of Dewey's Pedagogy to His Concept of Community.*

The six points Wingo claimed as achievements made by educators in the United States during the first seventy-five years of the twentieth century are: (1) There has occurred an expansion of what and who should be included in free public education. The idea that everyone should have educational opportunities that meet her/his needs and abilities has been forwarded, although this idea and even formal commitment has not always been realized in practice. (2) The curriculum has been expanded and enriched so that a broader range of educational experiences is more available than ever. (3) Ideas and practices of school discipline have been humanized and are more effective than the rod and dunce cap. (4) The idea that effective teaching and learning depend on engaging the students' interests has been rather convincingly demonstrated. (5) The materials used for instruction have been improved significantly. There has occurred a visual and tactile revolution in the schools. (6) Method and curriculum have been organized around scientific concepts of human development; the psychology of learning has strengthened pedagogy. In spite of his wariness about monocausal claims, Wingo asserted "that the liberal protest movement favored such developments and supported them at virtually every turn appears so well established as to be outside the possibility of serious argument."[39] Dewey's reform ideas and activities sought to establish a new humanism, one built on the scientific method and democratic ethics. Wingo cited Hook and told us that all too many progressives forgot to remain liberal, i.e., that school reform must be anchored to broad social understandings, penetrating theoretical knowledge, and principled commitments.

V

In this section we shall consider social reconstructionism as a radicalized development of the liberal progressive protest. Perhaps the following will serve as a guide for the reader.

Suggested Task for the Reader

Statement
Many of the pioneers and theorists in education have believed that schooling and education should relate to empowering persons to become critical and competent problem-solving citizens and workers.

Tasks
   A. Explain what Dewey's mastery of the scientific method has to do
      with citizen and worker empowerment.
   B. Explain how Dewey's emphasis on the scientific analysis of prob-
      lems can logically lead to Social Reconstructionism.

Wingo explained, Dewey believed that the education he proposed, if
successful, would help develop a new kind of individual who could then
act decisively to promote the democratization of society that Dewey favored. Dewey did not favor the schools entering politics; he was clear
about not supporting specific political parties; instead, the school should
help to promote broad social forces and their movements. Dewey's "conviction was that the school, by developing social intelligence and awareness in individuals, could make its greatest contribution to social reconstruction."[40] During the catastrophe of the Great Depression in the 1930s,
some critics argued that Dewey's views were inadequate for the perilous-
ness of the times. The Marxist left continued its critique of Dewey's and
liberalism's refusal to ally themselves with the position that class struggle
was central to any really progressive future for school and society. Dewey
was mauled by some on the left who were liberals, the most noteworthy
being George Counts. He was highly critical of the lack of a credible
conception of social justice and welfare in a progressivism easily dominated by the well-to-do, those who could afford to see progressivism mostly
as an affair of child-centered development, with little regard for those
whose development was stymied by increasingly hostile socioeconomic
conditions. Counts argued that teachers should use their influence to educate students in a clear understanding of the need for profound social
reform. It is possible to argue that during the tragic Depression years, the
use of Deweyan scientific method would usually result in fair-minded condemnation of practices, institutions, systems, and certain malefactors of
great wealth as well as their agents. As a result of this use of the scientific
method with which to study the crisis of the Great Depression, the need
to deconstruct what was bad and then reconstruct seemed obvious! To
those who worried about "imposition" or "indoctrination" by teachers on
their students, Counts responded that students always undergo imposition; the real issue is by whom and for what?[41] "Counts wrote in the early
1930s that this nation was the scene of an 'irreconcilable' conflict between democracy and capitalism. He warned that unless political democracy could establish a complementary foundation, it would not survive."[42]
Counts' influential polemic that succinctly articulated his reconstructionist
position is called *Dare the Schools Build A New Social Order?* (1932).

Dewey did not believe that the institutional school and its teachers were powerful enough to achieve what Counts asked them to dare. Ironically, Dewey's position here is remarkably like Marx's as well as many Marxists and other radicals. Dewey held that although schooling-education were necessary conditions for progressive reconstruction, they alone were not sufficient. Counts' powerful arguments, as well as the crisis of the Great Depression, caused many to agree that teachers should decide which side they were on in an unjust, polarized, and socially stratified society. Counts articulated the earlier American radical tradition, especially its broadly educative component, that sought to point out the evils of capitalism. This earlier tradition included the work of Thorstein Veblen, Upton Sinclair, et al. As Lawrence Cremin wrote, "The theme of all these works was essentially the same: that until the dead hand of the businessman was removed from the schools and the control of education placed with teachers, where it belonged, it was folly to talk about liberating intelligence or reforming the curriculum."[43]

In the 1920s progressive education could be said to have been dominated by those who championed child-centered schooling. Counts' social meliorist and reconstructionist curriculum was challenged by the child-centered developmentalists.[44] During the Great Depression, political and educational radicalism were widely discussed as possible solutions. Counts and other reconstructionists at Teachers College, Columbia University, were, in part, responsible for advocating a new "frontier" position for education in the face of the catastrophic Depression. *The Educational Frontier* (1933) was the characteristic progressive statement of the decade. *The Social Frontier* was the journal counterpart of this reconstructionist progressivism. Cremin was critical of the reconstructionists' call for teachers daring to build a new social order, in part, because schoolteachers were neither willing nor prepared to take on the dare. The progressives were not the kind of people who would take to the streets and/or other contested sites, organized as class actors with other *workers*. The reasons for this are many. Perhaps the fact that progressivism was mainly a middle-class movement tops the list.

The reconstructionists were concerned with educational and social change. Many of them believed that a new society needed to be built. They sought to reconstruct school and society in a way that empowered people to have greater control over their own lives as members of society. Those who promoted reconstructionist educational ideas sought to have teachers and their students critically examine the society they lived in. They insisted that schooling be characterized by attempts to identify important conflicts, arguments, inconsistencies, injustices, etc., and then to propose solutions that could be acted on. A reconstructionist, educational program would include: a critical examination of our cultural heritage, confronting the most controversial issues, commitment to serious socio-economic change, planning and hypothesis construction, and the enlistment of teachers and students in programs designed to bring about progressive change.[45] The reconstructionists realized that when the school acts in an avant-garde way, it will be controversial and attacked by some people. Teachers who have been committed to democratic empowerment, social justice, and respect for diversity have often been considered controversial when their views have been accepted and acted on by their students. Critically examining classism, racism, and sexism is still considered by some to be an activity that is better left to adults, especially if such inquiry reveals that the practices of these isms are deep, general, structural, historical, and systematic. Reconstructionists, neoreconstructionists, and many radicals do not agree with arguments that students should be overly protected as learners, critics, and occasional activists.

There is a Society for Educational Reconstruction. For those who are interested in learning more about contemporary reconstructionism, *Introducing Educational Reconstruction: The Philosophy and Practice of Transforming Society Through Education* (1997) will prove useful. In the introduction, Angela Raffel wrote: "Born out of the struggle for human rights and social justice, Educational Reconstruction has . . . emerged in the minds of many scholars and practitioners who, in concert, have concluded that education can and should be a tool for social transformation and the great problems faced by humanity should be the basis of the school curriculum."[46] Teacher education students who are exposed to reconstructionist pedagogy would engage with social conditions and problems, e.g., violence, the environment, unemployment, economic insecurity, etc. They would be encouraged to formulate plans that help to solve these problems. Theodore Brameld promoted a "culturalogical" approach for understanding a world featuring both crises and possibilities. In fact, "the insistence of Educational Reconstruction on cultural transformation, involving both radical and structural changes, is exemplified by its method of working toward the goal of peace through the elimination of discrimination and oppression. Although the means may disrupt the harmony of the community, . . . global citizens and world educators [must] work . . . toward a lasting peace. 'Think globally and act locally' is . . . [the reconstructionists'] maxim."[47] The works of Marx, C. Wright Mills, and Paulo Freire are supportive of the reconstructionism portrayed in the passage quoted above.

I conclude this section with paraphrased passages from an article I wrote which appeared in 1990. A close reading of the following can assist the reader to think contextually, historically, and critically about educational reconstructionism, as well as "motivationalism."[48] I refer to certain neoreconstructionists as "motivationalists" because they have criticized some forms of Marxist analysis as too deterministic, i.e., pessimistic arguments claiming that democratic schools cannot be developed in a larger capitalist socioeconomic system. The "motivationalists" are convinced that teachers' motivation is minimized when educational theorists write about the economic base as determinative of "superstructural" institutions such as our schools. George H. Wood and other motivational theorists paint a grim picture of contemporary schools and society, one that is believable. They claim that now is the time for the birth or rebirth of participatory democracy. Wood et al. have much in common with the earlier reconstructionists, as well as some predictable differences. But one is still tempted to ask why the motivationalist and neoreconstructionists think they can succeed in building a new school and social order when Counts failed during a time that United States institutions were broadly viewed as having failed. If one looks at reconstructionism as focusing primarily on education instead of interventionist political action, it is debatable whether educators have succeeded at the more modest goal of having more than a few of their students understand the most important socioeconomic and political issues. The reconstructionists were not in charge of school policy when Counts "dared the schools"; that is the point: radical educators have never been in charge of, or in, American schools.

Educational historian, Michael B. Katz argued that we must not allow ourselves to place our hopes on illusory optimism. Speaking of Counts' *Dare the Schools Build a New Social Order?*, Katz labeled it as a passionate manifesto that engenders unrealistic expectations which serve to cause despair in the end because of predictable failure. Counts and the neoreconstructionists exhibit an ambivalence with regard to what educator-led reconstruction can achieve. This is not surprising. I am convinced that most K–12 teachers have not tried to "dare build a new social" or even a new school "order" for a variety of reasons. One of the most important reasons is that they did not and do not believe that their jobs include or permit such roles and activities. Many teachers are conservative and status-quo oriented in many ways. My assessment is not presented happily or approvingly. Still, things can change.

What can be done in the K–12 schools during these times? After having sounded a sober and realistic note concerning unrealistic claims and hopes, I am convinced, along with the educational historian Wayne J. Urban, that Dewey, the reconstructionists, and the motivational neo-reconstructionists can and have helped teach us that the school's unique power is its ability to formulate an ideal of a democratic society and school, helping to inspire students to believe that they can contribute to reconstruction throughout their lives. This is different than claiming that vulnerable teachers and students can lead the way. Teachers and students are also citizens and workers. They can, and should, enter into broad-based progressive coalitions that could erupt into forces for meaningful change.

In a country where there are official commitments to de jure democracy, as well as de facto realities, educators can safely have a "democratic bias" without needing to be extraordinarily or unrealistically brave. Many teachers celebrate the advantages of democracy and fair play without ever having studied educational theory. When one considers our tradition consisting of education empowerment; heuristic or discovery pedagogy; respect for the individual student; recognition of various learning styles; growing awareness of racial, ethnic, gender and sexual preference differences; knowledge of social-class inequities, and so forth, it is possible to construct relevant models for what can and should occur in the schools. Our tradition of progressivism takes us from the Dewey School, through the reconstructionists, the 1960s' reformers, and to the present concern for education that prepares the youth for civic literacy, altruism, and compassion for others. The motivational theorists have made important contributions to this fine tradition. Their claims that those educational theorists who continue to take structural impediments (to volition and agency) seriously are dampening educators' motivation to seek progressive change in school and society are simply wrong-headed. In spite of the good ideas held by the progressive tradition, Dewey's educational philosophy and pedagogy were not able to be implemented in public school policy because his idea of democratic community—which his educational ideas presupposed—was not a reality during his lifetime. It still is not. We remain stuck where Dewey was, i.e., how to implement what we think is best educationally for our youth. A different kind of politics may be needed in order to make progressive education—from Dewey to the motivationalists—dominant in our schools. This concludes the paraphrased passages from my 1990 article.

VI

Critique is central to philosophical inquiry and discourse. I have written a substantial critique of Dewey's educational ideas as well as an analysis of their impact on educational theorists, practitioners, and the schools. This lengthy critique is chapter twelve, "Democratic Theory and Practice: Dewey and Beyond," in *A Radical Democratic Critique of Capitalist Education*. I will draw on some of that work in this section. First, let us consider the following passage from the British historian Eric Hobsbawm's work. It is offered as warning to those who think that the scientific method is easily harnessed to the activities of a bona fide participatory democracy. Hobsbawm writes of how difficult it was for bright, highly educated, and interested persons to understand what was being done by scientists at their own universities—even when the scientists' work aimed at solving problems of societal importance.

> Thus the present author [Hobsbawm] was a fellow at Cambridge college at the very time when Crick and Watson were preparing their triumphant discovery of DNA . . ., immediately recognized as one of the crucial breakthroughs of the century. Yet, though I even recall meeting Crick socially at the time, most of us were simply not aware that these extraordinary developments were being hatched in a few tens of yards of my college . . . in laboratories we passed regularly. . . . It was not that we took no interest in such matters. Those who pursued them simply saw no point in telling us about them, since we could not have contributed to their work, or probably even understood exactly what the difficulties were. Nevertheless, however esoteric and incomprehensible the innovations of science, once made they were almost immediately translated into practical technologies.[49]

Hobsbawm went on to analyze the research and development conducted by central governments especially for military purposes, and multinational corporations, actions that do not always result in what is in the overall public interest. There is evidence to support that Dewey was aware of these problems, although there was an absence of democratic power to solve them. However, some scholars have not been satisfied with Dewey's supposed awareness.

Drawing from my book review of William Paringer's work, *John Dewey and the Paradox of Liberal Reform* (1990), I present the following for the reader's consideration. Paringer argued that Dewey's pedagogical insights are praiseworthy. The freedom for the learner he championed cannot be achieved in the absence of successful challenges to the complex structures and practices of socioeconomic, political, and cultural domination. Paringer criticized Dewey for allegedly failing to direct the scientific method's analytical power at the inequities inherent in a society dominated by capitalist logic and practice. Paringer argued that Dewey's concept of democracy did not pose a serious challenge to U.S. society that was dominated by a capitalism which rendered its very limited democratic politics (and imperative) unable to balance the more powerful capitalist imperative on society and school. Dewey was criticized for not being alert enough to the fact that the scientific-technological revolutions were being monopolized by capitalism, business, and narrow "bottom line" priorities. According to Paringer, Dewey did not understand well enough that democracy and/or individual freedom are not organically connected to or dependent on science and technology. Dewey was not fully aware that knowledge is not inherently neutral! The scientific method itself may be of specific and limited use.[50]

Paringer charged Dewey with failing to distinguish between an organic Darwinian view of society and politically constructed and mediated one, of which Giambattista Vico (1668–1774) wrote. Because Dewey did not recognize well enough the ideological reality of social reality, he saw political economy as "natural and evolutionary." In fact, "Paringer is critical of equating adaptation in a biological and psychological sense with adaptation to capitalism. Public education's attempt to fit psychologically described students into a rationalized status quo can be attributed in part . . . to Dewey's concept of nature."[51] Perhaps an even more important critical perspective on Dewey's work and legacy is the argument that both of them are to be understood as part of the hegemonic discourse characterized by upper-middle-class values, and other components of what the educational historian Merle Curti called the "American ideology." Paringer fired this barrage: Dewey failed to adequately recognize the implicit elitism of scientists, industrialist, technocrats, managers, and even intellectuals. Paringer believed that: (1) A consolidation of power was occurring in the United States during Dewey's lifetime; specifically, it was led by the kinds of persons listed in the previous sentence. Scientists, industrialists, et al. maintained, misleadingly, that their methods were accessible to all. The Critical Theorists of the Frankfurt School (see chapter three) realized that the scientific method could be understood and evaluated only within the context of the society in which it was practiced. Science is not automatically a champion of progressivism. The Critical Theorists saw American pragmatist philosophy as an expression of a society dominated by technology under the domination of monopoly capitalism. (2) The consolidation referred to above required oppositional or countervailing power in order to realize the ideas that we admire in Dewey's work.

I argued that Dewey's dislike of social-class politics prevented him from being able to realize that the working class in the United States was the potential agency required to move his ideas about society and school forward.[52] Robert Westbrook offered: "[What] remained absent in . . . [Dewey's] *Democracy and Education* and thereby limiting its radicalism was anything resembling a *political* strategy for the redistribution of power Dewey proposed. He remained wedded to moral exhortation as the sole means to the ends that [instead] required democratic politics. He advanced impeccable arguments . . . yet relied too heavily on the force of such arguments to overcome the appeal of tangible, if morally shortsighted benefits employers derived from exploitation . . . thus, . . . he had yet to envision a politics commensurate with . . . [his] radical vision."[53]

I conclude my study of Dewey and the progressives with an appraisal of the inheritance they have bestowed on those of us interested in teaching and learning for democratic empowerment, social justice, and respect for diversity. This inheritance represents the most effective rationale for what has been advocated thus far in this book. Many K–12 teachers have found this legacy—especially its emphasis on problem solving, heuristics, scientific method, and individualized instruction—a useful tool for their own dispositions about teaching and learning. Many education students find Dewey's progressive, liberal, and democratic views preferable to the essentialist ones favored by conservatives. I contend that neither educational theorists nor practitioners have, in any important way, gone beyond the impressive analysis constructed by Dewey and the progressives with regard to educating the whole person for participation in the civic affairs of society. Those who have worked historically in this inheritance have dealt with somewhat different problems and possibilities. The trajectory of Dewey's legacy has provided a springboard for most of the adjustments required. Dewey pushed the historical liberalism of his time to something quite different; it has been capable of serving us beyond the progressive movement and Dewey's life. Dewey argued that "the cost of revolution must be charged . . . to those who have taken for their aims customs instead of . . . readjustment. The only ones who have a right to criticize 'radicals' . . . are those who put as much effort into reconstruction as the rebels are putting into destruction."[54]

If this society cannot move significantly beyond the historical and current impasse between the democratic and capitalist imperatives on society and school, it is important to keep redefining educational practice along the lines constructed by those who bestowed this inheritance on us. The inclusion of the wonderful diversity of persons into the ranks of educational practitioners and theorists will, more than likely, allow us to render this inheritance more useful to the commensurately multicultural nature of the student body and general population. I hope that, in the long run, inclusion and greater security for those included, may lead to the necessary consideration of a democratically constructed notion of a general welfare.

It is of crucial importance for those of us who labor to make schools and society more responsive to democratic and egalitarian principles to be energetic, resolute, informed, realistic, and sober. Our hope must be tempered by realistic and sober assessments of what can be done. In a society that is already committed to de jure democracy in which the K–12 public schools, as well as much of postsecondary education, is part of the state sector, educators can afford to have a "democratic bias." Many educators promote fair play, democratic and even egalitarian principles without having formally studied the issues raised in this chapter. Our educational tradition has featured wise theoretical insights and practices, many of them derivative of and/or compatible with the Deweyan legacy being addressed here. Getting beyond such intramural commitments and accomplishments may necessitate a reconstructed society along the lines championed by Dewey, the progressives, and even some radicals.

In the meantime, because schooling is compulsory for children and adolescents, we must act sensitively, humanely, and wisely toward the students in our care. There are educators who act this way everyday, although the conditions of their work make it difficult. We are heirs to a tradition and literature that celebrates the teacher as democratic, egalitarian, sensitive, wise, caring, and devoted to helping cause "good things to happen to and for kids." The educational literature is replete with good arguments for empowering all students; pedagogies based on heuristics as a featured activity; respect for the individual; recognition of multiple and varied learning styles; and awareness of social class, racial/ethnic, gender, and sexual preference inequities; therefore, the beginning teacher can stand on the shoulders of those who came before them, and/or those who are currently practicing.

Conclusion

This chapter includes suggestions and arguments supporting the notion that Dewey could serve as the schoolmaster for Marx's radical democracy. Certain similarities in both philosophers' intellectual roots, as well as their mature positions on the relationships between thinking and doing, make their work helpful to those interested in participatory democracy and education for democratic empowerment.

The potential for Dewey's version of the scientific method to help clearup what is indeterminate, and/or to solve human problems, was stressed in chapter four. It was argued that Dewey's favored mode of inquiry could best be practiced in societies that were democratic communities. Although Dewey did not make common cause with the revolutionary potential of the working class, his version of the scientific method has radical potential. Although most progressive educators were political liberals, the trajectory of Dewey's method of intelligence could and did support rather radical reconstructionism, as exemplified by Counts, Brameld, and some contemporary educational social reconstructionists.

Dewey, the progressives, and reconstructionists were placed into a context featuring their insistence that the quest for certainty could no longer succeed in a heterogeneous society. The social use of the scientific method was portrayed as the liberal and progressive attempt to establish an effective and acceptable way to solve social, public, and educational problems in this country. Pragmatist philosophy, as well as its educational uses by Dewey and his supporters, were also featured in this chapter. Dewey's attempt to convince his audience that schools must be characterized by community, democracy, and the moral use of the scientific method is central to chapter four. His educational views and actions brought him into conflict with proponents of the dominant conservative and essentialist practices of his time. Dewey's educational position made his alliance with the broader (than school reform) progressive protest a natural one. A critique of Dewey is provided, derived from those who admire his work. Philosophers and philosophers of education do not view critique or argument as necessarily destructive. We shall learn in chapter five, the existentialist philosophers and thinkers do not necessarily agree that Dewey's hope, to be saved by a method, has been realized.

Afterword

Taking the pragmatists seriously means purging ourselves of the quest for certainty in our intellectual and moral lives. It means giving up absolutism and dogmatism. . . . The alternative the pragmatists present us with is not one of despair or skepticism. There is rather the clear imperative never to block the road to inquiry, to realize that any of our beliefs, no matter how cherished and fundamental they may be, are open (and indeed require) further criticism. . . . Dewey was particularly sensitive to the moral and social consequences of this new understanding of critical inquiry. If Peirce's ideal is not to remain just an ideal, but is to become actualized, then we must begin with restructuring our social and our educational institutions.[55]

Notes

1 Salvatore D'Urso, "Can Dewey Be Marx's Educational-Philosophical Representative?" *Educational Philosophy and Theory* 12 (October 1980): 31.

2 Richard Brosio, "Dewey As the Schoolmaster for Marx's Radical Democracy," *Philosophy of Education 1994*. Proceedings of the Fiftieth Annual Meeting of the Philosophy of Education Society, 1995, 295.

3 G. Max Wingo, *Philosophies of Education: An Introduction* (Lexington, Mass.: D.C. Heath and Company, 1974), 301.

4 Sidney Hook, *From Hegel To Marx* (Ann Arbor: The University of Michigan Press, 1950), 281.

5 Wingo, *Philosophies of Education: An Introduction*, 229.

6 John Dewey, *Human Nature and Conduct* (New York: Random House, 1930), 167–68.

7 For an in-depth analysis of these ideas, see Richard A. Brosio, *The Relationship of Dewey's Pedagogy to His Concept of Community*, University of Michigan Social Foundations of Education Series, no. 4 (Ann Arbor, Mich.: Malloy Lithoprinting, Inc., 1972), chapter one, "John Dewey's Place in the Western Tradition of Concern for Community."

8 Crane Brinton et al., *A History of Civilization, Volume II: 1715 to the Present* (Englewood Cliffs, N.J.: Prentice-Hall, Inc., 1955), 49.

9 John Dewey, *Theory of the Moral Life* (New York: Holt, Rinehart and Winston, 1908), 29.

10 For an analysis of more recent attempts to control people in this society and elsewhere, see, Richard A. Brosio, *A Radical Democratic Critique of Capitalist Education* (New York: Peter Lang Publishing, Inc., 1994), chapter six, "The Consequences of the Capitalist Imperative on Everyday Life," and chapter seven, "Capitalism's Mediated Influence Within School Sites: Correspondence Theory and Empirical Description."

11 Walter Lippmann wrote a brilliant and still timely analysis of the historical breakdown of certainty in the West, Part I, see "The Dissolution of the Ancestral Order," in *A Preface to Morals* (Boston: Beacon Press, 1929). The philosopher of education Maxine Greene provided a compelling essay on the necessity for alternatives to choose from if choice and, especially moral choice are to be bona fide and meaningful. She spoke of the need to be "wide-awake" in order to realize that there are choices, as difficult as that may be. One must act on the decisions made. Maxine Green, "Wide-Awakeness and the Moral Life," in *Exploring Education: An Introduction to the Foundations of Education*, eds. Alan R. Sadovnik,

Peter W. Cookson, Jr., and Susan F. Semel (Boston: Allyn and Bacon, 1994), 221–28.

12   Dewey, *Theory of the Moral Life*, 78.

13   Dewey, *Human Nature and Conduct*, 11–12.

14   Dewey, *Theory of the Moral Life*, 8.

15   Wingo, *Philosophies of Education: An Introduction*, 186.

16   Ibid., 207–08. Wingo's chapter seven, "American Pragmatism and the Liberal Protest," is an excellent source for understanding the interplay between American pragmatist philosophy and the great educational and social protest against the dominant triad of essentialism, idealism, and conservatism.

17   John Dewey, *The Child and the Curriculum* (Chicago: The University of Chicago Press, 1900), 11.

18   Brosio, *The Relationship of Dewey's Pedagogy To His Concept of Community*, 30.

19   John Dewey, *Logic, The Theory of Inquiry* (New York: Henry-Holt and Co., 1938), 345.

20   For an interesting account of caring and community by a philosopher of education who understands and values Dewey's work, see "The Importance of Relationships and Community: Self-Transcendence, Growth, and Creative Bestowal of Value," in Jim Garrison, *Dewey and Eros: Wisdom and Desire in the Art of Teaching* (New York and London: Teachers College Press, 1997), 39–42. Garrison wrote the following on p. 60, "[Jane] Addams and Dewey were both committed to an organic holism that respected differences without allowing relationships to degenerate into alienating fragmentation or discord." I bring this to the readers' attention to make clear that what I admire about Dewey's concept of community cannot be equated with current demands for more *unum* and less *pluribus* in the United States. For example, see, Arthur M. Schlesinger, Jr., *The Disuniting of America: Reflections on a Multicultural Society* (New York and London: W.W. Norton & Company, 1992), passim.

21   Dewey, *Theory of the Moral Life*, 141. For a profound, compelling, and enlightening analysis of education, community, and civic virtue—one that is congruent in many ways with Dewey's concept of community and requisite morality and virtue—see, John I. Goodlad, *In Praise of Education* (New York and London: Teachers College Press, 1997), chapter three.

22   Joseph Ratner, ed., *Intelligence in the Modern World: John Dewey's Philosophy* (New York: The Modern Library, 1939), 401.

23   Katherine Camp Mayhew and Anna Camp Edwards, *The Dewey School: The Laboratory School of the University of Chicago 1896–1903* (New York: Atherton Press, 1936), passim. This book is a classic description written by the sisters

Camp, who were teachers at this famous school. In his introduction to the book, Dewey gives the work his official stamp of approval. For another account of the school, especially for the period after Dewey and his wife left in 1904, see, Ida B. DePencier, *The History of the Laboratory Schools: The University of Chicago 1896–1965* (Chicago: Quadrangle Books, 1967), passim. See also, Wingo, *Philosophies of Education: An Introduction*, 154–66, for an informative picture of the Dewey School.

24   Wingo, *Philosophies of Education: An Introduction*, 161.

25   John Dewey, *Experience and Nature* (New York: W. W. Norton & Co., Inc., 1928), 167.

26   Mayhew and Edwards, *The Dewey School*, 5.

27   Sidney Hook, *John Dewey, An Intellectual Portrait* (New York: The John Day Co., 1939), 154.

28   Salvatore D'Urso, "An Evaluation of Dewey's 'Social Intelligence,'" *Educational Theory* 28, no. 2 (Spring 1978): 129.

29   Wingo, *Philosophies of Education: An Introduction*, 148–49.

30   Lawrence A. Cremin, *The Transformation of the School: Progressivism in American Education, 1876–1957* (New York: Vintage Books, 1961), viii.

31   The following sources provide more critical views of liberalism/progressivism. Clarence J. Karier, "Liberal Ideology and the Quest for Orderly Change," in *Roots of Crisis: American Education in the Twentieth Century*, eds. Clarence J. Karier, et al. (Chicago: Rand McNally & Company, 1973), 84–107; Samuel Bowles and Herbert Gintis, *Schooling in Capitalist America* (New York: Basic Books, Inc., Publishers, 1976), passim; Frank Margonis, "John Dewey: Organic Intellectual of the Middle Class?" *Philosophy of Education 1994* (Urbana, IL: Philosophy of Education Society, 1995), 302–05; and David T. Sehr, *Education for Public Democracy* (Albany: State University of New York Press, 1997), especially chapters two, "Ideological Roots of Privatized and Public Democracy" and three, "Privatized Democracy."

32   Cremin, *The Transformation of the School:*, ix.

33   John J. McDermott, ed., introduction, and commentary, *The Philosophy of John Dewey, Vol. II, The Lived Experience* (New York: G.P. Putnam's Sons, 1973), 442–43.

34   John Dewey, *My Pedagogic Creed* (first published by E.L. Kellogg & Co., 1897), this passage is from its appearance in McDermott, *The Philosophy of John Dewey*, 445.

35   Ibid., 452.

36   Ibid.

37   Ibid., 453.

38   Wingo, *Philosophies of Education: An Introduction*, 231.

39   Ibid., 230.

40   Ibid., 191.

41   For an analysis of the arguments concerning alleged indoctrination of students, see, Daniel Tanner, *Crusade for Democracy: Progressive Education at the Cross-roads* (Albany: State University of New York Press, 1991), chapter 5, pp. 35–36, 38, and 48.

42   Richard A. Brosio, "The Legacy of Counts: Contemporary Motivational Theory in Education and the Power of the Status Quo," *Midwest Philosophy of Education Proceedings 1989–1990*, ed. David B. Annis (Midwest Philosophy of Education Society, 1991), 37.

43   Cremin, *Transformation of the School*, 225.

44   See, Sadovnik, et al., *Exploring Education: An Introduction to the Foundations of Education*, chapter 7 on curriculum and pedagogy. See pp. 304–09 for a discussion of the developmentalist and social melioristic curricula in progressivism.

45   Alan C. Ornstein and Daniel U. Levine, *Foundations of Education*, 5th ed. (Boston: Houghton Mifflin Company, 1993), 475. For a neo-reconstructionist analysis of involving students in programs for social change, see James W. Fraser, *Reading, Writing, and Justice: School Reform as If Democracy Matters* (Albany: State University of New York Press, 1997), 127–28, "Children as Allies and Agents for Change."

46   Angela Raffel, "In Praise of Educational Reconstruction," *Introducing Educational Reconstruction: The Philosophy and Practice of Transforming Society Through Education*, Susan Roberts and Darroll Bussler, eds., (San Francisco: Caddo Gap Press, 1997), 7.

47   Ibid., 9. Because the Society for Educational Reconstruction was founded by Theodore Brameld's students in 1969, it is fitting to cite this teacher-scholar's *Toward a Reconstructed Philosophy of Education* (New York: Dryden Press, 1956). Brameld's publications are numerous; one is able to understand the breadth, depth, and nuances of his arguments,

48   See, Richard A. Brosio, "Teaching and Learning for Democratic Empowerment: A Critical Evaluation," *Educational Theory* 40, no. 1 (Winter 1990): especially pp. 79–81.

49   Eric Hobsbawm, *The Age of Extremes: A History of the World, 1914–1991* (New York: Vintage Books, 1994), 526–27.

50   For an informative and disturbing analysis of the exploitation and misuse of both physical and social sciences by the national security State in Washington D.C. and its corporate allies during the Cold War, see Noam Chomsky et al., *The Cold War and the University: Toward An Intellectual History of the Postwar Years*

(New York: The New Press, 1997). John Marciano's *Civic Illiteracy and Education: The Battle for the Hearts and Minds of American Youth* (New York: Peter Lang Publishing, Inc., 1997) provides a complementary analysis and exposure of how the national security State has been represented in the media and the schools. Marciano's convincing analysis makes clear how academicians, including scientists, have been used to forward the mostly unacknowledged and not well-known agenda of the ruling elites in the United States. His impressive knowledge of schools makes this book especially relevant to those interested in education. The author's methods of inquiry represent critical theory and "impolite" scientific method at their barefisted best.

51   Richard A. Brosio, "Book Review of Paringer's, *John Dewey and the Paradox of Liberal Reform*," *History of Education Quarterly* 31, no. 3 (Fall 1991): 427.

52   Brosio, "Dewey As the Schoolmaster for Marx's Radical Democracy," 295–98. See also, Frank Margonis, "The Organic Intellectual of the Middle Class?", which is the official response to my "Dewey As Schoolmaster." Margonis's work can be found on pp. 302–05, immediately following my paper.

53   Robert B. Westbrook, *John Dewey and American Democracy* (Ithaca and London: Cornell University Pres, 1991), 179.

54   Dewey, *Human Nature and Conduct*, 167–68.

55   Richard J. Bernstein, *Praxis and Action: Contemporary Philosophies of Human Activity* (Philadelphia: University of Pennsylvania Press, 1979), 314.

Chapter Five

Existentialist Contingency, We May Just Be On Our Own— And Camus's Solidarity

Introduction

In reference to Ernest Hemingway's short story, "A Clean, Well-Lighted Place,"[1] a review of one of Kurt Vonnegut's books included the following comparison: The world is not that sort of place, not so clean or well-lighted. Rather it is messy and most of us keep on going during and after being overcome by dirt and darkness. The Italian writer Alberto Moravia is reputed to have said: Stabilized despair is intellectual lucidity without any consolation. Walter Kaufmann wrote that "all man's [sic] alibis are unacceptable: no gods are responsible for his condition; no original sin; no heredity and no environment . . . no father, no mother; no wrong-headed education . . . no teacher; not even an impulse or a disposition, a complex or a childhood trauma. Man is free; but his freedom does not look like the glorious liberty of the Enlightenment; it is no longer the gift of God. Once again, man stands alone in the universe, responsible for his condition, likely to remain in a lowly state, but free to reach above the stars."[2] It is necessary to assert that the preceding quote as well as existentialist philosophy are not to be confused with the freedom articulated by supporters of capitalism or the "free market." Some conservatives and others have historically sought to equate human freedom with economic opportunity and success. This is not true of the existentialists.

William Barrett played an important role in introducing and explaining European existentialist thought to audiences in the United States after 1945. The following passage from Barrett's writings is intended to help the reader understand some relationships between the last chapter and this one.

The genial inspiration that lies behind . . . [Dewey's] philosophy is the belief that in all departments of human experience things do not fall from heaven but grow up out of the earth. Thinking itself is only the halting and fumbling effort of a thoroughly biological creature to cope with his [sic] environment. The image of man as an earth-bound and time-bound creature permeates Dewey's writings . . . up to a point. Beyond this point he moves in a direction that is the very opposite of existentialism. What Dewey never calls into question is the thing he labels Intelligence, which in his last writings came to mean simply Scientific Method. Dewey places the human person securely within his biological and social context, but he never goes past this context into that deepest center of the human person where fear and trembling start. . . . Given Dewey's emphasis upon the biological and sociological contexts as ultimate . . . together with his interpretation of human thought as basically an effort to transform the environment, we end with . . . man as essentially *homo faber*, the technological animal. This belief in technique is . . . a supreme article of the American faith. Dewey grew up in a period in which America was still wrestling with its frontier, and the mood of his writings is unshaken optimism at the expansion of our technical mastery over nature. Ultimately, the difference between Dewey and the existentialists is the difference between America and Europe. The philosopher cannot seriously put to himself questions that his civilization has not lived.[3]

Barrett also claims that Marx and the Marxists have a secular religious faith in history and its developmental progress. Barrett charges Marxism with failing to develop philosophical categories for "unique facts of human personality." Although there is truth in Barrett's accusation, Marx situated human beings in the earthiest contexts of our lived experiences. Jean-Paul Sartre, Herbert Marcuse, et al. have recognized Marx's explicit view of human nature. Marcuse and other members of the Frankfurt School (see chapter three) attempted to develop a Marxist concept of human beings and our personalities. Eric Fromm's, *Marx's Concept of Man* (1961) is one of the best examples of this attempt. Fromm focused on the young Marx's philosophical work, rather than the latter's economic writings. Sartre's specific attempt to integrate Marx's social theory with existentialist individualism met with mixed reviews.[4]

Existentialism can be defined as a view that holds that human beings develop our essences as we make decisions throughout life. Existentialists argue that *existence precedes essence,* i.e., that there is no stamped-out or cookie-cutter essence of humanness; what our essence is to be is constructed by sentient and intellectual men, women, and children as we seek to live and make sense of our lives. Existentialists stress human responsibility for constructing our own natures; personal freedom, decision-making, and commitment are characteristic of authentic and wide-awake lives.[5] Many existentialists claimed that we are condemned to be free! This sense of freedom has little to do with the kind of political, economic, and personal freedoms celebrated by enthusiasts and cheerleaders for particular political and economic systems. Existentialists speak of human *contingency*. This means that *you, I,* and *we* are dependent for our existence on something that is uncertain. Contingency refers also to chance, without known cause, and even being accidental. This is radically different from believing that human beings are created in the image and likeness of a benevolent, intervening, and personally interested deity. Another meaning of contingency is that something, or someone, is neither logically necessary nor logically impossible, therefore necessitating sensory and intellectual observation and study in order to portray their existence. The comfort expressed by the old adage, the deity is in heaven and all is right with the world, is of no comfort to secular existentialists. Existentialists are among those thinkers who believe it has been futile to seek certainty as an alleged compass serving to guide human action. Neither Dewey's scientific method nor the Marxist claim to have understood certain historical laws of motion is accepted by existentialists. Many of them think that these maneuvers are a continuation of the older quest for certainty, albeit by somewhat different means. Secular existentialists have faced up to the distinct possibility that the world we inhabit has no meaning except for what human beings have constructed.

Albert Camus (1913–1960), who won the Nobel Prize for literature in 1957, articulated well some of the central existentialist insights in an essay called "The Myth of Sisyphus." A brief presentation of this essay, which is based on a Greek legend, follows: Sisyphus was punished by the gods by being forced to roll a huge stone up a hill. It would always roll back down the hill, necessitating endless labor to roll it up once more. He was condemned to labor, but also to accomplishing nothing. In his essay, Camus is particularly interested in Sisyphus at the moment he looks at the stone rolling downward. The essay portrays the laborer as walking with a heavy measured step, with his face looking as if it were becoming stonelike. However, Camus's reading of the myth views Sisyphus as being stronger than his condition and seeming fate. The myth is tragic because the tortured laborer is conscious of his condition! Camus wrote: "Sisyphus . . . powerless and rebellious, knows the whole extent of his wretched condition; it is what he thinks of during his descent. The lucidity that . . . constitute[s] his torture at the same time crowns his victory. There is no fate that cannot be surmounted by scorn."[6]

Camus argued that happiness and the absurd are both part of the human condition; they may be inseparable. The human condition is characterized by a wild, limited, but not yet finished universe, a place where our fate is a human matter to be settled among ourselves. The stone need not turn Sisyphus into a thing. His fate is to be self-determined, in a terrible situation. When Sisyphus pivoted and looked down on the stone, he represented the human opportunity to look over our lives, that series of seemingly unrelated actions which become our fate as we initiate and/or react to these activities. Camus gave us a person who, like the tragic Oedipus, concluded that all is well. "This universe henceforth without a master seems to him neither sterile nor futile. . . . The struggle itself toward the heights is enough to fill a . . . [person's] heart. One must imagine Sisyphus happy."[7] Camus related Sisyphus's toil to the workers of his time who labored at monotonous tasks, who began to understand the exploitation and absurdity of their condition, and finally became class conscious about their condition. Marx's workers/proletariat would not be happy with existential freedom alone; their historical task was to change the conditions of their labor and lives.

Camus's countryman, Blaise Pascal (1623–1662), provided an early modern preview of existentialist thought which did not come into its own until the nineteenth century. The comparative popularization of its central insights awaited the terrible slaughter of World War I (1914–1918) and its aftermath. In his *Pensées* (published thoughts), Pascal presented some of the following insights and worries. He began by raising the question of what human beings amount to and/or mean when viewed in the context of the infinite. He saw our human beingness as situated between the abysses of the infinite and nothingness. We are nothing in comparison to the infinite, and all in comparison to nothing, i.e., a midpoint between everything and nothing. Pascal's references to the infinite can be read as human conceptions of deities and/or unchanging and universally applicable forms. Nothingness can be interpreted as nonlife, thingness, and/or death. Pascal argued that we are unable to know about the extremes of the infinite and nothingness. He held that our attempt to comprehend these extremes can be based only on the so-called irrational and/or faith. He "asserted that the belief in God is a wager on which one can lose nothing."[8] We are described by Pascal as sailing in a vast ocean, drifting without a reliable compass. Whenever we think we have secured a solid position on which to anchor ourselves, it seems to vanish. Still, we yearn for solid ground, although we must know it is not attainable.

Pascal admitted that the eternal silence of infinite spaces frightened him. Perhaps some readers will be surprised at this admission from a seventeenth-century person. Pascal throws a small lifesaving tool to us. A human being "is but a reed, the most feeble thing in nature; but . . . [we] are thinking reed[s]. The entire universe need not arm itself to crush . . . [us]. . . . But, if the universe were to crush him [sic], man would still be more noble than that which killed him, because he knows that he dies and the advantage which the universe has over him; the universe knows nothing of this. All our dignity consists, then, in thought. By it we must elevate ourselves. . . . Let us endeavor . . . to think well; this is the principle of morality."[9] Both Deweyan pragmatists and Marxist historical materialists would insist that thought can and must be translated into action which should be aimed at making our concrete position better than it naturally is. They would argue that being aware through thinking well leaves us feeling inadequate with a spectator theory of epistemology, rather than a constructivist one—which holds that we change what we study and ourselves through inquiry.

Camus was in part a political activist, e.g., in the French Resistance during the Nazi occupation and on behalf of Algerian Muslims in their struggle for justice against French colonialism in that country. He did not favor Algerian independence from France because he was part of the French population that had settled in Algeria. The following presentations from his book, *The Rebel*, allows the reader to see possibilities for action beyond endeavoring to think well. According to Camus, we can master and repair a great many things in life that need such treatment. We can and must rectify that which needs such action. However, even after we have acted, good people will still suffer and die. In spite of our greatest ameliorative efforts we can only "diminish arithmetically the sufferings of the world."[10] His rebel learned to live and die as a human being, i.e., not as a self-appointed and false deity. For Camus, the frightened human attempt to find certainty has not been conducted only by religionists and idealist philosophers but by secular revolutionaries who have tried to elevate their causes to semidivine status. Camus denied that we can find substitute deities within the realm of intelligent thought, method or historical "laws." In his view, justice is not inherent in the universe or in our world. The human attempt to find, declare, and enforce arbitrary conceptions of justice and certainty has led to tyranny and *injustice*. He insisted that we are on our own. In "Letter to a German Friend," he wrote:

I . . . choose justice in order to remain faithful to the world. I continue to believe that this world has no ultimate meaning. But I know that something in it has a meaning and that is man [and woman], because he is the only creature to insist on having one. This world has at least the truth of man, and our task is to provide its justification against fate itself. And it has no justification but . . .[human beings];

hence . . . [we] must be saved if we want to save the idea . . . of life. With your [his fictitious pen pal] scornful smile you will ask me: what do you mean by saving man. And . . . I shout to you that I mean not mutilating him and . . . giving a chance to the justice that . . . [we] alone can conceive.[11]

In chapter four, Dewey perceived a universe in which we must make ourselves at home. He saw the need for the democratic use of a broadly conceived and used scientific method in order to have human-made order prevail over chaos. He asserted that events do not possess intrinsic meaning apart from human cognition and our naming these events; we shall continue naming and making sense of these events as long as we are human. The Dewey just presented is at least a cousin to some existentialist thinkers. The Marx who is presented next is also a family member.

Marx paints a societal picture at the end of the *Economic and Philosophical Manuscripts of 1844* which consists of true and ultimate human freedom. Sympathetic critics have called it a society of artists who create and work together. . . . [People] would find freedom and happiness in work. . . . There would be no rules imposed from outside the work process. . . . Marx's position is that "art cannot be created by plans imposed from outside; it knows no authorities and no discipline except . . . [that of] art itself. This discipline and authority every artist accepts freely and consciously; it is this . . . that makes him [her] an artist. What is true of art, Marx believed, is true of all free, productive labor. This vision . . . remained with Marx all of his life."[12]

How can a person who is a teacher and/or preparing to become a professional teacher find intellectual support for analysis, critique, necessary iconoclasm, reconstruction and democratic renewal from the confluence of Marxist, Deweyan, and existentialist thought? Section I presents an interpretation of existentialist thought that can contribute to the scaffolding and construction necessary for democratic empowerment. This includes discussion of how the root principle of human freedom can lead to the possibility for solidaristic, progressive social action. The second section continues the thesis but pushes it to the contributions made by the star player, Albert Camus. Section III offers an analysis of some possibilities for education that is derived from existentialist assumptions; it presents ideas about complementary and perhaps necessary education ideas if one is to be an existentialist educator.

Suggested Task for the Reader
   a. Describe how and why Dewey and the existentialists share certain views. Explain how they differ with regard to what can and/or must be done after having admitted that certainty cannot be achieved by human beings.

b. Speak to the existentialist critique of pragmatist philosophers' reliance on the "scientific method." It will be helpful to read further in this chapter before addressing (b).

I

William Spanos claimed that the beginnings of existentialist thought are found in the early history of Western Civilization. He argued that the existentialist "attitude" was especially relevant in the modern period. It is best to read Spanos's work:

> In the past—as recently as Soren Kierkegaard's day [Danish philosopher and theologian, 1813–1855]—the existentialist philosopher or artist was an isolated voice asserting the precariousness of human life . . .. As long as the community believed . . . in the existence of a God who offered the reward of eternity as compensation for the suffering . . . of temporal life, his warning went more or less unheard and the existential attitude . . . remained marginal. In the middle of the nineteenth century, however, after a long period of secularization, God—at least the traditional image of God—expired and man [sic] was left naked to confront in T.S. Eliot's [British poet and critic, born in the United States, 1888–1965] great existentialist metaphor, "a heap of broken images." The proclamation by [Friedrich] Nietzsche's [German philosopher, 1844–1900] madman of the death of God was the annunciation of the age of anxiety. After this, philosophers could no longer spin verbal webs . . . without . . . confronting the reality of Nothingness; nor . . . could artists project rational microcosms without confronting the irrational macrocosm.[13]

Spanos believed that twentieth-century humanist and religious thought and art could best be understood as an encounter with the possibility of Nothingness as well as an effort to overcome this threat to human life and meaning.

Existentialist thought has been touched on in the introduction to this chapter but it is necessary to go further in order to see how this "attitude" can be interpreted as relevant and/or useful to the democratic project presented in this book. Because existentialism is not really an organized or agreed upon systematic body of thought, it cannot be described easily. However, existentialists are interested in a philosophy of existence, rather than one of *essences*. This means that existentialists seek to deal with human life in all its plenitude and complex relationships to the world. Spanos believed that existentialist thought can be imperfectly organized around two possible responses facing us in the universe from which the deities have seemingly retired. The first is to seek the comfort that allegedly derives from conforming to institutionalized, collectivized, and increasingly technologized life, the second and preferred response is to maintain our uniqueness and authenticity in the face of the confrontation with the possibility of Nothingness. The second response includes resistance to the pressure to conform. Many existentialist thinkers and artists view the lonely individual as seeking comfort and orderliness that membership in mass technological and consumer society seemingly promises. This quest or obsession is best explained as being driven by the deconstruction of the historical religious and philosophical cosmologies that offered real or hoped-for security. Because the "heap of broken images" has not been reconstructed, modern men and women have sought security in a world of things which have been brought to (some of) us via the industrial revolutions, under the aegis of capitalism. The price has been high. The existentialists see a loss of freedom in the current human condition in which all too many worship surrogate deities, e.g., mammon. The modern obsession with material goods is seen as part of a desperate attempt to escape from the dreadful burden of freedom and necessity to choose in a world where the old putative certainties have disappeared. The putative choices in the global, capitalist, shopping malls, and more recently the Internet, do not impress existentialists as authentic choices. Existentialists have criticized the quest for materialistic utopias, whether capitalist or communist. They have realized that an abundance of material possessions allow many people to feel protected from the daunting and inescapable need to make sense of our lives—and to do this against the possibility that there is no preordained meaning in our worlds.

The existentialists would have us reject the behavioral sciences' view of human beings that seeks to describe us as just another object in a universe in which all living creatures, as well as inanimate phenomena, are supposedly governed by the same natural laws. Instead, we are encouraged to see ourselves as minorities in a universe governed by these deterministic laws. We are to assert life and meaning against the inhuman thingness of the universe. In this assertion we become "absurd" men and women. (Absurd means contrary to reputed reason and common sense.) It is helpful to know that the prefix "ab" means away from; "surd" means not capable of being expressed in rational numbers. Human beings are unique in not being able to be successfully described and measured in the same way as other beings and things. Pierre Teilhard de Chardin's (French Jesuit, geologist, paleontologist, and cosmological visionary, 1881–1955) argued that a human being is "a phenomenon to be described and analyzed like other phenomenon . . . [as] proper subjects for scientific study."[14] The existentialists take issue with this classification. The meaning of *existence precedes essence* is that human beings, as opposed to things, *become* rather than merely *are*. In other words, we do not "have a universal and thus permanent *nature*, as for example, a stone has (its 'stoneness'). Unlike a stone . . . [we] cannot be abstracted and quantified, i.e., measured, classified, and placed in a system that can accurately predict . . . [our] behavior. . . . Put positively, 'existence' refers to . . . [our unavoidable and burdensome freedom], that unlike objects which merely *are* and thus at the mercy of their pre-established essence, man [woman] alone is capable of choosing . . . and determining his own essence."[15]

Consider further how the word "authentic" relates to what has been presented. For existentialists, life is a journey characterized by the need to be aware of the mystery of our very existence; at the same time, there is an insistence that we create meaning for ourselves. Although it is not convincing to some critics, most existentialists argue that the mysterious journey that features the need for human-created meaning also requires taking responsibility for our actions. The authentic person lives with the constant awareness that s/he must be accountable despite the absence of stone tablets on which rules are chiseled. This view of life demands that we are awake, aware, alert, and ready to act, even though there are no pregame coach-called plays. Ernst Breisach wrote that for existentialists, life is a drama and struggle rather than a smooth existence; we are condemned to be free and responsible for how we conduct ourselves. The authentic person takes on this burden seeking to interpret freedom as an exercise in responsibility.

We have considered the existentialist concern with our contingency, i.e., the dependent nature and fragility of human life. Existentialists argue that the inescapable knowledge of our eventual deaths can and should cause us to think more deeply about life, its meaning, and how we can live it more humanely and responsibly. Breisach argued, "secular and religious existentialists alike have insisted on contingency as the crucial mark of . . .[human] life. It alone initiates man's [sic] wondering about the meaning of life, projects him out of superficial comfort, and is the major challenge to [leading] an authentic life."[16]

Closely linked to contingency is the disposition called anxiety. This is not the anxiety of which popular psychology speaks; it has nothing to do with maladjustment or inability to conform to societal established norms. The existentialist views popular definitions of anxiety as attributable to inauthentic living. For both secular and religious existentialists, anxiety derives from one's increasing and authentic awareness of the threat posed by nothingness. "Always nothingness is experienced in the contingency of man's [sic] life and with it the awesome certainty of the 'not to be,' an experience . . . at the core of man's life. Nothingness taken in this sense becomes the great positive force in . . . [our lives] through challenges to live authentically. . . . [Therefore,] anxiety is the call to become oneself rather than the signal for . . . conformity."[17]

The term "despair" is linked to the words we have been analyzing in our attempt to understand what existentialist authenticity means. If we are submerged in a "whirlpool of freedom" from which we must make responsible decisions on our own, then there exists the tendency to despair. Remember, as authenticity develops, we are less likely to depend on the comforting feeling made possible by false absolutes, supposedly universal systems, meretricious satisfactions in the shopping mall, daily routines, etc. Breisach articulated human reactions to despair as follows:

> In despair the certainty of any haven of safety turns out to be illusory. Existential despair is [the] becoming aware of one's being alone in those matters which count most. . . . . No other . . . [person] and no . . . institution can lift the burden of responsibility. . . . Nor does authentic existence . . . obliterate this whirlpool of freedom. . . . No smooth transition leads from existential despair to authentic existence. . . . Ever since Kierkegaard, existentialists have spoken of the leap into authentic existence. The leap is executed in a typical situation of human decision; that is, the leap itself and what it leads to never loses the character of being a great risk.[18]

The struggle to live authentically is lifelong because despair and authenticity are never far from one another. The authentic person endeavors to live creatively and responsibly despite the ultimate futility of her/his condition. The human journey is endless but one must continue to push forward—without guarantees or consolations.

Breisach spoke to accusations that existentialism is too pessimistic or an adolescent disorder. Breisach argued that lack of certainty, the need to struggle ethically for meaning, and eventual death need not cause pessimism. Life for Sisyphus and others is worth living because of its intense poignancy; small joys; temporarily holding back the goblins from our still fragile, clean well-lighted places; comradeship; clear thinking; and good conscience as a result of fighting alone or in solidarity for what I/we think is just—or at least more just. Camus, who claimed he was not an existentialist, justified his membership in the French Resistance against the Nazi Occupation (1940–1944) as fighting for a half-truth against a total lie.[19] Camus's use of the term half-truth referred to his criticism of the French government, its corporate and other elites, for not living up to the country's humanistic and inclusive rhetoric. Camus said, as he accepted the Nobel Prize for Literature (1957):

The writer's role is . . . at the service of those who suffer. . . . The silence of an unknown prisoner . . . is enough to draw the writer out of his exile. . . . Whatever our personal weaknesses may be, the nobility of our craft will always be rooted in two commitments . . . [:] the refusal to lie about what one knows and the resistance to oppression. . . . Each generation doubtless feels called upon to reform the world. Mine knows that it will not reform it, but its task is perhaps even greater. It consists in preventing the world from destroying itself. Heir to a corrupt history, in which [we find] . . . fallen revolutions, technologies gone mad, dead gods, and worn-out ideologies, where mediocre powers can destroy all yet no longer know how to convince, where intelligence has debased itself to become the servant of hatred and oppression, this generation starting from its own negations has had to re-establish both within and without, a little of that which constitutes the dignity of life and death. . . . It is not certain that this generation will . . . accomplish this immense task.[20]

This immense task can be started with the assistance of guidelines (there are not many) that can empower us to vaguely see the overall direction. There is no fully developed road map.

The root concept of existentialism is human freedom; this freedom is grounded in our contingency, most dramatically exemplified by our ultimate death. We are left naked and alone to face in fear and trembling the great void. Shakespeare's King Lear said that we can and must decide whether to make something out of nothing. Sartre's pronouncement that we are condemned to be free can be interpreted as an attempt to activate genuine awareness of our situation—but this realization can also activate "concern." This moment of concern is the place or time that separates the secular from the religious existentialist. According to Spanos, the secular/agnostic/atheistic existentialist's rational alternative to physical or spiritual suicide is to emulate Sisyphus, as he consciously, if agonizingly, does his work. Sisyphus takes comfort and pride in an assertion of rebellious, if precarious, selfhood in the face of the human predicament. Theologian Paul Tillich (1886–1965) called the Sisyphisian stance "the courage of despair." The religious or theistic existentialist follows another path, a leap of faith. This is not a rejection of the concrete world; it is the wager which we have learned earlier, one that the absent deity reconciles us with this worldly existence "and thus infuses meaning into an apparently chaotic and fragmented temporal world."[21] Spanos argued that for the religious existentialists there are neither possibilities for purely rational knowledge about how the world is, nor the specific characteristics of the divine—let alone whether or not things will turn out well for us. The struggle for meaning and/or salvation must still be waged in the darkness of this world. This position is a jumping-off place for liberation theology (section III of chapter 6).

The existentialist portrayal of our human condition could be made less dreary through the realization that it is a Technicolor life and we live among many other human beings; some of them are very attractive, good, and capable of assisting us. Furthermore, we can and do return the favor frequently. Sisyphus may also have been able to experience assistance from fellow workers. Perhaps he can even gather stones and build a place in which to rest, think, form a plan (with others), and oppose those responsible for the conditions of labor. Holding hands around the alleged abyss may be preferable to the solo leap of faith recommended by Kierkegaard! I will pursue the discussion about the possibility for existentialists to engage in solidaristic, progressive social action after considering the American philosopher Abraham Kaplan's assessment of existentialism.

Kaplan, who admired American pragmatist philosophy, is critical of existentialism for a variety of reasons. He admired existentialists for emphasizing problems and possibilities that are central to the human condition. Consider one important criticism of existentialism first. Kaplan claimed that existentialism does not

> express the philosophy of a mature personality. It seems to articulate, rather, the travail of childhood and adolescence in learning the facts of life—what we then felt to be bitter truths, but what maturity accepts without inner torment as simple matters of fact. . . . Eventually the pathos of adolescence must give way to the tragic sense of life—and to the comic spirit as well—so that, like the great Greek realists, we can see life steadily and see it whole. At best, existentialism teaches only how to be good losers. But even that is a great deal, and makes it deserving of careful attention. A philosophy which . . . struggles for a mature acceptance of defeat [the world is not made with us in mind, meaning must be created, and still death is inevitable] . . . has something to say to everyone.[22]

Kaplan's view of pragmatist philosophy was that it admits that the question of the meaning of life has no answer; this inability will continue as long as human life continues. The question for Kaplan and pragmatist philosophers "must be answered by each of us, not in terms of meanings already provided, but only in terms of meanings, which, with the deepest sensibilities and fullest exercise, we ourselves can provide."[23] Perhaps Kaplan thought that the pragmatists' best provision can be more easily lived with than is the case with existentialists, who see pragmatist-constructed order as inadequate solace.

Kaplan argued that existentialism speaks to those of us who fear that we inhabit a world we never had a hand in making, a place too vast and complex to understand adequately. Contemporary postmodernists share the same fear. Existentialists focus on human beings as central to their concerns and it gives them an advantage over many other philosophers who seem to have pushed man and woman to the periphery—focusing instead on systems, scientifically described nature, behaviorism, etc. Existentialism represents philosophy as a way of life, rather than merely a dispassionate system of propositions. People want to know what kind of life to lead and on what to base their decisions. Existentialists speak and write about ideas which interest people. My own experiences as a secondary school and college teacher have taught me that students are intellectually/passionately interested in the ideas of existentialist thinkers. Some graduate students in my collegiate philosophy of education classes were so affected by our analysis of existentialism that they were at first outwardly hostile to its suggestion that all too many religions represented merely a human-created meaning system which could not survive serious scrutiny. Many of my high school philosophy students in the late 1960s were more open to and admiring of existentialism as a possible way of thinking about their lives during those turbulent times. The existentialist emphasis on *humans becoming what we previously were not* has been received and appreciated by many students as they seek to find a ray of light in a society and world that seem so different from how they wished it were. This was especially the case in the 1960s and 1970s when various psychologists argued that we could overcome certain psychological disorders which were believed to be deeply embedded in conditions described by existentialists. Those prominent psychologists include: Carl Rogers, Fritz Pearls, Paul Goodman, Eric Fromm, Rollo May, Abraham Maslow, and Viktor Frankl.[24]

As we move toward deciding whether or not it is possible for existentialists to act solidaristically and effectively in order to make socioeconomic and political life better, consider the following from Kaplan's analysis of existentialism. Existentialists insist that our most human attribute is being able to choose, Kaplan believed. We are most human while choosing. He understood well that for existentialists the choices are not between a predetermined, clear-cut good and/or evil. "What makes us human is that life has meaning for us . . . that we determine for ourselves a perspective on life in which there is . . . a difference between good and evil. . . . The meaning of life lies in the values which we can find in it, and values are the product of choice."[25] Choosing from another's inventions and/or priorities, e.g., various types of superficially different automobiles, would not represent authentic existentialist choice. The same would apply when having to select from candidates whose political positions are all distasteful to the voter. Existentialists deny that authentic choice represents choosing values that are already provided by some authority figure, e.g., a deity, the State, or our ancestors; it is *we who create values ourselves, not just things that belong to predetermined (by others) value-categories.* Kaplan articulated the situation: "Thus the existentialist moves from the concept of existence to the concept of choice, and from choice . . . to the concept of freedom. . . . In the existentialist conception it is not merely true that . . . [we] are free, as though this happened to be one ot . . . [our] attributes among others; man is freedom. Freedom comes as close to constituting the essence of man [woman] as his existence makes possible whatever a man may be, he is free to do something else if he chooses; but he is not free to choose to give up his freedom."[26]

We are prepared to consider further if human freedom can lead to solidaristic, progressive social action. Existentialists have argued that human freedom is inseparably connected to responsibility; in fact, the importance of choice goes beyond the act itself and includes *what* is chosen. Existentialists claim that we are responsible for more than what becomes of us; we are also responsible for what happens to others as a result of our choices. To strengthen the stretch from choice to responsibility for ourselves *and* others, when we choose we must do so *as if* we were acting for humanity itself. "Thus existentialists universalize individual choice after the manner of the Kantian categorical imperative: You must never will what you cannot consistently will should be willed by all other rational beings."[27] This imperative is based on universal assumptions, assumptions that existentialists usually criticize and denounce. I believe that existentialist philosophy does not provide adequate scaffolding for this claim to be made; more than a few existentialists have done just that—even if their intellectual underpinnings did not logically allow it. The German philosopher Karl Jaspers (1883–1969) assisted the existentialist attempt to connect choice to social commitment when he argued that a person cannot become human by her/himself. Jaspers believed that the only reliable "other" for the existentialist is one's fellow human. I am not convinced that existentialist premises can easily move us to Jaspers' conclusions. Kaplan did admit though that it is incorrect to equate existentialist freedom with irresponsibility. Neither existentialism nor psychoanalysis teaches us to do anything and/or everything we unreflectively feel. Pragmatists would note that existentialists do not provide a suggested method that could help us choose. They are obviously critical of this absence. Existentialists might respond that no method is possible for everyone when it comes to such complex issues such as human choice and responsibility. Existentialism, at its best, would have us recognize the complete list of our possibilities. Like Marx and Dewey, they realize that the past has affected our choices and us. This recognition forces some existentialists to take social and historical questions seriously.

Drawing from Breisach's work, we learn that because existentialism is concerned with the whole person, it is inevitable that ethical questions abound. Because of the existentialist emphasis on the uniqueness of each situation in our lives, there arises the necessity for human creativity with regard to value construction. The existentialist who struggles with ethical choices must and does decide with authentic awareness that s/he is committing to how her/his life will be, perhaps irreversibly. Such awareness is a brake on the possibility for recklessness. Existentialists believe that it is within the human *attempt* to choose well, act altruistically, favor social justice, and develop our intellectual/spiritual potentials on which we must be evaluated. Greek writer Nikos Kazantzakis (1883–1957) agrees. Focus is on the attempt/struggle, not the actual arriving at a safe haven.[28] Authentic existence is the central ideal of existentialism along with its emphasis on singularity, so the development of a social philosophy has been a challenge. Neither Kierkegaard nor Sartre is adequately helpful with regard to the challenge. Jaspers and the Jewish philosopher and theologian, Martin Buber (1878–1965), are helpful: the former speaks of communication between authentic existences as central to our necessary creation of values and ethics. We are not able to live authentically when isolated from each other. "Buber is even more outspoken when he equates authentic existence with his [wo]man of the dialogue between *I* and *Thou*. In the view of both philosophers the relation between two persons can go far beyond the mere 'staring' at each other suggested in Sartre's work. Relations are possible between [and among] human beings that do not impair the freedom and integrity of those communicating. Love and respect can underlie relations . . . [among us]."[29] For Buber, genuine community exists where and when people affirm each other as persons, rather than treating them like manipulable *It(s)*. Buber argued that human relations all too often slipped into *I-Its* categories. For example, marriages become impersonal and characterized by the couple's attempts to take from one another. The trouble with our capitalist economic system is that it is based on appropriating (taking from) rather than respectful *I-Thou* dialogue. All too often workers are seen by management as a decimal point in the cost of production, rather than as persons. Capitalists view human labor as a debit rather than a credit to the sum total of human creativeness and productivity.

I admire the existentialists who believe that society must be organized in a way that facilitates personal communication. Democracy is a favored context in which this occurs because it is characterized by social justice, respect for bona fide diversity—and caring. In keeping with the thesis in the first four chapters, I argue again that, because existentialists admit they do not and cannot gain epistemological certainty, it is unlikely that they would support authoritarian institutions and processes. If there can be no quest for certainty, individuals and groups must adopt a tentative position with regard to beliefs and actions. I maintain that bona fide democratic behavior is more likely to develop from this state of affairs, as compared to those in which people think they know what the truth is; making compromise less likely and proselytizing a real and sometimes dangerous possibility. Existentialism, at its best, provides the democratic person the political, economic, and social democracy s/he requires. The existentialist free person will affect democratic life to be lively and sometimes confrontational; democracy may require this aliveness and wide-awakeness rather than dull conformity.

Walter Odajnyk wrote of the existentialists' insistence that when we choose authentically we select that which is better, not only for ourselves but for everyone. Referring to Sartre's work, Odajnyk told us that to act ethically we must consider our actions within the context of all humanity. "'An authentic morality . . . will be one that takes into account the dual aspect of man's existence as an individual and as a social being.'"[30] An action is considered good if taken by an authentic person who respects the existential freedom of others. Simone de Beauvoir (1908–86), French playwright, novelist, and essayist as well as Sartre's companion and acknowledged ethical guide, argued that although all criteria and rules must come from inside each person as s/he faces particular situations, "anarchy is avoided because when man realizes that he is free he also realizes that his [sic] freedom is in many ways dependent upon the freedom of others for its existence."[31] Marxist Adam Schaff saw existentialist thought as helpful to the Marxist project because the former speaks to responsibility for one's action—an area neglected by Marx's discussion of social class and macroeconomic factors. Schaff argued that we must choose; we do so as influenced by social conditions, because we are an ensemble of social relations. One could picture Sartre saying: You Marxists have what we existentialists need, a practical theory of society; while we have what you require, a realistic theory of the individual. Let us unite. Schaff and other Marxists have not been convinced that the two philosophies can be so easily joined. It must be said that the attempt to reconcile human

agency/volition and structure is never easy. Philosophers have perenni-
ally wrestled with the tensions between freedom and determinism. Sartre's
alleged failure does not mean that a union of the individual and society, of
subjective and (somewhat) objective, is impossible.

Suggested Task for the Reader
Explain how existentialist concerns and fears may seem foreign and even
expressions of weakness to many people who live as part of affluent
societies in which they seem to be protected (or anesthetized) from the
dangers and possibilities of which existentialists speak.

II

I return to Camus in order to strengthen the bridge construction between
human freedom and responsible solidarity. Camus in his famous declaration said that he was not an existentialist, but I argue that he belongs in
this chapter. Simone de Beauvoir stated that life itself is neither good nor
evil. Camus said that life is good in itself and that it can be made better or
worse. "Camus is less interested in an anguished and absolute choice of
values . . . and more interested in harmonious and pleasant participation with others. . . . Sartre is . . . enamored of liberty, Camus of
Life. . . . For Camus 'no appeal to . . . ends, of the future, can justify
any attack on the present, on life which is an inalienable value.'"[32] For
Camus, our human lives are the primary and final value: No sacrificing of
us to hoped-for revolutionary and/or utopian futures—ones that are unlikely to materialize as planned. Germaine Brée wrote that his "primary
revolt was directed against what imprisons men [sic], barring them from a
full experience of the world in its sensory and emotional richness. His
sense of injustice was closely tied to his passionate concern that no human being [should] be wantonly cheated of his fragile chance to experience happiness as well as pain, and thereby be excluded from the full
knowledge of the glory of life itself."[33]

Camus was born and grew up in the Mediterranean port city of Algiers.
His celebration of the sun, sea, wind, and stars and his participation in
the Algerian outdoors was set against the fact of his realization that this
sensual enjoyment was fragile and fleeting. This juxtaposition of sunshine
and water against the inevitability of death was mediated by poverty that
characterized his childhood and youth. Even tuberculosis did not cause
Camus to surrender his celebration of the real pleasures of material life.
The danger of the lived human condition served to enhance his aware-

ness of and appreciation for life. His membership in the working class caused him to appreciate the dignity, seriousness, suffering, and joy of people who sought to make sense of and enjoy their hard lives. His solidarity with those who labored did not come from reading Marx; his connections were visceral.

> Poverty . . . was never a misfortune for me: it was radiant with light. Even my revolts were brilliant with sunshine. They were . . . revolts for everyone, so that every life might be lifted into that light. There is no certainty my heart was naturally disposed to this kind of love. But circumstances helped me. To correct a natural indifference, I was placed halfway between poverty and the sun. Poverty kept me from thinking all was well under the sun and in history; the sun taught me that history was not everything. I wanted to change lives, yes, but not the world. . . . This is how I got started on my . . . difficult career, innocently stepping onto the tightrope upon which I move painfully forward, unsure of reaching the end. . . . I became an artist . . . [because] there is no art without refusal or consent. . . . It was not poverty that got in my way: in Africa, the sun and the sea cost nothing. The obstacles lay rather in prejudices and stupidity . . . that I tried in vain to correct, until I realized that there is fatality in human natures. It seemed better to accept my pride and try to make use of it, rather than give myself . . . principles stronger than my character. . . . However, I can testify that amongst my many weaknesses I have never . . . [felt] envy. . . . I take no credit for so fortunate an immunity. I owe it to my family . . . who lacked almost everything and envied practically nothing. Merely by their silence, their reserve, their natural sober pride, my people, who did not even know how to read, taught me the most valuable and enduring lessons. . . . I can imagine the accusations of our grim philanthropists, if they should happen to read these lines. [They will claim] I want to pass the workers off as rich and the bourgeois as poor, to prolong the happy servitude of the former and the power of the latter. No, that is not it. For the final and most revolting injustice is consummated when poverty is wed to the life without hope or the sky that I found on reaching manhood in the appalling slums of our cities: everything must be done so that men [women and children] can escape from the double humiliation of poverty and ugliness.[34]

Camus was a person of the Left all of his adult life. In 1938 he wrote an article, "Dialogue Between Prime Minister and an Employee at 1200 Francs a Month." He sought to defend the progressive reforms gained by workers in 1936 through the first Socialist government in France. He told Prime Minister Daladier that the workers were struggling to achieve economic, political, and social conditions/rights which would allow them to think, live, and be men and women—rather than exploited and stunted. He realized that economic deprivation affected the whole person. He understood that social class membership and oppression excluded many workers from certain "essential joys" and that this exclusion was unjust. Among these essentials was the freedom to develop their minds so that they could enhance their condition as freer persons. After the Second World War, he argued that the mechanical repetitious work in factories and offices would result in Tristan having little or nothing to say to Isolde. [Tristan and Isolde are romantic characters in Richard Wagner's opera (1865) whose title bears the lovers' names.] Many workers and colonial people were treated as *Its* rather than *Thous*. Chapter seven will consider the politics of identity which is characterized by the emergence of women and people of color on the historical stage as they struggle for recognition, good working conditions, political and social rights, and an end to being treated as manipulable *Its*. Camus told of people's needs and demands for dignity, and how history is about our struggle against those who would humiliate us. Brée wrote that Camus "spoke of himself as a 'man of passion,' and there was certainly in his instinctive way of life a streak of the Spanish 'point of honor,' of the independence subsumed in the Spanish [word] 'hombre,' which echoes in the Algerian worker's [insistence] 'to be a man.' The answer he gave when asked why he joined the Resistance is genuine: he couldn't imagine himself on the side of the concentration camps."[35]

Camus did not seek to organize all of life in a single frame of reference. He was not a systematic philosopher; he did not concern himself with the traditional terms and problems of professional philosophers. He started from the conditions, the "givens" of everyday life for most human beings. The world meant a concrete physical place for him, one he called our "common homeland." Camus celebrated human beings' passions, problems, egos, peccadilloes, failures, and triumphs. He saw people as different from one another in an interesting way. He knew that beyond these distinctions we share many common traits. In the human condition we all encounter certain fields of possibility, share basic and other needs, and try to construct some kind of meaning and order for our personal and social lives. Camus insisted that men and women need to communicate with each other through many mediums, including friendship. Camus wrote that men "want to become foremen so they can retire to a little house in the country. But once they are well on in years, they know . . . this is a mistake. They need other men for protection. And as far as he was concerned, he needed to be listened to in order to believe in his life."[36]

Camus loved women and men as they were; he cared about what occurred in each life—even if seemingly trivial. The denial of or contempt for the personal sphere, held by some intellectuals, angered Camus. His ethic of commitment was grounded in the lives of ordinary people; his solidarity was with real and flawed persons, not with theoretically constructed models. Camus thought that there have always been persons who would fight against the various plagues that afflict us, and for a variety of reasons. Each may have her own realm of concern, his particular way of understanding the significance of what is at stake. These real and authentic people can communicate and act solidaristically because of the mutual bond of respect. Camus was referring to his novel, *The Plague* (1947), a term he used as a metaphor to depict what was occurring during the rise of Fascism and Nazism in post-World War I Europe. Brée took us back to Camus's novel, *The Rebel*, which "restates Camus's dedication to the community of men [and women], in which contention and conflict are qualified and limited by the consent and acceptance of the imperfections, inadequacies, inconsistencies, and never-ending struggles inherent in the human lot, and of . . . [our] simple addiction to . . . [our] happiness."[37] This happiness is not to be confused with the packaged, commodified, and for sale promises of happiness brought to us by hypercapitalism as the second millennium comes to an end.

Happiness and moderation were integral to Camus's own attempts to rise above the temptations of pettiness, meanness, violence, and other violations of humanity, committing instead to a larger more holistic vision. He was convinced that our responsibilities must go beyond the always-flawed official attempts to impose exact order on the complex richness of life. It is best to read Camus's own words. "We know that we live in contradiction, but . . . we must . . . do what is needed to reduce it. Our task is . . . to find the few principles that will calm the anguish of free souls. We must mend what has been torn apart, make justice imaginable again in a world so obviously unjust, give happiness a meaning once more to peoples poisoned by the misery of this century. Naturally, it is a superhuman task. But superhuman is the term for tasks . . . [we] take a long time to accomplish."[38] Philip Thody wrote: Pessimism is only a point of departure for Camus, a place from which to attempt the construction of a new humanism that can make possible a more just social order within which we can be relatively happy and good. He insisted that absolute values must never replace human ones. Those whose goal is salvation may not be satisfied with Camus's insistence.[39]

Suggested Tasks for the Reader

1 Starting from the existentialist premise that human beings stand in an absurd relationship to the world because we insist on meaningfulness whereas the world is mostly unknowable, speak to the kind

of curriculum you would seek to develop—along with a supportive pedagogy—so that your students would be served well.

2 How would you organize learning experiences based on the existentialist assumption that to be human is necessarily to choose? Would your understanding of existentialist ideas cause you to think seriously about what kinds of choices are considered meaningful to existentialists? Explain.

3 How could you construct learning opportunities for students that would challenge them to understand how existentialist epistemological uncertainty could lead logically to the need for broadly inclusive, participatory democracy?

4 Demonstrate your understanding of the thesis that freedom and choice can lead to solidaristic, progressive social action, rather than to a fractured, selfish war of all against all. If the reader thinks that the radical existential freedom to choose is more likely to result in the lack of social harmony, egoism, and the possible call for repression aimed at knocking together a semblance of agreement, then s/he should develop an explanation of this likelihood.

5 Explain how the accomplishment of solidarity among only some people may not necessarily be supportive of radically inclusive democracy, social justice, and respect for bona fide diversity as I have championed in this book. As you work on these tasks, consider and comment on how your mastery of them could possibly enable you to translate this understanding into effective pedagogical practices.

III

It is possible to argue that Marx provides better ideas than Dewey does about historical, revolutionary agency. The latter offers better ideas with regard to education compared to Marx's underdeveloped writings on the subject. The existentialists have provided understandings about personal lives that can make both Marx and Dewey more understandable and their projects more accomplishable because of existentialists' insight into real people. Because of this attention to the personal, existentialist's ideas can be understood easily by teachers whose work is conducted on the personal level. It is necessary to add an important qualification. Consider Wingo's view: "In seeking to locate connections of some kind between existentialist philosophy and ideas on education we are at a disadvantage. This disadvantage lies in the fact that the leading figures of this tradition have little to say about [formal] education. . . . Further, the amount of commentary on the implications of existential thought for education is not very extensive. . . . This means that we are left, in considerable degree, to our own devices."[40]

Drawing again from Wingo, it seems that existentialist ideas about education should follow from the central thesis of these ideas, the fact of human freedom. This central idea should be represented in existentialist views on the nature of the curriculum, the teacher's role, and the way methods are to be practiced. Wingo argued that those who take existentialism seriously agree that the curriculum must be organized around the liberal arts. "There is evidence in the writings of both Sartre and Heidegger of their belief that the humanistic studies are the most valuable. In various forms of art, the existence of man [woman] in all its poignant character is most clearly portrayed. Since truth for the existentialist derives from human subjectivity . . . literature, the graphic arts, music, and myth are far more the source of truth than the sciences. . . . The main existentialist objection to science is that it is cold, aloof, and [putatively] objective in its approach to nature and to man, and that . . . it is concerned only with abstractions."[41]

With regard to the role of the teacher, Socrates could stand in for the quintessential existentialist. He seems to have been authentic as a person and teacher; it would be difficult to separate the two. His insistence on humans being central to philosophical inquiry is supportive of existentialist thought. "The way in which Socrates conducted his teaching . . . and the kind of relationship he established with his students are also in apparent agreement with . . . existentialist philosophy. . . . His method of teaching was one of asking questions, refining answers, asking more questions, and pushing the issue until some acceptable conclusion was reached. He himself did not give answers and always maintained that he was ignorant and was only asking for enlightenment from those with whom he was conversing."[42]

Wingo is correct in pointing out that one important factor distinguished Socrates-the-teacher from existentialism; that the Greek master really used the inductive method to go from the immediate and particular to the abstract and universal. Existentialists do not believe that the abstract and/ or universals can be known; they might be very critical of Socrates's so-called sleight of hand.

Wingo's balanced discussion of existentialism and education included arguments for this philosophical tradition's importance. He portrayed existentialism as one of the main protests against philosophical idealism and realism along with its essentialist educational and conservative political allies. The other main protests have been the progressive and Marxist ones. Wingo also included the perennialist protest in chapter eight of his book. His mild criticism of existentialism is that it is difficult to take its principles and then demonstrate logically the derivative educational philosophy and practice that follow. Existentialism's importance and the reason for its inclusion in Wingo's classic work is explained by its articulation of how human beings have had to struggle against the threat to become a manipulable *It* in a mass society, one that reduces us to being considered a computer card to be punched and filed. "It is suggested, therefore, that instead of attempting to tame this rebellious offspring of philosophy . . . we should take it for the passionate . . . protest against the established order that it is. There is the chance . . . that when we . . . think obstinately about the education of *the individual* in a mass society, the protest of existentialism will be appreciated for what it is."[43] Wingo concluded by granting the existentialist assertion that one's education is the product of her/his own choosing. People can be educated without being schooled.[44]

In order to better understand how existentialist ideas could play out in educational contexts I will consider the work of Van Cleve Morris. His book, *Existentialism In Education* has proved helpful to my students in philosophy of education classes over the last quarter century. Morris articulated what he believed existentialist education is: When one tries to answer the question of why human beings were "thrown" into a world we did not create, it becomes necessary to go beyond ordinary reason in order to satisfactorily respond. "And it is in this . . . thrust beyond reason . . . this inquisitive expedition which shoots free of mere cognition, that he [she] invades and marks out the particular zone which he creates for himself and which makes him human, the zone where values are created in the act of an individual living a life. To encourage the young to invade this zone and stake out their own plots there—this is an Existentialist education."[45] In contrast to Dewey placing the individual in society, Morris argued that existentialists are correct to stress the person as a single subject in the world. The student must be encouraged to become fully aware of her/himself as the shaper of her/his own life; when this occurs s/he reaches a supremely human zone where knowledge, understanding, choice, and value creation move beyond the teachers and textbooks. Morris wrote of an existential moment when a young person first realizes her/himself as existing in a world that is not necessarily made for Jacqueline or Jack. Morris argued that this realization is the beginning of youthful recognition of responsibility. Here we see the hoped-for leap from choice to responsibility once more. Morris encouraged teachers to assist the young to realize that the world is open. This is not to be dreaded, but welcomed. Students can be helped to understand that if they are free, each person can construct some unique contribution to the developing essence of the species. Teachers are urged to portray education as a discovery of responsibility—obviously not to old codes that are erroneously portrayed as universal and timeless.

Consider Morris's critique of Dewey and progressive education in order to grasp more firmly his existentialist commitment. He argued that progressive education is emotion free. "It is a . . . detached . . . way of dealing with human experience. 'Low-conflict' rapport with others . . . is the unarguable first principle [of progressivism]. A passionless acceptance of the *method* by which disputes are resolved and by which the whole . . . of social existence is managed therefore takes over as the primary obligation of the youngster in school. The canons of *inquiry* . . . now become the prime aim of instruction. This is what the [progressive] means by . . . 'problem solving.' It is a pedagogy dedicated to the 'training of intelligence' in the management of life's problematic situations. But, while the situation may be problematic, the method by which they are to be managed is not."[46] This fact does not allow the student to see a possibility for asserting a personal subjective view of the problematic. For the existentialists, the scientific method is another reliance on certainty, albeit, methodological rather than ontological or religious. Their view is that the scientific method can never deal with the tremendous complexity of life and natural phenomena.

Morris claimed that existentialist epistemology is most radically differentiated from the spectator of theory of knowledge. We are not spectators of a preestablished reality but, actors who are actively constructing what it means to be human. Much of our life's work is of the ad lib variety! Morris wrote that the "library of any university or the curriculum of any school . . . represents the 'scripts' that have thus far been written, the lines spoken by others in their interpretation of the 'role' of man [woman]. They are there for the taking, but each learner must do the taking."[47] He thought that history and literature provide the best contexts for existentialist teachers because it is possible to learn that we make our own histories and write the literature that helps us understand them.

Morris called Summerhill a model school for existentialism. Although currently there seems to be little discussion of A.S. Neill's private English school, this has not always been the case. Again, Morris is helpful. Neill tested a hypothesis concerning whether or not freedom works. "Suppose you had a school in which there were no rules, no requirements, no homework, no regulations . . . no grades, no academic expectations, no tests, no institutional codes of decorum. . . . Suppose all you had were a small 'campus,' some living quarters, half a dozen teachers, and forty to fifty youngsters ranging in age from five to seventeen. It would be a small but thoroughly free and open society. . . . It would be, rather . . . a collection of . . . individuals with one another, old and young alike, as free and autonomous persons. Could anything like 'education' possibly occur there? Neill found the answer is, 'Yes.'"[48] As you can imagine, not all educators and citizens agree with Neill's approach to education. Eric Fromm wrote the following: "Neill does not try to educate children to fit well into the existing order, but endeavors to rear children who will be happy individuals, men and women whose values are not to *have* much, not to *use* much, but to *be* much."[49] Neill understood that the educational existentialist project can occur best—or perhaps only—in contexts that are free. It is within these contexts that *I-Thou* relationships and communion can occur.

Both Neill and Morris argued against compulsion in education. They claimed that it leads to disunion, humiliation, and rebelliousness. Communion in education allows the opening-up and drawing-in of all those involved. Morris gave fair warning with regard to the consequences of freedom in education. It means that students must have the opportunity and the right to contribute to the construction of standards, curriculum, pedagogy, and governance. "Finally, the teacher comes to realize that successful teaching in the Existentialist mode ends, as it began, in *paradox*: Such teaching succeeds by doing itself out of a job. It succeeds by becoming unnecessary, by producing an individual who no longer needs to be taught [an autodidact], who breaks loose and swings free of the teacher and becomes self-moving."[50] I counter that as one becomes more fully educated or authentic, it need not mean '"swinging free," but cooperating on a more equal basis.

Maxine Greene wrote eloquently about existentialist possibilities in education, although her philosophical beliefs are not attributable to existentialism alone. Her intellectual debts to Dewey, various democratic Marxists, Paulo Freire, Maurice Merleau-Ponty, and Alfred Schutz are obvious to readers, and they are specifically acknowledged by Greene. Consider the following paraphrased presentation of one of her insights. She argued that a person's self is created through choices and resultant actions. Such actions must be informed and critically reflective; social spaces and opportunities must exist in order for such actions to occur. Social change must be a possible outcome of reflective choice. Students must be encouraged and enabled to work in a "curriculum as possibility."

The curriculum should provide occasions for students to articulate themes of their existence in order to know where they are in space and time. Such an education empowers people to name what was formerly obscure and/or unknown. Education must focus on the lived lives of students and help prepare them to recognize lacks and deficiencies that are barriers to their development. Greene insisted that learning must be in some manner emancipatory. She saw the arts and humanities as central to this kind of learning. Her own work in philosophy of education is based on her effective use of literary interpretations.[51]

She wrote of writers and artists who have been especially aware and sensitive to various forms of unfreedom. Greene thought that we can use their work to help clarify educational problems and possibilities. "Without that awareness and . . . hope, teachers find it difficult to cope with the demands of children. . . . They may become drifters as a result, or authoritarian. If they undergo a purely technical training or a simplified 'competency-based' approach, they are likely to see themselves as mere transmission belts—or clerks. The question of the freedom of those they try to teach, the question of their students' endangered selves; these recede before a tide of demands for 'basics,' 'discipline,' and preparation for the 'world of work.' Teachers (artlessly, wearily) become accomplices in mystification. They have neither the time nor energy, nor inclination to urge their students to critical reflection; they, themselves, have suppressed the questions and avoided looking backward."[52] Greene referred to Camus's concept of "the plague" as a distancing and indifference among people and how the possibilities for commitment, community, and love are weakened. She stressed her belief that wide-awakeness, cognitive clarity, and existential concern are related and necessary to the kind of education she championed.

Greene argued that all too often the public views particular institutions and processes as "natural," "given," and unchangeable. Even though there may be a widespread realization that a particular status quo does not allow justice for everyone, the tendency is to believe that it "works well enough," or "it's getting better," or "it'll get better." Schools, like the mass media, play important roles in maintaining such disempowering views. "It is not that teachers consciously mystify or deliberately concoct the positive images that deflect critical thought. It is not even that they . . . are . . . sanguine about the health of the society. Often submerged in the bureaucracies for which they work, they simply accede to what is taken for granted. Identifying themselves as spokespersons for—or representatives of—the system in its local manifestation, they avoid interrogation and critique. . . . They may, deliberately or not, adapt [their uncritical views] to accommodate to what they perceive to be the class origins or the capacities of their students, but, whether they are moving these young people towards assembly lines, or administrative offices, they are likely to present the world around them as *given,* probably unchangeable and predefined."[53] Efficiency, management, and expertise come to dominate too much schooling, rather than critique and emancipatory thinking. It is technology, under capitalist direction forever; therefore, students and citizens must accommodate themselves to this alleged universality.

Greene realized that teachers can neither frontally attack the schools in which they work, nor, change quickly or profoundly the places where their students will eventually labor. What is to be done? She argued that certain philosophers have maintained that the need for freedom is deeply rooted in the human condition, if not human nature itself. Deceptive and/ or meretricious freedom is recognized for what it is—at least in the long run. These facts are the base on which Greene built her views on how teacher education should be taught in order to overcome the bleak picture she has painted. Greene would have us go beyond the merely technical and how-to emphases of many teacher education programs. She favored teacher education that is interpretive, critical, and normative in its thrust.[54] This emphasis will make more possible the interrogation of ideational and sociocultural contexts of teaching and learning. Teachers must be educated to realize the need for them to act as their students' advocates. "Teachers are not only obliged to become scholars and theorists in specialized fields but persons . . . concerned with the polity and the kinds of action that make a difference in the public space. I would suggest that there must always be a place in teacher education for 'foundations' specialists, people whose main interest is in interpreting—and enabling others to interpret—the social, political, and economic factors that affect and influence the processes of education."[55] These interpretations must be developed within dialogic environments. Greene understood that those who interpret and critique do so from various vantage points and experiences, both of which are affected by social class, race/ethnicity, gender, and sexual orientation. Greene proposed that teacher educators take epistemology seriously; to think profoundly about how we think, why, and what kinds of claims can be made for the warranted assertibility of what we claim to know.

Greene called our attention to what Freire has called a "culture of silence"; those who have remained powerless in voice and deed. Many who have been silent or silenced are people of color, women, children, workers, and the poor. History studied from the ground up can help educators invite various mute people to find voice and power. "A new pedagogy is . . . required, one that will free persons to understand the ways in which each of them reaches out from his or her location to constitute a common . . . world. It might well be called a democratic pedagogy, since, in several respects, the object is to empower persons to enact democracy. To act upon democratic values . . . is to be responsive to . . . principles of freedom, justice, and regard for others. If individuals can . . . [do so] the way may be opened for *praxis*, for bringing the world closer to heart's desire."[56] Like Camus's Tarrou in *The Plague*, there is plague and there are victims; we must not join forces with the former. Dr. Rieux's common decency caused him to fight the plague. Kyo in Andre Malraux's novel *Man's Fate* (1934), gives up a somewhat comfortable life to participate in revolution in order to relieve human pain. Irving Howe wrote: "Asked by the Shanghai police chief, 'You want to live?' Kyo replied, 'It depends how.' Challenged by the . . . chief, 'What do you call dignity?' He answered, 'The opposite of humiliation.'"[57]

Greene was right when she wrote that a person who is conscious of her/his own existential condition, characterized by the freedom and duty to choose, can still act strategically as a teacher. There is no way to imply specific behaviors from one's encounters with existentialists; there can be no definitive existentialist theory of, or philosophy of, education. "The very notion of doctrine is excluded by the existentialist view. Prescription is excluded by the centrality of free choice. All we can say is . . . if the individual who engages with existentialist writers is committed to the study of teaching and learning, and to the action which is teaching, he—or she—cannot but see education with new eyes when the reading is, for the moment, done."[58] The teacher must decide for herself how existentialist insights can enrich practice. The student can benefit from rich curricula that allow for depth, breadth, and diversity. The teaching-learning environment can encourage one and all to realize that the moments and experiences in it are unique and not likely to be duplicated or repeated. Maxine Greene articulated well how the student as seeker and knower can use intuitive, rational, empirical, aesthetic, discursive, emotive, logical, mathematical, and scientific tools in order to construct meanings that can challenge and change her/his life and world. As free individuals, we must take our choices seriously and then act in the spaces in which we find ourselves—spaces between limitations and possibilities.

Suggested Task for the Reader

Because it is unlikely that one would be a teacher in an "existentialist school," or even in a place with few if any existentialist colleagues, how could a person who considers existentialist insights seriously "act strategically" as an educator?

Conclusion

Existentialists have said that, although Dewey has properly placed human beings within biological and social contexts, he never went beyond them and into the depths of our personhood(s) where fear and trembling begin. Existentialists also criticize Marx and Marxists for failure to adequately develop philosophical categories for presenting and explaining the uniqueness of human beings and our personalities. Existentialists have argued that for human beings, our existences precede our essences and are responsible for the latter. This position is the opposite of the quest for certainty advocates, who insist that human nature is "given" to us by a creator rather than being an affair of men and women and our lifelong construction of meaning and self. Existentialism opposes most radically and completely the historical quest for certainty. Like Sisyphus, our fate is self-determined but in very difficult situations which are givens. Sisyphus personifies the existentialist belief that it is the struggle that counts most, rather than a predestined arrival in a safe haven.

Pascal's precocious awareness of existentialist concerns suggest that we have only our intellect and awareness to rely on in a world that was not created with us in mind. Still, he argued, or wagered, we can assume that there is some kind of deity who is responsible in the last analysis. It costs nothing to make such an optimistic wager or surmise. Pascal's countryman, Camus, argued that action can and must result from good and effective thinking. Camus cautioned us that human action can never solve every problem that plagues us. He expressed it: In spite of our ameliorative actions, we are capable only of "diminishing arithmetically" the problems, injustices, and oppressiveness of this world. He courageously contended that this world has no ultimate/inherent meaning; we must endeavor to insist on and construct our own meanings. In this endeavor, Camus, many existentialists, Marx, and Dewey are at least members of the same extended family.

In section I, I considered the root principle of human freedom and how it can lead to solidaristic action to achieve democracy, justice, and enhance human dignity. That section also featured an analysis of other key existentialist terms, e.g., authenticity, contingency, and despair. You were introduced to various existentialists and some commentators on this philosophical position. The cast of characters include: Spanos, Huxley, Breisach,

Kierkegaard, Camus, Kaplan, Frankl, Kazantzakis, and Odajnyk. Section II features our solidaristic star player, Camus. He best represents the possibility to move from existentialist philosophical positions to concrete action with others in order to strengthen the march toward more human dignity. The last section provided descriptions and analyses of possibilities for education that are derived from existentialists assumptions. I argued that there can be no specific lesson plan on how to be an existentialist teacher. One can refer to an "existentialist mood" that must be constructed and used by specific persons who work as educators. That section featured work by Wingo, Morris, and Greene.

Notes

1   Ernest Hemingway, "A Clean, Well-Lighted Place," in *A Casebook on Existentialism*, ed. William V. Spanos (New York: Thomas Y. Crowell Company, 1966), 17–21.

2   Walter Kaufmann, ed., intro., and preface, *Existentialism from Dostoevsky to Sartre* (Cleveland and New York: Meridian Books, 1956), 46–47.

3   William Barrett, *Irrational Man: A Study in Existential Philosophy* (Garden City, N.Y.: Doubleday Anchor Books, 1958), 19–20. Some would argue that Dewey's *Art As Experience* (1934) is indicative of a softer, less *homo faber* view of human beings. With regard to Barrett's equating *homo faber* with technology and technique, see his, *The Illusion of Technique* (Garden City, N.Y.: Anchor Press/Doubleday, 1978), passim. I argue that the human-as-maker is not limited to technique. There are many forms of transformative labor. Technology and technique are only some examples.

4   See, Jean-Paul Sartre, *Between Existentialism and Marxism* (New York; Pantheon Books, 1974), and Walter Odanjnyk, *Marxism and Existentialism* (Garden City, N.Y.: Anchor Books, 1965). *The Economic and Philosophical Manuscripts of 1844* must be considered in any fair evaluation of Marx's work because they present the philosophical underpinnings of his subsequent socioeconomic writings. See, Richard A. Brosio, "One Marx, and the Centrality of the Historical Actor(s)," *Educational Theory* 35, no. 1 (Winter 1985): 73–83.

5   See, Maxine Greene, "Wide-Awakeness and the Moral Live," in Alan R. Sadovnik et al. *Exploring Education: An Introduction to the Foundations of Education* (Boston: Allyn and Bacon, 1994), 221–28.

6   Albert Camus, *The Myth of Sisyphus and Other Essays* (New York: Vintage Books, 1942), 90.

7   Ibid., 91.

8   Albert E. Avey, *Handbook in the History of Philosophy* (New York: Barnes & Noble, Inc., 1954), 135.

9   Blaise Pascal, "Pensées," in *A Casebook on Existentialism*, ed. Spanos, 223.

10 Albert Camus, *The Rebel* (New York: Vintage Books, 1951), 305.

11 Albert Camus, *Resistance, Rebellion, and Death* (New York: The Modern Library, 1960), 22.

12 Brosio, "One Marx and the Centrality of the Historical Actor(s)," 78.

13 Spanos, *Casebook on Existentialism*, 1.

14   Julian Huxley, "Introduction," *The Phenomenon of Man*, Pierre Teilhard de Chardin (New York: Harper Torchbooks, 1955), 12.

15   Spanos, *Casebook on Existentialism*, 5–6.

16   Ernst Breisach, *Introduction to Modern Existentialism* (New York: Grove Press, Inc., 1962), 194.

17   Ibid., 196.

18   Ibid., 196–97. Kierkegaard spoke of the "leap of faith," because he argued that the deity is rationally incomprehensible.

19   For a useful context in which to understand Camus's differences with some existentialists, as well as the former's ability to fight for more justice, if not perfect justice, see, H. Stuart Hughes' *The Obstructed Path: French Social Thought in the Years of Desperation 1930–1960* (New York and Evanston: Harper & Row Publishers, 1996), chapter 6, "The Way Out."

20   Albert Camus, "Acceptance Speech," in *Nobel Prize Library: Camus, Churchill* (New York: Alexis Gregory, and DelMar, Calif.: CRM Publishing, 1971), 8–9.

21   Spanos, *Casebook on Existentialism*, 8.

22   Abraham Kaplan, *The New World of Philosophy* (New York: Vintage Books, 1961), 115.

23   Ibid., 45.

24   See, Viktor E. Frankl, *Psychotherapy and Existentialism* (New York: A Clarion Book, 1967) and Mike Rose, *Lives on The Boundary* (New York: Penguin Books, 1989), chapter 4, in order to get a sense of the liberatory potential represented by some psychologists.

25   Kaplan, *New World of Philosophy*, 105.

26   Ibid., 106.

27   Ibid., 108.

28   See the following works by and about Kazantzakis. *Zorba the Greek* (1952), *The Greek Passion* (1953), *Freedom Or Death* (1955), *The Last Temptation of Christ* (1960), *Report To Greco* (1961), *The Fratricides* (1961), and Helen Kazantzakis, *Nikos Kazantzakis: A Biography Based on His Letters* (1968).

29   Breisach, *Introduction to Modern Existentialism*, 226. Buber wrote, "the primary word *I-Thou* can be spoken only with the whole being. . . . I become through my relation to the *Thou* [not the mere *it*]. . . . All real living is meeting." *I and Thou*, 2nd ed. (New York: Charles Scribner's Sons, 1958), 11. See Buber's *Between Man and Man* (New York: The Macmillan Company, 1947), part I, "Dialogue."

30   Odajnyk, *Existentialism and Marxism*, 118.

31   Ibid., 120.

32   Ibid., 123.

33   Germaine Brée, *Camus And Sartre: Crisis and Commitment* (New York: A Delta Book, 1972), 65–66.

34   Albert Camus, *Lyrical and Critical Essays* (New York: Alfred A. Knopf, 1968), 6–8.

35   Brée, *Camus and Sartre*, 128.

36   Camus, *Lyrical and Critical Essays*, 26.

37   Brée, *Camus and Sartre*, 223.

38   Camus, *Lyrical and Critical Essays*, 135.

39   Philip Thody, *Albert Camus: A Study of His Work* (New York: Grove Press, 1957), passim. For two other studies of Camus's life and work, see Herbert R. Lottman, *Albert Camus: A Biography* (Garden City, N.Y.: Doubleday & Company, Inc., 1979), and Olivier Todd, *Albert Camus: A Life* (New York: Alfred A. Knopf, 1997). Lottman includes the following from Sartre's eulogy on the occasion of Camus's death. "'He represented in this century . . . the present-day heir of that long line of moralists whose works constitute what is perhaps most original in French letters. His stubborn humanism, strict and pure, austere and sensual, delivered uncertain combat against the massive and deformed events of the day'" p. 708. In the spirit of interpretive disagreement, which characterizes philosophy, see John L. Hess, "*L'Étranger et l'Étrangère* (masculine and feminine for strangers) Camus Against the Other," *Monthly Review* 50, no. 7 (December 1998): 50–54. Hess is critical of Olivier Todd's book on Camus—and of Camus himself. The latter is criticized specifically for his positions and literary representations of Arabs (in his native Algeria), and of women.

40   G. Max Wingo, *Philosophies of Education: An Introduction* (Lexington, Mass.: D.C. Heath and Company, 1974), 334. For an example of how existentialism's relationships to education have been portrayed, see, Ralph Harper's "Significance of Existence and Recognition for Education," *Modern Philosophies and Education the Fifty-fourth Yearbook of the National Society for the Study of Education,* ed. Nelson B. Henry (Chicago: University of Chicago Press, 1955), chapter 7. Also, consult the Appendix of Chapter 1 of this book for more about official Philosophy of Education positions on what was important to its members.

41   Wingo, *Philosophies of Education: An Introduction*, 336.

42   Ibid., 337.

43   Ibid., 339.

44   Ivan Illich is not an existentialist, but his book, *Deschooling Society* (New York: Perennial Library, 1970), is supportive of Wingo's comment concerning "in spite of schooling."

45   Van Cleve Morris, *Existentialism In Education* (New York: Harper & Row Publishers, 1966), 104–05.

46   Ibid., 118.

47   Ibid., 124.

48   Ibid., 147–48.

49   Eric Fromm, "Foreword," in *Summerhill: A Radical Approach To Child Rearing*, A.S. Neill (New York: Hart Publishing Company, 1960), xiv. Fromm's work on the tendency for men and women to "escape from freedom" is relevant to an understanding of existentialism, Marx, and Freud.

50   Morris, *Existentialism In Education*, 153.

51   See, Maxine Greene, *Teacher As Stranger* (Belmont, Calif.: Wadsworth Publishing Company, Inc., 1973), and her *The Dialectic of Freedom* (New York: Teachers College Press, 1988).

52   Maxine Greene, *Landscapes of Learning* (New York: Teachers College Press, 1978), 38.

53   Ibid., 56.

54   For an official statement on the Social Foundations of Education (as interpretive, critical, and normative) in teacher education, see *Standards for Academic and Professional Instruction in Foundations of Education, Educational Studies, and Policy Studies*, 2nd ed., presented to the Educational Community by the Council of Learned Societies in Education (San Francisco: Caddo Gap Press, 1996).

55   Greene, *Landscapes of Learning*, 59. The Social Foundations of Education courses consist mainly of: philosophy/sociology/history of education and policy studies.

56   Ibid., 70–71.

57   Irving Howe, *Politics and the Novel* (New York: Horizon Press, Inc., 1957), 211.

58   Maxine Greene, ed. and commentator, *Existentialist Encounters for Teachers* (New York: Random House, 1967), 157. For another fine study specifically with reference to existentialists not providing marching orders for teachers, see, George F. Kneller, *Existentialism and Education* (New York: Philosophical Library, Inc., 1958), 41, and passim. Kneller provides an insightful analysis of existentialism and democracy. He argues that existentialists do not support democracy as knuckling under to the group. pp. 98–99

Chapter Six

Liberationists: Freire and Various Spiritualists

Introduction

The work of Paulo Freire and those he influenced have played important roles in late-twentieth-century education for democratic empowerment, social justice, and respect for authentic diversity. Their ideas are featured in sections I and II of this chapter. Freire was born in Brazil in 1921 and died there in 1997. Peter McLaren wrote that Freire "became a legendary figure in the field of education. A courageous scholar, a social activist, and a cultural worker admired for his integrity and humility, Freire became internationally renowned for developing an anti-imperialist and anticapitalist literacy praxis employed by progressive educators throughout the world."[1] Many critical, progressive educators and activists have welcomed Freire's work because his ideas spoke of hope as well as critique. Some of these critical progressives are presented in section II of this chapter. This is true also of liberation philosophy and theology developed in Latin America. This philosophy and theology are discussed in section III of this chapter.

To set the stage for how Freire is presented in section I, I offer a paraphrase from the eulogy I wrote for him. Freire's work came to me by way of various paths and interests. The culture of silence he attempted to overcome was dramatically introduced to me as a young man while reading Ignazio Silone's novel, *Bread and Wine* (1937), especially on reading about Sciatàp. This poor fellow was told to "shut up" so many times that he took on the Italianized version of the English language command as his name. Sciatàp is representative of many of the working-class, Italian immigrants that I grew up with. Camus's portrayal of his silent mother also helped me to understand why Freire's insistence on the radical democratization of voice is of great importance. I welcomed Freire's demand that each and every one of us must be able to name our socioeconomic and political experiences, in part because of what I had already learned from the Frankfurt School philosophers, especially Max Horkheimer. He wrote: Philosophy is the conscious attempt to weave together all of our understanding and knowledge into a linguistic whole permitting us to call things and events by their correct names. Gramsci's pioneering work on the power of hegemony to control working-class people's lives was done in Turin, Italy from where my ancestors emigrated to the United States. His analysis of this attempt to control people like members of my family helped prepare me to embrace Freire's further development of hegemony as a problem and a challenge to be overcome collectively. My work experiences as a teacher-scholar made it imperative that I grasp Freire's pedagogical insight that students are not just empty vessels to be filled by essentialist teachers. The study of Dewey's ideas helped me understand Freire's position on proactive students. If the "student is the curriculum," then her/his needs, hopes, and strengths must drive what the appropriate education should be. Freire's and Dewey's views on teaching and learning which would strike a powerful blow to the reproductive function of schooling was not lost on me.

The paraphrase continues. Marx's ideas also assisted me to readily embrace Freire's insistence that we can and must make our own histories. Too many subaltern people have been forced to "shut up" so that history could be made behind their backs. Freire belonged to the great Promethean tradition that features the stealing of fire from the "gods." He is a comrade for all of us who believe that intelligence, bravery, altruism, and educability are widespread human characteristics, rather than just among the so-called elite. Freire knew that all human beings want and need both "bread and roses"! However, we still must face the difficult problem of collective human agency; not the fact of its possibility, but how it is to be concretely accomplished in these times. Those of us who mourn the death of Paulo Freire can honor his memory by ascertaining who will stand in for Marx's lost proletariat as the main engine of progressive change. Is it possible to construct broadly inclusive progressive coalitions that seek to strengthen participatory democracy, social justice, and respect for diversity? Can this necessary coalition be formed from among the wonderful variety—and all too often divisiveness—of people who are classed, raced, and gendered? Freire knew that the struggle to translate liberatory ideas into successful praxis would be very difficult. He warned the progressive writer Jonathan Kozol that one would have to pay "a serious price" in order to do the things they had talked about.[2] This concludes the paraphrasing from the eulogy I wrote for Freire.

I first commented in print on Freire's work in a 1986 publication.[3] A transformative, liberatory education and politics must be based on the assumption of individual and collective human volition/agency. Freire's radical pedagogy is an excellent example of the education part of the equation, although his pedagogy is also political. I included a direct quote from Henry Giroux. For Freire

> all pedagogy . . . is essentially a political issue and all educational theories are [also] political. . . . Inherent in any educational design are value assumptions and choices about the nature of humankind, the use of authority, the value of specific forms of knowledge and, finally, a vision of what constitutes the good life. Freire's work represents a critical attempt to illustrate how ideologies of various . . . persuasions reflect, distort, and prevent men and women from becoming socio-political actors in the struggle against an oppressive society. Thus to understand his pedagogy, one must begin with a recognition that it is a call for liberation and an ongoing process of radical reconstruction.[4]

Freire wanted lifelong learners to be able to discover for themselves that democratic participation in a community of shared values and economic fairness should be honored as one of the most important public goods. His educational ideas include humanistic, personal, and caring *processes*, as well as content that is characterized by breadth, depth, and the potential to equip learners for effective liberatory action.

Freire's actors must learn how to construct their own meanings, definitions, and lenses in order to see things more accurately. This entails overcoming the hegemonic attempts by the powers that be to present "reality" in a way that supports their continued dominant position. Human struggle is necessary for this to occur. As Freire wrote:

> To exist humanly is to *name* the world, to change it. . . . Men [sic] are not built in silence, but in word, in work, in action-reflection. But while to say the true word . . . is to transform the world, saying that word is not the privilege of some . . . but the right of every man. Consequently, no one can say a true word alone—nor can he say it *for* another. . . . Dialogue is the encounter between men, mediated by the world, in order to [more effectively] name . . . it. Hence, dialogue cannot occur between those who want to name the world . . . and those who deny other men the right to speak their word. . . . Those who have been denied their . . . right to speak their word must first reclaim this right and prevent the continuation of this dehumanizing aggression.[5]

You are encouraged to reflect on instances when others have successfully provided their picture of reality and meaning of events to you, and how such an imposition all too often helped form your agreement with them on specific issues and problems; not all "impositions" of new ways to see things are harmful to our development, and it is important for youngsters to be able to recognize that the "emperor has no clothes." An example might be the present celebration of how well the U.S. economy is doing when, in fact, many people are living in poverty. Those who are poor and powerless seldom get to publicly communicate their view of the economy. Marx and Freire would probably name the current U.S. economy as amoral or immoral. This would be resisted by those who profit most from the dominant forms of capitalism at the end of the second millennium.

Freire urged teachers to present knowledge, facts, and the taken-for-granted as problematic, i.e., problems to be interrogated and solved. Students must learn to question whose reality is being legitimized, and/or whose interests are being served by certain forms of naming the world. This learning process is related to the epistemological component of philosophy, namely, how do various knowledge claims hold up under inclusionary and radical (to the root) interrogation. Freire argued that education is not, and cannot, be a neutral process. Richard Shaull wrote in the introduction to Freire's *Pedagogy of the Oppressed*: "Education either functions as an instrument that is used to facilitate the integration of the young . . . into the logic of the present system [when it is unjust] and bring about conformity to it, *or* it becomes 'the practice of freedom.' . . . The development of an educational methodology that facilitates this process will inevitably lead to tension and conflict."[6]

My 1986 publication concluded with an attempt to convince the reader to see Freire's work as relevant for us, and not just his native Brazil. Although the forms and degrees of oppression and injustice are not the same everywhere, we know that millions of people in the so-called "developed" Northern Hemisphere are neither able to name their world, nor to alter it. Both Freire and Marx believed that we can and must liberate ourselves; this is the case because "only those who are historically 'immersed' in complex forms of oppression . . . can identify the special garb worn by 'cultural silence' in . . . [their own] society. Clearly it is not illiteracy, as in northeast Brazil, or economic marginalization as in rural Chile. What is it, then, that blocks oppressed Americans from controlling their own social destiny?"[7] To answer the question, those who consider Freire's work valuable and relevant to their own schools' and societies' problems and possibilities will have to study carefully, reconfigure, translate, and critically appropriate his ideas.

I

This section features presentations of important Freirean ideas from two of his books: *Pedagogy of the Oppressed* (1970) and *Education for Critical Consciousness* (1973). I will comment on and relate Freire's ideas to other important literature. You are invited to consult the literature analyzed and cited in this section so that you may engage in an analysis of my interpretation as well as of the original sources. Freire wrote within the context of Latin American and former Portuguese colonies in Africa. His statement of problems, suggested analyses, and required actions are familiar to readers worldwide. Freire's belief in intelligence, education, reflected-upon experience, and subsequent praxis are central to the European Enlightenment and its legacy, including the work of Marxists and Deweyans. The Brazilian's great sensitivity to matters of social oppression and injustice also stems from his Christian upbringing and the parts of this religion's positions on human dignity and social justice. In section III of this chapter, Freire's work is shown to coincide with the rise of Latin American liberation philosophy and theology. Freire's deserved membership in the company of those who theorize about and practice the kind of education favored in this book is exemplified by his belief in human agency. He argued that we must be educated to understand that our situation is neither determined nor unalterable; it is only limited. He thought that the struggle to progress beyond limits is mainly a collective historical struggle. Existentialist readings of Marx, Dewey, and Freire can reveal their recognition of individual/personal factors involved in achieving awareness of problematic situations and determination to resolve them. Citing Marx, Freire argued that the social reality we live in has been constructed by human beings; it can be altered for the better. Both philosophers believed that we are transformed through liberatory struggle.

You should consider the possibilities for these philosophical positions to be translated (with the necessary changes being made) into your own social and work life. Teachers in North America may come to understand that their students, although neither peasants nor industrial workers, may face various forms of injustice and even oppression in schools in which their cultural capital serves them poorly in the grades and credentials race. The problematic situations we all face can also be viewed as where certain possibilities begin. These problems and possibilities are critically assessed in concrete historical situations; as this is done we begin to expect solutions. Dewey's scientific method is similar to what is described.

Freire judged the fundamental theme of our historical time as one of domination/oppression. Like Marx, he was convinced that this implies its opposite, namely liberation. He wrote that we are Subjects in *expectancy*; Freire did not underestimate the difficulty of making expectancy real. He lived many years in exile, a result of the liberatory pedagogy he attempted to implement in his native Brazil.

Freire's belief in human agency is related to his understanding that history is open! Like Marx and Dewey, Freire argued against both the idealist philosophers and conservatives who held that mind and will alone can overcome all obstacles and the determinists who held that the mechanistic material world is a force independent of human beings. Freire's sober views on history's openness to human intervention are based on a dialectical/interactionist view of human understanding and action with the social and physical worlds. Freire stated: "Throughout history men have attempted to overcome the factors which make them accommodate or adjust, in struggle—constantly threatened by oppression—to attain their full humanity."[8] (You will notice the attempt to make this work gender-fair throughout. Because Freire's early works used masculine terms to stand for human beings in general, the decision is to alert the reader to substitute gender-fair pronouns throughout this section. A feminist critique of Freire's work will be provided in chapter seven.) Some people have interpreted Freire as subscribing to certainties about important phenomena such as the nature of humankind, oppression, liberation, etc. Overall his work belongs to the epistemology celebrated in this work, that of accepting and dealing with human uncertainty. One thesis of this book is that experiencing a lack of certainty need not paralyze us into inaction or debilitating cynicism. Freire criticized "sectarians" for their lack of doubt. "Radicals" who are committed to human liberation do not become prisoners of a "circle of certainty"—although they commit themselves in history to struggle in solidarity with others who are imprisoned in Plato's or other caves.

Freire's emphasis on education for the liberation of the oppressed classes was made necessary in part by Brazil's undemocratic cultural history. Brazil's civil society and various cultures did not feature the habits of political and social solidarity appropriate to a hoped-for democracy. Dewey also favored education as a, or *the*, main activity for enlightenment and democratic participation. Marx did not think that oppressive societies could or would tolerate schools—or education in the broader sense—which threatened the oppressors' advantages. I argue that historically varied circumstances help explain the differences among these philosopher democrats.[9] Freire wanted the oppressed in Brazil and elsewhere to learn social and political responsibility through *experience,* e.g., participation in schools, unions, places of work, associations, clubs, neighborhoods, places of worship, etc. People would learn through the practice of democracy. The appropriate habits could then be developed. The chief threat he saw to the development of democracy in countries where he worked to cause progressive change was undemocratic education. Like Dewey, Freire argued that democracy is a form of life, one that is necessary to underpin formal political and socioeconomic democracy. Freire was wise enough to realize that education (especially schooling) neither is nor can be by itself a miraculous process in terms of moving a society or nation from lack of democracy to an authentic one.

Freire, in agreement with Marx, Dewey, and many existentialists, sought to study the human condition in its social and physical concreteness. He explained that *Pedagogy of the Oppressed* is "rooted in concrete situations and describes the reactions of laborers (peasant or urban) and of middle-class persons whom I have observed. . . . Continued observation will afford me an opportunity to modify or corroborate in later studies the points proposed in this introductory work."[10] The need to deal with the concreteness of life, and how continuous study and action provide an imperfect self-correction of hypothesis and praxis was just described. Like the thinkers featured in chapters three, four, and five, Freire was not an uncritical supporter of all forms of science because of their potential harmful uses; he recognized the dangers of technology that were uncoupled from the necessary humanist compass guidelines. He saw advanced technological societies in much the same way as Marcuse and some of his Frankfurt School colleagues did, that critical social consciousness is not the same as mere technical accomplishment.

Like Dewey, Freire did not reject machines but insisted that we must be educated on how to humanize them. The kind of education he favored "would enable men to discuss courageously the problems of their context—and to intervene . . .; it would warn men of the dangers of the time and offer them the confidence and the strength to confront those dangers instead of surrendering their sense of self through submission to the decisions of others. By predisposing men to reevaluate constantly, to analyze findings, to adopt scientific methods . . . and to perceive themselves in dialectical [interactive] relationship with their social reality, that education could help men assume an increasingly critical attitude toward the world and so to transform it."[11] This activist learning process would be guided by theory grounded in the specifics of human life. There is also a strong emphasis on holistic inquiry in Freire's work. He would have us learn about the contexts in which things occur—or do not. I interpret Freire as advising us to construct a "big picture" in order to better understand the constituent elements. Some postmodernist and feminist thinkers are distrustful of grand explanatory narratives and alleged big pictures for fear of their oppressive possibilities. These thinkers stress the importance of the local and specific. Freire is rightly critical of those who resist the attempt to understand the historical essence of a problematic situation. He explained that they become angry when a person attempts to establish a fundamental proposition that has the potential to explain epiphenomenal, "fortuitous or secondary" characteristics to which those who are annoyed had assigned primary importance.

Suggested Task for the Reader

Although Freire's ideas may not yet be well known to you, it could be beneficial to construct a tentative articulation of how you understand some important similarities and/or differences between his work and the work of Marx, Dewey, and perhaps some existentialist thinkers. Keep in mind that I am not claiming that the writers featured in chapters three, four, and five have had direct/causal influence on Freire's intellectual production.

Now that I have presented some of Freire's general similarities with other democratic philosophers, consider more specifically the somewhat unique contributions he made to philosophical scaffolding for democratic education. The first is his description and condemnation of the "banking concept" or "method" of education and especially pedagogy. As we proceed, you might keep in mind the discussion of essentialist pedagogy in chapter two. Knowledge is considered a gift or thing that is bestowed upon or imparted to the recipient in the banking concept of education. The teacher is considered as the one who knows, the student is considered ignorant. The teacher-imparter fills the empty tank of the students with facts, official knowledge, and even the truth. The knowledge/thing that is imparted is comprised of and/or reflective of a world-view and ideology held by the rich and powerful in the society. The assumption that the student is empty and/or ignorant reflects the assumption held by elitist societies concerning its rank and file members. The teacher or official talks about reality as if it were universally applicable and mostly unchangeable. It is often presented to students in compartmentalized ways. There is little or no attempt to relate this official knowledge to the students' experiences, needs, and hopes. The teacher attempts to fill the students' alleged emptiness with facts and truth; they are expected to memorize, bank it, and then regurgitate at the proper moment. Students record, memorize, and repeat! Dewey would support Freire when the latter charged that this kind of education is not respectful of knowledge as process, constructed by the many instead of the few, and marked especially by inquiry into the problematic unknown. Freire worried that in the banking method, the teacher presents himself/herself to the students as their necessary opposite; the students then justify the teacher's role because of their alleged ignorance. The logic of liberatory education is radically different as it strives to reconcile the polar opposite of teacher and student. "Education must begin with a solution of the teacher-student contradiction so that both are simultaneously teachers and students."[12]

For Freire, everyone must become a Subject rather than a mere Object who is acted *upon*. The student and citizen-worker must be seen not only as a spectator of what others have created, but as persons capable of constructing and reconstructing their own meanings, names, and realities. As Freire articulated: "It is not surprising that the banking concept of education regard men as . . . manageable beings. The more the students work at storing the deposits . . . the less they develop the critical consciousness which would result from their intervention in the world as transformers of . . . [it]. The more completely they accept the passive role imposed on them, the more they tend . . . to adapt to the world as it is and to the fragmented view of reality deposited on them."[13] I agree with Freire's main argument, but it is a fact that some people who have been schooled in the "banking" or essentialist methods have used the "deposits" in unintended (to their teachers') ways, they have helped construct liberatory projects with what was "deposited" on them. Perhaps the best examples are those revolutionary thinkers and actors who were schooled in banking methods but who succeeded in breathing new life into potentially liberatory but contextless "facts." This does not justify what Freire rightly condemns. Freire may be one of the best examples of how conservative education can ironically result in radical politics.[14] Freire anticipated my comment about the ironic outcomes stated above, but in a slightly different way. According to Freire the "deposits" are found by students to be internally contradictory, not congruent with lived experiences, and even manipulative in their outcomes—and even in their intentions. He argued that some "bank-clerk teachers" are well intentioned, although unaware of their roles as agents of mystification and oppression.

Drawing from the work of Erich Fromm (a member of the Frankfurt School), Freire claimed that "bank-clerk teachers" and their masters are *necrophilic* people, i.e., they consciously or unconsciously "love death."

This necrophilia is meant as the tendency to "Thingify" everything and everyone, or to turn what is organic into something inorganic. The necrophilic person can relate only if s/he can possess and control. In this desire to control, life is snuffed out. The banking method attempts to control thought and action.[15] Joel Spring argued that,

> for Freire, sexuality has a determining effect on the development of consciousness and reason. The necrophilic personality is open to cultural invasion by the forces of oppression. Since necrophilics love oppression, they willingly accept the domination of their consciousness by outside forces. . . . In broader terms, cultural invasion is a form of economic and political domination. The invader, similar to the teacher in banking education, does not respect the creativity, the potentialities, and the world-view of the . . . [person]. The invaded consciousness is treated as an object to be penetrated by . . . the invader. . . . The invaded begin to see the world through the eyes of the invader. . . . Reflecting a necrophilic personality, the invaded consciousness loves and accepts domination. . . . Invaded people want to become like the oppressors.[16]

Frantz Fanon wrote about the attempts by colonized peoples to throw off the yoke of Western imperialism, especially about the war in Algeria against the French in the 1950s: "The fight carried on by a people for its liberation leads it, according to circumstances, either to refuse or else to explode the so-called truths which have been established in its consciousness by the colonial . . . administration, by the military occupation, and by economic exploitation. Armed conflict alone can really drive out these falsehoods created in man which force into inferiority the most lively minds among us and which literally, mutilate us."[17] Freire did not advocate armed struggle in Brazil or elsewhere. He understood the need to decolonize the consciousness of the oppressed. Colonialism seeks to systematically negate colonized persons by denying them the attributes of humanity, thus eventually forcing the oppressed to ask themselves who they really are. Freire explains how decolonization occurred after the oppressors left by speaking of Cape Verde (a former colony of Portugal). "The repressed native culture is beginning to reemerge. Certain cultural behavior patterns that were forbidden by the colonizers, including language expressions . . . poetry and music are reappearing. People walk without having to bow. . . . They now walk upright, looking up. There is a pedagogy of walking in this new behavior, walking freely."[18]

Freire's pedagogy sought to free our minds and more specifically to change the necrophilic person into a biophilic one. This education and consciousness-raising required leaders who have already struggled toward humanization. "Freire solves the problem of finding teachers and initiating social change by linking the biophilic personality with revolutionary consciousness. . . . In this context, Freire's teachers are lovers who desire to free human consciousness and transform the world so that all people will be free of oppression."[19] Freire's idea of leadership is not avant-garde, i.e., he knows that we are all human and that knowing more about some things and/or being especially brave does not entitle an elite to become the self-appointed, know-it-all, new oppressors. Arbitrary means cannot be used to accomplish democratic goals. Leaders and teachers must enter into communion, dialogue, and solidarity with those they seek to empower.

Freire's liberatory education sought to "extroject" various forms of subaltern mentalities that have been "introjected" by oppressors. The educational process is a practice of liberty as both students and teachers graduate beyond silence and monologue. Like Dewey, Freire's education for democratic empowerment began with where students are at in space and time, as well as with who they really are. Liberatory education begins with students in concrete historical situations in which everyone is a classed, raced, and gendered actor. The education Freire championed seeks to undo schooling that is aimed at adapting the students to a socioeconomic, political, cultural, and educational order which neither they nor their families had a voice in constructing—a status quo that is not in their best interests. The banking method is not the one to be relied on. As Freire insisted: verticality must be broken down. "The teacher is no longer merely the one-who-teaches, but one who is himself taught in dialogue with the students, who in turn while being taught also teach. . . . In this process, arguments based on 'authority' are no longer valid; in order to function, authority must be on the side of freedom. . . . Men teach each other, mediated by the world, by the . . . [knowable] objects which in banking education are 'owned' by the teacher."[20]

Freirean education provides contexts in which educators can engage with their students so that the latter can develop the ability to become self-educating; capable of critical analysis, solidaristic action, and responsible citizenship—in the world and in their workplaces. The complex relationships between teachers and students have challenged educational reformers and revolutionaries for a long time. The following passage from Marcuse is an important contribution to this challenging debate.

> While it is true that people must liberate themselves . . . it is also true that they must first free themselves from what has been made of them in the society in which they live. This primary liberation cannot be "spontaneous" because . . . [it] would only express the values and goals derived from the established system.

Self-liberation is self-education but presupposes education by others. In a society where the unequal access to knowledge and information is part of the social structure, the distinction and . . . antagonism between the educators and those to be educated are inevitable. Those who are educated [I argue that the definition of education should not include a radical dichotomy between those who allegedly are or are not] have a commitment to use their knowledge to help men and women realize and enjoy their truly human capabilities. All authentic education is political education, and in a class society, political education is unthinkable without leadership, educated and tested in the theory and practice of radical opposition. The function of this leadership is to "translate" spontaneous protest into organized action, which has a chance to develop and to transcend immediate needs and aspirations toward the radical reconstruction of society.[21]

Suggested Task for the Reader

Enter into the small but important argument between Freire and Marcuse with regard to differences in knowledge among people, specifically those between teachers and students. It may not be necessary to know more about the two philosophers' positions in order to develop your own point of view based on your reflected-on experience.

Freire used the Portuguese word *conscientização* (conscientization) to mean: learning to perceive socioeconomic and political contradictions and injustices that can be acted upon in order to better our life conditions. The Frankfurt School might call this the achievement of critical consciousness while Marx's term is class-consciousness. Freire referred to the ability to reflect upon "situationality" which is social, material, and concrete. We emerge from our submersion in particular "situationalities" and learn to intervene in realities that become unveiled and clearer. "*Intervention* in reality—historical awareness itself—thus represents a step forward from *emergence*, and results from the *conscientização* of the situation . . . [i.e., the deepening of the attitude of awareness.]"[22] This transformative intervention is what makes us uniquely human as we create and recreate material goods, social institutions, and ideas. For Freire, it is necessary for all to "name" the world, call things by their right names. "There is no true word that is not at the same time a praxis. Thus to speak a true word is to transform the world."[23]

Continuing on with Freire's unique contributions to philosophy of education and pedagogy we shall consider his concept of "problematizing." It should be pointed out that Freire wrote the following about originality or uniqueness: "I have always agreed with Dewey, for whom originality does not lie in the 'extraordinary and fanciful,' but 'in putting everyday things to uses which had not occurred to others.'"[24] Freire explained that "problematizing" is different from how so-called technological experts view problem-solving. "Problematizing" involves solidarity with those s/he intends to help. The dialogical relationships among teachers-students and/or leaders-people produce the "codification" of the problems and possibilities they confront. To codify means to develop learning materials such as sketches, photos, dramatization, tape recordings, etc. in order to facilitate deep and liberatory understandings and action. "Problematizing" is aimed at developing people into Subjects, rather than Objects. Freirean problem posing results in overcoming the dichotomy between teacher and student. The student becomes a "co-investigator" with the teacher. The students are introduced to relevant problems that they must eventually deal with in the "thickness" of the lived world. This concrete "thickness" is similar to Marx's, Dewey's, and the existentialists' positions with regard to human beings' embeddedness in history and the world. Freire also subscribes to this view, one which is opposite of the spectator theory of knowledge, one in which the person as onlooker is sealed off as s/he contemplates a finished product that is believed to be unaffected by cognition.

Freire argued that problem-posing education does not serve the interests of oppressors, because they dare not encourage and/or permit the asking of profound "Why?" questions. Even in a society that features oppressive customs, practices, and institutions, it is possible for liberatory teachers and leaders to employ "problematizing" as their method. The students' worldviews, although inarticulate and inchoate, are where the "problematizing" teacher begins. The dialogic educator helps the students to develop a more clear view of her/his reality through codification, thematic development, and generative words that emerge from the interactive pedagogy. This process of interdisciplinary co-investigation is aimed at representing the world as a problem to be solved. "Problem-posing education bases itself on creativity and stimulates . . . reflection and action upon reality, thereby responding to the vocation of men as beings who are authentic only when engaged in inquiry and creative transformation."[25] Freire shared the view I hold that epistemological doubt and problem posing are a crucial component of democratic people and their processes. Freire used the term "sectarian" to epitomize a position that is antithetical to democracy. He charged that the sectarian disrespects the views of others and attempts to impose her/his positions on others. The sectarian is driven to an unreflective activism because s/he is convinced of rightness and certainty—a conviction that often leads to the attempted imposition of sectarian "truths" upon nonbelievers.

The importance of dialogue for Freire's educational philosophy and practice cannot be overestimated. He called dialogue a horizontal relationship, i.e., A *with* B, rather than A *over* B. Authentic dialogue is inter-communicative, characterized by empathy, loving, humble, hopeful, and trusting, yet critical. This ability to communicate deeply, honestly, and respectfully is based on our having faith in human beings and especially in the proposition that I can be myself when others can do the same. Pedagogy of the oppressed and/or education for democratic empowerment, social justice, and respect for diversity must proceed through dialogue! Teachers and students and/or leaders and people must be free to have a dialogue without fear of arbitrary power interfering. There are differences between the oppressed people in "underdeveloped" countries where Freire worked and students in "developed" and rich (for some) North America; still, there are similarities as well. Oppression takes many forms.[26] If it is difficult or impossible to convince most others of our possession of certainty on major issues we all confront, then for epistemological reason—as well as moral and political ones—we must rely on dialogue among the many. In chapter three of this work, we learned that Habermas is another champion of dialogue. Freire, Habermas, et al. favor dialogue, in part because they believed that ordinary (used honorifically) persons have the potential and ability to think well and act wisely.[27] This belief is not shared by everyone. Those who subscribe to the banking method and/or essentialist types of pedagogy do not subscribe to the belief in widespread human intelligence and capacity for civil, responsible behavior.

Freire wrote that dialogue cannot occur in the absence of hope. Hope is not a passive condition for him. "The dehumanization resulting from an unjust order is not [necessarily] a cause for despair but [instead] for hope, leading to the incessant pursuit of the humanity denied by injustice. . . . If the dialoguers expect nothing to come of their efforts, their encounter will be empty and sterile."[28] For the dialogical, problem-posing educator the content of the pedagogical practice consists of "organized, systematized, and developed 're-presentation' to individuals of things about which they want to know more."[29] Through authentic dialogue we can learn about what was originally unclear.

Freire captured the spirit of this book. "The best philosophy student is not one who discourses '*ipsis verbis*' [verbatim] on the philosophy of Plato, Marx, or Kant but one who thinks critically about their ideas and takes the risk of thinking too."[30] My experience is that teachers in the spirit of Freire and the others featured in this book help their students realize that, although the famous intellectuals, philosophers, and activists are perhaps deserving of their fame, they share with the rest of us living in historical conditions as well as with memberships in a common humanity. Students must realize that they may be able to accomplish critical analyses that can help make a better world. Mike Rose has given us this wonderful passage which articulates well the point I wish to make.

> Professor Ralph Cohen spoke with a Brooklyn accent, and when he spoke he did so with the severity of an Old Testament prophet, pounding the podium with his fist . . . leaning forward to glare at us and level his charge against rival literary theorists. "Aristotle," he said . . . "is in serious difficulty." Aristotle—in difficulty? That knocked me out. . . . [My other teachers] took issue with the philosophers and critics we were studying, but . . . Cohen seemed to be taking it all personally—he looked like my uncles when someone crossed them. Aristotle and Kant and [T.S.] Eliot pissed Cohen off. How could they think so sloppily? How could they not see the issue as he was now setting it before us? He jerked them back from the grave, woke them up just to slap them around. "Aristotle," he repeated, "is really in trouble."[31]

Joel Spring wrote that "the central goal of Freire's pedagogical method is to teach reading and, at the same time, to raise the student's level of consciousness. . . . According to Freire, learning to read is a process of learning how to name the world."[32] Freire realized that literacy is not just a mechanical skill but it is related to knowledge as power. For example, critical literacy empowers people to recognize that they have been cheated out of water rights in northeastern Brazil; it can be used as a tool for a trip to city hall in order to secure those rights. Critical literacy is crucial to the empowered citizen-workers who were championed by Marx and Dewey. Freire knew that illiterates were not verbally illiterate; they were not lacking in intelligence. Teachers in North America must realize this about their students, although Freire's educational insights cannot be transported without the necessary changes being made for somewhat different conditions. The absence of critical literacy plagues populations other than in the impoverished societies in which Freire labored. Freire's famous adult literacy programs were based on the assumption that intelligence is widespread and that people wanted to become Subjects who could help construct better lives for themselves and their children, rather than remain Objects to be hammered upon by those who considered themselves their betters. Freire criticized literacy programs that confronted students with material that did not reflect their experiences. "It required patience . . . after the hardship of a day's work (or . . . [one] without work) to tolerate lessons dealing with . . . 'Johnny saw the wing.' . . . Lessons talking of Graces and grapes to men who never knew a [female called] Grace and never ate a grape."[33] The educational tradition favored in this work is characterized by an agreement that becoming literate and educated is easier to do when the material used is of interest and relevance to the learner. This is central to Dewey's pedagogy. He was known for the following quote. "Only in . . . [formal schooling], never in the life of farmer, sailor, merchant, physician, or laboratory experimenter, does knowledge mean a store of information aloof from doing."[34]

Mike Rose and Freire are kindred spirits. I draw once again on the former's writing to explain further what Freire's literacy programs were based on.

> The English curriculum that I saw [in Los Angeles, CA], and the . . . textbooks particularly, were almost entirely oriented around grammatical analysis, [i.e.,] subskills . . .. There ended up being little room . . . to explore the real stuff of literacy: conveying something meaningful, communicating information, creating narratives, shaping what we see and feel and believe into written language, listening to and reading stories, playing with the sounds of words. . . . The curriculum I saw drained the life out of all this, reduced literacy to the dry dismembering of language, ... The children's textbooks were colorful, and little boys and girls and dogs and cats cavorted around the exercises, but . . . [they] were not all that distant from the ancient descriptive grammar books. . . . It seemed to me that such a curriculum was especially troublesome for children . . . who had not been prepped in their homes to look at language . . . [this way]: children for whom English was a foreign language; children . . . who fell out of curricular lockstep . . . children who, like me long ago, just did not see the sense in such analysis. . . . And so these children would fail at the kind of literary activities the school system had woven throughout its curriculum and turn off to writing and reading. . . . But that did not mean that they were illiterate.[35]

Freire's National Literacy Program in Brazil was terminated by a military take over of the government in 1964. Freire was jailed briefly and then driven into exile by the new regime. They feared his critical literacy campaign that sought to investigate "Themes of the Brazilian people." Many false charges were brought against Freire, but he said that "my actual crime was that I treated literacy as more than a mechanical problem, and linked it to *conscientizaçâo*, which was dangerous. It was that I viewed education as an effort to liberate men, not as another instrument to dominate them."[36]

Freire was not hesitant to talk about spirit and love. This may be the case, in part, because of his membership in Brazilian and Catholic cultures. He argued that radicalization increased one's commitment to the positions and persons one has chosen. These words and ideas are more commonly used and accepted in these cultures than in other liberatory traditions, e.g., Marxism and American progressivism. This is primarily a critical, loving, and humble stance. True solidarity can be found only in the "plenitude of love." It is based on ethical awareness that can result in liberatory praxis based on concern, study, knowledge and hypotheses-construction. Freire drew on Fromm, e.g., love is an active power that can break through the barriers which separate us from others.[37] Perhaps Marx's tragically grim proletariat could be assisted by learning about such forms of nonerotic love for purposes of becoming more collectively effective. Fromm and Freire assume that we are capable of such love (agape) and in this they are allied to others who may not share their entire radical project. The concern and love for one's fellow human beings are essential to Freire's pedagogy of the oppressed. He recognized that this form of agape can be practiced only in freedom, never as the result of compulsion. Fromm wrote: "Those who are seriously concerned with love as the only rational answer to human existence must then arrive at the conclusion that . . . radical changes in our social structure are necessary, if love is to become a social and not a highly individualistic, marginal phenomenon. . . . The economic machine must serve him, rather than he serve it. . . . Society must be organized in such a way that man's social, loving nature is not separated from his social [economic] existence, but becomes one with it."[38]

Both Fromm and Freire were critical of capitalist societies for their alleged domination by destructive competition and materialism. For them, the real materialists are those who are unrestrained in their possessiveness and seek to transform everything into commodities to be purchased. Those materialist oppressors measure everything in monetary terms. What is worthwhile is translated into more of everything. Freire named the oppressors as the class of the 'haves"; a class that blames those who are "have-nots" for their poverty. In crude, social Darwinist fashion the oppressors blame the oppressed by naming them as lazy, ignorant, and without discipline. Freire argued that violence has never been initiated by the oppressed; violence is visited upon the poor through the socioeconomic, political, and educational systems. When the oppressors are occasionally forced to give up some of their unfair advantages over others, the former charge that now they are oppressed. The pedagogy of the oppressed seeks to promote a praxis that will dismantle oppression as a system and oppressors as a class. Some would argue that oppression has many facets and that we are neither all subjected to the same kinds of oppression, nor, at the same time. We will learn about multiple sites of oppression and how some feminists have criticized Freire for ignorance about the oppression of women and people of color—concentrating instead on social-class oppression.

To conclude my consideration of Freire's dependence on love to move forward his liberatory educational, cultural, socioeconomic, political project, I must briefly mention Spring's argument that Freire belonged to a historical tradition in philosophy that included an insistence on the importance of sublimated erotic love as an important contribution to all kinds of human creation and achievement. Spring wrote of sublimation: "Philosophers have considered sexuality as a generalized state of energy and pleasure that can be directed at purely physical pleasure, and also the creation of great works of art and revolutionary desire to free people. This generalized state of sexuality is called Eros."[39] Spring was correct to claim that Freire's assumptions about human nature drive the latter's philosophical, political, and educational project(s). It is always possible that Freire and/or other philosophers could be wrong. Be that as it may, Freire is in good company in his assumptions because Socrates and other deservedly famous thinkers argued that Eros, consciousness, and good deeds can be related.[40]

I have come to the end of presenting and commenting upon Freire's somewhat unique contributions to the philosophical scaffolding for democratic education. I now turn to an explicit argument for Freire's relevance for educational philosophy and practice outside of the Third World contexts in which his work was mainly constructed. I mentioned tangentially in this chapter, history is marked by many and various oppressions and injustices that were endured by all too many people around the world. If one were to subscribe to the mainstream, "free" media's portrayal of reality in the United States, it would be difficult to accept arguments for Freire's relevance here.[41] A critical study of life in these United States may uncover a different picture. In spite of this country's de jure democratic forms of government and progress made with regard to some forms of social class, racial/ethnic, gender, and sexual orientation injustices, many serious problems remain. A critical radical reading of events in the United States reveals continuous struggles by subaltern people whose goals are to make the de jure commitments and promises de facto, i.e., real. I argue that the profound incompatibilities between capitalism-as-a-system and democracy (which requires equality of opportunity as well as ethically justifiable differences in results) continue to plague this polity, society, economic system, and cultures. With regard to education, social-class stratification, as it is affected by other asymmetrical relations of power, privilege, income, wealth, and access, continues to be reproduced through some forms of schooling. Our schools are still in correspondence with powerful socioeconomic and political institutions and processes that do not honor bona fide democracy, social justice, and respect for diversity—let alone authentic and successful caring. Freire's work can, must, and is being applied to educational problems and possibilities in the United States and in other "developed" and rich countries. It is up to the reader to answer the question of Freire's relevance.

Freire's epistemology is specifically congruent with other thinkers' positions on this crucially important part of philosophy and education. He refused to quest for transcendentally guaranteed certainty. He refused also to be paralyzed by this uncertainty; he, like Marx, Dewey, and many existentialists, saw the world as a problem to be solved. Just because one is without deity-given instructions, codes, or laws does not mean that everything is relative. Our various educational, intellectual, and political tools have allowed us to make moral and ethical distinctions according to common sense—bolstered theoretically and empirically. The democrats championed by Freire and me subscribe to democratic dialogue as the best alternative to the supposed moral relativism, cynicism, and nihilism that allegedly follow logically from the absence of certainty. The generalized nature of human intelligence and the historical record of altruistic, brave, and individual social responsibility together give us confidence that we can reflect critically on our experiences as well as construct a human-based ethics. The scientific method, in its various forms, has been central to those who seek to construct better understandings of our world and ourselves. This is in no way a call for the exclusion of those critical democrats who believe that they benefit also from some form of divine guidance. In section III of this chapter, I will specifically address liberation theology and its progressive "believers." The philosopher Abraham Edel wrote that "wisdom is not a separate light shining from outside. It is rather a full sense of how, in the historical present, knowledge and value and the practical situation operate in their constant interaction, and what our directive values require in knowledge and for action."[42]

Section I concludes with the following perspective of Freire's contributions to the kinds of sociopolitical action and education championed in this book. Although not every student is oppressed, Freire was correct to argue that recognition and action are central to learning—whether in a relatively safe school or in the midst of oppressive social conditions which require overcoming. He understood that not even the best-intentioned leaders can give freedom or independence to someone else. The learner in all contexts must be volitional and reflective in order to overcome impediments to learning and concomitantly engage in the "ontological and historical vocation of becoming more human."[43] The students and/or

revolutionaries must believe in themselves. Freire's sophisticated awareness of relationships between individuals and groups was articulated by
his conviction that, although it is impossible to liberate/educate oneself
alone, it is not possible for this to occur solely by the efforts of the leader/
teacher either. Liberatory education is dependent on broad and deep existential experience as well as critical reflection on it.

Freire was well aware of oppression that was caused by more sophisticated means than guns, bayonets, and police dogs. He, like Gramsci,
understood that hegemony consists of oppressed people being convinced
that their present living conditions are the way things are, ought to be,
and are unchangeable. He wrote of the "tragedy" of how people are manipulated by organized advertising. People unwittingly give up their capacities for choosing. The important issues that shape life are decided on
by self-appointed elites. Drawing from Fromm once more, Freire wrote of
veneers of human optimism that paper over profound feeling of power-
lessness. Noam Chomsky spoke of power elites engaged in "manufactur-
ing consent" among ordinary citizens. The following passage from Freire
articulates his broad understanding of how injustice and oppression work,
wherever it occurs.

> The oppressed suffer the duality which has established itself in their innermost
> being. They [we] discover that without freedom they cannot exist authentically.
> Yet although they desire . . . [it], they fear it. They are at one and the same time
> themselves [oppressed] and the oppressor whose consciousness they . . . inter-
> nalized. The conflict lies in the choice between being wholly themselves or . . .
> divided; between ejecting the oppressor within or not . . . between human soli-
> darity or alienation; between being spectators or actors; . . . between speaking
> out or being silent. . . . This is the tragic dilemma of the oppressed [of all kinds
> and degrees] which their education must take into account.[44]

Paulo Freire knew that we must seek life-affirming humanization through
struggle. In the spirit of various Reds, he knew that the oppressed have
not just sought more bread—as crucial as food is to human life. Freire
would have had us struggle for "bread and roses"! The term "bread and
roses" refers to a 1912 strike in Lawrence, Massachusetts, by textile
workers. Some scholars connected the Lawrence strikers' insistence on
bread and butter issues, as well as personal and cultural dignity, to a 1920
strike which occurred in Turin, Italy, when railroad workers and their
families were fired upon by soldiers. Actually, the Turin strike featured
carnations. The point is that "historians influenced by E.P. Thompson
[British labor scholar] have been . . . right to reject the notion that working people engaged only in 'rebellions of the belly,' while thoughts of
'love and life and flowers and song and beauty and the ideal,' about which

Arturo Giovanitti wrote from his prison cell during the Lawrence strike, were meaningful only to people with incomes and education."[45] Stanley Aronowitz wrote the following introduction to a work published after the Brazilian educator's death in 1997.

> Freire . . . takes his stand with those who would create social and economic arrangements that while dedicated to more equality, go beyond the urgent task of eliminating poverty, hunger, and disease. The good life is not merely having a job, enough to eat, and decent shelter. Authoritarians have, from time to time, been able to deliver this much, at least for limited periods. Freire holds that a humanized society requires cultural freedom, the ability of the individual to choose values and rules of conduct that violate conventional social norms, and, in political and civil society, requires the full participation of *all* of its inhabitants in every aspect of public life. . . . For Freire . . . "the foundation stone of the whole [educational] process is human curiosity. . . ." A learner who has reached this point is ready to demand power, which, after all, is the object of any pedagogy of freedom.[46]

Freire rejected schooling that concentrates mostly on the preparation and training of classed, raced, and gendered students for the highly stratified world of work featured by capitalist economies. In the 1990s he was especially critical of the worldwide tendency for schools to adapt to demands made by the spokespersons and agents of the capitalist "new world order."

Suggested Task for the Reader

Freire's philosophy, politics, and philosophy of education include emphases upon the following terms and ideas: conscientization, dialogue, deconstructing/overcoming the banking (or essentialist) method of education, hope, love, and what has been referred to as bread *and* roses. Construct an argument, based upon careful interpretations of the terms and ideas stated above, one which seeks to convince the reader that *either* (a) Freire's work is indeed applicable to situations beyond the places where he put his ideas into practice; or (b) his work is relevant only, or mostly, to his native Brazil, other former Portuguese colonies, and Latin America. Those readers who are preparing to become professional teachers and/or are already engaged in the profession are encouraged to include attention to teachers' work as they construct their arguments.

II

This section is focused on various critical, progressive educators and activists who have welcomed and/or embraced both Freire's critique and courageous hopefulness. I continue with Aronowitz's assessment of Freire's work on the occasion of the Brazilian educator's death. "He was . . . an intellectual and proud of it. His response to efforts to reduce his philosophical and theoretical ideas to a teaching method geared to helping students [merely] obtain careers was [one of] annoyance. His passing should be a time . . . to rededicate . . . [ourselves] to his revolutionary, radical democratic commitments, to make education part of a larger project of social and cultural emancipation."[47] Aronowitz emphasized Freire's denunciation of educational "reactionaries" who would have us make education mainly the training of students to take their places in the highly stratified, and unfair, capitalist job market. Education for self-exploration and understanding is pressured by banking method reactionaries to become mostly a process of learning for tests through the ingesting of externally imposed curricula. Freire believed that everyone can learn about the deepest, most interesting, and important things. His belief in our ability to emancipate ourselves was rooted in an ethical and hopeful "existentialist" commitment, rather than in any form of alleged personal/historical inevitability. I conclude the presentation of Aronowitz's evaluation and admiration for Freire with the following:

> Freire believes the teacher [necessarily] takes sides between those who have appropriated the wealth, the land, and the knowledge of the social and cultural system and the dispossessed. Freire judges current social and political arrangements by the criterion of whether they have taken steps to meliorate, much less reverse, the long tradition of authoritarian societies to exclude substantial portions of their population from participation in economic, social, and cultural life and whether they further or retard humanity's project of self-fulfillment. Finding that in his native land . . . neo-liberalism [unregulated markets] has done little to change the conditions of life for ordinary people, he joined the opposition Workers Party and became its first secretary of education . . . in . . . Sao Paulo in 1991.[48]

Let us turn our attention once more to Peter McLaren's analysis and assessment of Freire's work. McLaren situated his comments within the context of postmodernist thought. He argued that postmodernists are correct to criticize epistemologies that claim to rest on certainty and/or foundational principles, as well as "grand narratives" that claim privileged, cognitive explanatory powers. However, McLaren worried about postmodernist thought's shortcomings with regard to the perhaps ironic results of overthrowing overly authoritarian epistemological positions—in the name of justice and equity. These results are characterized by "'fragmentation, jaggedness, decentering, deconstruction, a frenetic giddy whirl of overturning . . . the "common" experience of our time.'"[49] I shall revisit postmodernist thought in chapter eight. McLaren was critical of postmodernism's lack of solid cognitive ground, a weak epistemic subject, and the absence of hope/possibility for making things better. McLaren criticized postmodernist thinkers for failing to address the need to translate theory into transformative liberatory politics in school and society. "In summary, if we accept the view of reality implicit in much of postmodernist theorizing, then we will get a reality independent of . . . political commitment . . . [and] of a preferential concern for subordinate groups and therefore intrinsically meaningless as the grounds for creating an emancipatory praxis linked to a struggle for democracy."[50]

McLaren is not proposing a return to false or unprovable claims of certainty on which to ground progressive action in schools and society. He does criticize postmodernist thought for deconstructing any "privileged ground" on which to base and justify convincing arguments for the kind of education and politics favored throughout this book. It is at this point that McLaren brings Freire into his analysis. Calling Freire a self-assured modernist revolutionary, McLaren lauds the Brazilian for his tireless struggle to translate solid ideas into liberatory praxis.

Unlike the postmodernist description of human beings as floating freely and aimlessly in a sea of ever-changing meanings, Freire's people are firmly rooted in existentially rich lives and struggles. His people sweat, suffer, hope, work, and live complexly in concrete historical situations—ones that allow the possibilities for long-term solidaristic and comradely relationships. This portrayal of men and women is in keeping with Marxist and existentialist views on the human condition. Some would ague that Dewey also shares in this earthy view of our condition. It is with such people that Freire engaged in his concrete educational, social, and political projects. His utopianism is based on faith in human beings and our abilities to dialogue, learn, and to understand the need for democracy, social justice, and respect for diversity. As Henry Giroux said, Freire is utopian in the sense that he persists in his liberatory project against all odds: refusing to surrender to the unjust status quo.

McLaren explained that,

Freire's language of hope and his utopian vision are . . . engrained in . . . the prophetic new Church of Latin America. He assails the traditional church for presenting a world view that "satisfies the fatalistic and frightened consciousness of the oppressed" . . . while drowning them in a culture of silence. . . . The prophetic church is occupied by "a critical analysis of the social structures in which conflict takes place" . . . and demands of its followers ". . . knowledge

. . . and ultimately 'an ideological choice.'" Accompanied by . . . liberation
theology, . . . the prophetic church challenges the present historical situation in
Latin America. Freire writes that "such a . . . perspective does not represent an
escape into a world of unattainable dreams. It demands . . . knowledge of the
world as it really is."[51]

I shall consider liberation theology further in the next section of this
chapter. It must be made clear that Freire's hope is not a new quest for
certainty. He too realized that history is open: that human effort can
result in progressive accomplishment. However, there are no guarantees.
As McLaren pointed out: "Freire understands full well that a pedagogy of
liberation has no final answers: Radical praxis must always emerge from
continuous struggle within specific . . . [educational] sites and among
competing theoretical frameworks. Truth has no necessary closure, no
transcendental justification. Even the God of History and the Oppressed
can offer no final solution since history is, for Freire, 'becoming' and is,
furthermore, 'a human event.'"[52]

Giroux has helped us understand Freire's work and its significance. "At
the core of Freire's notion of knowledge is a recognition of the dialectical
interconnections between the doer, the receiver, and the objective world
itself. Knowledge is seen as an active force that is used . . . to make
sense of: [our] 'life-world'. . . . Knowledge . . . is more than a social
construct, it also represents the basis for social action. A radical conception of knowledge does not rest simply on the ability to demystify the
ideological hegemony of the dominant order. . . . [It] also rests on how
well it can be used by the oppressed themselves to question the very
processes used to constitute and legitimate knowledge and experience in
the first place."[53] As we generate our own meanings, such knowledge
serves us to become self-determining and better able to choose among
various truth claims. Giroux realized that Freire's work was relevant to
educational and societal problems and possibilities in North America because the latter's work helps us understand the political nature of schooling. Freire's analysis assists people everywhere to understand the "normative and ideological underpinnings that exist at the various levels of the
classroom encounter."[54]

In an article published after Freire's death (May 2, 1997), Giroux emphasized the following: "Hope for Freire is a practice of witnessing, an act
of moral imagination that enables progressive educators and others to
stand at the edge of society, to think beyond existing configurations of
power in order to imagine the unthinkable in terms of how they might live
with dignity, justice, and freedom. Hope demands an anchoring in transformative practices, and one of the tasks of the progressive educator is to

'unveil opportunities for hope, no matter what the obstacles may be.'"[55] Freire did not underestimate the obstacles. He suffered imprisonment and forced exile. Giroux was right to remind us that Freire's work is not about self-improvement in constricted vocational and/or psychological terms alone; instead it urges transformation of the many forms of oppression and domination that prevent all too many from realizing their overall human potentials. Freire never forgot the need to transform the material conditions of our lives that make our historic attempt to advance closer to what we can and should become difficult. Giroux presents a useful summary of Freire's legacy.

> Freire leaves behind a corpus of work that emerged out of a lifetime of struggle and commitment. Refusing the comfort of master narratives, Freire's work is always unsettled and unsettling. . . . Unlike so much of the politically arid and morally vacuous academic and public prose that characterizes much of contemporary educational discourse, Freire's work is . . . fueled by a healthy rage over the needless oppression and suffering he witnessed as he traveled all over the globe. . . . Freire's gift is to elaborate a theory of social change and engagement that is neither vanguardist nor populist. He has a profound faith in the ability of ordinary people to become critical agents in shaping history, but he also refuses to romanticize the culture and experiences of those who bear the weight of oppressive social conditions. Combining theoretical rigor, social relevance, and moral compassion, Freire's work and politics give new meaning to daily life while affirming the importance of critical theory and radical pedagogy in opening up the space . . . [for] critique, possibility, and practice.[56]

It would be a great loss if we failed to keep Freire's work and example alive during this time of continuous attacks on education committed to meaningful democratic participation by the many and aimed at the achievement of greater social justice.[57]

Suggested Task for the Reader
Explore the possibilities for different kinds of schooling in the United States (and elsewhere) if "minority," "underclass," and/or "underachieving" students were seen as part of an *oppressed* group. Can arguments be made to successfully reconfigure many student failures as a part of socioeconomic, political, school oppression—albeit not intended by the overwhelming majority of educators?

III

As we turn to the main ideas of liberation theology it is necessary to explain why they could or should be included in this philosophy of education book. This explanation is especially required because of the secular emphasis in my work. Let us reflect on chapter five and the existentialists so as to provide a transition to section III. To facilitate this transition I revisit the work of William Spanos. Spanos explained that for religious existentialists, the so-called "death of God" means not being able to hold on to a concept of the deity that is entirely knowable and a source of certainty. The religious existentialist still must choose to hammer out personal and social meaning in the thickness and chaos of everyday, concrete life. Chapter five shows that the secular or humanistic existentialist revolts occurred against the threat of absurdity and lack of built-in meaning exemplified by Sisyphus. For the religious existentialist "the mythic symbol of the absurd man [sic] . . . is the biblical Abraham, although he cannot perceive God rationally, nevertheless obeys."[58] Sisyphus represents the agonized acknowledgement of human alienation from the world and universe. The religious or "theistic" existentialist takes a Kierkegaardian and/or Abrahamian "leap of faith, a wager, that though unprovable, God exists. God is merely incomprehensible rationally or absent for the Christian existentialists described by Spanos. Such persons must still "choose between a life of despair in the realm of Nothingness and life of precarious joy in the realm which, to the empirical eye appears meaningless, but to the eye of faith constitutes on the microcosmic level a reconciliation between existence and essence . . . on the macrocosmic level. . . . For the Christian existentialist, in other words, existence precedes essence only in the sense that man cannot know his divine essence and achieve an I-Thou relationship with God without immersion into the destructive element of existence. For both atheistic and theistic existentialists, then, the royal way of 'salvation' lies in the heart of darkness which is this world."[59] It is the story of Christ's life on earth and His sacrifice that provides the possibilities of reconciliation, liberation, and justice for the theistic existentialists. I shall conduct my consideration of liberation theology from within the context of what has been presented above. The following is a brief background of liberation theology.

The Brazilian liberation theologians, Leonardo and Clodovis Boff, dramatized well the radical tenor of section III. "The liberation wrought by [the historical] Jesus outside the law and customs of the time, and his radical requirements for a change of behavior along the lines of the Beatitudes [from the Sermon on the Mount], led him into serious conflict with all the authorities of his age. He knew defamation . . . persecution and the threat of death. His capture, torture, judicial condemnation, and crucifixion can be understood only as a consequence of his activity and his life."[60] Present day, liberation theologians pose this aggressive question to the powerful: What kind of solidarity do capitalists and Christians seek with the world's oppressed? What are you doing to promote the development of social structures and procedures that are likely to result in more justice for the greatest number of people? Leonardo Boff thinks that most capitalists would respond: The best way to help the poor is to avoid being one of them! Liberation theologians understand well that the rich countries also include many who are poor and oppressed. Many children and adolescents in this country's schools can be included in these categories. Jonathon Kozol's *Savage Inequalities: Children in America's Schools* (1991) exposes this fact in devastating fashion.

American philosopher Cornel West helps to provide background and context for connections between the historical Jesus and the present demand for liberation and socioeconomic, political, cultural, and educational justice. He argued that capitalism has failed to provide "existential moorings and emotional assurance" to people where it is dominant as well as in societies where capitalism is becoming dominant, e.g., Latin America. Capitalist-directed industrialization, urbanization, and consumerism have helped destroy old face-to-face communities and customary social and familial relations. It has not replaced them, offering instead a society in which one's worth is judged primarily in terms of one's usefulness to amoral and or immoral market demands and outcomes. Participation as consumers, for those who can afford it, becomes the substitute for communal and/or citizen participation. Capitalist work and consumer relations and activities represent a growing totalism that pushes aside older practices and meanings. Religious movements have occurred in the second half of the twentieth century in part as a response to rich, "developed," capitalist countries' neoimperialist attempts to dominate so-called underdeveloped countries in terms of working for low wages and in turn purchasing the commodities produced by capitalist corporations. These occurrences have been accompanied by people being expelled from the land where they toiled as farmers and forcing them to serve as proletarians (people who have nothing but their labor to offer) in the growing cities of Latin America. The Catholic Church has emerged as an institution (*not without internal strife*) that provides contexts in which the oppressed can discuss their conditions, seek new personal and social meanings, and construct explanations for their misery as well as hypothesize and plan strategies for liberation.[61]

In Latin America, "base communities" provide places where oppressed people can combine religious, literacy, and political education. This religious and lay movement is most prominent in Brazil where Freire, although not a theologian, participated as a teacher of the (formerly) illiterate of his country. Passages from the Bible that speak of the hungry being fed are relevant to impoverished Latin Americans and help convince them that the god of history is on their side. The Italian film, "The Gospel According to St. Mathew," directed by Pier Paolo Pasolini, is a brilliant example of what "base communities" attempt to teach about their religion and its potential for liberation. This film features an angry revolutionary, Jesus, who drives the moneychangers from the temple. The struggle revolving around liberation theology in Latin America has involved great risk to clergy and laypeople. Some members of the clergy have been silenced by those above them in the church hierarchy. Many have been beaten, jailed, tortured, killed, and "disappeared." This movement declares its "preferential option for the poor" and shares some characteristics with the black civil rights struggle in the United States from the 1950s to the 1990s, and the Latino United Farm Workers' Union activities, led by Caesar Chavez in California and the southwestern United States in the recent past. Frantz Fanon's *The Wretched of the Earth* (1961) has allowed Latin Americans seeking to overcome oppression to understand their situation in a global context—Fanon's book addresses the Algerian struggle for liberation from French imperialism. Like the United States, Brazil has a large black population whose members were brought to the Western Hemisphere as slaves. The revolutionary work of Amilcar Cabral during the 1960s in the former Portuguese colonies of Guinea-Bissau and Cape Verde Islands in Africa has influenced Americans in terms of understanding the sources and realities of their oppression in concrete historical and global terms. Brazil was a former Portuguese colony. Freire worked in Guinea-Bissau as an educator after its liberation from the colonial power. The revolutionary writings and activities of Argentinean, Che Guevara, in Cuba, South America, and Africa are relevant to issues raised with liberation theology and philosophy.[62] There are differences between Marxists and religionists, but as we shall see, similarities do exist.

Starting in the 1960s "winds of change" blew through many societies including churches and other religious institutions. The Roman Catholic Church, as well as various Protestant Churches, have had historical records of socioeconomic and political concerns and action. This tradition was reactivated in the Catholic Church by the Second Vatican Council during the explosive sixties. Vatican II was conducted in the spirit of *aggiornamento* (updating) and it provided support and justification for social and religious change. The Council's participants spoke of the "underdeveloped" countries, mostly in the Southern Hemisphere, that were exploited by the rich capitalist countries. The countries of the "center" were exploiting countries of the "periphery." The term *oppression* began to be used rather than underdevelopment. Causal relationships between wealth and poverty were recognized. The "poor have always found a merciful welcome, and place of their own in the Church. But they have never been accorded [until the 1960s] a collective status as principal historical subject of the . . . [enactment] of the protest of the Poor One of Nazareth."[63] Similar to Freire's insistence, liberation theologies see the oppressed poor as potential agents of their own liberation, albeit with help. Freire argues earlier in this chapter that the student is volitional and is responsible for and capable of her/his own learning. Although the proletariat was the revolutionary agency for Marx, he too insisted that oppressed people must free themselves, as they come to learn about causes, conditions, theories, facts, and strategies for liberation. The Latin American poor, many of them agricultural workers as well as of "Indian" or native origin, came on the historical stage *after* the industrial workers' first appearance in the nineteenth century. Similar to Europe, the United States, and elsewhere in the Northern Hemisphere, workers who were originally agricultural workers are the ones who have been pushed and pulled into urban centers, jobs, and joblessness as Latin America has undergone industrialization under foreign and domestic capitalisms.

Vatican II provided space for liberation theology to develop. A theology of hope and politics began to take root in Latin America. The Catholic Church, *with internecine struggle*, moved in the direction of being world-centered rather than its earlier church focus. Theologians and activists attempted to translate eschatological (study of last or final matters) hope into a demand for justice in history, more specifically in the very near future. Issues of social justice were on the table for discussion in the Church. In 1968 the Latin American Catholic bishops met formally in Medellín, Columbia and announced that the Church had a message for those who hunger and thirst for justice. This declaration made clear the institution's commitment to take a stand against oppression in the here and now. The Church promised to join hands with those who were relegated to being "nonpersons" or the "damned of the earth" in Latin America. Leonardo Boff wrote, "justice, by definition, is justice for all. Likewise freedom, rights, and dignity must be prerequisites of all human beings; otherwise they belong to none."[64] The Latin American bishops met officially again in 1979 in Puebla, Mexico, and reinforced what they had started in Medellín. The Puebla meeting must be understood in terms of the ten-year period of experimentation that preceded it.

After Medellín the Catholic Church attempted to reposition itself among the subjugated. According to Leonardo Boff, the religion of the people can become a catalyst for theories and practices aimed at constructing alternative societies—especially alternatives to capitalism, neoimperialism, and injustices suffered by indigenous people, people of color, women, and others who historically constitute the oppressed. At Medellín and Puebla the Latin American Church made a "categorical option" for the people—the oppressed and poor—for their liberation socially, materially, politically, religiously, and educationally. A commitment was made to establish "base communities." The Church showed that it was ready to assist in constructing a more equal society where everyone could participate meaningfully. Opposition to this new direction was fierce and even murderous. Oppositional forces from all over the Americas, including in the United States, reacted on many fronts, including fighting civil wars in many Latin American countries. The papacy in Rome, under the increasingly conservative John Paul II, reacted critically to what he and his allies deemed radical beyond the intentions of the earlier *aggiornamento*. Nevertheless, Gustavo Gutiérrez's *Theology of Liberation: History, Politics and Salvation* appeared in 1971 and was, and continues to be, widely read.

Suggested Task for the Reader
Construct an informative, persuasive argument that employs liberation theology's concepts to strengthen progressive projects in your own society and school. Specifically, address how the theology's and movement's insistence on radical inclusivity might be threatening to those who benefit today from the status quo.

The liberation under consideration here is an integral one—of the whole person and all of us, into every facet of our societies—although the focus in Latin America is on the very poor and most severely oppressed. Liberation includes rising above material poverty, getting free of social and political oppression, and the emergence of a new human being—one free from sin and seeking realization and actualization in God. Readers who study liberation theology and philosophy in greater depth will learn that the tensions between those who see liberation as a wholly secular project and those who understand it as both on earth and in terms of a good life leading to eternal life have not been resolved. For the later, the religious spiritualists, the struggle for earthly social justice is to be understood within the larger framework of both human and divine liberation. In spite of the emphasis on the very poor, the liberatory project includes an option for the youth. This is important to educators everywhere. As Leonardo Boff wrote about Latin America: "Young people—persons under eighteen years of age—make up more than one-half of the . . . population. But the majority of youth are condemned to live their lives without ever having been young. At the first possible moment, they are absorbed into the productive process under conditions of exploitation. . . . Our pastoral activity with our youth aims basically at making them agents of change in society—not by way of violence but through the liberation process, in solidarity with organized . . . [adults]."[65] George Counts and other educational reconstructionists (see chapter four) have argued that the youth can and must play a part in liberatory struggle, in the United States and elsewhere. This insistence is tied to the belief that all human beings can understand issues as well as act on this comprehension. Marx, Gramsci, and Dewey agreed with this belief.

Clergy and laypersons struggling to transform a dream of freed men, women, and youth into concrete societal reality characterize the background of liberation theology. Latin American liberationists agree with Martin Luther King, Jr. and other revolutionaries that without a dream, energizing myth, and/or a liberatory, democratic imagination, it is either difficult or impossible to mobilize people effectively for the long haul that is necessary for struggle against the powers that be. Some adjectives that define liberatory struggles in Latin America are comradely, prophetic, committed, joyful, contemplative, utopian, and bravely active. The Boffs have claimed: "Those committed to integral liberation will keep in their hearts [and minds] the *little utopia* of at least one meal for everyone everyday, the *great utopia* of a society free from exploitation and orga-nized around the participation of all, and finally the *absolute utopia* of communion with God in a . . . redeemed creation."[66] Although non-religious spiritualists and secular radicals may not endorse the absolute utopia, they may be interested in the power of hope as we all struggle for justice against difficult opposition. The work of educational theorist Giroux has been helpful to educators in terms of his reminders of the importance of possibilities as well as problems. He is conversant with and knowledge-able about the issues presented in chapter six.

To summarize, the background of liberation theology includes the fol-lowing. It developed in Latin American peripheral societies. Its adherents insisted that the plight of the poor and oppressed be put on the agenda of Church, society, and politics. Its prophetic function was to uncover and denounce the causes responsible for the wretched conditions which so many lived under. Writers and activists were not hesitant to point out world and national capitalism, neoimperialism, and oppressive governments that supported unjust economic systems. The liberationists' focus was on the material concreteness of everyday life, although the related cultural realities were included. Liberationists insisted that action be taken as a logical and moral consequence for the official options for the poor, youth, et al. This championing of inclusivity and justice for all has ramifications for those interested in justice for their own schools and societies— wherever they may live. The liberation movement represents a progressive, discernible, world historical movement (not an inevitability) demanding justice for those formerly excluded. I have confidence that special education teachers in the United States would understand this point as they place legal guarantees for the inclusion of all youngsters in the mainstream of public school life.

Argentinean Enrique Dussel provided a context and explanation of liberation theology that allows us to better understand its philosophical underpinnings and meanings. Connecting secular and religious ideas to socioeconomic, political, cultural, and education ideas and realities, he viewed liberation theology as a challenge to the closed system and totalism represented by European and North American theology and capitalism. The dominance of the center over the periphery is contested on many fronts, including ideas and their concrete manifestations.[67] Dussel acknowledged the importance of Freire's pedagogy of liberation and those who practice it with the well-being of their students in mind. He agreed with Freire that the relationships between teacher and student are complex and that the former is neither all-wise nor the latter ignorant and/or an empty vessel. He wrote that the prophetic-pedagogical function of the Church in the concreteness of history is to liberate people from oppression, including pedagogical dependence, even if it is not oppressive.[68]

Domenico Jervolino argued that although theological and philosophical hermeneutics are distinct disciplines of interpretation; their histories are intertwined.[69] Liberation theology and philosophy developed concomitantly as a result of the events briefly described in this background part of section III. Liberation philosophy also developed from the debate in Latin America concerning whether underdevelopment meant delay in catching up with the rich center, or with the center's oppression of the periphery. Argentina is the birthplace of liberation philosophy, one that attempts to break free of European and other center academic models of interpretation. It posits instead, the Latin American people as the agents and subjects of their own history, thus helping to remove the imperialist or colonial yoke from those seeking autonomy, independence, and liberation. One can easily understand that such philosophy is helpful to any oppressed and colonized people; e.g., people of color in the United States as well as women and persons with nonheterosexual orientations and practices. The next chapter will address these philosophical similarities.

Jervolino pointed out that Dussel thought of the Other, i.e., the Latin American poor and oppressed, as the living and "fleshy" subjectivity that provides an outside point of reference to the closed system of capitalist totalism, as well as social and religious thought produced in the rich countries. Latin Americans argued for a somewhat different key agent of liberation from Marx's industrial proletariat. Both liberation philosophy and Marxism start from the realities of living workers in their concrete historical struggle for more secure, participatory, and dignified lives. Referring back to chapter three and the emphasis upon spaces for inclusive conversation among people, Jervolino pointed out that it is an empirical fact that three-quarters of humanity are excluded from participating meaningfully in democratically empowered communication. Horkheimer's ideal speech context is far removed from the possibilities of the Latin American poor and for oppressed people everywhere. The twentieth-century philosopher Karl Popper's "open society" is not enjoyed by most of the subaltern people—including youths—in the Americas and around the world. Because of the "immense world of the excluded" we can say that Western civilization's philosophy of freedom is suspect because of its reluctance or failure to expand its rights and privileges. Countries of the rich center in the Northern Hemisphere must come to terms with its conquest of most of the rest of the world. The West's liberating ideas and practices must include all Others.

Consider more carefully the emphasis on human agency and volition as we study liberation theology and philosophy as ideas for action. Throughout this book, one of the most important themes has been the insistence upon human beings' abilities to *act upon* other people and forces. We in turn are acted upon. First, the poor and oppressed are portrayed as having led the way to their own liberation by reading the Bible from their own positions, the bottom of the socioeconomic, political order.[70] The oppressed refer their interpretive (hermeneutical) understanding of the Bible to their lives in all its concrete materiality. Plans for action derive from the interpretive insights learned. Only then is action taken. Freire, Dewey, and Marx all celebrated the learner, beginning by making sense of their own experiences. The following may clarify my argument:

It is a reading [of scripture] that takes the material world and human society seriously. Until roughly a generation ago religion and religious symbols essentially affirmed the existing order, including the [social] class system. Although many readings of Christianity continue to do that, this new reading subjects existing social arrangements to a critique whose standard is how it affects the . . . poor. Not only does this reading not see the existing order as fixed by God, but sees human beings as [mostly] responsible for the earth, including the societal arrangements they live under. . . . In Latin America one . . . hears the notion that human beings are called to be "subjects of their own destiny," "co-creators in history."[71]

This articulation has little or nothing to do with the capitalist assertion and conservative insistence in the United States that people are responsible for and subject to punishment for "choosing" to be poor! The liberation reading is similar to Marx's Eleventh Thesis on Feuerbach: The theologians have only interpreted the world; the point is to change it, to change the system of oppression that contributes to ghettos, barrios, slums, and school failure.

Joel Kovel argued that "spirit reaches beyond the material, historical world of economy and technology, yet it is deeply affected by the time and place at which it arises. Thus spirit stands outside history, acts within history, and is acted upon by history."[72] This helps explain the power of liberation theology, its precarious balancing act between the concrete and the hoped-for, not-yet-realized tomorrow. Some religious have placed this tomorrow in the afterlife. Liberationists have insisted that justice can and must be achieved here on earth. Liberation theology does *not* claim that perfect justice can be realized; instead, it is within the human effort to secure more justice that liberation is pursued. Kovel told the story of an old, Spanish anarchist as he was confronted by skeptics because of his alleged utopianism, or even quixotism. He responded by suggesting that realization may be impossible; that most everything that is possible in these times is worthless. "The reason we should fight for spirit is the here and now, because spirit creates a new sense of the possible. . . . Thus the impossible must be imagined if it is to be realized, and it is true sanity to do so."[73]

The murky border between human agency and alleged divine assistance is troublesome for secular spiritualists, secularists per se, and obviously for agnostics and atheists. The Great French Revolution of 1789 was conducted by people who believed in an inherent rationality in human history and that they were on the right side. Those who made the Russian Revolution of 1917 were convinced that they were acting in accordance with deterministic economic laws that they credited Marxist thought for having discovered. I shall leave this murky border to you for further discussion. Liberation theologians argue that the Bible is mainly the work of oppressed people, as they wrote about how that condition might be overcome. Their constructions of the deity allowed them to argue that their God was on their side. This interpretation by contemporary poor and oppressed people is attractive and heartening. The rich and powerful are not usually attracted to this radical reading of scripture. The classical concept of God as an omnipotent figure who is removed from the messy everydayness of history is replaced by one who enters this place and assists those in bondage, e.g., Exodus and Jesus. Christ is portrayed as "very human, sharing utterly in the lot of the poor and oppressed . . . helping them fashion tools for overcoming their . . . [conditions]."[74] In Luke 4:18–19, "Jesus proclaims what can only be seen as a revolutionary message. . . . He announces that God has sent him to bring the good news to the poor, to release the captives . . . to set at liberty those who are oppressed . . . debts . . . forgiven . . . land redistributed so that all can share in the collective fruits of God's gifts and of human labor (Leviticus 25:1–24). . . . The basic theme is those who do not do justice do not know God."[75] As children, it was significant to many of us to learn that Joseph and Jesus were tradesmen-carpenters. It is *also* relevant that the dialect of the New Testament, *Koiné* Greek, is the language of the work world, of the untutored, rather than the classical language of famous Greek epics and tragedies.

Leonardo Boff explained, liberation theology and philosophy focus on the historical Jesus (namely, the one that is known beyond the claims of faith alone) for the following reasons. This helps us understand the somewhat similar structural system of oppression between his time and place and ours. A study of his life shows that words and ideas have concrete consequences; they are likely to "stir conflict" and even severe punishment—including death. This study makes clear that the path to the deity is found in risk, iconoclastic thinking, and radical action, i.e., contemplation and carrying religion exclusively inside ourselves are not adequate. The historical Jesus demands that we change ourselves through thought and action; he stands for crisis (a point at which hostile forces and/or elements are most tensely opposed to each other) recognition and response—in the world today! The title of one of the chapters in L. Boff's book, *Faith on the Edge,* is called "Jesus the Liberator." The gospels present Jesus as standing in conflict with the authorities of both religion and government. The historical Jesus experienced the necessity to struggle, sacrifice, suffer, and finally, be executed by the authorities argue many existentialists. The portrayal of Jesus-as-man features his doubting about divine protection at times; he, like religious existentialists must find salvation via the crisis-ridden, dangerous road featuring opposition to the unjust order. The liberationist reading of the Bible is profoundly radical; God is active in history on the side of the oppressed. Theology, the study of divine things, becomes secularly concrete in the sense that one is to act against oppression in the here and now. The biblical secular historical records are called on to remind contemporaries that both Jews and Christians suffered persecution for their beliefs and practices. The many conservative religious leaders and their followers are criticized for attempting to "domesticate" the original radical tendencies in Judaism and Christianity. L. Boff wrote that "the relationship Jesus established with his fellow human beings . . . is a relationship of radical communion. Jesus receives everyone as his brother or sister—Jew, pagan, poor, sinful, oppressed, and oppressor. . . . The supreme commandment is to love one's brothers and sisters, a love that ought to characterize his community. . . . Among sisters and brothers is no longer any servitude, only service. This is what Jesus . . . demands—the kind of relationship that ought to obtain among human beings—and this is what he himself lives, in unquestioned radicality."[76]

Focus specifically again on epistemology as it relates to theological and philosophical liberation. An important and continuing thesis of this book is that critical democracy is best served, as is the necessary education, by holding to an epistemological, cognitive stance that forgoes the quest for certainty. The narrative which follows attempts to demonstrate that although the religious liberationists believe in an interfering and benevolent deity, they do so from a rather untidy epistemology. One could insist in stark either/or terms that the spiritual religionists must choose: "is there, or isn't there." This analysis allows for middle ground and aporia (one has real doubt about where to begin or what to do or say; it describes a difficulty encountered in establishing the theoretical truth of a proposition encountered by evidence both for and against). This conflict is part of the historical tension between faith and reason found in most organized religions. The spiritual religionists hold to the Pascalian wager (it does not hurt to assume that there is a deity who is ultimately in charge). This wager does *not* prevent liberation theology's adherents from taking the need to struggle seriously without guarantees.

Cornel West supported my refusal to abandon the middle ground. Religious commitment and affiliation are not the mark of ignorance or intelligence. Wisdom compels us to understand the circumstances in which people make their decisions with regard to spiritual, religious, or secular responsibility. In fact, "the grand quest for truth—which ultimately separate religionists from secularists—is a . . . historical one that takes the form of practical judgements inseparable from value judgements upon, and social analytical understandings of, prevailing socioeconomic realities. There are . . . standards of adjudication, but such historically constituted standards yield multiple viewpoints worthy of adoption. Hence the quest for truth continues, with only human practice providing provisional closure."[77]

Dussel provided further support for the epistemological middle ground I seek. This liberation theologian depends on solid and inerrant sources; however, the search for these hoped-for true foundations requires a life of constant labor in order to *partially* grasp them. As he struggled, he turned to the oppressed who comprise the mass of people in peripheral areas, such as his own Latin America. He argued that the poor have a special vantage point because of their outside and suffering status. They are tapped as a kind of universal epistemic subject, rather like Marx's choosing the industrial proletariat who could understand and then act to overcome the injustices of their time. In a comparison between liberation theology of the periphery to that of the Western European center, Dussel informed us that "our theology will be . . . more critical than theirs, not because we are more intelligent . . . but simply because we are victims of the system and . . . outside."[78] Similar arguments have been raised by African Americans, Hispanics, women, and others in the United States who argue that they have been systematically discriminated against and oppressed. Such claims have not gone unopposed. These are important issues for educators. The epistemic need to get outside of the realities and totality of what we are studying and seeking to change is historical in Western philosophy. Philosophers, and theologians, seek to establish an outside point of reference from which to understand complex things holistically. Many educational theorists and activists in the United States speak of the necessity to get beyond certain "borders" in order to understand how oppression works, as well as how to oppose it. Those who have been forced to be on or beyond the borders are often referred to as the Other.

L. Boff provided another articulation of liberation theology's epistemology and helps to explain why it belongs in this book, which is concerned with philosophical scaffolding for democratic education. He explained that just because theology is about the deity, the absolute, this does not mean that theology is itself absolute, universal, or without error. Theologians must not and cannot ascribe to themselves qualities and abilities that are reserved only for God. The human *idea* of what may be divine is not the same as the reality. One must not construct idols! In fact, "on the concrete level, faith is always historically situated in a language peculiar to the particular circumstances in which it is lived and experienced. . . . This being the case, there is not reason why there should be a variety of theologies."[79] Liberation theology is based on the realization that human truth cannot be eternal, or unchangeable—or universally applicable; instead it is intrinsically and humanly historical. Rembert Weakland, Archbishop of Milwaukee, Wisconsin, spoke out against the idea and practice of a hierarchical, top-down church in a way that hits the center of my epistemological point. Weakland wrote that the proponents of an authoritarian Catholic Church "'see a strongly hierarchical model . . . where the faithful are taught by the bishops, who are [allegedly] in possession of the gifts of the Spirit needed for authoritative . . . teaching. The model adopted by the U.S. conference [of bishops] believes [instead] that the Holy Spirit resides in all members of the church and that the hierarchy must listen to what the Spirit is saying to the whole church. This does not deny the teaching role of the hierarchy, but enhances it. It does not weaken the magisterium [the authority and power of the church to teach religious truth], but ultimately strengthens it.'"[80] We see in Weakland's words a recognition of authority and a realization that broad participation is required for wise and just decisions, because no one has a monopolistic grasp of *the* truth!

Our focus now shifts from epistemology to liberation theology's method. They are connected. Dussel argued that crisis is a necessary condition for real/profound thought. For him, crisis necessitates judgment by s/he who faces it; this in turn entails a certain distancing of oneself. The person moves away from ordinary day-to-day comprehension in order to see the crisis/problem from the borders or even beyond. The methodology of thinking well requires that we move beyond a comfortable situation. Dussel said it is necessary to assume the position of stranger, rather than one who is comfortably at home. This line of thought would be embraced by existentialists, Dewey, and Marx. In Dussel's words: thinking seeks to get beneath the concreteness of the foundation, to what is "covered up by the dust" of what is conventionally accepted as obvious or the way things are. Educators should be challenged by Dussel's insistence that we must "encamp outside the security of the fortress and know how to penetrate and dwell in an inhospitable land."[81] He feared that for some people being in an inhospitable land is beyond their psychological capabilities based on the fear of losing the security of her/his cognitive "skeletal system."

Juan Segundo wrote of a methodology called the *hermeneutic circle*. Hermeneutics mean interpretation; Segundo saw the need to interpret the scriptures constantly as concrete lived conditions change. The *circle* of which he wrote must be based on (1) the questions addressed being profound, general, and rich enough to potentially change how we see the problems; and (2) the theological frames of references used in question-asking must be of the kind that changes customary interpretation of the scriptures. After these two are in place, we can (a) endeavor to experience the world with "ideological suspicion," and doubts about official definitions of reality and righteousness; (b) turn this suspicion on theology itself; (c) focus this suspicion on what is *missing* in conventional and conservative readings of the Bible; and (d) have the previous steps result in a new and liberatory interpretation of scripture and theology. These underlying assumptions and methodological steps can be used, with the necessary changes being made, to address other forms of official knowledge! Segundo argued that the *hermeneutical circle* can assist those engaged in class struggle.[82]

The methodology of liberation theology was presented by the Boff brothers as follows: first, there is the socioanalytical attempt to ascertain how and why the poor are oppressed; second, the hermeneutical attempt to discern what God's plan is for the oppressed; third, the practical step in which the inquirers attempt to formulate a plan, a praxis, with which to resolve the crisis, to overcome oppression. The Deweyan scientific method, or "complete act of thought," can be compared to the methodology of the spiritual liberationists. The latter consider evidence that the philosophical pragmatists would not use; the borders separating what is to be considered proper data is of great interest to philosophers. At its best, the methodology of liberation theology and philosophy is praiseworthy, in part, because its practitioners stress referring facts to systems and totalities. They try to lay bare everyday practices in reference to the bigger socioeconomic, political, cultural, religious, and educational picture. These actions allow and demand judgment of school and societal policies and practices. The methodologists are aware that judgments are made, for the most part, among seemingly competing goods—not just good and bad. This methodology insists on taking action. The relentless and savage attacks made on supporters of liberation theology prove that they have, indeed, acted.

Suggested Task for the Reader

The word aporia (ah-pohr´-ee-ah) means a difficulty encountered in establishing the theoretical truth of a proposition created by the presence of evidence, both for and against it. The term also means having real doubt about where to begin, what to do, or say. Using the word aporia as a central concept demonstrate your understanding of how many liberation theologians have sought middle ground between the historical quest for certainty and the recognition that, even if this were achievable, it requires a lifetime of struggle through swamps of uncertainty—and requires individual and/or group decisions.

Conclusion

The conclusion of this chapter consists of my commentary on a few subjects and sources that may be useful to the reader. One necessarily studies and takes notes for purposes of writing and teaching that comprise more than can be written and spoken about within space and time frames; so what follows is brief. The first subject is already implicit, if not suggested in this section, Marxist thought's connections with liberation theology.

Liberationists have assigned much of the blame for Latin America's poverty and unjust social-class stratification to oligarchic governments that are part of the global capitalist and neoimperialistic system. Liberation theologians call capitalism "atheism in practice" because of its emphasis on materialism. This is the charge that conservative Christians make against Marxism! Liberationists find Marxist class analysis and historical materialism especially useful. L. Boff argued that historical materialism is not a dogma but an open theory which serves as a tool kit to better understand and change oppressive regimes. He added that using such Marxist tools is not dangerous for people of faith because religion's "broad horizons" can accommodate secular help. He reminded us that ultimately the "grammar" of theology is different from Marxist and/or other secular analyses and that theologians must construct their own synthesis. The two grammars correspond to two distinct dimensions of reality: rationality and hope. He hoped that there will eventually occur a synthesis of socialism and progressive religion which can be strengthened by science and yet be open to a potentially limitless future! Secular rationalists do not usually have this kind of hope. The story told here is one of Latin American Christians becoming militant and joining populist organizations and "left-leaning" political parties. They were responding to "the death of the People," not to the European, Nietzschean "death of God."

José Miranda asserted that Marx's systematic critical analysis of capitalism caused him to conclude that it does not respect human beings as persons, subjects-agents, or Thous. Miranda claimed that this critical analysis is "eminently Christian," at least for Christians who take the social gospel seriously—as do the liberationists. He argued that Marx is a normative humanist, he thinks that Christianity at its best is a form of humanism.[83] The opponents of liberation theology do not agree.

You may have read Marx's famous, or infamous, utterance that religion is the "opium of the people." The interpretation of this passage is better understood as follows. Marx's attitude toward religion in general, although not including all religious institutions, was one of sympathy and understanding. Marx and his collaborator, Friedrich Engels, thought of historical religious expression as a necessary human reaction to oppression and misery. This reaction sought to assert that the oppressed were "somebodies" who deserved to be freed. The Marxists argued that these religionists did not yet fully understand the contributing and/or determinative socioeconomic causes of their oppression.

Historically the secular Left has distrusted institutional religion because of its record of supporting the powers that be. Section III addressed the Left's cooperation with some religious movements. Many socialists, Marxists, and other democratic Leftists are still suspicious of the mysticism and authoritarianism that some religions still represent. Catherine Lugg explained, e.g., how fundamentalist Christians in the United States effectively entered politics beginning in the 1980s. Their intent and impact were very different from that of the liberation theology movement. The fundamentalists supported and were supported by the ultraconservative, and even reactionary, Reagan administration. This Rightist alliance sought to restore public school prayer; fought against sex education and forms of multicultural education; attempted to have "creationism" included in the curriculum as an alternative to the Darwinian theory of evolution; pushed public tax support for students to attend private and religious schools and supported those institutions; opposed the feminists' attempt to have an Equal Rights Amendment for the U.S. Constitution; acted at the forefront to stop the federal government's attempt to integrate schools racially—pursuant to the *Brown v. Board of Education* (1954) Supreme Court ruling; and adamantly contested the attempt by schools and society to include gays and lesbians into the mainstream of American life. These actions were complemented by fundamentalist Christians who supported the Reagan administration's reduction of federal spending for public schools. Lugg claimed that these religionists, for the most part, supported the Republican administration's drive to return to unfettered (by socioeconomic safety nets) capitalism.[84] Lugg recognized that the social-class anxieties experienced by these actors about their places and futures in the rapidly changing capitalist economy served as factors contributing to their reactionary project. What has just been described makes clear that various religions' interpretations of socioeconomic, political, cultural, and educational issues can be quite different from one another.[85]

Prudent watchfulness of organized religion's tendency to reduce spirituality to superstition, dogma, and narrow-minded faith in authority should not cause secular radicals and democrats to be insensitive or hostile to what lies beyond tight definitions of the "rational." Critical theorists have already made clear their opposition to "positivism," i.e., namely, the Western mistaken belief in the exactness of rational science, when science is in essence, hypothetical. Secular democratic radicals have a good record of going beyond positivist interpretations of science and mathematics as they have courageously immersed themselves in literature, poetry, film, and other forms of art that necessitate interpretation. The practice of interpretation shares commonalities with the hermeneutical study of the "nonrational," as well as matters of faith and religion.

My basic reason for the inclusion of various spiritualists in this section and chapter is that many believers have struggled (and still do) for the ideas championed in this book. One's ultimate beliefs and motivations are one's own affair. I insist that those who were involved in progressive collective actions as my comrades should not expect their beliefs and certainties to be accepted as any kind of special, privileged truths. Many spiritualists are able to satisfy my criterion on this litmus test.[86] Cornel West summed up the possible and perhaps necessary cooperation between religious and secular spiritualists—ones who are committed to democratic empowerment and social justice for all, including the Other.

> Notwithstanding the secular sensibilities of most left intellectuals and activists, religion permeates the lives of the majority of people in the capitalist world. And all signs indicate that the prevailing crisis in the capitalist world is not *solely* an economic or political one. Recent inquiries into racism, patriarchy, homophobia, [misogyny], state repression, bureaucratic domination, ecological subjugation and nuclear exterminism suggest that we understand this crisis as . . . [one] of *capitalist civilization*. To extend left discourse about capitalist civilization is to accent a sphere rarely scrutinized by Marxist thinkers: *the sphere of culture and everyday life*. And any serious scrutiny of this sphere sooner or later must come to terms with religious ways of life and religious struggles.[87]

Some of the best educational writing that further articulates West's passage has been done by David Purpel and Svi Shapiro. "As educators, we must stand fast in our faith that understanding and insight are vital for liberation and that the development of intellectual capacities for this purpose remains a central concern. However, our view of education is that its process must extend beyond the intellectual realm since . . . humans do not learn to live and love by intellect alone. We as a people respond also to the rhythms of the body, the light of the soul, and the voices of the spirit."[88]

Notes

1   Peter McLaren, *Life in Schools: An Introduction to Critical Pedagogy in the Foundations of Education*, 3rd ed. (New York: Longman, 1998), xxi. See the whole of McLaren's "In Memoriam" to Freire for a description of the latter's academic, political, and professional life, xxi–xxiv.

2   Richard Brosio, "Eulogy for Paulo Freire, *Taboo: The Journal of Culture and Education*, vol. II (Fall 1997): 40–41.

3   Richard A. Brosio, "*Pro Bono Publico:* Educational Reform and the Historical Actor(s)," *Philosophical Studies in Education* (Coraopolis, Pa.: Ohio Valley Philosophy of Education Society, 1986), 106–16. This volume is the published proceedings of the Society's 1984 conference.

4   Henry A. Giroux, *Ideology, Culture, and the Process of Schooling* (Philadelphia: Temple University Press, 1981), 129.

5   Paulo Freire, *Pedagogy of the Oppressed* (New York: Herder and Herder, 1970), 76–77.

6   Ibid., from the introduction, 15.

7   Denis Goulet, "Introduction," to *Education for Critical Consciousness*, Paulo Freire (New York: The Seabury Press, 1973), x.

8   Freire, *Education for Critical Consciousness*, 5.

9   For an analysis of similarities and differences between Marx and Dewey on democracy and education see: Richard Brosio, "Dewey as the Schoolmaster for Marx's Radical Democracy," *Philosophy of Education 1994*. Proceedings of the Fiftieth Annual Meeting of the Philosophy of Education Society (Urbana, Ill.: Philosophy of Education Society, 1995), 292–301. In my view Freire deepens and broadens Dewey's educational insights in important ways; he too could serve as an educational leader for Marx's radical democracy.

10 Freire, *Pedagogy of the Oppressed*, 21.

11 Freire, *Education for Critical Consciousness*, 33–34.

12 Freire, *Pedagogy of the Oppressed*, 59.

13 Ibid., 60.

14 For an interesting but controversial work on this ironical result, see Harold Entwistle, *Antonio Gramsci: Conservative Schooling for Radical Politics* (London and Boston: Routledge & Kegan Paul, 1979).

15 Millán Astray, a general on the side of the political Right led by Francisco Franco, responded to his admirers during the Spanish Civil War that *Viva* was not the

correct response to his speech from the balcony. "'What's that?' cried the General, 'no *vivas* for me! But let all shout with me "*Viva la muerte!*"' (Long live death!) The crowd echoed this mad slogan." Hugh Thomas, *The Spanish Civil War* (New York: Harper & Row, Publishers, 1961), 272. On another occasion when Astray and a crowd joined in the General's slogan *Viva la Muerte*, the great Spanish philosopher Miguel de Unamuno responded to those assembled. "'You all know me and are aware that I am unable to remain silent. At times to be silent is to lie. For silence can be interpreted as acquiescence. I want to comment on the speech—to give it that name . . . I heard a necrophilious and senseless cry: "Long live death." And I, who have spent my life shaping paradoxes . . . must tell you . . . that this outlandish paradox is repellent to me. General Millán Astray is a cripple . . . a war invalid. So was Cervantes. Unfortunately there are all too many cripples in Spain just now. And soon there will be even more of them if God does not come to our aid. It pains me to think that . . . Astray should dictate the pattern of mass psychology. A cripple who lacks the spiritual greatness of a Cervantes is wont to seek ominous relief in causing mutilations around him.'" Astray responded shouting, "Down with intelligence!" Ibid., 354.

16   Joel Spring, *Wheels in the Head: Educational Philosophies of Authority, Freedom, and Culture From Socrates to Paulo Freire* (New York: McGraw-Hill, Inc., 1994), 156.

17   Frantz Fanon, *The Wretched of the Earth* (New York: Grove Press, Inc., 1963), 238.

18   Donaldo Macedo, *Literacies of Power: What Americans Are Not Allowed to Know* (Boulder, Colo.: Westview Press, 1994), 124. From the author's interview with Freire.

19   Spring, *Wheels in the Head,* 159.

20   Freire, *Pedagogy of the Oppressed,* 67.

21   Herbert Marcuse, *Counterrevolution And Revolt* (Boston: Beacon Press, 1972), 46–47.

22   Freire, *Pedagogy of the Oppressed,* 100–01.

23   Ibid., 75.

24   Freire, *Education for Critical Consciousness,* 57.

25   Freire, *Pedagogy of the Oppressed,* 71.

26   See, Edward E. Sampson, "Identity Politics: Challenges to Psychology's Understanding," *American Psychologist* 48, no. 12 (December 1993): 1219–1230, for an analysis of how women, African Americans, gays, and lesbians have been denied being allowed to speak "in their own voices" with regard to constructing their life conditions and in determining their own identities and subjectivities. Similarly to Fanon, Sampson addressed the need to rid oneself of the destructive

self-concept many oppressed people have had introjected in them by various forms of oppression.

27   For a helpful look at various views on the nature of our genus and species, see Leslie Stevenson, *Seven Theories of Human Nature* (New York and Oxford: Oxford University Press, 1974).

28   Freire, *Pedagogy of the Oppressed*, 80.

29   Ibid., 82.

30   Freire, *Education for Critical Consciousness*, 125.

31   Mike Rose, *Lives On the Boundary: A Moving Account of the Struggles of America's Educational Underclass* (New York: Penguin Books, 1989), 69.

32   Spring, *Wheels in the Head*, 159.

33   Freire, *Education for Critical Consciousness*, 43.

34   John Dewey, *Democracy and Education* (New York: The Free Press, 1916), 185.

35   Rose, *Lives on the Boundary*, 109–10.

36   Freire, *Education for Critical Consciousness*, 57.

37   Erich Fromm, *The Art of Loving* (New York: Bantam Books, Inc., 1956).

38   Ibid., 111.

39   Spring, *Wheels in the Head*, 163.

40   For an example, see Jim Garrison, *Dewey and Eros: Wisdom and Desire in the Art of Teaching* (New York and London: Teachers College Press, 1997).

41   The work of Noam Chomsky, not well known to those who rely solely on "mainstream" media for their news, provides powerful, critical analyses of governmental and corporate wrongdoing in the United States and around the world. John Marciano's, *Civic Illiteracy and Education: The Battle for the Hearts and Minds of American Youth* (New York: Peter Lang Publishing, Inc., 1997) provides clear arguments and facts demonstrating how the dominant elite of Chomsky's description has succeeded in placing its view of the world front and center in our schools. Marciano provides a fascinating analysis of how American history textbooks have provided inaccurate pictures of U.S. foreign policy and wars.

42   Abraham Edel, *Relating Humanities and Social Thought: Science, Ideology, and Value, Vol. 4* (New Brunswick, N.J.: Transaction Publishers, 1990), 315. See my review of this book for further analysis of how we have been able to act responsibly without possessing transcendental guarantees, *Educational Studies* 22, no. 4 (Winter 1991): 473–79.

43   Freire, *Pedagogy of the Oppressed*, 52.

44   Ibid., 32–33.

45   David Montgomery, "Bread and Carnations Maybe?" *Radical History Review*, no. 65 (Spring 1996): 98.

46   Stanley Aronowitz, "Introduction," in *Pedagogy of Freedom: Ethics, Democracy, and Civic Courage*, Paulo Freire (Lanham, Md.: Rowman & Littlefield Publishers, Inc., 1998), 18–19. This book offers a clear presentation of Freire's central ideas. It reflects, in part, his experiences in the 1990s as first secretary of education in São Paulo, Brazil. This urban experience complements his earlier focus on rural areas. See, Freire's, *Pedagogy of the City*, (New York: Continuum Press, 1993), for more on his attempt to apply democratic ideas to schooling in a large school system.

47   Aronowitz, "Remembering Paulo Freire," *Taboo*, Fall 1997, 182.

48   Aronowitz, "Introduction" in *Pedagogy of Freedom,* 11.

49   Peter McLaren, "Review Article—Postmodernity and the Death of Politics: A Brazilian Reprieve," *Educational Theory* 36, no. 4 (Fall 1986): 390.

50   Ibid., 392.

51   Ibid., 398.

52   Ibid., 400. For a clear statement of how Freire's work helped the young Peter McLaren as a teacher, see McLaren, *Life in Schools*, "In Memoriam," xxiii. Peter L. McLaren and Colin Lankshear, eds., *Politics of Liberation: Paths From Freire* (London and New York: Routledge, 1994) provides a rich array of educators' and activists' assessment of Freire's work.

53   Giroux, *Ideology, Culture And The Process of Schooling*, 131.

54   Ibid., 135.

55   Henry A. Giroux, "Radical Pedagogy and Prophetic Thought: Remembering Paulo Freire," *Rethinking Marxism* 9, no. 4 (Winter 1996/97): 79–80.

56   Ibid., 85.

57   Perhaps some readers who think that keeping Freire's work alive is important would benefit from reading his, *Teachers as Cultural Workers: Letters to Those Who Dare Teach* (Boulder, Colo.: Westview Press, 1998). Freire presents "ten letters" and "last words" as short chapters in which we learn of his everyday practical concerns about teaching and learning. Pepi Leistyna's, *Presence of Mind: Education and the Politics of Deception* (Boulder, Colo. and Oxford, U.K.: Westview Press, 1999) provides an interesting integration of a critique of his graduate education experiences at Harvard, Critical Pedagogy, Freire, and the work of Noam Chomsky.

58   William V. Spanos, *A Casebook on Existentialism* (New York: Thomas Y. Crowell Company, 1966), 5.

59   Ibid., 9.

60   Leonardo and Clodovis Boff, *Introducing Liberation Theology* (Maryknoll, N.Y.: Orbis Books, 1986), 54.

61   Cornel West, "Religion and the Left," in *Churches in Struggle: Liberation Theologies And Social Change in North America*, ed. William K. Tabb (New York: Monthly Review Press, 1986), 198–206.

62   Peter McLaren, "The Pedagogy of Che Guevara: Critical Pedagogy and Globalization Thirty Years After Che," *Cultural Circles*, Summer 1998, vol. 3, Boise State University, 22–103.

63   Leonardo Boff, *When Theology Listens to the Poor* (San Francisco: Harper & Row, Publishers, 1984), 30.

64   Leonardo Boff, *Faith on the Edge* (Maryknoll, N.Y.: Orbis Books, 1989), 193.

65   L. Boff, *When Theology Listens To The Poor*, 27.

66   The Boffs, *Introducing Liberation Theology*, 94–5.

67   Enrique D. Dussel, *History and the Theology of Liberation* (Maryknoll, N.Y.: Orbis Books, 1976), passim.

68   Enrique D. Dussel, *Ethics and the Theology of Liberation* (Maryknoll, N.Y.: Orbis Books, 1974), 78. Dussel's work is among the very best with regard to profoundly understanding the phenomenon called liberation theology. He writes with piercing clarity and holistic richness.

69   Domenico Jervolino, "Towards a Philosophy of Liberation from a Cosmopolitan Perspective," *Rethinking Marxism* 8, no. 3 (Fall 1995): 80.

70   The Boff brothers provide a good example: Speaking of Mary, the mother of Jesus, they explain how she was embraced by the oppressed in Latin America from the inception of European Christianity in the Southern Hemisphere. "She took on the dark face of the slaves and persecuted Amerindians. She is the *Morenita* ('little dark girl') in Guadalupe, Mexico; she is *Nossa Senhora da Aparecida*, bound like the slaves in Brazil; she is the dark-complexioned Virgin of Charity in Cuba." *Introducing Liberation Theology*, 58.

71   Phillip Berryman, "How Christians Become Socialists," in *Churches in Struggle*, ed. William K. Tabb (New York: Monthly Review Press, 1986), 158.

72   Joel Kovel, *History and Spirit: An Inquiry into the Philosophy of Liberation* (Boston: Beacon Press, 1991), 6.

73   Ibid., 13.

74   Robert M. Brown, "The 'Preferential Option for the Poor' and the Renewal of Faith," in *Churches in Struggle*, 11.

75   William K. Tabb, "Part I: Theologies of Liberation," in *Churches in Struggle*, 1.

76   L. Boff, *Faith on the Edge*, 149.

77   West, "Religion and the Left," in *Churches in Struggle*, 205–06.

78   Dussel, *Ethics and the Theology of Liberation*, 166.

79   L. Boff, *Faith on the Edge*, 55.

80   Tabb, "The Shoulds and the Excluded Whys: The U.S. Bishops Look at the Economy," in *Churches in Struggle*, 289.

81   Dussel, *Ethics and the Theology of Liberation*, 127.

82   Juan Luis Segundo, *The Liberation of Theology* (Maryknoll, N.Y.: Orbis Book, 1975), chapter one, "The Hermeneutic Circle."

83   José Porfirio Miranda, *Marx Against the Marxists: The Christian Humanism of Karl Marx* (Maryknoll, N.Y.: Orbis Books, 1978), passim.

84   Catherine A. Lugg, *For God and Country: Conservatism and American School Policy* (New York: Peter Lang Publishing, Inc., 1996), see the prologue, and chapters 4, 6.

85   Ronald J. Sider, *Rich Christianity in an Age of Hunger,* 3rd ed., (Dallas, Tex.: Word Publishing, 1990), argues that the rich people in the United States are insensitive to the plight of the world's poor. He is critical of their religious commitments in the light of their lack of ethical concern and action. After earlier editions were criticized by conservatives, Sider made it clear in the third edition that he did not blame capitalism for the poor conditions affecting the poor. He endorsed capitalism, albeit with laws in place to protect and help those who are unable to do so themselves.

86   See, Michael Kazin, "The Politics of Devotion: The Christian Right Is Only One Feature of Today's Great Awakening," *The Nation* 266, no. 12 (April 6, 1998): 16–19, for an insightful description of spiritualists—from the abolitionists, Eugene Debs, Norman Thomas, Dorothy Day, Michael Harrington, and M. L. King; to Jesse Jackson, and Cornel West—who would certainly satisfy my criterion. The mature Malcolm X would also be a good candidate.

87   West, "Religion and the Left," in *Churches in Struggle,* 199. For an interesting study of a political theology that is closely connected to Marxist thought, especially in reference to their alleged commonalities about utopian ideas, see John Joseph Marsden, *Marxian And Christian Utopianism: Toward a Socialist Political Theology* (New York: Monthly Review Press, 1991), passim.

88   David E. Purpel and Svi Shapiro, "Beyond Liberation and Excellence: A Discourse for Education as Transformation," in *Critical Social Issues In American Education: Transformation in a Postmodernist World,* 2nd ed., (Mahwah, N.J.: Lawrence Erlbaum Associates, Publishers, 1998), 390. See also David E. Purpel, *The Moral and Spiritual Crisis in Education: A Curriculum for Social Justice* (Granby, Mass.: Bergin & Garvey, 1998).

Chapter Seven

The Politics of Identity: The Struggle for Human Dignity Is Expanded

Introduction

In this chapter I will focus on two rather recent collective actions that are built on earlier claims and struggles: Feminist and African-American movements. This is to deny neither the uniquenesses nor the vital importance of these expansions. Continuities in the historical human struggle for liberation, justice, and dignity is one of the major arguments in this book. The story of these struggles has been set in the West's history. This does not mean the histories of other civilizations are less important. I do not think "the West is best," and Samir Amin's *Eurocentrism* (1989) provides a helpful analysis of Western self-centeredness. The need for historical expansions of claims for equity and justice means that there were, and continue to be, serious flaws in the West's record of providing contexts for democracy, social justice, respect for diversity—and the conditions that encourage human beings to care for one another.

The Marxist social-class–based analysis historically championed European, male, industrial workers—even though Marx argued that the proletariat served as a universal group in terms of their liberatory potential and mission. Marxism expanded throughout the world as a theory for analyses of injustices and suggested strategies for empowerment. Factors of ethnicity, race, gender, and other differences were realized by some Marxists; however, those whose everyday life problems and possibilities seemed more dependent on gender or racial identities and characteristics than on class ones pushed for greater considerations given to these memberships. Stanley Aronowitz argued that Marxism can neither claim to be *the* master discourse with which to explain our societies (and schools), nor to provide the only theory and praxis necessary to change them. Historical materialism must enter into dialogue with new social forces, e.g., feminism, ecology, and religious movements.[1] Social-class memberships, with regard to the dominant, capitalist socioeconomic, political, and cultural systems, were to be enriched and redefined by women, persons of color, gays, lesbians, et al., because their concrete experiences could not be understood by class analysis alone. Thus, a politics of identity was born.[2] For example, school success is obviously related to social-class status. Empirical evidence demonstrates that in the United States there are important differences in educational outcomes even when students' class positions are roughly the same. The experiences of African Americans, Native-Americans, Hispanics, women, and other historically subaltern people serve as examples.

In the period immediately following World War II, people of color in the former European colonies forced their way on the historical stage in order to achieve their freedom. The beginning of the Civil Rights Movement in the United States began most famously with the 1954 Supreme Court decision *Brown v. Board of Education*, in which "separate but equal" was struck down in favor of integration, and the 1955 Montgomery bus boycott. Various forms of decolonization were the issues in Africa, Asia, and the United States. Somewhat similar issues and movements led by women, Hispanics, and Native-Americans followed the black civil rights movement. The complexities involved in these movements as well as questions of causalities among them are beyond the focus of this chapter. There exists an increasingly rich literature from which one can learn more about these great eruptions of democracy. The emphasis in chapter seven is on women and African Americans. The presentation is within the context of their roles as citizens and workers. This strategy is employed because, in spite of the great importance of gender identities and race, this does not render unnecessary considerations of women's and African-American's relationships to the economy (class), or their relationships to the political system (citizen) of the country. Even those who are not citizens in a particular country must relate to the government and economy. It is through these relations and memberships that subaltern people have historically sought empowerment in order to make their lives better. Those who have been unjustly excluded—as the Other—required places and memberships that allow conversation, analysis, the construction of hypothetical blueprints, and then collective action.

Edward Sampson wrote that "a variety of collective movements including women, gay males, lesbians, African Americans, and members of the third [underdeveloped or peripheral] world . . . [have argued] that members have been denied their own voice in establishing the conditions of their own lives and in determining their own identity and subjectivity."[3] Sampson related his psychological concerns to politics because he realized that psychological injury and lack of voice must be addressed through effective collective struggle. He asserted that if I, as the Other, have to speak and be like you in order to be understood/accepted, then I am forced to become like you. This is neither what Sampson's oppressed person wants nor can accomplish. To posit the white, Euro-American heterosexual male from the dominant socioeconomic classes as the implicit standard against which all others are judged means that these subaltern people are evaluated invidiously against standards that are difficult or impossible to meet. What is more, these standards are erroneously and unjustly considered universal and given rather than specific and historically constructed.

The inclusion of women and African Americans into the ranks of paid (not always very much) labor helped bring members of these identities into more public places in which they could use their citizenship in a formal democracy to demand socioeconomic, racial, and gender justice. People occupy multiple memberships: all of us are classed, raced, and gendered. Cameron McCarthy and Michael Apple developed what they call a "*parallelist*" position in order to sort out these dynamics with regard to school and society. These dynamics are class, race, and gender. They are to be understood in terms of their relationships to the economy, cultural, and political spheres, as well as among each other. For McCarthy and Apple, class is neither necessarily primary, nor most importantly causal/determinative of success—or failure—in school and society. They argued that the operation of class, racial, and gender relations in our daily experiences are "*nonsynchronous*"; i.e., not occurring at the same time. The relationships of people and groups to the economic system and polity are different enough so that our consciousnesses, needs, and demands are varied.[4] African-American males have different problems than their female counterparts, or their white, male schoolmates or colleagues; various people experience problems at different times. Rich people of color have different opportunities than their poor counterparts. Poor and working-class students who are white may, and do, perform less well than do middle-class and/or rich people. Upper-class women often do much better in school and society than working-class men—white or black.

Nancy Fraser helps us understand these differing needs and necessary remedies. She argued that while socialist and Marxist demands for social-class justice seek to abolish the exploited workers' conditions, the politics of identity based on race/ethnicity, gender, and sexual orientation wish to maintain and assert these distinctive identities. The first seeks a politics of equality, the second one of difference. In her view each needs the other. The demands made by identity politics are occurring in increasing material inequalities everywhere. Social-class politics sought economic redistribution; identity politics seeks to achieve recognition. Fraser insisted that social justice requires *both* redistribution and recognition. Economic disadvantage and cultural/identity disrespect are entwined. Because we are all classed, raced, and gendered, most of us need both redistribution of the necessary societal resources and recognition of our differences. Racial and gender memberships and identities are good examples of Fraser's claim that many people need recognition and redistribution of resources downward. Too many women and African Americans are poor. There are race-and-gender-specific modes of exploitation, marginalization, and deprivation; race and gender are characterized by certain social-class characteristics. Justice demands the smashing of current job-related divisions and injustices based on race and gender. Race and gender conceived of in certain biological terms cannot be easily abolished in the same way that Marx's proletariat can. If derogatory *construction/interpretations* of these biological differences are what cause injustice, then they can and must be abolished. "For Fraser, gender is both a political-economic differentiation and a cultural-valuation one. The major factor of gender injustice is androcentrism. Injustices such as sexual assault and domestic violence are relatively independent of . . . [social class]; therefore, they cannot be remedied by redistribution remedies alone. In fact, the logic of remedy is [based upon] . . . respect for sexuality (thought of as different from gender in Fraser's view), namely, to give positive recognition to a devalued group. *Mutatis mutandis*, this applies to . . . difficulties and hoped for remedies experienced by people of color. The economy and culture must be changed radically in both [for women and blacks] cases."[5]

Not even the inclusion of race, gender, and sexual orientation to social-class considerations permits us to understand the whole, wonderful complexity of people. My analysis in chapter seven is based on the assumption that class, race, gender, and sexual orientation identities determine many life chances. We can use these identities as analytic tools because every member at some time will experience—or not experience—things caused by her/his class, race, gender, and/or sexual orientation. Many political Rightists and conservatives do not agree with this assumption. You will determine for yourself where and when individuality and agency bump up against the structures, comprised in part by how class, race, gender, and sexual orientation are constructed and treated by the schools and societies in which we live and work.

It is interesting that in chapter six, the brothers Boff view class oppression somewhat differently than identity oppression. Nancy Fraser argued that these differences require dissimilar remedies. The Boffs argued that social-class antagonisms are irreconcilable: Worker and capitalist can never get along because their very relationship is based on the exploitation of the former by the latter. Capitalism must be overcome in order for justice to be accomplished. They argued that the positions of blacks, indigenous people, and women are not irreconcilable; it is the underlying class antagonisms that make reconciliation of black-white, native-European, woman-man relationships irreconcilable, not their extra-class identities.

The Boffs point out that it is one thing to be a black taxi driver, quite another to be a well-paid soccer idol. The woman as domestic servant obviously faces different challenges and has fewer opportunities than does the "first lady of the land." A landless Amerindian is much worse off than one who has land to work. In their opinion, this is why class struggles are at the bottom of most historical strife. "On the other hand, the struggle of blacks, . . . [indigenous people,] and women bring groups that are not naturally antagonistic into play, whose basic interests can in principle be reconciled. . . . We are dealing here with non-antagonistic contradictions mixed in with the basic, antagonistic class conflicts. But . . . non-economic types of oppression aggravate preexisting socioeconomic oppression. The poor [most of them workers] are additionally oppressed when, beside being poor, they are also black, indigenous, women, or old."[6] Many theorists, activists, and teachers who seek greater justice for classed, raced, and gendered persons do not agree with the Boffs and me on the above arguments. This chapter allows that many feminists argue that sexism and misogyny are fundamental and most causal of oppression. Some people argue that racism is the most basic and determinative of oppression. You can, and should, come to your own temporary conclusions as knowledge and experiences cause us to think about these troubling situations.

Section I begins with a feminist critique of Freire's work, followed by some excerpts from an interview Donaldo Macedo conducted with Freire. My intent in proceeding in this manner is to provide continuity with chapter six and then to begin a presentation of some feminist philosophies which can be related to educational concerns.

I

Kathleen Weiler expressed admiration for Freire's work. Yet, she said that, as a feminist, she is compelled to critique certain aspects of it. She argued that Freire's assumptions of common liberationist goals fail to recognize the specificity of different people's lives. She pointed out that people can be and often are both oppressors and oppressed. Weiler was correct in stating that Freire's initial understanding of oppression was in terms of social class. The privileging of class characterizes Freire as well as other spiritualists in the liberation theology movement. Weiler is critical of Freire because "when we look at *Pedagogy of the Oppressed* from the perspective of . . . feminist theory and pedagogy, certain problems arise. . . . [For example, the book] is striking in its use of the male referent, a usage that was universal in the 1960s. . . . Much more troublesome, however, is the abstract quality of terms such as humanization, which do not address the particular meanings imbued by men and women, Black and White, or other groups . . . .. The nature of their perception of the world and their oppression is implicitly assumed to be uniform."[7] Freire did not portray teachers and students as subjects with conflicting interests based on multiple identities and positions of power.

Weiler argued that we must construct a more "situated" theory of oppression, subjectivity, and difference. Feminists and postmodernists have criticized the attempts by school and society reformers to assume universal experiences and overly general goals. She also wrote specifically about differences within differences. Various classed, raced, and gendered actors have very different experiences of oppression and (perhaps) also as oppressors. Weiler explained how black women, lesbians, and postmodernists have made strong arguments for the lack of unified experiences within the identity called female. "The turning to experience [rather than just theory] thus reveals not a universal and common women's essence, but rather, deep divisions in what women have experienced, and in the kinds of knowledge they discover when they examine their own experience."[8]

In the end, Weiler reaffirmed her admiration for Freire's liberatory project; nonetheless, she criticized him for neglecting to explore and problematize his own rather privileged position as a white, male, highly educated person. The postmodernist, feminist Weiler called Freire a modernist because of his underdeveloped views of complex identities. She thought that Freire's ideas exemplify the universalizing tendencies of "malestream" thought.

Macedo referred to Weiler's critique during his interview with Freire. Freire admitted that he concentrated on class and to a lesser degree, racial oppression as he grew up in the Brazilian Northeast. Because his native culture was androcentric, patriarchal, and macho, he was influenced adversely by these discriminatory attitudes and practices. His denunciation of class and racial oppression eventually permitted him to understand the plight of women. Freire explained that his experiences with North American feminists in the 1970s helped him focus more sharply on gender issues. Freire claimed that since he wrote *Pedagogy of the Oppressed*, copyright 1970, he has benefited from the growing knowledge based on feminist issues and insights. Freire argued in the interview that it is not enough for women to liberate themselves from men, who themselves are discriminated against in terms of class and race, although one can understand focusing one's struggle against the most immediate and perhaps dangerous oppressor. Freire insisted that all the various forms of oppression must be understood so that there can be a solidaristic struggle. This may not satisfy all feminists who still insist that Freire's analysis is not specific enough and responsive to differences; even though he claimed in public that "I too am a woman." By this he meant that "the concept of the gender struggle is political and not sexual. . . . The fundamental issue is the political [socially constructed] vision of sex, and not the sexist vision. . . . What is at stake is liberation and the creation of liberatory structures . . . for both men and women."[9]

I now turn to select feminist philosophers' analyses of gender injustices, including misrepresentations of women. These dangerous actions are attributable to many of the most famous and influential male, white philosophers who are responsible for the historical canon of Western philosophy. Nancy Tuana charged that the canon excludes fair representation, misrepresentation, and nonrepresentation of women, non-Caucasians, workers, poor people, gays, lesbians, et al. who have been treated as subordinate and/or Other. These oppressed people have been invidiously compared to the privileged, Caucasian male who is called the Subject or protagonist—as opposed to the Object-to-be-acted upon. Tuana pointed out that one of the reasons for these philosophical exclusions and misrepresentations is the monopoly enjoyed by a male, white elite that has had the historical leisure, freedom, and training to become philosophers and studied philosophy that confirmed and/or agreed with their interests and advantages. The female Other who appears in this canon is defined as *not* being male, i.e., lacking and worse than men.

Tuana argued that:

The woman reading philosophy . . . finds herself alienated from the text. To insert herself into the text—to insist that she is capable of rational thought, to perceive herself a moral agent, to believe that she too can understand and participate in the workings of the . . . [government]—is to believe that she can act "like

a man," for . . . each of these abilities is defined within philosophy as "male."
At times, the option of acting "like a man" may seem acceptable to the woman
reading philosophy. . . . But this solution often only adds to our alienation. As
we attempt to force ourselves into the [male] categories . . . many of us discover
that these categories omit qualities and abilities we value . . . [those] defined as
"feminine"—emotion, empathy, connectedness—qualities and abilities which are
part of ourselves as women and as human which we do not believe should be
rejected. In other words, we discover that [Western] philosophy omits the experiences of being women.[10]

Feminists argue that these so-called female characteristics and qualities are the result of historical human construction, i.e., they are neither
universal nor timeless. Privileged, white men have officially constructed
these historical concepts of gender. These manmade portrayals have not
favored women. Feminist philosophers, writers, teachers, and activists
have helped us understand that even in the cases of obvious physiological
differences between women and men, e.g., the fact that women can become pregnant and give birth to children, these factors need not have
been construed as females' inability or deservedness to play equal roles in
the public, political, and economic lives of their particular societies. The
fact of motherhood need not mean that child rearing is to be done exclusively by the mother and other women. The social, political, economic,
and educational status of women, and in this case, women as mothers,
did not inevitably need to limit Western women's roles within the governmental sector and marketplace. The casting of most women into subaltern roles was caused by some men who have had the motive and power
to allocate resources that are necessary to live a life of security, comfort,
dignity, and freedom. The direct and indirect political and economic power
of classed and raced men, in conjunction with the intellectual, artistic,
educational cultural power exercised by philosophers and other "learned"
men, resulted in historical experiences in which many Western women
were treated unjustly.

The feminist liberatory project presented in this chapter speaks to
Western women's intellectual and material struggles to become actors,
protagonists, and subjects who can construct their own lives and projects
in the name of liberation and justice. This struggle has become worldwide; it is part of (but still unique in some ways) the larger struggle for
human rights and justice. The important issues feminists raise are often
about personal, familial, and local life, but space limitations make it difficult to treat this important literature. The emphasis here is on women as
citizens (relationships with the politics and governance of their societies)

and *workers* (paid laborers in the public economy, not just in the home).[11] As is the case with social class and racial struggles for justice, women have sought to use their political rights to secure better material/economic conditions for themselves and their dependents. These citizen-worker concepts are offered as steps in the direction of larger socially constructed "universal" and inclusionary terms such as human being. Feminists have been suspicious of this usage and project because of experiences in which women were folded into a larger category but as the weaker and oppressed Other. This is clearly not my intention. I remind you that feminism is about much more than struggles for democratic power and socioeconomic justice; a powerful feminist slogan is: The private is political. Feminism has been a name for women articulating their critique of what they consider to be a chauvinist and oppressive culture, as well as actions aimed at overcoming these injustices. Some feminists are heterosexuals, others are lesbians, and some are sympathetic and supportive men.

Many feminist philosophers, including Tuana, commence their critique of Western philosophy with Plato and Aristotle. She indicted these intellectual giants for erroneously equating humanness with maleness. Although the two differ with regard to the alleged causes of female inferiority, they agreed that women are not capable of developing the "higher" faculties of rationality and morality. Based on this unjust portrayal of women, classic Greek philosophers sought to deny women equal places in public life of the city-state. If women could neither reason nor understand the putative universals and truths accessible to disciplined and trained philosophers, then their thinking was relegated to the "less important" affairs of the household, family, body, emotions, and "gossip." Without the ability to reason about the affairs of government and the public economy, women would be unprepared to make solid moral or ethical decisions about the affairs of state. Plato blamed women's alleged inadequacies on their "inferior souls," whereas his student Aristotle pointed to "biological differences." The privileged male Greek philosophers were also ungenerous toward most other men of their time with regard to their supposed intellectual and moral disabilities. They all insisted however that males were the true and best forms of humanity. The women referred to as "fallen souls" and/or "mutilated" or "defective" men would be confined to nurturing and child-rearing labor in the household. This philosophical heritage has continued on into our own time.[12] One can easily understand why Tuana claimed that a "woman reading philosophy . . . finds herself alienated from the text."

Perhaps the least favorite philosopher in feminist evaluation is the French-man, René Descartes (1596–1650). As Tuana asserted, Western phi-losophy from Plato through Descartes represented reason as the oppo-site of emotions; this stark dichotomy ranked emotion as less trustworthy and good. (She included Jean-Jacques Rousseau in her book in chapter three on Descartes, which she called, "The Maleness of Reason." I focus on Rousseau at the end of section I.) This resulted in women, as well as many men, being portrayed as creatures of emotion and habit as com-pared to the white, privileged male who is celebrated in Western philoso-phy. Tuana was convinced that this systematic exclusion of women and other putative subaltern people so weakens and delegitimates Western philosophy that it cannot be saved by mere inclusion. I respect her argu-ment, but I do not find it convincing. I will address this disagreement more completely later in the text.

Eve Browning Cole also provided an account of Descartes' philosophy (called Cartesian) and some of the key reasons why it poses a threat to women's rights. She too began with Descartes' radical separation of mind from body, one that had dominated Western philosophy even before the seventeenth century. The question was: How were philosophers and other intellectuals to evaluate the sense impressions and other data that came to the mind from the body? Descartes' "solution" was to suspend belief in his "embodied existence," seeing himself instead as "locus of thoughts and other mental events." He sought to discover the one indubitable truth, one that would serve as an immovable/certain Archimedean point on which he and others with disciplined intelligence could depend on as knowledge unsullied by the emotional data of the body and senses. This is the famous *cogito ergo sum* (I think, therefore I am) of Descartes.

For the idealist philosopher Descartes, the body is a liability that must be policed by the mind. Cole called Descartes' quest for certainty his "Holy Grail," and the extra-baggage body is, at best, a "second-class citi-zen." According to Cole:

> First rank in Descartes' universe is held by "thinking things," nodes of conscious-ness that can through purely rational processes follow deductive argumentation to absolutely certain conclusions. The body cannot participate in this process with its own humble abilities, here conceived as sensation . . . it either impedes the rational process or, tamed and disciplined, stands dumbly by and lets knowl-edge happen. Highest epistemological honors go to the . . . deductive reason-ing process: mathematical laws, [and] logical principles. . . . These construct the knowable core of the world, and to them . . . is superadded a "flesh" of more dubious nature: bodies, colors, touches, smells, and the entire organic con-

tents of the universe. . . . The mind or soul is in Descartes' [and Plato's] view
the locus of certainty and value . . . the body is to be subordinated and ruled.[13]

The philosophers who have so far been featured and championed in this
book have all been against the idealist philosophical Cartesianism of which
Cole wrote. The so-called "romantic" intellectuals and artists of the late-
eighteenth and early-nineteenth centuries paid a good deal of attention to
feelings and thought them necessary to living a good life. Progressive
education in the United States and elsewhere has argued against the Cartesian mind-body dichotomy and based its practice on seeing the student
as integrally one.

The problem of mind-body, intellect-emotion, and other purported
human dichotomies are already in the proper province of philosophical
discourse—and certainly in philosophy of education. We know a good
deal more about these phenomena today as a result of centuries of theoretical and empirical studies. These accomplishments have allowed us to
understand ourselves beyond the crude dichotomies of seventeenth-century Western philosophy. Feminist philosophers have contributed much
to our current understandings. All thoughtful educators are correct when
they are interested in what can be known about these phenomena with
regard to teaching and learning. Common sense suggests that it is wise to
see ourselves as comprised of feelings and intellect, and although they are
not starkly dichotomous, it is possible to get into trouble if and when their
sometimes separate demands get too far out of balance. This applies to
both males and females.

Suggested Task for the Reader
Construct a convincing argument that connects the mind-body dichotomy
of Western philosophy to the school dichotomy that is called the head-
hand division. Do class, gender, race, and ethnic biases play a role in
helping to decide who is selected for the low status, body side of the
dichotomy?

Cole is correct when she argues that the Cartesian ego is an erroneous
abstraction; she advises that we begin with the "relational self." This more
believable self's consciousness is not only open to the data provided by
our senses, but is connected inextricably with other human beings. As
Marx and Dewey have insisted, we are born into the materiality of physical and social life. Had Descartes started from the concept of relational
selves, his philosophical project would have been different—and more
realistic. As Cole argued: Descartes saw other persons as "colorful wall-

paper" which the knower contemplates from a "mental fishbowl." This distancing himself from other conscious people, believing instead that his own thinking was all that could be relied on, takes Descartes to an illogical conclusion—because this distancing is, in fact, impossible.

Descartes held to his own kind of logic and believed that theoretically, all people could and should be *taught* to reason in order to achieve reliable knowledge and certainty. He was confident that *he* was capable of providing such instruction. Descartes "allows" that women could undergo the training he gave; the gender and social-class divisions of labor which prevailed during his lifetime meant that very few—if any—women could learn to become a Cartesian rational philosopher. Even women from the most privileged social classes during the early modern period in the West were forced into responsibilities and labor that made the kind of thinking Descartes championed virtually impossible to practice. As Tuana explains:

> The leisure necessary for the pursuit of [Cartesian] reason is not available to a wife and mother. This point was well made by Princess Elizabeth of Bohemia, who corresponded with Descartes about his method. "The life I am constrained to lead does not allow me enough free time to acquire a habit of meditation in accordance with your rules. Sometimes the interests of my household, which I must not neglect, sometimes conversations and civilities I cannot eschew, so thoroughly deject this weak mind [an example of learned self-deprecation] with annoyances or boredom that it remains, for a long time afterward, useless for anything else."[14]

Tuana is correct to argue that the woman as mother, working in the realm of the home, must be sensitive to each child in her care as well as to the many crucially important resources which good child-care requires. Such a caregiver, woman or man, will not get very far with Cartesian deductive, abstract reasoning when the children require personal care, emotional support, warmth, and love.

The preceding argument provides a segue to a consideration of what feminists have currently called "caring." Many feminist issues are, in fact, ethical ones; feminists have analyzed and critiqued the putative moral-ethical canon of Western philosophy. Cole said, "much moral philosophy has tended to obscure, rather than clarify or at least honestly acknowledge its political [gender, class, race] basis and implications; much moral philosophy has employed an atomistic concept of the self; and much moral philosophy has either explicitly or implicitly derogated the activities and concerns of women to second-class status. . . . In ethics . . . feminist thought has gone . . . beyond critique in constructive ways."[15] Feminist reinterpretation and repair can be characterized by the following: The liberal, American philosopher John Rawls' landmark book, A *Theory of Justice* (1971) stands accused of presenting a male, Western model of persons and families as though these were universal. Rawls portrayed the nuclear family with its paternal-head as egoistic and a putatively rational bargainer as the model of human personality. The "cultural wars" that have been fought during the last thirty years have radically called such allegedly universal types into question. Feminists have been joined by African Americans, Hispanics, gays, lesbians, Third World people, and radicals in deconstructing the universals of the kind Rawls is accused of having taken as givens. Feminists have also critiqued the work of Lawrence Kohlberg on his criteria for moral maturity. Kohlberg's findings have been very influential among educators; the deconstruction of his research is important to teaching and learning theory and practice.

Carol Gilligan's *In a Different Voice* (1982) suggested that Kohlberg's framework and criteria for moral development presented moral reasoning in particular, rather than universal ways. Gilligan argued that the female subjects in *her* research reasoned their way through moral dilemmas differently than men. The former tended to focus on specific personal relations and their connectedness. These connections demanded responsibilities in specific ways, e.g., my mother and I—rather than generic mother-daughter relations. Gilligan's research subjects thought in concrete particulars rather than general, abstract, and universal terms. She should be read in her own voice:

> As we have listened for centuries to the voices of men and the theories of development that their experience informs, so we have come more recently to notice not only the silence of women but the difficulty in hearing what they say when they speak. Yet in the different voice of women lies the truth of an ethic of care, the tie between relationship and responsibility, and the origins of aggression in the failure of connection. The failure to see the different reality of women's lives and to hear the differences in their voices stems in part from the assumption that there is a single mode of social experience and interpretation. By positing instead two different modes, we arrive at a more complex rendition of human experience which sees the truth of separation and attachment in the lives of women and men and recognizes how these truths are carried by different modes of language and thought. To understand how the tension between responsibilities and rights sustains the dialectic of human development is to see the integrity of two disparate modes of experiences that are in the end connected. While an ethic of justice proceeds from the premise of equality—that everyone should be treated the same— an ethic of care rests on the premise of nonviolence—that no one should be hurt. In the representation of maturity, both perspectives converge in the realization that just as inequality adversely affects both parties in an unequal relationship, so too violence is destructive for everyone involved. This dialogue between fairness

and care not only provides a better understanding of relations between the sexes but also gives rise to a more comprehensive portrayal of adult work and family relationships.[16]

Teachers' work in the K–12 schools is deeply connected to the necessity of caring for their students, especially in societies where all too many youngsters come to school from places of deprivation.

Nel Noddings' *Caring: A Feminist Approach to Moral Education* (1984) called for changing the educational system to reflect the importance of "the immediate behavior of caring for relevant individuals." Many teachers whose work had been necessarily based on personalism and caring accepted these ideas. The ethic of care became more readily recognized and accepted as a philosophical statement and justification of what was already being done due to the gendered nature of teachers in the United States. The *relational self* becomes the basis for moral reasoning. "The central directive of an ethic of care is that I should act always in such ways as to promote the well-being of both the others to whom I am in relation and the self which is relationally constituted. . . . Rules are less significant than a caring and attentive conscientious *presence* within one's moral situation, a sensitivity to the needs of others, and a basic dispositional willingness to do what I can to create situations in which those needs can be met."[17] Noddings wrote that "caring is not just for women, nor is it a way of being reserved only for the private life."[18]

Sara Ruddick's *Maternal Thinking: Toward a Politics of Peace* (1989) provided insight into an ethic of care that is supportive of ideas and themes featured in this book. She attempted to identify central characteristics of maternal work usually performed by women. Cole presented Ruddick's work as follows. Maternal work includes both cognitive and moral interests and abilities. Central to such work and its organizing virtue is "attentive love": one that is capable of accurate observation and assessment. Maternal labor must be done with "the patient eye of love" for what the child and/or student is as well as what s/he may become. Such a disposition allows differences to emerge and develop without forcing premature, comforting, and restrictive commonalities on the young person. The maternal worker lets Otherness be! "In 'maternal thinking' Ruddick . . . says the primary concern is preservation of the vulnerable child, the midwife teacher's [maieutic teaching in a Socratic sense] first concern is to preserve the student's fragile newborn thoughts."[19]

These virtuous dispositions and practices are good and useful in many places other than the home and classroom. Cole explained Ruddick's commitment to a politics of peace. "Mothers know that it is in the interests of their children and themselves to find ways out of conflict situations which do not provoke injury or destruction. . . . Maternal work can be seen to be 'governed by ideals of nonviolence. . . . Mothers must . . . learn to forge a 'sturdy' peace, in which lively interests of all parties are served."[20] As the *Madres des Desaparecidos* (mothers of the disappeared) of Argentina have dramatically demonstrated, maternal activists can be effective in dangerous public places. It is far easier to do the kind of work Ruddick champions if it occurs in a social context that was characterized by discussion, mediation, compromise, and respect for the Other, rather than by intimidation, lies, and ultimately coercive violence.

You have learned, philosophers are argumentative; thus, they have critiqued the caring literature.[21] Tuana warned that in a culture like ours even the most positive "female virtue" such as caring is seen negatively by some as symptomatic of the failure to acknowledge one's own needs and to act upon them. The whole question of women's roles as protagonists and agents in the public arenas currently dominated by men makes caring a practice that must be made safe to carry out in the world of power-driven give and take. Coalition politics are necessary in order to change profoundly our socioeconomic, political, cultural, and educational systems in order to make altruistic caring safe for those who wish to practice this virtue. Cole alerted us to the danger of grounding the whole of moral action and evaluation on the ethic of care as feminists have defined it. She asked whether we need "robust" conceptions of duty, obligation, and civility in situations where we intensely dislike certain people.

An ethic of care could be translated into at least two related strategies by teachers. In the short run it seems necessary to practice caring up-close and personal in many of the nation's K–12 classrooms. Another aspect of caring might mean that teachers and/or progressive people would struggle to change society for the better, especially its economic system which helps cause at-risk conditions for young people and others. The kind of caring that many good teachers exhibit might better occur in families that can be made more secure by enlightened public policies, e.g., job security, fair and adequate compensation which does not discriminate against women and other people who have suffered because of similar discrimination, family leaves, better medical services, public transportation, and greater investment in people and the public good overall. Caring would be more concretely grounded. Cole articulated well one more important worry about caring as it is currently interpreted. "Critics of the ethic of care are alarmed about the possibility that women's subordination is simply valorized and ratified by making caring a central moral directive. There is something uncomfortably familiar about the vision of the caring, relating, attending moral agent who places others' needs in the center of her moral universe; she is the stereotypical female and we can effortlessly predict her lines. . . . 'Can I get you anything?'. . . . 'No, I'm not busy' . . . and so forth."[22]

I used Descartes as the central target for feminist anger at Western philosophers' depiction of women, still it is fitting that this section be concluded with a brief look at Rousseau's famous book called *Émile* (1762). The education of Émile and Sophie that Rousseau advocated is considered among the best examples of gender bias in not only Western philosophy but education as well. Tuana and some other feminist writers argued that it is not right, fair, or justifiable to let philosophers such as Rousseau, Descartes, Aristotle, and Plato off the hook for their gender bias just because these attitudes were accepted as common sense itself during the times in which they lived. Tuana insists that the overall frameworks of their philosophies cannot and should not be saved.

Even though Tuana condemns Rousseau's treatment of Sophie, her chapter subsection is called "The Marriage of Reason and Emotion: Rousseau." You may recall that Descartes was skewered for banishing emotion from any place of respect. Rousseau was credited as one of the pioneers in the romantic movement in Europe, one that was characterized by celebrating passion, fervor, spirit, and emotion. Tuana's complaint is that Sophie was made to be the character epitomizing these romantic characteristics, whereas Émile represented the reason part of the equation. Rousseau included faculties historically thought of as feminine (passion and the senses) in the realm of the rational. Rousseau, like Plato and Aristotle, believed that reproduction and child-care must not be burdens for those who run society, so he placed these responsibilities on Sophie. The family was seen as the pillar of society for Rousseau. He was a pioneer in developing an educational philosophy for Sophie, who will be responsible for the good home that will enable Émile to do his job in the public realm. Jane Roland Martin wrote,

> Rousseau's fundamental insight in *Émile* was that the plausibility of Émile's education is due to the existence of Sophie and the fact that Émile and Sophie are united in partnership. . . . Sophie has full responsibility for carrying out the reproductive processes of child rearing and maintaining home and family for Émile, and is to be educated in the qualities necessary for doing so. Equally important, the man Émile, even when educated according to plan, is not and cannot be a complete moral person. Only in partnership . . . can Sophie and Émile be completely moral, and even then, neither individual alone is a complete

moral person; rather, the *union* of Sophie and Émile constitutes a complete moral entity.[23]

It is quite easy to criticize the division of labor that comprises this union. Contemporary feminists have done so. Tuana argued that this asymmetry, or different and unequal relationships, between Sophie and Émile, accepted the former as in the public realm or civil society; she is still limited to the private realm of the family. "Émile must enter not only into the private realm as head of the family but also into public . . . life. Sophie is important only insofar as she serves to assist Émile in these two functions. . . . The political realm is a masculine realm. Women ought to participate in it only very indirectly. . . . The general will, Rousseau explains, must transcend the particular needs of the family and focus on the common good. Sophie will see only the needs of her family, and thus her concerns will be in tension with those of the State."[24] The alleged complementariness of Sophie and Émile's relationship is exposed, in Tuana's mind, for what it is: the continuing subservience of the woman to man. Tuana offers a postscript: The type of rationality that Rousseau has "granted" to Sophie, a "civilized" European woman, is in the end capable of only instrumental value, serving to assist the man to guide his rational ability.

Tuana stated that an acceptable nonsexist concept of rationality requires a mix of (historically constructed) feminine and masculine characteristics, without "privileging" one set over the other. Tuana was not writing as a gender "essentialist," i.e., the erroneous belief that women, men, heterosexuals, and homosexuals are distinguished by hard and fast, easily recognizable "essentials." Her point is well taken. Discussion about and treatment of women, men, et al. in the West has been marked by *group* treatment in many ways. There seems to be possible differences that are difficult and/or impossible to change, but our reactions to these facts need not lead to unjust treatment of women and/or others who have been discriminated against. The fact that it is women who become pregnant, carry children, and give birth cannot be easily altered—even in this age of genetic engineering. This fact need not lead to Western philosophers interpreting this as a weakness and justification for keeping women out of public and/or influential roles. Women who choose to become mothers should be supported by society at large so that this valuable role can be performed under the best conditions. The need for quality child rearing need not be interpreted to mean that only mothers and other women should do most or all of the heavy lifting. These progressive insights abound today and there has occurred substantial concrete experiential results in Western societies and elsewhere. Further progress may require more profound and systematic socioeconomic, political, cultural, and educational changes. Women who decide to become mothers as well as those who do not *must* have access to public life on the same basis as men!

Discussions of public roles by Western philosophers have overwhelmingly favored men over women but this does not mean that we must heed what they have said. We cannot pretend that their ideas about citizenship, the public, moral macroeconomy, democracy, the rule of law, inalienable rights, a modicum of egalitarianism, and education for critical citizenship are useless and/or harmful just because of certain regrettable exclusions. The progressive history of the West has been one of including the many who were formerly considered beyond the pale of protection by just laws and practices. Workers, people of color, women, et al. have stormed the fortresses of privilege via eruptions of democracy and demands for inclusion and equality. They were not seeking to overthrow but to gain admittance, although gaining admission and participation can and does alter profoundly and radically the previous status quo.

Martin argued that Rousseau's recognition of the need for a good home life in order to have a good society is praiseworthy, but he did not have to choose Sophie to be exclusively responsible for ensuring it. She asserts that "recognition of Rousseau's insight does not entail an endorsement of . . . a patriarchal society in which only males can be citizens or for a . . . family in which wives must endure their husband's wrongs. . . . It does not require a two-track educational system and a division of labor based on sex or gender. It does . . . require that we take Sophie's virtues seriously and seek ways of incorporating them into the ideals we develop to guide the education of the women and men who should today be sharing responsibility for the reproductive processes of society."[25] Sophie's virtues cannot just be "added on" to Émile's. As we expand and alter our dominant educational ideals, both Sophie and Émile's virtues will be transformed. Martin agrees with multiculturalists who explain how a democratic heterogeneous society will be constantly in the process of constructing a new culture, rather than fixing racial/ethnic, religious, cultural, and other differences in concrete, and still be "tolerated." Martin said, "if men and women are to be complete people, regardless of their gender, they must acquire Sophie's virtues as well as Émile's—or some appropriate transformation thereof."[26]

Simone de Beauvoir (1908–1986), the French playwright, novelist, essayist, and philosopher, published the influential book *The Second Sex* in 1949. Her inclusion in this part of the text suggests what the fictitious Sophie of Rousseau's creation might have become in the twentieth century. De Beauvoir asserted that one is not born a woman; rather, she becomes one. An existentialist would say, our essence is created by what we do. Her feminism was indebted in part to existentialist philosophy. In her view there is no way of deciding once and for all the matter of sexual difference. She asserted that we cannot know what the ontological differences between women and men are, in part because of the *différend* (difference as in a dispute or quarrel) which precludes easy solutions due to the lack of a rule of judgment applicable to both or more contending parties. The *différend* "is a figure for the difficult politics of representation . . . the attempt to put into words something that cannot be because of the incommensurability of knowledge that precludes an objective perspective."[27] In de Beauvoir's view, the past cannot determine the future, although one cannot act as though there were no history at all. In keeping with existentialist philosophy, she insisted that bodies are not essentialistic and/or fixed forever but only differentially "marked" by gender. De Beauvoir took seriously our embededness: "She begins *The Second Sex* with data of biology: 'For, the body being the instrument of our grasp upon the world, the world is bound to seem a very different thing when apprehended in one manner or another. This accounts for our . . . study of the biological facts; they are one of the keys to our understanding of woman. But I deny that they establish for her a fixed and inevitable destiny. They are insufficient for setting up a hierarchy of the sexes; they fail to explain why woman is the Other; they do not condemn her to remain in this subordinate role forever.'"[28] For de Beauvoir, woman is not a completed reality, rather, she is a becoming. This becoming can never be known in advance. A "pro-ject" is a throwing forward of the dynamic self.

Suggested Task for the Reader

Comment in some detail about the following feminist positions as well as the tension between them. Organize your comments around the construction of public and school policies. (1) Women are similar enough to men—in their ability to reason and to act morally as agents with regard to complex choices—consequently women fully deserve equal opportunities and roles in public life. (2) Because of women's biological differences from men and consequential historical life experiences, women have developed a view from the margins of public life which enable them to see and feel the injustices inherent to a system of gender, class, racial/ethnic hierarchy and oppression. This epistemological position and view from the borders and beyond provide women with superior understanding about how things are as well as what is to be done in order to make more just conditions. Your commentary here could connect with arguments made throughout this book that people who are or have been oppressed can and must free themselves.

I continue to maintain that Rousseau's deep commitment to radical democracy, one in which the individual citizen never would turn over political power even to a representative assembly, and his passionate argument requiring rough equality in any kind of authentic democracy, is still highly relevant to contemporary progressive struggles for democracy and social justice. Further, I argue that most of what feminists have demanded, which could be achievable politically, can be most realistically achieved in a society that builds on or from Rousseau's ideas.

His seminal, democratic, and comparatively inclusive insistence that a society must strive to articulate and enact socioeconomic, political, and cultural reforms in congruence with democratically constructed ideas of the common good stand in stark contrast to Adam Smith's (1723–83) capitalist assumption that the pursuit of self-interest is the only trustworthy motive, and that this pursuit would invisibly/magically result in the common good. Rousseau's focus on the citizen as the person who should hold power was a wonderfully radical, democratic idea for its time, one that has been pushed beyond including only the propertied and artisan European man. Rousseau's emphasis on citizenship for ordinary Frenchmen was aimed at the situation which prevailed in the Europe of his day that featured political power in the hands of the royalty, church, and aristocracy. The emphasis on *citoyen* (citizen) finally came to include *citoyenne* (female citizen) as well. Citizen was the universal term used by progressives in the eighteenth century. We know it was flawed because of those not included: women, slaves, unskilled workers, the poor, et al. The current feminist insistence on rightfully including women with the concept of the universal Subject developed from earlier claims of universality—this development required struggle against the canonical monopolists who defended narrow and stingy ideas and practices of universal rights and entitlements. The framers of the Constitution of the United States were complicit in this miserly construction of universality, as women, slaves, Native Americans, and those without property and artisanship were excluded. United States history is marked by popular democratic pressure to make the rights and inclusion of the few into more inclusive ones. This is the essence of modern democracy. The feminist struggle is a wonderful part of it, as is the struggle by African American and other historically oppressed people. The inclusion of the variously abled in public schools and the larger society is a result of similar struggles. The French and American Revolutions helped make Sophie a potential Simone de Beauvoir, although she does not represent the zenith of women's liberation.

I respect the feminists' anger at Rousseau and other privileged, male philosophers for their unjust exclusion of women as rational and moral Subject as compared to their favorite male candidates. My counterargument is that it is a serious error to disqualify them entirely as thinkers who contributed to bringing about a world in which feminist claims can be more easily understood, accepted, and enacted. In spite of the fact that the canonical Western philosophers' portrayals of women and some men were disparaging, we must remember that they were merely historical constructions. They were neither accurate nor binding. We can and do portray women and other former subaltern people differently, more accurately, and more justly in many places today. We can make our own histories, albeit not just as we would like or as if the past did not exist. We can overturn oppressive systems.

We must realize that many oppressors are not familiar with Western philosophy. Not every unjust person acts as s/he does because of reading the philosophical "list of suspects" that has been presented here. We must not exaggerate the direct power of ideas on historical occurrences. It is better for alert, active citizens to know the general and overall story of Western ideas that have contributed to many of the actions, quarrels, fights, and resolutions human beings have experienced. I hope that many people will find the history of philosophy and educational philosophy interesting and fascinating enough to study further. Perhaps some of those who do will agree with me that universal declarations of rights must be appreciated, not discarded because of their failures, but improved upon until each and every person enjoys universally guaranteed rights that are historically and materially grounded. Commensurate duties are also inextricably in partnership with rights.

II

Because the philosophies presented honorifically in this book feature a praxis dimension, logic compels us to consider a politics best suited to progressive feminist philosophy. The politics of a materialist-socialist feminism is organized around the following concepts, although not in a linear or schematic way. The concepts are italicized. The first concept is the *public-private divide* which follows from the philosophical dichotomy that erroneously depicted men as more rational than women, thus relegating women to domestic life. This philosophy helped to justify keeping women's work relegated to the household, whereas men performed in public, paid-labor contexts and in government. Women learned how to fight their limited, oppressed assigned roles by demanding the *right to define themselves* as women and as individuals in their gender/sex. This demand was logically possible because of women's concomitant insistence that they too were capable of *volitional, proactive agency.* They argued that because of their *gendered, classed,* and *raced* identities, roles, and positionalities (as well as the interaction among these various identities) there occurred certain *cognitive/epistemological advantages,* e.g., seeing things from the bottom, from those who were oppressed. Women came to realize that these standpoints in the socioeconomic, political system provided certain opportunities for *collective struggle* against oppression and exploitation as solidaristic actors. Women made *double demands,* as did African Americans and other oppressed people. The first demand was that women be included in the rights, opportunities, and privileges that middle-class and some working-class, white men already enjoyed. Second, more radical women insisted that the old rules be changed so that they could be included on their own terms, as women, not as women-like-men. They demanded getting beyond mere add-on inclusion into a system which they considered less than the best possible.

The materialist-socialist feminist tradition is *grounded in political economy* (see chapter three) and the *concreteness of everyday life.* This is different from and opposed to feminist theory and politics that "privilege" discursive rendering of realities, rather than the older Marxist emphasis on labor. The materialist-socialist feminists consider the "discursive" (emphasizing writing and speaking) emphasis alone dangerous because of alleged discontinuities between ideas/conversations and what occurs in the world of work: systematic/direct oppression of women as classed and raced workers.[29] The "discursive" and "ludic" feminist positions are criticized by materialist-socialists as the project of wealthy, university-educated, white women who live mostly in North America and other places where one can afford to overlook the relentless, crushing, materiality of job exploitation suffered by millions of other women—and some men. Feminists who still regard social class as central to understanding oppression—and possible liberation—have had to include the independent dynamics of gender oppression to their theory and politics.

You are reminded that theoretical and political positions, although real and different from one another, share commonalities. (It is beyond the scope of this book to provide an analysis of all the differences and similarities among feminist theoreticians and activists.[30]) Returning to the key concepts around which the discussion of materialist-socialist feminism proceeds, the emphasis is on *women as citizens and workers.* You know, I have favored these memberships which are different from gender or race alone, although feminists and African Americans have worked effectively to stress that citizens and workers are gendered and raced. Materialist-socialist feminists have focused on citizenship in the sense of its inclusion of socioeconomic rights, rather than just the narrower, earlier political meaning of the term. Women, people of color, et al. *deserve full inclusion—defined as important by themselves*—because a good society needs many voices due to the fact that no one and no group has/have a direct conduit to certainty and/or right. This is an epistemological and political (democratic) concept. Inclusion is warranted on the simple grounds of *fairness and justice*! The conceptual preface presented is intended to assist the reader as s/he progresses.

Materialist-socialist feminists acknowledge the importance of Marx's social class analysis but look to patriarchy as the most direct source of women's oppression. They also consider race as an important factor in people's oppression. These feminists understand that although there are many differences among women—class and race being two of the most important—there remains a constancy and similarity among all women's experiences. "Rich or poor, all women are held responsible for the majority of all domestic labors and have less sexual freedom than men. Women's oppression in the 'private' realm of family and sexuality in turn affects her options in the 'public' realm of production."[31] Tuana and Tong go further as they draw from the socialist feminist Alison Jaggar's work: "Full reproductive freedom for women will require even more than altering our economy so that all people have access to birth control, abortion, child care and adequate means to support a family; it will also require abolishing 'the compulsory heterosexuality and mandatory motherhood that have characterized all male-dominated societies' and restructuring the gender divisions that exist in the wage labor force. Women and men must become equal participants in a [paid] workforce that is responsive to the needs of parents (parental leave, flexible working hours, provisions for child care, and similar concerns)."[32] In the society at large there is great opposition to some or all of what Jaggar has advocated.

In order to solve the problem of women's dual oppression by patriarchy and capitalism, materialist-socialist feminists focused on "social reproduction" (of the necessary people, practices, and institutions) theory, and eventual action. Sue Ferguson invites us to reread Marx so that the stark dichotomy of dual oppression can be overcome. These feminists sought to overcome this dualism because they were convinced that in spite of real differences between unpaid, household female labor and paid, capitalist work, mostly by men, these various jobs and oppressions were ultimately linked. A unified systems theory can allow a feminist historical materialist analysis, and/or a profoundly gendered theory of oppression. Ferguson argued that empirical study and even more casual observations demonstrate that complex practices of oppression (capitalism, sexism, and racism) are integrally related. Ferguson would have us reconsider descriptions and analyses of everyday life—the actual sociohistorical relations among people, rather than narrowly conceived economic ones. The capitalist, paid labor, economy is not cleanly separate from the daily, generational production *by* and *of* real and specific people! She reminds us that Marxist historical materialism is a tool for understanding human activity, especially labor and how it has always featured cooperative efforts by men, women, and children to satisfy all of their needs. The central, important activity has been the production (birth and subsequent child development, including education and training) of individuals that occurred mostly in the household, the extended family, the community, and later in the schools.

When capitalism first developed in England during the seventeenth and eighteenth centuries, it featured an unprecedented development: the establishment of paid labor sites, mostly for men, and the relegating of women to the household and the reproduction and caring for children, but no longer as producers of material goods. This unprecedented occurrence caused families to become dependent mostly on wages earned in the paid labor sites. The worker was seen as a tool serving the drive for profit, rather than a full human being. The reproductive function in the household was viewed by the capitalists as one of preparing fresh supplies of workers who served to increase profit but were uncritical of a process that was not in their best interests. Some women also worked in paid labor sites during capitalist development, although the emergence of the "family wage" meant that the men's pay no longer necessitated their wives working outside the home. The reentry of women into the workplace in the United States and elsewhere is due in large part to the inadequacy of the "family wage" to sustain the modern family in a consumer capitalist society.

Feminists who continue to draw on Marxist thought insist that women's reproductive, education, and training work was and is of vital importance

to the continuation of capitalism. In spite of its reproductive role for capitalist labor supply needs, the family has answered to other needs and
desires, the characteristics of love, care, cooperation, and hopes for
children's lives to be better—ones in which they would not just serve as
tools for others' profits. In general, women and parents have resisted the
capitalist imperative that sought to reduce the family to a *producer* of an
endless stream of hardworking, compliant, and uncritical labor. The contemporary K–12 public school features a similar situation with regard to
the conflicting imperatives of capitalism (profit) and democracy (and overall personal development) on its teachers—many of them women. Neither
the family nor the school has ever been completely subservient to the rule
of capital. People work together in order to live in the paid labor, official
economy, as well as in the private unofficial economy comprised of communities and households/families. These various forms of labor are called
the "material bases of life," ones that are complex and often *contradictory.* Some Marxists had thought that opposition to capitalist exploitation
and oppression could be mounted from paid, mostly male, work sites. If
we understand the actual *seamless web of labor,* extending to and including the household, then sites for opposition and liberation are not just
limited to the formal capitalist-dominated workplace! The theory of dual
oppression is weakened because the work done in the household is revealed to be part of capitalism's support system. The historical dichotomies of public-private, men-women, reason-emotion are softened, if not
entirely overcome.

I draw on Kathleen Weiler in order to strengthen Ferguson's argument
about the connectedness between private (women) and public (men).

> To argue the need to take seriously the everyday lives of women is not to accept
> as valid the dichotomy between private and public . . . as separate universes. As
> socialist feminist theorists emphasize, the role of women in reproducing social life
> and life itself is essential to the public world of production. De Beauvoir reminds
> us that 'women have never constituted a closed and independent society; they
> form an integral part of the group, which is governed by males and in which they
> have [unfortunately] a subordinate place'. . . . What focusing on the everyday
> life of women should do . . . is reveal that connection between public and pri-
> vate, between production [of goods] and reproduction [of children, workers, and
> attitudes]. In socialist feminist research, the everyday world is not a self-contained
> world; quite the contrary, it is an integral part of the social whole. What is more,
> the relationships and values of the private, everyday world are shaped by large
> social and economic forces. . . . The focusing on the everyday world reveals the
> way larger forces, both ideological and material, place limits and conditions on
> our actions. But . . . making the everyday world of women the center of social
> research demonstrates that a concentration solely on the public arena is equally

inadequate. Feminist scholarship, by revealing the everyday lives of women, opens up the other half of social [economic] reality which has been ignored.[33]

The materialist-socialist feminist project is aimed at constructing better explanations about why the separation of household labor from paid labor resulted in a devaluation of the former and why women were assigned to the household. Heidi Hartmann insisted that gender-blind Marxist analyses provide no clue concerning why women were, and are, subordinate to men inside and outside the family. It was necessary to ascertain if capitalism and patriarchy were historically connected, rather than separate, although concomitant systems of women's oppression. Hartmann wrote a famous article, "The Unhappy Marriage of Marxism and Feminism," in which she argues that gender differentiation has been transhistorically universal and of equal importance with social-class distinctions. There is, she claims, a codetermination on our lives by both gender and class. Hartmann defined patriarchy as "a set of social relations among men which have a material base, and which, though hierarchical, establish . . . interdependence and solidarity among men that enable them to dominate women."[34] She asserted that men dominate women successfully because of material reasons: women's labor is controlled for the most part by men. This control, which is supported by ideological justification, depends on male restrictions on females' access to economic and social resources that are crucial to their well-being. This male domination or hegemony includes the control over women's sexuality and especially reproductive capacities.

Hartmann thinks that patriarchy, like capitalism, is reproduced and justified in the home, school, community, and society. As a result, children learn through experience that they have different places in the gender and social-class hierarchies. The gender division of labor (which has been opposed by feminists) is the scaffolding for sexual "subcultures" in which females and males experience life differently. For Hartmann and other socialist feminists, there is no such thing as a pure form of capitalism; instead, we have lived in a patriarchal capitalism. If this is the case, then it is possible to overcome capitalism and experience, e.g., a patriarchal socialism! "Capitalist development creates the places for a hierarchy of workers, but traditional Marxist categories [and explanations] cannot tell us who will fill the places. Gender and racial hierarchies determine who will fill the places. . . . It is in studying patriarchy that we learn why it is women who are dominated and how."[35] Hartmann explained that patriarchal capitalist benefits are open to various people based on class, race, nationality, gender, age, marital status and, of course, sexual orientation! The availability of benefits according to identity criteria enables the agents of capitalism to exacerbate and manipulate differences to control workers. Women have become aware of themselves as classed, gendered, and raced workers within the experiences of their work sites, ones historically devoted to actual biological and "educative" reproduction in capitalist divisions of labor. Because reproductive schooling in the United States was not expected to cause rebelliousness against the status quo, it was believed by men in command that women would serve as the most trustworthy teachers. The stereotypes describing women as driven by emotions and dominated by the need to nurture others were decisive in the hiring of women.

Hartmann reminded us that the sexual division of labor reappears in the paid work sites where women often are employed at many of the same tasks they performed in the household, namely, food preparation, service, cleaning, caring for people, etc. Because all too many of these jobs are considered low-status and low-paying, sexual and gender discrimination remains prevalent. Many women so employed are still dependent on a partnership to make ends meet. This situation is caused not only by low wages but by the absence of a social democratic welfare (honorific meaning) state and system of benefits in capitalist America. Women's earnings allow very few women to support themselves and their children adequately. For many women who are waged and/or salaried workers, the "double day" has been a reality. This means that they continue to bear the greatest responsibility for household work even after the paid job is completed.

According to Hartmann:

> Women are teachers, welfare workers . . . and in the health fields [although not as medical doctors to the same extent as men]. The nurturant roles that women play in these jobs are of low status because capitalism emphasizes personal independence and the ability of private enterprise to meet social needs, emphases contradicted by the need for collectively [publicly] provided social services. As long as the social importance of nurturant tasks can be denigrated because women perform them [and/or because capitalism does not value them for each and everyone of us], the confrontation of capital's priority on exchange value [profit] by a demand for use value [helpful and useful to concrete human beings' everyday real needs] can be avoided.[36]

Materialist-socialist feminists focus on a careful reading of historical materialism and its portrayal of labor as consisting of all the economic, social, and reproductive work done by everyone in order to sustain life and make a living. They emphasized this in order to overcome the stark dichotomy between women's work in the household and men's work in the formal capitalist economy. The socialists' goal was to valorize women's work as equal to that of men; make clear that both women and men were oppressed under capitalism; show that all men were favored in some ways over women because of patriarchy; but that women and men could become enlightened enough about their conditions to band together as workers from household and paid labor sites to overcome capitalist exploitation—and concomitantly to deconstruct patriarchal injustice. This potential achievement requires the education of chauvinist men so that they (we) can understand the unfair advantages enjoyed over women historically, and specifically under patriarchal capitalism. This project also depends on the various actors (classed, gendered, raced workers) having the cognitive ability and desire to learn from their personal, work, and societal locations what the injustices they all suffer from consist of and how they can be overcome.

While assessing the capitalist economy as very powerful, socialist feminists maintain that it is not absolutely determinative of our lives. Human agency and volition are possible and real. They argue that agency occurs by people who may be motivated mostly by class oppression, or gender injustice, and/or racial inequities. The socialists do not claim class as the only, or even most, advantageous location to resist multiple, but integrated, oppressions. "Struggle and strategy must be, therefore, assessed within the specific contexts. And if gender and class etc., are not separate systems, so much as they are a series of layered experiences, it is essential to move away from framing analysis in terms of structures and functions [alone] and begin instead with real [concrete] social relations and the [actual] human agents that produce, shape, and sustain those structures and functions [in society and the schools]."[37] This sophisticated theoretical and political position allows both solidarity and the possibilities for women to contribute from their own power bases.

Marianne Ferber and Julie Nelson edited a book, *Beyond Economic Man,* that is useful to the materialist-socialist feminist tradition featured here. They argue that men have created and dominated the scholarly field called economics. In support of women defining their individual and collective needs, Nelson asserted in chapter one that "what is needed . . . is a definition of economics that considers humans in *relation* to the world. Focusing economics on the provisioning of human life, that is, on the commodities and processes necessary to human survival [and well-being], provides such a definition. . . . When human survival—including survival through childhood—is made the core of economic inquiry, non-material services such as childcare and supervision, as well as health concerns and the transmission of skills, become just as central as food and shelter."[38] The Greek root of both economics and ecology is *oikos* (house). Economics could and *should* be about how we live in our house and on the earth. I will touch on the importance of ecology and the "Green Movement" in chapter eight. Nelson encouraged us to move beyond overly mathematical and impersonal studies of economics to a focus on human beings and their concrete needs, aspirations, and overall well-being. This change would neither be masculine nor feminine, rather a human science capable of serving all the human beings who inhabit and labor on the earth.

Suggested Task for the Reader
Based on what you have studied, how would you present an argument demonstrating the historical "progression" of rights claims on the path to the *possibility* for people living more dignified lives? How does the emergence of the "new social groups" since 1945 (woman, people of color, and most recently homosexuals and lesbians), relate to the earlier demands for fair and equitable treatment made by classed workers. Be sure to include the unevenness of this development, i.e., its nonlinearity and the view held by some that not every "classification" or "identity" deserves the same kind of recognition as others—specifically when it comes to treatment in schools. What should the criteria be for deciding upon/ among the various class, race, gender, and sexual orientation claims?

III

In section II I presented feminist political positions that follow from the philosophical discussions and problems discussed in section I. I organized the politics of materialist-socialist feminism around the following concepts: public-private; self-definition; agency, gendered, classed, and raced positionalities; epistemological advantages; opportunities for collective struggle; double-demands; political-economic concreteness; citizen-workers; and inclusion of women for epistemological reasons as well as fairness. In this brief section, I show that the feminist project presented so far can be viewed as part of the historic ideas and values characterizing the humanist West. Not everyone will agree that such connections can, or should, be made. Philosophers, including educational philosophers, are an argumentative group!

The decision to focus on Western philosophy is not driven by disregard for other philosophies and ideas. The focus on Western ideas occurs because our educational philosophy is dependent on Western philosophy, and I am a man of the West. The Western tradition of ideas presented so far features many arguments, disagreements, and some recognizable, agreed-upon developments that bode well for those who are interested in education for democratic empowerment, social justice, and respect for diversity. Western civilization continues to operate in the complex world which features other civilizations that interact with the West in unprecedented and possibly promising ways. You are encouraged to place this book in the wider contexts of your knowledge of and experiences with global realities. The West has played a major role during late-twentieth century international interactions and exchanges. The West's role is not appreciated by each and every person around the world, especially when this role smacks of neoimperialism.[39]

Pauline Johnson's work placed feminist thought and action in the tradition of Western humanism and is included here as a capstone to my own overall thesis in this book. This thesis is that there exists a recognizable conversation and resultant record of action in the West's history which provides scaffolding for education devoted to democratic empowerment, social justice, and respect for diversity. Johnson admitted that not all feminists embrace humanism, mainly because this tradition has been guilty of using man to represent all of humankind, subsuming women under the masculine category. The historical use of humanism to smooth over or deny human differences and pluralities makes Johnson's arguments for feminism's belonging properly within the humanist home somewhat difficult. According to Johnson: "It needs to be underlined that modern humanism is not merely a doctrine which asserts the . . . unity of the species. Parallel with the aspiration to consider all humans within these universalizing terms has been the equally strong desire to affirm particularity, to raise awareness and respect for the uniqueness of all forms of individuality: this desire has served as a basis from which to . . . [denounce] the totalitarian character of all images of a common humanity."[40] Johnson explained well the complex realities involved in differences among certain commonalities. Humanism is an idea and consciousness that takes us beyond identification based on custom and tradition, beyond mere local membership as definers of who we are. Modern humanism asserts that beyond differences assigned by memberships and localities (ascribed characteristics) there exists a "primary status as members of a generic humanity."

Johnson argued that modern humanism has given us a dynamic concept of the person: one that portrays us as unique in many ways, potentially autonomous, struggling against material and other structures, but still members of the human family with its basic commonalities. Her definition of radical humanism asserted that it is a historical project that is characterized by conscious value choices. These choices are related to and often congruent with one another in the historical, collective struggle for human freedom and justice. Johnson cautioned her sister feminists that to overlook the benefits brought to them and all of us by various forms of humanism, e.g., the Enlightenment, French and American Revolutions, Marxism, etc. is mistaken; such oversight threatens many of the fragile accomplishments currently enjoyed. Johnson thought that many women rely for their well-being on the liberal and radical reforms that were driven by humanist ideals, ideas, and politics, e.g., governmental interference on the side of ordinary people whenever market outcomes throw too many of us into poverty. She suggested that some comparatively affluent feminist theorists are out of touch with the fears, needs, and hopes of women who work at low-wage, difficult, and other jobs that people with choices do not fill.

Johnson opposed those who see humanism as just a cover for men's power over women, et al., and/or as window-dressing for masculinist logic. Her view of Western ideas and actions includes recognition of their complexities as well as spaces in which modern feminism has developed. She pointed to the rich lode of human diversity conceptions in the Enlightenment, Romantic, and liberal traditions. Feminists are urged to understand their memberships in the richly complex conversations and actions characteristic of Western humanism. Johnson believed that feminists have the opportunity to help shape—for the better—the current forms of humanism not just in the Western world, but globally. Feminists have also succeeded in educating us to understand that many legitimate demands require us to go beyond mere inclusion and add-on-ism. We have learned about specific and new needs and demands from feminists, blacks, Hispanics, Native Americans, gays, lesbians, et al.

The feminism Johnson championed represents a double relationship with Enlightenment thought. Its protest against imposed gender identities and relations is congruent with and extends the Enlightenment's emancipatory commitment to human beings' right and ability to determine their own lives and social world. Radical feminism continues the Enlightenment's promise of and trajectory toward the achievement of radical, participatory democracy. In spite of its congruence with the best of the Enlightenment, radical feminism refuses to be assimilated into any fixed doctrines. Feminist critique seeks to unmask the various failures of the Enlightenment tradition—especially the failure to translate the Enlightenment's best promises into action and fulfillment for everyone. "The narrow rationalism of seventeenth-century metaphysics . . . the so-called gender-blindness of Marxian categories, as well as liberalism's own construction of an abstract 'rights-bearing subject,' have all been appropriately targeted by this critical feminist perspective."[41]

Johnson continued to insist that beyond the "constellations of contingencies" and structures that help shape our individual biographies, each of us also has her/his primary status as a member of a common humanity. She saw the possibility for pluralism and unity existing in a necessarily fragile—but necessary—balance. I agree with her articulation of the possibility of this balance: modern humanism continues to insist on the universalist character of its aspirations. It realizes that it can only be played out in specific, material, culture-bound contexts. If there are universal values *within history* that are worth defending, these historical, humanly constructed values exist in particular forms and in specific places. Johnson attempted "to establish that feminism *is* a humanism. It offers a distinctive set of interpretations of these historically evolved value ideas and stands as an index to their practical force. Historically, feminism has extended and added new meaning to the idea of the civil rights of all individuals, it has qualitatively expanded our understanding of . . . publicly significant needs and enriched our sense of the many sided uniqueness of the human personality."[42]

IV

Our attention will be focused on black liberatory philosophy which is congruent with and supportive of the thesis offered in this book. The liberatory struggles by women and black people through various forms of identity politics have expanded the struggle for human dignity. You may recall that Nancy Fraser argued that gender and racial oppression could not be remedied by the *redistribution* of resources alone. There is the need for *recognition of difference* as a remedy. Because we are all classed, gendered, and raced, most of us need both fair distribution of resources and recognition/acceptance of our gendered and raced identities. I present the work of Lucius Outlaw as a good example and explanation of African-American liberation philosophy. Outlaw recognized both the dangers and opportunities for black liberation in Western philosophy and especially in the modern period that featured the enslavement of black Africans. His work provides a useful entry for those who want to study further African-

American and African philosophies. Timothy Reagan's *Non-Western Educational Traditions* (1996), cited in the 5th endnote of chapter one, may also be helpful. It would be well to relate what will be presented to what has been read in chapter seven. Women and African Americans have both had to combat Western, white, male philosophical (and consequential socioeconomic, political, cultural, and educational) claims and practices in order to clear spaces for *inclusion into*—as well as fundamental *improvement of*—the mainstreams of our common civilization. For better or worse, the late twentieth century is a time when various historical civilizations are losing much of their distinctiveness, partly as a result of growing economic interdependence, the communications revolution, and the shrinkage of time and space with regard to travel. Those who are most responsible for the current global capitalist project seek to make everyone and every place answerable to market outcomes. Recognition of human and cultural differences is viewed by capitalist actors as realities that should be tamed by turning them into criteria for jobs assigned and consumer choices.

Outlaw's autobiography centered on his attempts to make sense of the racial segregation he experienced from the time of his early childhood in Mississippi. "The picture of America and its promises, as well as those of Mississippi, that were presented to me in classes in civics and history *made no sense* when compared to my experiences of the sharply drawn, tightly structured, and forcefully maintained race-focused realities [segregation and discrimination] of daily life and the scripted limitations on the futures of colored folk. The disparities and contradictions between the two—the pictures and the realities; the high principles and rhetoric of grand promises, and the arrogant . . . legalized inhumanity intended to thwart . . . [our] sharing the dreams of opportunity, let alone working to realize them—were painfully obvious, as was intended."[43]

Outlaw claimed that it made no sense to him that "Christian white folks" practiced segregation and oppression because they erroneously believed that African Americans were incompatibly different from and inferior to themselves. Outlaw argued that the schooling he experienced was characterized by teachings and curricula aimed at keeping black students in their places. These hegemonic strategies were intended to convince black youngsters that segregation was the way things were supposed to be. Outlaw refused to internalize these messages, as he realized that racist Mississippi was not an example of the natural order of things. The young Lucius did not achieve this ability to resist the cruel teachings and experiences on his own. He wrote about some of his black teachers and coaches who provided counterhegemonic messages. He credited his parents, clergypersons, Scout leaders, and older peers with teaching him survival skills as well as a good self-concept. The black community protected, instructed, and taught its young to strive to "move on up a bit higher." He wrote specifically about his father who taught him that white men who were wealthy and well-schooled had most of the power in Starkville, Mississippi. Members of the black community would have to become even better educated in order to contest the hegemony and direct power exercised over them.

Outlaw explained that when he went to Fisk University in Nashville, Tennessee, one of the premier "Negro" colleges in the country, he was entering an institution that was dedicated to developing leaders. He decided to major in philosophy! This decision followed from his attempts to make sense of things. Lucius was now among bright students from around the country and the world; the teachers pushed the students to the limit of their capacities, through the introduction of Sartre, Kierkegaard, Plato, C.P. Snow, Karl Marx, Joseph Conrad, Aristotle, Einstein, Thomas Aquinas, et al. He wrote that he became a "mildly radical" humanist: one who was committed—passionately—to yet incomplete notions of freedom and autonomy. Outlaw's work in philosophy convinced him that the ability to reason, i.e., the defining human capacity to make sense of his life and world, empowered him to live according to his own careful and responsible choosing.

You will most likely realize that Outlaw included himself amongst those who systematically philosophize about what human beings could and should be. He realized that Western philosophy had excluded all too many people from being able to qualify for this elite company. He hoped that philosophical understanding would empower him to contribute to the ending of racial segregation and varied accompanying practices of injustice so that America might be transformed into a racially just nation. It is intriguing to learn about this undergraduate student who came to the realization, at a comparatively early age, that philosophy is not just about understanding but potentially a basis for transformative action. Outlaw came to understand that the white man's Euro-American philosophical "club" made good arguments for liberty, equality, community, social justice, and democracy—even though they, in most cases, left black people out of these rights' claims, and/or specifically argued that people who lived in and/or originated from Africa were not qualified to enjoy the privileged lives championed by Western philosophy.

Outlaw's philosophical consciousness was further developed by what was happening in the political and judicial processes as well as on the

streets. The Civil Rights Movement caused most Americans, and especially black Americans, to confront intellectually and morally the massive
and systematic injustices in the United States. Many had to decide whether
or not to act. Outlaw found himself in the thick of passionate conversation and debate about the goals of the Civil Rights Movement and the
brutal opposition against it while he was a visiting student at Dartmouth
College and as a traveler to Europe which was part of his schooling at
Fisk. Radical students who sought to rethink what it might mean to be
black in America challenged Outlaw when he was a member of student
government during his senior year at Fisk. Outlaw spoke of being pressured to change his identity from "Negro" to "Black," i.e., to shed the
oppressors' name for African American in order to do as liberationist
philosophy and politics commanded—to determine one's own identity
and call things by their right names. Alas, the philosophy he had studied
up to the time of his senior year at Fisk did not adequately help him to
face challenging existentialist decisions. While he wrestled with certain
outward manifestations of the new, black identity, e.g., wearing his hair
"Afro" style, he found little to assist him in the philosophies written by
white men he had read. Outlaw realized that the key question was whether
"Black Power" was the right cause to support, not hairstyle—although
symbols and identity are connected. Outlaw was compelled to expand his
ideas about philosophical thought, and who its authors were.

He left Fisk for Boston College, a Catholic Jesuit institution in Chest-
nut Hill, Massachusetts—a well-to-do suburb. He was pursuing a doctor-
ate in philosophy and along with a few comrades in the program, Outlaw
pressed their concerns on professors and the curriculum: racial injustice,
the war in Vietnam, the injustices of capitalism, imperialism, etc. These
graduate philosophy students were convinced that their formal studies
should be integrated into concerns for democracy, social justice, respect
for diversity, and peace. In many cases they had to find resources on their
own.

> In addition to reading texts and completing the work assigned in courses and
> seminars, I began to turn more of my attention out of class to numerous texts on
> the informal curricula of the Black Power and Anti-War Movements, still in search
> of resources to help me make sense of things. Frantz Fanon, Karl Marx, Herbert
> Marcuse, W.E.B. DuBois, and Harold Cruse, among many others . . . were the
> focus of my efforts. Intense debates with various folks in various networks helped,
> as well. So, too, attending all those meetings and lectures on various campuses,
> in public places, and organizations' meeting places. I began to take every oppor-
> tunity I could to integrate these efforts into my studies in philosophy at Boston
> College. . . . I reached a major turning point in my efforts when one evening I
> attended a standing-room-only lecture . . . given by Herbert Marcuse (he had

been a major influence on Angela Davis when she was a student studying philosophy at Brandeis University). Inspired by what he had to say, I began to read his
work and . . . found my way into the Frankfurt School of Critical Social Theory
and on to an entire generation of humanistic, Marxist, democratic socialists throughout Eastern and Western Europe. About the same time I began to tap into traditions of . . . Black nationalist critiques of white supremacy along with my Marx-
inspired critiques of capitalism. But the integration of the results of my efforts
into a coherent perspective would take a while still.[44]

Seeing and hearing Marcuse at the University of California, San Diego in
the late 1960s caused me, because of the depth, clarity, and passion of
his lecture, to take his work seriously in my attempt to make sense of
things.

Upon completion of the Ph.D. at Boston College, Dr. Outlaw returned
to Fisk as a faculty member. His doctoral dissertation, awarded in 1972,
is entitled: "Language and the Transformation of Consciousness: Foundations for a Hermeneutic of Black Culture." Hermeneutics is a branch of
philosophy and theology that seeks to interpret and make the meaning of
various writings and events clear. This beginning professor had to learn
how to engage his students with the philosophies he had learned and
considered relevant to their education. He was intent on helping them to
think critically about the institutional forces and people who structured
people's lives in oppressive ways. As he sought to engage in this pedagogy he realized that his knowledge of black scholars' and activists' work
was inadequate. He began to construct a project that would correct this
deficiency. He had to dig among sources in order to unearth the work of
African-American and African thinkers and freedom fighters in order to
teach about these important, but little known, accomplishments. Professor Outlaw made clear that he continued to study and teach about the
canonical figures in Western philosophy at the same time as he brought
new voices into the historical conversation. His self-directed learning project
included reaching out to the handful of other black philosophers in the
United States, e.g., Cornel West, Leonard Harris, et al. These academics
sought to develop "Black Philosophy," which was the name they gave to
the efforts made to revise the philosophical canon in order to include the
contributions of African and African-descended thinkers. Outlaw also made
contacts with philosophers in Africa as part of his learning project.

Outlaw's work eventually caused him to critically consider the enterprise of philosophy itself—not just to its conspicuous exclusion of black
thinkers. He turned his attention to the "insidious yet constitutive ways in
which valorizations of raciality have been at work, mostly silently but quite

effectively, to bring about and maintain over centuries a complex intellectual and cultural hegemony with particular racial and ethnic profiles."[45] Outlaw's lifelong attempt to make sense out of what he experienced, first as a child in Starkville and throughout his life in racist America and elsewhere, caused him to investigate the "coloring of reason" in Western philosophy: a resource that he had earlier considered the key tool for the realization of justice. He was convinced that the use of reason is still central to living a moral life and to constructing a just society. He believed that reason is *yet to be fully realized* because the progressive potential of Western philosophy and politics has not been extended to all of the world's people. The world must be "made reasonable"—fair and just—for all people, not just for wealthy and powerful people in the West. He struggled to walk the fine line between demanding *inclusion* of black people into the progressive benefits of what the white West has achieved, and arguing for going *beyond* these achievements. He thought that the inclusion of people of color into the liberatory project of Western philosophy, the Enlightenment, and modernism will be more than just "add-on-ism"; instead, this hoped-for inclusion will take us all beyond the liberal-Enlightenment-Marxist liberatory horizon.

Outlaw criticized Western philosophy and politics for not living up to its universal promise; Western philosophers tried to represent white, European, heterosexual, affluent man as *the* prototypical universal human being. This false universality excluded all too many Other people. He focused on the exclusion of African and African-descended people who have suffered catastrophically because of their exclusion from the safety of Western progressivity. Outlaw and other black philosophers indict Western philosophers for having constructed an exclusive club and then representing it as universal. This sleight of hand made the exclusion of black people from the club possible; this nonmembership was cruelly justified by claims of black people's inability to use reason. European philosophy had argued historically that the ability to reason was the sine qua non of being human! Outlaw's philosophical project is intended to rescue the very personhood of black people! His perceived need to do this is indicative of the shameful flaw in Western ideas and practices. Outlaw and many other black philosophers argue against this reality with resources drawn from the better parts of Western philosophy itself.

Outlaw's argument concerning how the Western definition of reason was constructed in a way that excluded black people from membership in the privileged rungs of the human race follows. The philosophical construction of "universal man" by Western thinkers was based on his alleged ability to grasp and understand the foundational, i.e., unchanging realities in the world. This model man was equipped with reason and rationality, along with the abilities to be truthful, good, and virtuous. A connection was made between the microcosm of human existence and the cosmos itself—one governed by a deity. The rational mind then is the essence of being human for Western idealist philosophers. Western philosophers argued that one must *know* what is real and good in order to act virtuously. This epistemology was based on a belief that the quest for certainty is achievable. This quest was portrayed as inherently progressive, certain European men moved almost inevitably toward higher levels of humanity and social excellence. This belief in Western man's superior epistemological grasp of reality, through reason, led to a certain arrogance toward those who did not possess this ability to reason. The putative possession of superior reason, intelligence, and understanding of universals led to the Western attempt to dominate other, "less worthy, less human people," e.g., those who lived in Africa. Outlaw argued that all too many definitions of rationality are constructed by certain people who follow certain agendas that are necessarily self-serving. Those with power have labeled themselves and others along hierarchies of intelligence, morality, and worthiness—all justified by claims of access to universal truths.

Outlaw's articulation of this shameful exclusion of all too many people from the human family itself stated:

> Such was the case with the European encounter with the different others of Africa. There the "Man" of Western Europe assumed His Position as paragon of human development . . . for Whom the resources and peoples of the world were to be made part of His private dominion. This self-image and posture were off-loaded to Africa from the decks . . . of slave ships and from inland caravans through rationalizations of greed and imperialism under the camouflage of sacred texts and practices guided by the cross, [Islamic crescent,] the pseudo-science of the "other" (i.e., early anthropology), and the outright practices of near genocide and dominating exploitation. The most frequent rationalization offered was that European encroachments in Africa brought "progress" in the form of Christianity and "rational" *civilization*. . . . By then Philosophy had become the . . . highest expression of this rationalization (and would remain so until replaced by achievements in the nineteenth and twentieth centuries in the natural sciences). The effort to realize this deep-rooted project of Western "civilization" was conditioned by a principle of discrimination. . . . For not all persons or peoples were thought to share the level of development and/or potential required to realize rationality, especially at its highest levels: only certain males of the white race of Europe were. . . . It was averred that only certain restricted groups of individuals (for example the free Greek male in Aristotle's *Politics*) or certain "civilizations" (that

of Europe) had the wherewithal to engage in philosophical praxis. In even more pointed and restrictive claims by [the Scottish philosopher David] Hume [1711–1776] and Hegel, African peoples were explicitly denied the status of rational . . . [human] beings.[46]

Africans and those of African descent had to "deconstruct" such life-threatening parts of Western philosophy and politics. Philosophers such as Outlaw have attempted to replace the degrading caricature of Africans with a reconstructed one that portrays them accurately as fully human. The philosophical attempts to correct Western philosophy's despicable portrayal of black people was accompanied by political struggles in Africa, the United States, and elsewhere aimed at decolonization, civil rights, and full membership in the respective societies as equal human beings. The people of Africa and the African Diaspora have demanded that they will define themselves! Remember that this deconstruction and reconstruction has occurred *within* the contexts of Western philosophy as a whole. These challenges by women, African Americans, non-Westerners, et al. serve to make possible a more defensible global way of thinking—one that goes far beyond Western philosophy and civilization.

Outlaw admitted that philosophy is left without universality and tight unity, especially during this wave of deconstruction. He hastened to add that philosophizing in general—as compared to the canons of Western *Philosophy*—has always been plural, multivocal, ubiquitous, nuanced, and even contradictory. The challenges posed by blacks, women, indigenous Americans, et al. mean that philosophers and ordinary citizens must enter into democratic contexts of dialogue in order to construct historical and human "universals" that serve to help all people achieve the conditions necessary to live better and more dignified lives. Outlaw wrote of "universals-through-consensus," a concept championed throughout this book. The participants in this democratic philosophical, political, and educational project will necessarily speak from raced, gendered, and classed positions. There are no universal models floating on high; the struggle to recognize the universal personhood of all people must occur within the materiality of everyday life.

Outlaw referred to current political movements whose mobilizations are driven by the valorization of various differences, e.g., race, ethnicity, and gender. He defended these politics of identity because all too many people and groups have been pressured into individualism and/or false universal memberships. The attempt to cajole or force each and every person into consumers is representative of both the kinds of individualism and universalism rejected by many progressive, identity politics activists. Outlaw argued that historical, cultural, social life-worlds are the very foundation of our lives and being. He wrote of the thickness and richness of African-American culture, realities that must be taken into consideration when discussing what rationalism means. As he stated: reason is never "pure" and never without specific historical/cultural "clothing." It is incorrect to oppose the claims of identity politics in the name of so-called universal claims of abstract rationality. Difference and self- and/or group-constructed identities should be prized over forced homogenization!

He sought to convince his readers that race, ethnicity, and gender are constitutive of our personal and social beings, not secondary or inessential characteristics. Outlaw argued that the path to an ethical and just concept of generalized personhood must go from and through the realities of the differences among us. There is no shortcut to the goal of simply stating, I am a human being who is deserving of equal rights, opportunities, and protection. Because of real and positive differences among members of the human family, it is not surprising that reason itself operates pluralistically. We must expand our idea of reason and humanness so that the shortcomings of our philosophical, socioeconomic, political, and educational practices are remedied in order to make possible a society wherein each and every person is valued. It is easier to propose these things than to achieve them.

I leave Outlaw in order to consider the work of two other African-American philosophers. Cornel West argued that black philosophers "can contribute to the redefining of philosophy principally by revealing why and showing how philosophy is inextricably linked to politics and power—to structures of domination and mechanisms of control. This important task does not call for an end to philosophy. Rather it situates philosophical activity in the midst of personal and collective struggles in the present."[47] West viewed the main task of African-American philosophy to preserve the idea of a revolutionary future, one better than the one that currently prevails. He stated that the black philosopher must take Hegelian and Christian ideas of negation (of what is unjust) and transformation (beyond the current state of affairs) and into the imaginary of the radical "not-yet" seriously. The famous "I Have a Dream" speech by the reverend Dr. Martin Luther King, Jr. in Washington, D.C. is in the tradition of which West wrote.[48] West insisted that "if Afro-American philosophers are to make a substantive contribution to the struggle for . . . [their] freedom, it is imperative that we critically reevaluate the grand achievements of the past philosophical figures in the West."[49]

Angela Davis is a well-known philosopher and activist noted since the late 1960s. She has played important roles in both women's and African-Americans' struggles for liberation. She had to go underground, was arrested, jailed, and acquitted for her alleged assistance to men who had broken the law. She contributed a chapter to Leonard Harris's *Philosophy Born of Struggle* (1983) in which she argued that black literature speaks of the translation of the principles of freedom into active, concrete struggles for liberation. The "wish dreams" of African Americans were placed in the real world of lived experience and collectively acted on through political struggle for achievable goals. She was interviewed in George Yancy's book which is based on the assumption that much of Western philosophy is dominated by white cultural hegemony. Most of the contributors to Yancy's work agree that there is a need to "decenter" this philosophy and expose its dominant discourses as examples of "colonialism" and even "cultural arrogance." Yancy thinks that all African-American philosophers have experienced various forms of marginalization because of racist attitudes and practices. He argued that this phenomenon applies also to women, and perhaps, most specifically to black women.

Davis explained in her interview with Yancy that her parents, both teachers, taught her that there was a need to contest the racist, segregated order of Birmingham, Alabama, and the American South. The segregated realities of everyday life led to a sense of community among blacks that allowed solidarity, strength, and hope. Her parents were involved in radical politics at home and in New York City. Davis learned about the relationships among critique, theory, and praxis in her community and in her family. Yancy asked Davis if she already had a "philosophical disposition" in her youth. Her response epitomizes the practice of philosophy being championed in this book.

> In the sense that we all have potential to engage philosophically in the world, I would say yes. I explain this philosophical disposition as a consequence of my parents' encouragement to think critically about our social environment, in other words, not to assume that the appearances in our lives constituted ultimate realities. Our parents encouraged us to look beyond appearances and to think about possibilities, to think about ways in which we could, with our own agency, intervene and transform the world. In this sense my own philosophical disposition initially expressed itself not so much as a specific mode of thought, but rather as a quotidian way of living in the world.[50]

She explained how her childhood ideas and experiences prepared her to think of liberation and justice as *human* necessities. She progressively developed a universal vision of humanity from the black liberatory project in which she labored. While in New York Davis learned more about the problems and possibilities of multiracial class struggle. Her reading of Marx, in a progressive high school, provided her with some basic conceptual tools with which to think about the relationships between race and class. She admits that thinking systematically about gender and how it fit into race and class occurred later in her life.

You are encouraged to think about similarities and differences between the women's and black people's liberatory movements. You may benefit from consulting the following sources on the black liberatory struggle. George Yancy, *African-American Philosophers: 17 Conversations* (1998), bell hooks and Cornel West, *Breaking Bread: Insurgent Black Intellectual Life* (Boston: South End Press, 1991), Angela Y. Davis, *Women, Race and Class* (New York: Vintage Books, 1981), and the writings of Martin L. King, Jr. and Malcolm X. Due to limitations of space and knowledge, this book does not include analyses of the struggles conducted by Spanish-speaking people, Native Americans, Asian Americans, and other people discriminated against in this country.

Suggested Task for the Reader
Lucius Outlaw and other African-American philosophers have learned that philosophy is not just about understanding; comprehension is potentially a basis for transformative action. Relate the statement above to the kinds of educational philosophy, curricula, and pedagogy that would best serve African-American and other discriminated-against students with regard to overcoming this oppression. See chapter four and the discussion of educational Reconstructionism.

V

The analyses of feminist and black philosophy and congruent politics that have been featured so far provide scaffolding for discussing educational consequences and possibilities. I will draw on Kathleen Weiler's *Women Teaching for Change: Gender, Class & Power* throughout this section. Her sensitivity to gender, class, and race justifies her work being featured in this section. The alert reader can relate and apply the educational ideas and arguments presented to specific problems and possibilities that are characteristic of her/his own particular interests.

Weiler began by explaining that schools are subject to conflicting imperatives. The first imperative or demand seeks to use schooling as preparation for jobs in the highly stratified, and unjust, capitalist work force. The intent is to "reproduce" competent but uncritical workers. This is often called the capitalist imperative. The second imperative, the democratic one, seeks to provide learning experiences that make it possible for all students to become *critical* citizen-workers.[51] Weiler argued that these conflicting imperatives act upon the gendered, raced, and classed students and their teachers. The imperatives fall upon students whose identities serve to determine what kind of schooling they are presented with; students are then selected and sorted for jobs along an extremely vertical rank order. The phenomenon called reproduction is beneficial to those who already do well in school and society, but harmful to the many classed, gendered, and raced people who have not.

Weiler wrote about how hegemony functions in schools in ways that make it seem as though the way things are, are inevitable, universal, and beneficial to everyone. Oppressive ideology and hegemony can be, have been, and are resisted. Weiler saw progressive teachers playing antihegemonic roles. This possibility is based on her belief that while the power of the status quo is considerable in terms of institutions and practice, people are capable of understanding and resisting conditions that are not really beneficial to them. People are volitional and we can make our own histories, although not as if institutional/structural realities and impediments do not exist.

Weiler wrote of educators and students enjoying certain spaces and autonomy within structures and between imperatives, some of which make possible an education for democratic empowerment, social justice, and respect for diversity. Progressive educators, students, and other citizens can negotiate around what is considered inimical to the development of the whole student within the spaces of which Maxine Greene and Hannah Arendt write. Our agency allows us to maneuver around and sometimes directly oppose the antiprogressive imperatives in school and society that seek to maintain a system that has proven unjust to certain students as well as adults. Weiler's socialist, feminist, and critical analysis goes beyond the liberal one that she finds lacking because it is unwilling and/or incapable of revealing the complex underlying causes of what liberal critics of school practice, oppose, and seek to change. Weiler's "critical feminist educational theory begins with certain assumptions that distinguish it from liberal . . . [theory]. The first assumption is that schooling is deeply connected to the class structure and economic system of capitalism; thus one focus . . . is on the relationship of women's schooling and women's work. The second assumption, again derived from more general socialist feminist theory, is that capitalism and patriarchy are related and mutually reinforcing of one another. In other words, both men and women exist in interconnected . . . relationships of gender and class . . . [and] race."[52]

Weiler thinks that the feminist movement as a whole has influenced education as follows. The first is that curriculum and pedagogy have been criticized for sexist biases and patriarchal assumptions. Second, feminists have created courses addressing women in many discipline areas; feminists have allegedly sought less authoritarian relationships/practices in classrooms—although a "feminist pedagogy" per se has not yet been developed. Perhaps the tradition that began with Dewey and the progressives, one which continues presently with certain changes having been made, is capable of providing educators with the antihegemonic tools and ideas for more democratic classrooms without specific pedagogies for women, African Americans, Hispanics, et al. Weiler explained that feminist educators "like all progressive teachers" are fighting against increasing technocratic practices and controls, reliance on standardized testing for purposes of selecting and sorting students, and the seemingly perennial public cry for "back to basics."[53] There has always occurred fierce arguments about what constitutes the basics, as well as who should decide. Cole wrote: "What it means to know, who are the knowers, and what counts as an object of knowledge are all defined by a highly restrictive community. That the definitions have been various has been philosophy's saving grace; opening up the membership criteria for the knowledge community is the feminist philosopher's goal."[54] African-American philosophers have sought this opening. So have subaltern people who are represented in this book.

Weiler's and Cole's general ideas about feminist methodologies is not intended to mean specific "how-to" tactics for classroom teachers' use. A more complex meaning is offered—one that may provide ideas for educators as they construct their own reflective practices. According to Weiler, feminist epistemology and methodology have been constructed from the study of women as they function in social settings, and how they are portrayed in texts, and the media. Simone de Beauvoir's central insight that women must endeavor to define themselves as women and human beings—rather than continuing to be defined by invidious comparisons with men is taken seriously by this methodology. Teachers who are interested in racial justice can also use this methodological assumption.

Weiler thinks that three themes dominate feminist methodology. The first theme is that studies aimed at ascertaining how an oppressive system works must begin with our concrete experiences in patriarchal, capitalist (and other) economic systems. According to Weiler, "women's consciousness includes both hegemonic ideas from the male tradition and the possibilities of critical consciousness or what Gramsci called 'good sense.' Before women researchers can understand the experiences and consciousnesses of other women we must come to understand ourselves and the ways in which we know."[55] Weiler realized that this first theme is characteristic (*mutatis mutandis*) of other liberatory methodologies.

The second theme of feminist research methodology is related to the first, attention to everyday life. The problems and possibilities faced by women occur in both the private and public spheres. Feminists have argued that the private is political and vice versa. Feminist methodology attempts to make clear that powerful men have portrayed social reality in an incomplete and distorted way as they have neglected to describe and analyze the conditions under which women live and work. Feminist methodology, like other liberatory varieties, is aimed at constructing a language of experience which includes what women undergo. This must come from explorations of personal, everyday, and concrete experiences— as well as reflections on them. Weiler hopes that focusing on the everyday world can reveal the ways in which larger forces, both material and ideological, cause certain limits on women's actions and their potentially liberatory politics. She argued that emphasis on everyday experience necessitates that the researcher place herself within her subjectivity, taking intuition seriously, emotions, and feelings. Many forms of Western methodologies have demeaned the value of the subjective.

The third theme of feminist methodology is the necessity of political commitment. In keeping with other liberatory projects, women (and black people) have insisted on ideas being translated into action. Along with Marx, Weiler's feminist methodology is committed to the famous dictum: the point is not just to understand the world, but also to change it. Weiler concluded by emphasizing the importance of understanding gender in social class and racial terms. She explained that inherited class positions are crucial to the opportunity women and men enjoy with regard to school and socioeconomic success. "Thus . . . [class] intersects with, in a material way, gender and race expectations. . . . Class places limits on what is possible through access to material resources, but it is also experienced through ideology and as subjective reality."[56] Weiler concluded by reminding us that feminist methodology shares many concerns with critical educational theory. This educational theory which is derived from Marxist and Freirean sources insists that *recognition* of oppression and injustice is only a first step to the goal of *overcoming* them.

Cole argued that central to feminist method is the inclusion of the many who were and/or are still excluded from the construction of philosophical understanding. She invites her readers to begin doing philosophy. "In this vineyard the work has just begun, the controversies are rife, and the issues are confusing and . . . changing as new, formerly silenced voices are heard. But it is intensely rewarding work, and the harvest—a free and living human future—may be sweet beyond our wildest expectations."[57] Perhaps! In any case, Cole gave us the following general ground rules for *doing* philosophy, which are not unlike Weiler's. (1) The methodology must be founded in the concreteness of social historical realities. These realities must be articulated by *all* who experience them—not just the few. (2) Like Weiler, Cole stressed the inclusion of emotions and feelings when reflecting on experiences. All the philosophers who are honored in this book have refused to confine themselves to "armchair philosophizing." (3) She asked us to carefully consider "nontraditional" sources of philosophical inquiry and insight. (4) Cole reminded us of the socioeconomic, political, and cultural implications of our philosophical methodology.

Cole placed philosophical thinking and doing within the traditions of Western philosophy—and its offshoots—some of which have been presented in this book. The work that subaltern and oppressed people were required to perform in order to join the conversation and to practice the philosophical craft should not be taken lightly. The ensemble of political, socioeconomic, cultural, and educational struggles has opened up the possibility for, and accomplishment of, an unprecedented inclusion of those who do philosophy at the end of the second millennium. This is *not* to claim that more should not be done. The inclusion into philosophical conversations must be aimed at having action outcomes that help make the lives of everyone better.

Let us briefly consider the gendered, raced, and classed nature of K–12 teachers in the United States. It is well known that women have constituted the majority of the classroom teacher work force. Many teachers, both women and men, came from working-class families, although the lower middle class has been a source as well. Black women and men have also found teaching as a worthy and accessible profession.[58] Weiler explained how teachers, specifically black and white women, have decided to enter the profession. Her studies reveal that white women took their race membership and privilege for granted, whereas black women were fully aware of their race and how it affected career choices.[59]

Weiler pointed out that the great struggles occurring in the United States and elsewhere (civil rights, black power, feminism, and antiwar efforts) influenced many of the teachers she studied but this may not be the case for teachers in general. The ideas generated by these struggles helped the teachers to have a heightened awareness of injustice in the society and schools, and the determination to make a difference. She argued that although the women she studied thought they made choices freely, they were profoundly acted on by internalized ideological and material/structural restraints. The ideology concerning a "women's place," when internalized and supported by more concrete career restrictions, conspires to select and support people into certain kinds of jobs. Weiler explained that the women she studied exercised their agency in the school once they became teachers. Another generation was attracted to teaching, women "did not view themselves as passive creations of 'fate' or social structures, but as individuals who had changed and could [now] have some influence over events in their own lives. They saw their teaching as important in encouraging students, particularly girls, to take control of their own lives. They defined their own work as teachers as part of a struggle to create a more just society. In this way, they all in some sense defined themselves as agents of social change."[60]

Many of them began to better understand their work in the classrooms as related to the well-being of society. They identified themselves as feminists, but also expressed their commitments to a wider concept of humanity. One teacher defined feminism as helping women develop and act to their full potential. She continued: I could go further to say humanism is the same kind of thing. This teacher saw the ultimate progressive goal as being able to include everyone in the human family. The women Weiler studied were born into certain identities and circumstances; they succeeded in reflecting on them as well as becoming committed to structural changes which would benefit gendered, raced, and classed actors.

Weiler's fifth chapter, "The Struggle for a Critical Pedagogy," further connects the feminism she favors to critical theory. She told her readers about certain practices engaged in by the women teachers she studied, and how this pedagogy caused conflict with the institutions where they worked. It may not be surprising to learn that feminist and antiracist teachers and administrators are sometimes opposed by those who cling to sexist and racist positions, albeit usually not of the overt and/or obvious kind. Weiler described the efforts of the teachers she studied as "feminist counter-hegemonic." This assumes that an oppressive hegemony exists and is maintained in some, if not many, of the nation's K–12 public (and private) schools. Weiler's women teachers spoke about their commitment to developing a democratic classroom, one in which "it's okay to be human." These feminist educators saw their pedagogical goals as human/humane ones—goals and necessary practices that were driven by concerns for students as complex human beings.

In my view, such goals and practices are solidly within the tradition of progressive education at its best: a tradition that views curricula as resources for helping to solve students' problems. The progressive commitment to educating the "whole child" means that the teacher viewed the student not just as a cognitive being but one whose intellectual potential and power were inextricably part of our complex humanity which includes emotions, feelings, socioeconomic needs, etc. Dewey and the Critical Theorists argued that we must view people within the contexts of their societies. Better education just may be dependent on the development of societies, communities, and families in which students are well prepared to do appropriate school work. This recognition of students' lives outside the classroom necessitates that progressive and humanistic teachers be concerned—or care—about all the factors that assist and/or impede students' development. Some examples are: poverty, discrimination, oppression, and other harmful practices that gendered, raced, and classed people undergo. The feminist teachers described by Weiler saw the necessity to understand some of the reasons why democratic classrooms were so often difficult to construct. Teachers can make their classrooms islands of humanness, fair play, democracy, social justice, and respect for diversity. It would be much better if these classrooms were part of a democratic sea. I am convinced that those who teach in the progressive tradition of which Weiler's feminist teachers belong are also at the forefront of recognizing that variously abled and special education students are among those who need and deserve the humanistic pedagogy, writ large, that Weiler favors.

Special education teachers may not use terms like "multiple subjectivities" to describe the differences they deal with; however, the development of progressive education from the late-nineteenth century to the present has always been based on the recognition of our multiple and varied subjectivities—as well as commonalities. Weiler's position as a critical and feminist educator is in keeping with this historical progressive project. Our common membership in the human race must be arrived at through the recognition of our differences—some of which are worth keeping, others are not. Social-class oppression can and must be overcome. Being a Native American should not be overcome, nor should this identity be changed. One's treatment as a Native American can and should be improved upon.

The complexities of lived subjectivities in concrete situations must be analyzed in terms of great discrepancies in wealth, income, privilege, access, and power (and related school outcomes) if we are to have a critical and potentially liberatory pedagogy. Class, race, gender, and other complex identities must be understood in order to provide equal opportunities in progressive schools and society. Rosemary Tong articulated this necessary balance between recognition of difference and our common membership in the human family. "In our desire to achieve unity, we have excluded, ostracized, and alienated so-called abnormal, deviant, and marginal people. As a result of this . . . exclusion, we have impoverished the human community. We have . . . very little to lose and much to gain by joining a variety of postmodernist feminists in their celebration of multiplicity. For even if we cannot all be One, we can all be Many. There may yet be a way to achieve unity in diversity."[61]

Weiler realized that schools are central to the achievement of Tong's vision. She argued that if schooling can play such a role, teachers, in addition to students, must be empowered. Teachers' intellectual work must be respected; moreover, they must be free to work for more democracy, more social justice, and greater respect for diversity. The teachers in Dewey's Laboratory School at the University of Chicago did not apologize for the school's democratic "bias." Weiler knew about the struggles conducted by brave educators who sought to realize the goals of progressive education, critical pedagogy, and gender/race/class justice. It is important for those who are interested in liberatory education to be aware of teachers like the "brave and imaginative women" who come alive in Weiler's book. Weiler understands that "a society [still] so shaped by racism, sexism, classism, and with great economic, political, and military power in the hands of a few cannot be transformed by . . . dedicated and critical teaching alone."[62]

I have stressed throughout this chapter and this book that the kind of education and schooling championed and celebrated here can be achieved only by broad-based, progressive coalitions that support educators in the schools and by causing supportive changes to occur in the larger society. "Critical educators, reformers, citizens, et al. who are interested in education for democratic empowerment and civic responsibility must know that these goals have to be understood, desired, and fought for by more than just educators. Authentic school reform that is committed to empowerment must be linked in solidarity with persons and groups that seek to democratize American society as a whole."[63]

Suggested Task for the Reader
Construct a critical explanation of how the "educational consequences" presented in section V follow logically from feminist and African-Ameri-

can philosophical interpretations found in chapter seven. Comment also on how these "educational consequences" and methodologies are somewhat similar to characteristics of progressive education, Critical Theory, Freire's work, and other educational ways of doing found in this book and/or other sources which you are familiar with.

Conclusion

This chapter has presented analyses concerning the importance of identities beyond social class. Aronowitz argued, historical materialism must enter into dialogue with new social forces such as feminism. I argued that the experiences of women, people of color, gays, and lesbians cannot be understood by class analysis alone. The remedies for various forms of oppression and exploitation are somewhat different, e.g., equality-redistribution, or difference-recognition. An underlying thesis in chapter seven is that we all live in multiple sites and have multiple memberships. In spite of these differences I maintained throughout this work that it is useful to study women, African Americans, et al. in terms of their relationships to the economy (class) and the political system (citizen). Workplaces and other public places have provided sites for workers and citizens to communicate effectively about their problems and possibilities. It is from these sites that liberatory actions have been mounted.

Section I featured Weiler's critique of the insensitivity to women in Freire's analysis—especially his early work. Feminist philosophers have also critiqued Western philosophy for its exclusion, misrepresentation, and potentially oppressive depictions of women. The alleged dichotomy between male reason and female emotion has helped make possible the exclusion of women from participating in public life. This chapter included specific criticism of classical Greek philosophers, Descartes, and Rousseau. Section II presented materialist-socialist feminism as the politics best suited to act on feminist, philosophical critique. These politics share some characteristics with those presented in chapters three, four, and six. All of them place persons and groups in the concreteness of everyday life. Socialist feminists seek to ameliorate or eliminate the dual oppression of women, i.e., as classed and gendered actors. I also gave attention to the historical tendency to restrict women to unpaid household work, while men labored for pay in the capitalist economy. The materialist-socialist feminists believe that their analyses can lead to liberatory action.

My brief, third section provided arguments for seeing the feminist project within the best values of the humanist West. Although Pauline Johnson is aware that humanism has been used to exclude women and others from the privileges and protection of Western institutions and processes, she insists that humanism made possible the eventual liberatory movements of inclusion. She argued that humanist thought is responsible for recognizing differences among human beings as well as viewing us as dynamic, volitional, and somewhat autonomous. Johnson would have her comrades embrace *and* critique the Enlightenment project. Finally, she reminded us that beyond differences, we are all members of a common humanity.

Section IV provides the reader with some features of black liberatory philosophy. Outlaw explained that his decision to study philosophy in college was related to his earlier attempts to make sense of the racist Mississippi of his childhood. Philosophy and the Civil Rights Movement were related and mutually influential to his sense-making project. As he developed as a philosopher, Outlaw had to seek out black philosophers— ones beyond the Western canon. His lifelong study forced him to conduct a critique of Western philosophy. He concluded that reason had not yet been realized. He counsels his readers to maintain this central Western idea, to insist that African Americans, women, and various formerly excluded Others demand to be recognized as persons capable of exercising reason in personally and publicly moral ways. This need to embrace and critique Western philosophy is shared by the philosopher-activist Angela Davis.

The final section dealt with some educational consequences and possibilities as articulated by Weiler's *Women Teaching for Change*. She argued that schools include spaces in which progressive, antihegemonic teachers can maneuver between the conflicting imperatives placed on our schools. She made clear her belief that the teaching she advocates is in the progressive tradition—although with greater awareness and attention to difference, specifically gender. The methodologies she and other feminists advocate are reminiscent of what was presented in chapters three, four, and six. In keeping with a major thesis of this book, Weiler insists that teachers must reach out to find solidarity with democratic progressive forces in the larger society.

Notes

1   Stanley Aronowitz, *The Crisis in Historical Materialism: Class, Politics, and Culture in Marxist Theory*, 2nd ed., (Minneapolis: University of Minnesota Press, 1981), passim.

2   For a brief description and analysis of the "Politics of Identity" see, Richard Brosio, "Globalism, Postmodernism, The Politics of Identity and the Need for Broad Democratic Political/Educational Coalitions," in *Philosophical Studies in Education*, ed. Richard Brosio (Terre Haute, Ind.: Ohio Valley Philosophy of Education Society, 1994), 13–26.

3   Edward E. Sampson, "Identity Politics: Challenges to Psychology's Understanding," *American Psychologist* 48, no. 12 (December 1993): 1219.

4   Cameron McCarthy and Michael W. Apple, "Race, Class and Gender in American Educational Research: Toward a Nonsynchronous Parallelist Position," in *Class, Race, and Gender*, ed. Lois Weis (Albany, N.Y.: State University of New York Press, 1988), 9–39.

5   Richard A. Brosio, "The Complexly-Constructed Citizen-Worker: Her/His Centrality to the Struggle for Radical Democratic Politics and Education," *Journal of Thought* 32, no. 3 (Fall 1997): 18. I have drawn on Nancy Fraser's, "From Redistribution to Recognition? Dilemmas of Justice in a 'Post-Socialist' Age," *New Left Review*, no. 212 (July/August 1995): 68–93.

6   Leonardo and Clodovis Boff, *Introducing Liberation Theology* (Maryknoll, N.Y.: Orbis Books, 1986), 29–30.

7   Kathleen Weiler, "Freire and a Feminist Pedagogy of Difference," *Harvard Educational Review* 61, no. 4 (November 1991): 452–53.

8   Ibid.,468–69.

9   Donaldo Macedo, *Literacies of Power: What Americans Are Not Allowed to Know* (Boulder, Colo.: Westview Press, 1994), 111–12.

10   Nancy Tuana, *Woman and the History of Philosophy* (New York: Paragon House, 1992), 4.

11   For a theoretical explanation and defense of the liberatory potential and actual success of movements organized around the axis of citizen-worker, see Richard Brosio, "The Centrality of Rousseau's Citizen and Marx's Worker," in *Philosophical Studies in Education*, ed. Susan Martin (Terre Haute, Ind.: Ohio Valley Philosophy of Education Society, 1992), 145–55.

12   For an analysis of gender bias in the Bible, see Cullen Murphy, *The Word According to Eve* (Boston: Houghton Mifflin Company, 1998). Here is a representative sample from this book. "Although the Bible offers transcendent moments of

prayer, psalm, myth, and revelation, it is also a document that cannot fail to register in the minds of modern readers as profoundly alien, the product of a world and of sensibilities that in many ways are not our own. This is nowhere more the case than with regard to women" pp. ix–x. On pp. 14–15 Murphy presents the "Ten Least Wanted" biblical citations that demonstrate bias toward women. He ends the main part of his book with this: "Think of it as we will . . . the Bible remains an ageless provocation. That is why feminist scholars were drawn to . . . [it] in the first place . . . and is not provocation Eve's true vocation? . . . Creativity, curiosity, and understanding: these are the provocative attitudes for which Eve is remembered. They might not be needed in Paradise. They are made, as we are, for a world that falls short of Eden" p. 241. Joseph Campbell argued that Western patriarchal systems of religion, e.g., Judaism and Christianity, not only overthrew the earlier systems based on earth-goddesses, but continued to view the female Other as a threat to the masculine "castle of reason." See his, *The Masks of God: Occidental Mythology* (New York: The Viking Press, 1964).

13   Eve Browning Cole, *Philosophy and Feminist Criticism: An Introduction* (New York: Paragon House, 1993), 55–56.

14   Tuana, *Woman and the History of Philosophy*, 40.

15   Cole, *Philosophy and Feminist Criticism*, 99.

16   Carol Gilligan, *In a Different Voice: Psychological Theory and Women's Development* (Cambridge, Mass.: Harvard University Press, 1982), 173–74.

17   Cole, *Philosophy and Feminist Criticism*, 107.

18   Nel Noddings, "Care and Moral Education," in *Critical Conversations in Philosophy of Education*, ed. Wendy Kohli (New York: Routledge, 1995), 143. For a useful presentation of caring within the philosophical discourse called moral education, see Nel Noddings, *Philosophy of Education* (Boulder, Colo.: Westview Press, Inc., 1995), 190–97. For a somewhat different presentation of caring in teaching and learning—one that is developed from the author's practical experiences, see Barbara J. Thayer-Bacon with Charles S. Bacon, *Philosophy Applied to Education: Nurturing a Democratic Community in the Classroom* (Upper Saddle River, N.J.: Prentice-Hall, Inc., 1998), passim.

19   Mary Field Belenky et al., *Women's Ways of Knowing: The Development of Self, Voice, and Mind* (New York: Basic Books, Inc., 1986), 218.

20   Cole, *Philosophy and Feminist Criticism*, 113.

21   For example, Audrey Thompson has constructed an extensive critique of the caring ethic in education with reference to what she calls its "colorblind" psychological assumptions. She suggests that we think of educational caring from perspectives that are generated by non-white and poor people. "Not the Color Purple: Black Feminist Lessons for Educational Caring," *Harvard Educational Review* 68, no. 4 (Winter 1998): 522–54.

22   Cole, *Philosophy and Feminist Criticism*, 109. Jim Garrison provided a useful analysis of "practical" reasoning that may help us better understand a way to overcome the Western historical dichotomization of reason and emotion, mind and body, etc. that many feminists find so unacceptable. See chapter five, "The Education of Eros: Critical and Creative Value Appraisal," in *Dewey and Eros: Wisdom and Desire in the Art of Teaching* (1997). In my review of his book I wrote that "the author is convincing when he argues that women's ways of knowing and the current emphasis on the ethic of caring both have important precedents in Dewey's ideas. Readers will be especially interested in chapter two, "Care, Sympathy, and Community in Classroom Teaching: Feminist Reflections on the Expansive Self." Richard A. Brosio, *Educational Horizons* 76, no. 3 (Spring 1998): 107–08.

23   Jane Roland Martin, "Women, Schools, and Cultural Wealth," in *Women's Philosophies of Education: Thinking Through Our Mothers*, eds. Connie Titone and Karen E. Maloney (Upper Saddle, N.J.: Prentice-Hall, Inc., 1999), 153.

24   Tuana, *Women and the History of Philosophy*, 51.

25   Martin, "Women, Schools, and Cultural Wealth," in *Women's Philosophies of Education*, 154.

26   Ibid., 155.

27   Ruth Evans, ed., *Simone de Beauvoir's The Second Sex* (Manchester and New York: Manchester University Press, 1998), 10.

28   Ibid., 17.

29   Rebecca Martusewicz explained to me that some feminist interpretations of Michele Foucault's work assert that it is inaccurate to "reduce the 'discursive' to writing and speaking." Discursive refers to "how social relations of all kinds function to produce meaning and thus construct people's consciousness/identity. . . . We should not exclude 'practices' from their discursive function." The quotes are from correspondence between Martusewicz and me.

30   You will find the following books organized according to various feminist political-philosophical traditions. Rosemarie Tong, *Feminist Thought: A Comprehensive Introduction* (London: Unwin Hyman, 1989) deals with a variety of feminist thinking: liberal, Marxist, radical, psychoanalytic, socialist, existentialist, and postmodern. Nancy Tuana and Rosemarie Tong, eds. *Feminism and Philosophy: Essential Readings in Theory, Reinterpretation, and Application* (Boulder, Colo.: Westview Press, 1995) is a book that features informative editorial chapter introductions and contributions by many of the most influential feminist writers. Feminist perspectives offered are: liberal, Marxist, radical, psychoanalytic, socialist, anarchist and ecological, phenomenological, and postmodern. The last chapter deals with perspectives on the intersections of race, class, and gender.

31   Tuana and Tong, eds., *Feminism and Philosophy*, 261.

32 Ibid., 262.

33 Kathleen Weiler, *Women Teaching for Change: Gender, Class & Power* (South Hadley, Mass.: Bergin & Garvey Publishers, Inc., 1988), 61–62.

34 Heidi Hartmann, "The Unhappy Marriage of Marxism and Feminism: Towards a More Progressive Union," in *Women and Revolution: A Discussion of the Unhappy Marriage of Marxism and Feminism*, Lynda Sargent, ed. (Boston: South End Press, 1981), 14.

35 Hartmann, "The Unhappy Marriage," 18.

36 Ibid., 29.

37 Sue Ferguson, "Building on the Strengths of the Socialist Feminist Tradition," *New Politics* 7, no. 2 (Winter 1999): 98.

38 Julie A. Nelson, "The Study of Choice or the Study of Provisioning? Gender and Definition of Economics," in *Beyond Economic Man: Feminist Theory and Economics*, eds. Marianne A. Ferber and Julie A. Nelson (Chicago and London: The University of Chicago Press, 1993), 32.

39 See, Thomas Patterson, *Inventing Western Civilization* (New York: Monthly Review Press, 1997) for a class, race, and gender analysis of "the West." Patterson argued that the rise of Western power, including its imperialist form, in the modern age is concomitant with the rise of capitalism. The tendency to view people beyond the West as Other and inferior is laid bare and condemned.

40 Pauline Johnson, *Feminism As Radical Humanism* (Boulder • San Francisco: Westview, 1994), viii.

41 Ibid., 45. For another explanation, critique, and defense of the Enlightenment, see, Richard A. Brosio, *A Radical Democratic Critique of Capitalist Education*, (Peter Lang Publishing, Inc., 1994), chapter thirteen.

42 Johnson, *Feminism As Radical Humanism*, 139. If you wish to consult other authors who generally support the thesis forwarded in section III, that the feminist project for greater participation in the public realm and the achievement of social justice can be best understood in the context of the Western progressive and humanist traditions, see: Teresa L. Ebert, Mary Dietz, Seyla Benhabib, and Chantal Mouffe.

43 Lucius T. Outlaw, Jr., *On Race and Philosophy* (New York and London: Routledge, 1996), xi.

44 Ibid., xxvii.

45 Ibid., xxx.

46 Ibid., 57.

47 Cornel West, "Philosophy, Politics, and Power: An Afro-American Perspective," in *Philosophy Born of Struggle: Anthology of Afro-American Philosophy from*

1917, ed. Leonard Harris (Dubuque, Iowa: Kendall/Hunt Publishing Co., 1983), 51. Harris' book features work by various prominent African-American philosophers, and useful editorial introductions to the contributors' reinterpretations of Western philosophy. Some of the reinterpretations are characterized by extending further the borders of philosophical inquiry. Editor Harris wrote in the book's introduction: "The principal, though not exclusive, thrust of African American theories involve confrontation with unfulfilled democracy, human ravages . . . [caused by] capitalism, colonial domination, and ontological designation by race" p. xv.

48   A classic example of critiquing existing conditions in the name of a different and better criteria is provided by M.L. King, Jr., "Letter from the Birmingham Jail," in which he invokes a higher law than the ones in 1963 racist, oppressive Birmingham, Ala. This letter can be found in David A. Hollinger and Charles Capper, eds., *The American Intellectual Tradition: A Sourcebook, Vol. II: 1865 to the Present* (New York: Oxford University Press, 1989), 237–45.

49   West, "Philosophy, Politics, and Power: An Afro-American Perspective," 58.

50   Angela Y. Davis, "Interview Number One," in *African-American Philosophers: 17 Conversations*, George Yancy (New York and London: Routledge, 1998), 17. For a more comprehensive look at Davis's work, see *Women, Race & Class* (New York: Vintage Books, 1981).

51   Brosio, *A Radical Democratic Critique of Capitalist Education*, especially chapter one, "The Janus-faced Public Schools in the United States."

52   Weiler, *Women Teaching for Change*, 29.

53   For an informative description and analysis of how current "back to basics," mandated standards and control of knowledge in our K–12 schools are harmful to the essence of a multicultural society, namely, its insistence upon difference within certain forms of democratically constructed unities, see, Harold Berlak, "Standards and the Control of Knowledge," *Rethinking Schools* 13, no. 3 (Spring 1999):10–11, 29.

54   Cole, *Philosophy and Feminism*, 83.

55   Weiler, *Women Teaching for Change*, 59.

56   Ibid., 65.

57   Cole, *Philosophy and Feminism*, 124.

58   For analysis of the gendered, raced, and classed nature of the teaching profession see: (1) Clinton Allison, *Present and Past: Essays for Teachers in the History of Education* (New York: Peter Lang Publishing, Inc., 1995), chapter three, "Women Teachers and the Struggle for Occupational Justice," and chapter seven, "Gender and Education." (2) Michael W. Apple, *Teachers and Texts: A Political Economy of Class and Gender Relations in Education* (New York and London: Routledge, 1986), chapter two, "Teachers."

59 Joe L. Kincheloe, Shirley R. Steinberg, et al., eds., produced a book called *White Reign: Deploying Whiteness In America* (New York: St. Martin's Press, 1998), in which various writers examine white privilege and its being taken for granted. The consequences for teaching and learning are addressed.

60 Weiler, *Women Teaching for Change*, 89.

61 Tong, *Feminist Thought*, 233.

62 Weiler, *Women Teaching for Change*, 153.

63 Richard A. Brosio, "Educating for Power," *Changing Schools* 15, no. 3 (Fall 1987): 5. See also my "Diverse School Populations and the Corresponding Need for Multiple-Identity Coalitions: With a Touch of Class," *Paideusis: Journal of the Canadian Philosophy of Education Society* 12, no. 1 (Fall, 1998): 23–36.

Chapter Eight

Back to Postmodernism: Problems and Possibilities—With a Touch of Green

Introduction

In keeping with postmodernist thinkers' antisystematic posture (based in part on their belief that "ordered systems" are simply human constructs), my presentation is in piecemeal fashion. You are encouraged to make sense of the postmodern condition and some of its spokespersons *within* the framework of your developing intellectual map, especially in reference to its philosophical latitudes and longitudes. The first section of this chapter is called the postmodern condition and provides background and context for understanding some general, and a few specific, postmodernist philosophical ideas.[1] The section also includes critiques of postmodernist thought. The second section features an analysis of postmodernist ideas in terms of their support, nonsupport, and/or danger to the project of democracy, social justice, and respect for diversity with reference to our society and schools. The work of the American philosopher Richard Rorty is prominently featured. The touch of green (referring to the importance of ecology) promised in this chapter's title is discussed only briefly in section III. It serves as an invitation for the reader to consider further important ecological ideas and politics that are logical extensions of this book's major theses.

"Back to postmodernism" refers to the word's appearance in the title of chapter two, as well as references to postmodernism throughout the text. "Back to" also refers to postmodernist thinkers' fundamental uncertainty about their and our ability to understand the world and ourselves well; they are diffident about human abilities to construct and activate collective, progressive, liberatory projects. This uncertainty and diffidence is a throwback to premodern and even preclassic Greek times. "Back to postmodernism" may mean that "po mo" is neither entirely new nor even post; it harkens back to a time before Greek philosophers achieved plausible holistic and systemic portrayals of human and physical existence. Rather than continue a quest for *comparative* meaning, some postmodernists have declared that the quest for certainty was predictably unsuccessful and also caused human suffering; everyone is on her or his own in a universe where there are neither intrinsic nor meaningful signposts to guide us.

Postmodernists seem to not realize that powerful people and institutions continue to organize the world and all of its people while they, the postmodernists, lament that it is impossible to see things holistically, insisting that causality is beyond our understanding in these complex times and that few if any ideas and practices are demonstrably better and more just than others. From their denunciation of the quest for certainty, many postmodernists have refused to admit that some things are still more warranted in their assertibility. To their credit, most, but not all, postmodernists have not been tempted to call for a *deus ex machina* solution.

I

In my attempt to explain the postmodern condition I draw upon Zygmunt Bauman's work. I have critically interpreted his ideas. Postmodernism must be understood in its relationships with modernism. European modernists sought to overcome and replace the ancient regime—a social order that was constructed by the medieval Catholic Church in a predominantly peasant population and the aristocracy which ruled over them politically. The Church, aristocracy, and some monarchs enforced a social order in which custom often was sufficient to keep peasants and other workers in line. The Church's intellectual hegemony made the use of naked repression unnecessary except for periodic revolts from the subaltern people. The project of modernism featured the rise of the bourgeoisie, the growing influence of rationalist philosophers, the centralization of monarchies, and the attempted replacement of divine law with rational secular explanations of human beings and their world.[2]

The modernist victory involved repression of the old. Modernism continued its coercion of all that it considered irrational, atavistic, and chaotic. Because the modernist, rational way of doing things was new and had not yet become customary, intellectual and armed coercion was visited on those who sought to preserve the old, and now discredited, ways.

This coercion necessitated central power, e.g., the rise of the absolutist monarchies, and a rationalist philosophy that could provide right answers as surely as the old religious system was reputed to have done. The new source of certainty was reason, not revealed religion, and this new source was used as a justification against all that was considered irrational—even though this resulted in punishing all too many for their living unavoidably complex human lives. Orderliness and homogeneity became the hallmarks of modernity. The early modernists were confronted with the need to keep order after the weakening of a divine-based social order. Reason became the arbiter of last resort in disagreements, those who spoke for official reason had the most power.

A good example of reason used as an arbiter is the work of the English utilitarian philosopher Jeremy Bentham (1748–1832). Bentham provided a model of society called panopticon which featured a reason-led society in which all of its people (inmates) were allegedly happy because they were saved from chaos, knew what to do, and did not have to wrestle with the most difficult moral questions. A panopticon is a place where all parts of the interior are visible from a single point. Customary coercion was replaced by a rational version. The work of the French philosopher Michel Foucault brought rationalist modernist forms of surveillance, discipline, and punishment to the critical attention of a wide readership; the modernist schools have been part of his indictment. As Bauman wrote, "if the civilizing formula of modernity called for the surrendering of at least a part of the agent's freedom in exchange for the promise of security drawn from (assumed) moral and (potential) social certainty, postmodernity proclaims all restrictions on freedom illegal, at the same time doing away with [hoped-for] social certainty. . . . Existential insecurity—ontological contingency of being—is the result."[3]

I have argued that postmodernist thought has many things in common with existentialism. One big difference is that a form of capitalism supports the former, one where the market has replaced an unprecedented number of other ways human beings have historically interacted.[4] Although Bauman et al. have recognized the importance of capitalism as part of modernism, they have often equated the coercive side of modernist Enlightenment with the whole rationalist project instead of with capitalism's leading role in this distortion. The relationships between capitalism and modernist rationality are complex and beyond the scope of this analysis. Bauman must know that various counterdiscourses *within* modernist Enlightenment, e.g., Deweyan science, the Frankfurt philosophers critique of positivism, romantic emphasis on feelings, and existentialists, all sought to counter the coercive potential of the modernist project. These internal counterdiscourses were critical of capitalism's role in modernism. Bauman's awareness of capitalism's importance does not go far enough; what he calls modernist domination may be better understood as capitalist distortions of what was best in modernist Enlightenment. Bauman and many postmodernist thinkers see morality—as the right and need to choose—as the highest human good, they celebrate the increase of choices in the postcommunist era, even though the choices may not be exercised within authentically neutral or free contexts.

My response is that what one gets to choose or even think of as subject to choice is powerfully influenced by socioeconomic, political, cultural, and educational factors. The conversion of much of our world into consumer markets makes choice all too vulnerable to being reduced to consumer choices. As the central state, religious institutions, and modernist/repressive school all lost power in terms of keeping order against real or imagined chaos, our fears have been privatized. As the second millennium comes to an end, the system is, in fact, actually existing capitalism. Its regime appears to make all choices and dreams possible within the endless variety (for those who can afford it or have a credit line) of the worldwide malls. Many postmodernist celebrants do not adequately address the lack of freedom and stern repression built into late capitalism. Postmodernist oppression is of a "lite" form for those who live in the rich countries, people in the "underdeveloped" places recognize the ungloved iron fist of the capitalist system and its governmental gendarmes.

Italian philosopher Gianni Vattimo argued that postmodernism provides the opportunity to reject, once and for all, the quest for certainty. He insisted that we guard against the temptation to "bring Zeus back in." This is a noble thought. Vattimo and Bauman believe the need to choose among meaningful alternatives is central to our humanity, the former should face up to what choice might mean in these postmodernist times.

> Postmodernity means many things to . . . different people. It may mean: a life that looks suspiciously like a TV serial, and a docudrama that ignores your worry about setting apart fantasy from what "really happened." It means license to do whatever one may fancy and . . . not to take anything you do or the others do too seriously. It means the speed with which things change and the pace with which moods succeed each other so that they have no time to ossify into things. It means attention drawn in all directions at once so that it cannot stop on anything for long and nothing gets a close look. . . . It means the exhilarating freedom to pursue anything and the mind-boggling uncertainty as to what is worth pursuing and in the name of what one should pursue.[5]

Bauman's passage could be strengthened by studying the following writers' analyses which seek to further explain the reasons for that which is portrayed above. The following theorists place their analyses of postmodernism in a historical, materialist context as well as viewing what we call postmodernity as a cultural manifestation of capitalist development: Marshall Berman, *All That Is Solid Melts Into Air* (1982); David Harvey, *The Condition of Postmodernity* (1980); and Fredric Jameson's work, especially, *Postmodernism, or, The Cultural Logic of Late Capitalism* (1991). Peter McLaren explained how it is necessary for educational theorists to take Marx and the persistence of capitalist power seriously in order to understand what the dangers and opportunities are in the postmodernist condition. The dangers are that capitalist power is organizing the world to profit criterion and market outcomes without safety nets for all of us. The possibilities are dependent on our using Marxist and other concrete analyses aimed at overcoming human suffering due to injustice and oppression during these tumultuous times.

Bauman explains how modernism needed disciplined workers and soldiers, postmodernism features consumers and "sensation gatherers"; although it should be obvious to him that the world's poor still work very hard. In Bauman's view, modernism insisted on conformity as a social regulator; postmodernism (and consumer capitalism as its main characteristic) depends on personal feelings of inadequacy—as against the commercial advertisements and standards about how one should be—to discipline people to the logic of the new order. "The supervisor, the foreman, the teacher all vanish—together with their powers to coerce. . . . It is now a matter of self-supervising . . . and self-teaching. . . . Everyone is now free, but . . . inside their own prison, the prison s/he freely builds. So it is no longer the task to conform that spurs the individual's life efforts, but . . . the *effort to stay fit*. . . . The effort not to grow rusty, stale . . . not to get stuck at any stopover for too long . . . [and/or] keep wide the 'space' in which to move."[6] The privatized, consumer body provides postmodernist culture with its unprecedented energy. Postmodernist society is characterized by compulsive restlessness, chaos, a parade of fads, "new and improved" commodities, ephemeral desires and products, absurd doses of viewer violence, and short-lived hopes. Affluent America is the unhappy model and world leader of this kind of society.

Postmodernist thought like Vattimo's raises questions about the teachers' role and the curriculum that seems to suggest that they can only join in the complex intellectual quest for comparative meaning. The scientific method should no longer be distorted into a new quest for certainty. Vattimo suggested a postmodernist mode of inquiry that resembles interpretations of art. In his view, the work of art does not correspond to a stable foundational essence; the artistic work displays its own fragile subjective character by the fact that it is open to varied interpretations. "Since the work of art is subject to the disruptive effects of the passage of time . . . and expresses no . . . permanent knowledge . . . aesthetic consciousness offers us a weak experience of truth . . . and that serves as a model for all areas of postmodern thought."[7] I believe that Bauman would concur.

Suggested Task for the Reader

If Bauman's portrayal of the postmodernist condition (see footnote number five) is even somewhat accurate and indicative of how many people act in response to these condition(s), what kinds of problems would contemporary educators face? Keep in mind that historically, schooling has meant the postponement of immediate gratification as the student concentrates on and makes sense out of both concrete and abstract problems.

Given Bauman's portrayal, how might educators employ a version of Vattimo's "weak thought" (artistic hermeneutics) in order to deal effectively—or at least adequately—with the postmodernist condition of shifting sands rather than terra firma?

The postmodern condition presents us with numerous problems and possibilities. One hopeful possibility is that the modernist insistence on dichotomizing, "Othering," and rank-ordering will be minimized and humanized. The modernist dichotomies of reason and emotion, civilized and barbarian, etc. led to many injustices—ones that continue to plague us. Serious multiculturists have considered many facets of postmodernist thought helpful to their project. Progressive educators have always championed the formerly excluded Other, and it is to postmodernism's credit that it possesses resources with which to further include those who have been excluded. Section III of chapter fourteen in my book, *A Radical Democratic Critique of Capitalist Education,* provides an evaluation of postmodernist strengths and weaknesses in reference to the kind of democratic education promoted in that book. The reader of this book could find it relevant as well.

A serious problem presented by the postmodernist era is the threat of a new totalizing power, namely global capitalism, with support from its various national governments, friendly international organizations such as the World Bank and the International Monetary Fund, and to some extent the United Nations. The colonization of everyday life by capitalist advertising and consumer addiction penetrates into the very minds and bodies of participating persons in ways that we may mistakenly believe that capitalism is uncoercive and the epitome of freedom. The current deregulation in overall capitalist structures results in the recurrence of the war of all against all of which Thomas Hobbes (1588–1679), Niccolo Machiavelli (1469–1527), and other great modernists warned. Marx was also a great modernist thinker who warned specifically that capitalism meant the threat to turn all that is solid into air as well as turn people into commodities.

The seemingly free society of consumer choice (for some) may present serious obstacles for solidaristic responses to injustices. Postmodern societies are privatized and then reorganized under the banner of capitalist production and consumption activities. It is not easy to see how personal and small group grievances relate to the organizational whole; political action is usually organized around single issues. Single-issue politics and abbreviated attention spans are complementary in a society of spectacle and characterized by the compression of time and space as a result of fast travel and instant electronic communications. Bauman is poignantly on target when he writes: "In a shifting, drifting world—what possible benefit can an individual derive from joining forces with other pieces of flotsam?"[8] Bauman's hope is that we can construct an unprecedented society that offers unity and the public good, but with diversity considered as an integral and inalienable part of the polity, economy, culture, and educational sites. He spoke of reforging polyphony into harmony, without succumbing to cacophony.

In keeping with discussing the postmodern condition in piecemeal fashion we shall consider the work of the French philosopher, Jacques Derrida. Mark Lilla argued:

> In the United States . . . his ideas, which were first introduced into literary criticism, now circulate in the . . . environment of academic postmodernism, which is a loosely structured constellation of . . . [short-lived] disciplines like cultural studies, feminist studies, gay and lesbian studies, and post-colonial theory. Academic postmodernism is . . . syncretic, which makes it difficult to understand or even describe. It borrows notions . . . from the (translated) works of Derrida, Michel Foucault, Gilles Deleuze, Jean Francois Lyotard, Jean Baudrillard, Julia Kristeva—and, as if that were not enough, also seeks inspiration from Walter Benjamin, Theodor Adorno, and other figures from the Frankfurt School. Given the impossibility of imposing any logical order on ideas as dissimilar as these, postmodernism is long on attitude and short on argument. What appears to hold it together is the conviction that promoting these very different thinkers some-

how contributes to a shared emancipatory political end, which remains . . . ill-defined.[9]

Lilla focused on Derrida's "deconstructionist," philosophical practice which seeks to call everything about Western philosophy into question. Derrida zeroes in on philosophical claims that assert language reflects and/or could be in a one to one relationship with reason. He argued that philosophers should not assume that they can construct hierarchies of rationality because they allegedly do not have the tools to do so. Philosophers can only uncover aporias and paradoxes embedded in reality. Philosophy can no longer claim to be logocentric! Logos means word, language, reason, and principle and served as the backbone of Western philosophical assumptions. Derrida argued that all texts are full of ambiguities and can be interpreted in various ways. There can never be a definitive reading of complex life; Western philosophers who claimed to be able to rationally describe universals and essences must be discredited. Derrida sought to "rob" Western philosophy of its self-confidence. This self-confidence and claims of certainty have led, according to Derrida, to the construction of oppressive regimes—ones that were effective beyond just intellectual oppression.

The deconstructionist practices of Derrida and other postmodernist thinkers certainly have precedent in Western philosophy: the German philosopher, Friedrich Nietzsche (1844–1900) immediately comes to mind. Lilla's worry about where Derrida's deconstruction takes us has been aimed at Nietzsche by countless other critics. The worry is that the "neutralization of all standards of judgement—Logical, scientific, aesthetic, moral, political . . . leaves these fields open to the winds of force and caprice."[10] The tendency of postmodernist philosophers to debunk the historical notion of human beings as rational, volitional, somewhat autonomous actors who are capable of recognizing what is better and more ethical than their opposites—as well as acting on these judgments—leaves human responsibility itself deconstructed. But Derrida provides a slightly open door from this dangerous subjectivity and relativism.

According to Lilla's reading of Derrida, the latter argued that the concept of justice is resilient enough to "withstand the acids of deconstruction." Derrida understood that the notion of justice is different from actual specific laws. Philosophers have wrestled with the problem of trying to distinguish the two, as well as seeking epistemological grounding for their alleged understandings of justice. Lilla accused Derrida of turning to "revelation" in order to grasp the idea of perfect justice—one that is immune to specific deconstruction. The deconstructionist Derrida has posited the existence of a universal. Lilla claimed that Derrida described the idea of justice as one existing beyond all experience. In order to protect his favorite idea, justice, he must rely on a timeless universal of the kind Western philosophers have constructed and relied on over the centuries. Relying on a *deus ex machina*, Derrida attempted to place his ideal of justice beyond the give-and-take of argument.

I do not claim that postmodernist thinkers have sought to return to absolutes in order to protect their most important notions. However, the postmodernists' view of the world as overwhelmingly complex and un-clear—a place where causality is difficult or impossible to establish—is it-self an aggressive and unprovable belief. This unprovable belief is taken for granted by many postmodernist philosophers. All too many postmodernist thinkers fail to question, criticize, and deconstruct the ideas and facts of global capitalism and its agents' attempts to organize the whole world and all of its people under the rule of the so-called free market. As some postmodernists continue to bash rationalism, the En-lightenment project, and various reds because of their claim that it is impossible to see things holistically or prove complex causality, capitalist totalism marches forward. Lilla claimed that, at best, Derrida is a kind of left democrat who values difference and toleration. Derrida thinks that his goals can be achieved by helping to destroy the language and concepts the West has used to think of democracy and tolerance. Derrida sees both justice and democracy as undefinable; they are treated as articles of irrational faith.

Calvin Schrag analyzed postmodernist attacks on various forms of philosophical reason. He argues that in spite of the damage done there remain various resources of rationality. Schrag contrasts Habermas's critical defense of modernism and reason with Rorty's proposed rupture with modernist discourse.[11] Rorty argued that we are now at the "end of phi-losophy" as it has been constructed within the mainstream of Western thought. Although Schrag views postmodernist thought and philosophy as unsystematic and rather inchoate, he ascertained that its central project has been to challenge, deconstruct, and even dismiss Western concepts of rationality. Postmodernists attempt to say farewell to reason, or to the despised logos (alleged rational principles that govern the universe). Ac-cording to Paul Feyerabend's *Farewell to Reason* (1987), "the multiple appeals to reason in the history of . . . [philosophy] have pretty much run aground. Reason . . . is [allegedly] bereft of any universal content; [and] is unable to dissociate itself from the particularities of human con-cerns and interests."[12] We must face up to the partiality and subjectivity of our supposed knowledge. Not only is the "reality out there" difficult and/or impossible to understand, but as knowing subjects we are not epistemologically up to the task of understanding phenomena objectively.

Schrag viewed postmodernism as favoring "dissensus" over consensus, being radically antifoundationalist with regard to our knowledge claims, suspicious of theory and explanatory grand narratives, and distrustful of any and all claims for reason's universality. He saw similarities between postmodernism's "assemblage of attitudes and discursive practices" and those of existentialist philosophy. He is correct to point out that existentialists portrayed human beings as able to cope with chaos; whereas, the postmodernist subject/actor is as fragmented as the reality s/he faces. Both postmodernist and existentialist pessimism can be studied in reference to the capitalist crises during the emergence of these two discourses.

In Schrag's analysis of postmodernism's threat to the ideas of reason itself, he speaks to the "despised logos" first. Postmodernist philosophers attack the claim by Western philosophy that through rational knowledge we can understand a rational cosmos. The postmodernists are not the first philosophers to call into question the claim that our minds are rational to the extent that they participate in and understand the rational structure of the cosmos. Schrag argued that this form of rationalism can be abandoned without also throwing out different concepts of rationalism that prevent us from sliding down the slippery slope of radical relativism and/or nihilism. I agree with Schrag's insistence that we are not reduced to Lyotard's proposed substitute of a politics of opinion for that of reason.

Schrag's second subsection is called "undecidability and indeterminacy." The quest for certainty and "unimpeachable foundations of knowledge" has been challenged before the late-twentieth century. Rorty was a harsh critic of epistemological claims that seek to convince us that the knower has gone to rock-bottom foundational depth. The claims that the human mind mirrors reality outside of us have rightfully been criticized by postmodernists et al. Postmodernists sought to discredit Western philosophy's claim that the trained mind is able to occupy a secure Archimedean site from which to gaze objectively and accurately at reality that is outside of us. Rorty, postmodernists, and others claim our representations and portrayals of complex, indeterminate phenomena are inaccurate. Postmodernists do not view human beings as capable of understanding and/or accurately deciding on what is real and/or good in a world that is characterized by indeterminacy, i.e., basic causality and effective prediction are not possible. There are no widely accepted public criteria with which to adjudicate our differences and fights. There is neither a generalizable outside nor inside point of reference; postmodernists claim there are only context-dependent "regimens" of speech, writing, meaning, and reference—ones that are not translatable into the others' way of expression and evaluation. Consensus is not usually achieved from the conditions described; hermeneutical anarchy and relativism are the likely outcomes. The consequences for education—and specifically schooling—are profound to say the least. Schrag asked if postmodernist claims of undecidability and indeterminacy doom every effort to understand and make evaluations that are warranted in their assertibility.

Schrag's third subsection is entitled, "plurality and paralogy" (the latter means drawing conclusions that do not follow logically from given assumptions). The ancient Greeks thought seriously about the one and the many, unity and plurality, permanence, and change; although these facts are not always acknowledged by "re-inventors of the wheel." Postmodernists are also very interested in pluralism within social and natural phenomena. Schrag articulated well what this subsection is about: "The recognition and accentuation of plurality and multiplicity as indelible marks of . . . our social practices again brings to the fore the consequences of pluralism for the resources of rationality. Concerns about whether . . . reason may still have something to offer become intensified when we observe the slide of plurality and multiplicity into heterogeneity and then into paralogy."[13] Schrag argued, against postmodernists, that thinking and talking about how to describe and understand phenomena are possible in spite of the difficulties inherent to the tasks and the real differences among us as inquirers. Drawing on Habermas, Schrag wrote that in spite of language and inquiry being subject to many different usages they still have the resources to allow common discourse. Thought has the potential power to take us beyond the local and situational. You will recognize my agreement with Habermas and Schrag.

Schrag's fourth subsection, "power and desire," confront him and us with serious challenges to the possibility of reason that is used to help us decide which are the more effective, better, and, yes, more moral actions to take in order to solve the problems we face. The rational resources for critique and emancipation are called into question by Foucault's identification of knowledge with power as well as Gilles Deleuze's assertion that what we think and what we do are powerfully affected by what we desire. These two challenges threaten to make rational claims into mere justifications for the exercise of power and desire. Foucault and Deleuze did not invent these claims and challenges by themselves. The work of Nietzsche and Freud immediately come to mind.

If knowledge consists of the body of thought and discourses that is used by the rich and powerful, then objectivity, let alone universality, and transhistorical applicability of ideas seem impossible. "If the logos itself is an effect of power . . . if the rational subject is a product rather than an agent of power, then the . . . [possibility] of autonomy and emancipation is deprived of any significant function."[14] If human beings are primarily "desiring machines," as Deleuze claimed, then our desiring may well be fulfilled, albeit meretriciously, in the malls of consumer capitalism. If reason cannot balance our most profound and sometimes dangerous desires, it seems obvious that the progressive Western project championed in this book is unlikely to be achieved. It is no secret that desire and power are often intertwined; however, we have endeavored to *educate* desire! This education refers to the need for us to strengthen our perception of how the past, present, and future can be seen as a pedagogical experience through which our understanding of liberatory, historical struggles is enhanced. It also refers to the opportunity for comprehending better the things that were, and can be justified as desirable.

Schrag's fifth and last subsection is called "a new historicism." Modernist thinkers believed they could describe and explain the past as it actually occurred. This allowed historians to make claims of causality and determination between past and present. The present was thus susceptible to progressive human intervention. Modern optimists saw the future as a time and place that would be changed for the better through the powers of reason, science, technology, and industry. This knowable, linear, causally interconnected concept of history, already under attack in the nineteenth century, has been more fiercely attacked by postmodernist philosophers. Nietzsche, Kierkegaard, the existentialists, et al. insisted that there are no guarantees that causality and determination can be uncovered. There is no empirical or even rational evidence that history is moving progressively, let alone toward the hoped-for perfectibility of what Carl Becker called, the "heavenly city of the eighteenth-century philosophers." Postmodernists see time in radically different ways than did most modernist progressives. Schrag points out, "along with . . . Nietzsche and . . . existentialism there were other voices [including those of some pragmatists] raised against the postulates of historicism. . . . But in addition to the various philosophical rejoinders to historicism there were certain socioeconomic-political events of the . . . twentieth century that issued their own indictments of inevitable progress . . . and perfectibility."[15] Schrag's passage demonstrates once again a central theme of this book, that there were earlier counterarguments within Western thought that criticized many of the things that postmodernists dislike. Some postmodernist critique is of a straw person who does not represent accurately what is being denounced. The historical arguments against dominant ideas and practices in the modernist West must be taken into account by postmodernist critics of this dynamic tradition.

While we must be sobered by the events of the bloody twentieth century, the postmodernists may not be correct in insisting that we are condemned forever to be buffeted by forces we are incapable of understanding or controlling. The postmodernists need not have the last word with regard to portraying the future as completely unknowable and immune to human interventionist efforts.[16] Postmodernists charge that nonjustifiably optimistic progressives and democrats view the future as naive utopians and idealists. The present offered by postmodernists is one of fleeting images, experiences, and the inability to commit to any long-term progressive and/or somewhat altruistic projects. People who have nothing to remember, a chaotic present, as well as no hope for the future except perhaps more purchases in the global consumer market are unlikely candidates to help construct the projects championed in this book. Schrag takes postmodernist challenges seriously as do I. Schrag and I are convinced that our condition is not so bleak; there are resources of rationality available to us. It is to Schrag's idea of "transversal rationality" that I turn my attention.

Schrag's transversal rationality project sought to locate a modified version of reason within the human condition itself. He placed this human-centered rationality within our discursive (verbal and written arguments) and other social practices that are embedded in the concreteness of everyday life. These practices are guided by rational guides thus rescuing reasoning and praxis from earlier versions of universal concepts of reason that were located beyond the human experience, or mysteriously in us, e.g., the soul. Transversal rationality is intended to rescue reason from a postmodernist fragmentary dispersion in which we are swamped by the play of multiple differences, and rampant pluralisms. Schrag steered a course between the Scylla of ahistorical "out there" universal reason, and the Charybdis of lawless, subjective particularism. The democratic logic of Schrag's insertion of human-constructed reason into everyday life is driven by the need for inclusive participation in the construction project. Like the Frankfurt School philosophers' insertion of reason and "universals" into the human experience and Dewey's concept of the democratized use of the scientific method in order to solve social problems, Schrag spoke of inexactness and lack of smooth linearity with regard to his transversal rationality project. "Hence, it will require attentiveness to certain juttings and joggings, byways and detours. . . . The principal signposts [are] . . . *critique, articulation,* and *disclosure* that mark the terrain of reason."[17] Schrag was convinced that we could all become rationally critical and articulate as we attempt to solve problems; such tactics will in some cases help disclose to us the more effective and better things to do. Notice there are no guarantees for us in transversal rationality.

Schrag used transversality as a concept/metaphor. Transverse means a line intersecting two or more lines, or lying across, and it is used to help us picture the knitted-together complexities of everyday life. *Critiques, articulation,* and *disclosure* lay "athwart," or crosswise our lived experiences and are deeply embedded in our worlds. It is from this complex transversality that imperfect human reason provides tools geared to an understanding of shared experiences, evaluation, and liberatory collective action. You will be served well by reading Schrag's chapter six, "Transversal Rationality," in order to better understand this complex concept and project. I ask for the reader's patience and concentration as I present two important passages from Schrag's chapter six. He argued that the "binding rationality" of critique, articulation, and disclosure is not universal (applicable everywhere and in all cases) but transversal. They make possible the shared understanding and solidaristic action, which are different from consensus derived from universally valid claims. "This shared understanding and solidarity is the achievement of hard struggle for communication across the spectrum of varying forms of life, attentive to the play of similarity within difference and the play of difference with similarity."[18] One more key passage will help us understand the subtlety of Schrag's work.

> The dynamics of the transversal logos, in its extending over and lying across the multiplicity of social practices and conventions, make it possible for us to visit different times and places without either requiring a panoptic standpoint outside of history or having recourse to . . . [only] local narratives. Understanding and communication across variegated forms of life are achieved not via an appeal to an overarching or undergirding universal . . . but rather through the hard struggle of a transversal communicative praxis that stays with . . . the historical without being bound to . . . localized conventions. . . . Socio-historical critique may indeed remain *context-dependent*, but this does not preclude an assessment . . . or indeed overturn of different localized contexts [which may be unjust]. . . . Every context-dependency is situated within a wider context-interdependency.[19]

Schrag argued as I do that in the absence of certainty and universally just signposts to direct our behavior, we must not fall prey to the most destructive practices of moral relativism and/or nihilism. We must use our considerable intelligences and abilities to evaluate from among many choices in order to do what is *better* for *more* people rather than being paralyzed because of the realization that it is impossible to know and do *the best* as we rely on secular tools of inquiry.

Suggested Task for the Reader

This work features a series of arguments which claim that secular, philosophical certainty cannot be achieved. There have been human-constructed "resources of rationality" from the time of the classical Greeks, through democratic Marxism, Dewey and the progressives, some existentialists, Freire and various spiritualists, et al. that provide compasses which can assist us as we make complex choices within the concreteness of everyday life. Considering the arguments made throughout this book, how would a citizen-worker and an educator deal with the postmodernist thinkers' claim that we face interpretive/hermeneutical anarchy and relativism at best and a Hobbesian war of all against all at the worst due to the discrediting of Western philosophy's claims to reason as possible guidelines for thought and action?

II

Richard Rorty argued that we are at the "end of philosophy." Although he claimed he is not a postmodernist, we shall briefly consider his work because his essay "Trotsky and the Wild Orchids" explains effectively some contemporary philosophers' desire and necessity to get beyond the modernist philosophical and political projects. After presenting some of Rorty's central arguments from his essay, I will point out what is dangerous about them in reference to the theses of this book. The postmodernist condition (or current cultural manifestations of global capitalist developments) must be taken seriously and studied thoroughly. The postmodernist philosophers, including Rorty, do not have a monopoly on necessary inquiry.

Consider Rorty's essay title. The reference is to the Russian revolutionary leader, Leon Trotsky (1879–1940), and Rorty uses Trotsky as a focal point for his youthful admiration of socialism and/or democratic Marxism. In addition to young Rorty's political commitments, which were also held by his family, he had aesthetic interests as well: wild orchids, where they grew, their Latin names, etc. How was Rorty to make compatible his esoteric interest in "socially useless flowers" with his sociopolitical resolve to help people overcome unjust capitalism? How was he to construct an intellectual and aesthetic framework which could "hold reality, and justice in a single vision"? He became a student of philosophy in order to "get to the top of Plato's 'divided line'—the place 'beyond hypothesis.'"

After struggling to accomplish a single unified vision and studying Plato and other idealist philosophers, Rorty turned to Dewey and American pragmatism. "I gradually decided that the whole idea of holding reality and justice in a single vision had been a mistake—that a pursuit of such a vision had been precisely what led Plato astray. . . . I decided that only religion—only a non-argumentative faith . . . could do the trick. . . . So I decided to try to write a book about what intellectual life would be like if one could manage [like Dewey] to give up the platonic attempt to hold reality and justice in a single vision."[20] Rorty criticized those who demand that what matters most to them should be embraced also by others. My equivalence of Rorty's love for orchids may seem weird or idiosyncratic to others—as well as to Rorty. He insisted that although people have "obligations" to overthrowing tyrants, feeding the hungry, etc., one should not try to bully others into accepting our social priorities or our version of orchids. Rorty goes further and claims that: There are no universals or deities out there that mandate our doing good works. There is no cosmic order that allows us to fit what we like and think is right into a single vision—one that others should embrace. He declares his solidarity to an interpretation of Dewey.

> Dewey thought, as I now do, that there was nothing bigger, more permanent and more reliable, behind our sense of moral obligation to those in pain than a certain contingent historical phenomenon—the gradual spread of the sense that the pain of others matters, regardless of whether they are of the same family, tribe, religion, nation, or intelligence as oneself. This idea, Dewey thought, cannot be shown to be true by science, or religion, or philosophy—at least if "shown to be true" means "capable of being made evident to anyone, regardless of background." It can be made evident only to people for whom it is not too late to acculturate into our own particular, late-blooming historically contingent form of life.[21]

Rorty, and even Dewey, might think differently if they were subject to the most cruel forms of oppression—ones that did not allow waiting for those comparatively well off to get their contingent individual moralities into gear in order to help those who suffer more, or most.[22] Rorty's version of Deweyan pragmatism floats on "wobbly pivots"; objectivity can never be more than constructing as much intersubjective agreement as possible. He denied that he was a "cultural relativist"—as this term is pejoratively used—he asserted that "our moral view" is much better than those held by Nazis and other bullies. This leaves Rorty on ground that is not firm, in part because to those who do not subscribe to his "our" position, his claims of superiority may sound self-centered and hollow.

Carlin Romano argued that "Rorty often gives the impression that any attempt to persuade beyond simply standing up and reciting one's story or screening one's film or offering fresh vocabulary smacks of surrender to old-fashioned realism."[23] Pragmatists and postmodernists have sought to discredit philosophical realism because of its dependence on a putative world of objective phenomena that human intelligence can know and grasp accurately. Michael Albert argued that Rorty sought to discredit realists and others who believe that our thoughts, perceptions, and portrayals grasp, represent, and reflect objective reality because they allegedly are among those who merely "spectate," i.e., remain inactive as spectators of what is out there. Albert countered Rorty by insisting that many—if not most—activists and reformers operate from a quasirealist view of the world. If there are no stories/interpretations that are more accurate or better than others, it is difficult to choose between the historical accounts offered by the radical historian Howard Zinn or former secretary of state Henry Kissinger!

Albert supports Rorty's belief that the United States "'cannot contain castes and classes, because the kind of self-respect which is needed for free participation in democratic deliberation is incompatible with such social divisions.'"[24] Rorty claimed however that we must focus only on piecemeal reform. Albert countered with: The difference between a reformer and revolutionary is that the former seeks to achieve reforms as ends in themselves; whereas revolutionaries see reform as necessary but insufficient achievements with regard to changing society's defining institutions. Overcoming caste and/or class injustices require revolutionary action, built upon meaningful reforms. Albert laid bare Rorty's limitations as a social philosopher in the following passage. Rorty "leaves us with only two activist options. . . . We can fight for changes that benefit folks now, with no broader 'foundationalist' [structural] aims. . . . Or we can fight for instant transformation of all defining structures, acting as though we sit on a perch outside history from where we need pay no attention to immediate needs and desires of suffering people."[25] I maintain throughout this book that the alternatives Rorty seems to offer have been criticized and overcome by social philosophers from Marx to Freire and educators like Kathleen Weiler.

Suggested Task for the Reader

If educators were to accept the logic of Albert's position about the relationship between reform and revolution, how would they negotiate the need to go beyond mere reform when considering the obstacles and resistance one would encounter? Provide examples of how certain educational reforms could become revolutionary were the former to occur often enough, on a broad front, and pushed to their maximum potential. Be as specific as possible.

Rorty shows his lack of confidence in ordinary people's abilities and potentials in his insistence that we are not able to think, let alone act, to get beyond capitalism and the limited democracies of the United States and other rich industrialized countries. He does not think we can do without the kinds of bureaucrats and entrepreneurs (capitalists) who run our societies. Albert, Marx, Gramsci, Dewey, Freire, Cornel West, Angela Davis, and I believe that ordinary people can and have learned how to run complicated processes and institutions as they become participatory democrats who are educated progressively through their constructive labor. Albert and Dewey both claim that we are "expert" at recognizing our own needs and desires; the knowledge required to participate sensibly is not so esoteric as to be beyond our reach.

It is Rorty's belief that we cannot think beyond capitalism that puts him at odds with one of the central theses of this book, capitalism and authentic democracy are incompatible. As Albert argued, how does Rorty know that it is "unimaginable" that people can picture a viable noncapitalist socioeconomic system? There are many people in the world who suffer much more, and more directly, from the attempt by global capitalism's totalistic attempt to render everyone and everything to market logic, allocations, and outcomes who are more motivated and perhaps capable of imagining something better than does Richard Rorty—considering his relatively privileged location in the New World Order. Rorty argued that we must get over hoping for a successor to Marxist theory, "'a general theory of oppression which will provide a fulcrum that lets us topple racial, economic, and gender injustice simultaneously.' For me [Michael Albert], quite the opposite holds. While struggling with realities, we shall have to develop ways of thinking about the world that combine concerns about racial, economic, political, and gender injustice to replace the underlying causes of each with institutions we prefer in their place."[26]

The postmodernist critique of philosophy and educational philosophy has been analyzed by Tony Johnson. His critical analysis also focused on Rorty. In keeping with the policy of allowing the reader to have access to the various cited authors' actual words, the following is offered as a representative sample of Johnson's critique of Rorty's postmodernist position.

History has shown us that oppression and exploitation have often occurred in the name of the collective, but are communities necessarily oppressive and constraining? In opting for procedural guarantees to ensure that the voices of the others will be heard, Rorty . . . [demonstrates his] fear of the tyranny of the community. The desire for the "other" to be heard is commendable, but unless it is accompanied by or includes a compelling vision of some legitimate albeit contingent and temporal, common, ground, [merely] expanding and continuing the conversation becomes a hollow process. If educators see themselves as change agents, as involved in transforming society from what is into what should be, then such an activity requires a compelling vision of what should be. Their emphasis on local and regional perspectives . . . prevent postmodernists from providing such a vision. . . . More than deconstruction is needed. . . . In focusing all their energies in combating the [alleged] fallacies of the past, postmodernists render themselves impotent in the equally significant task of recreating the present and future. For this reason . . . Rorty and other postmodernists are not, as they claim, the legitimate heirs of the pragmatic tradition created by John Dewey and others.[27]

I conclude my consideration of Rorty with the following critique—one that serves as a stepping-stone in section II for my critical analysis of postmodernist thought vis-à-vis the progressive, democratic, societal, and educational projects featured in this book. For Rorty, theory is not capable of directing human behavior let alone progressive politics. He claims that theorists are *tyrannical* in their attempts to govern practice. Rorty was reduced to relying on conversation and moderate piecemeal reform because he was convinced that human beings lack any solid ground from which to theorize deeply and broadly into human affairs. John McGowan argued:

Rorty does not want abnormal discourse to become the basis for the next normal discourse; rather, he wants abnormal discourse to function perpetually to unsettle the normal without . . . constituting new ground. . . . Rorty appears to endorse all change, anything that keeps the conversation rolling in new directions. Along with the fear of tyrannically imposed stasis, there also appears a fear of boredom. . . . Change, no matter to what or from what, earns his approval. . . . [As we know] this point of view toward change presents the basic world view of dynamic, advanced capitalism, not some oppositional challenge to it.[28]

The passage from McGowan portrays a bored tourist who has time to seek out interesting people who say and do interesting things. It speaks also to wealthy, cynical, radically chic people who can afford such a posture. With reference to schooling it suggests doing "neat" things with idiosyncratic, "gifted and talented" kids—the kinds of attitudes and activities so brilliantly exposed by Jonathon Kozol.[29]

David Purpel and Svi Shapiro argued that the postmodernist condition must be taken seriously by progressive educators, although, postmodernist thought is not uniformly supportive of the kind of education they favor. They worry that placing too much emphasis on differences among us can lead to disregarding our commonalities. Postmodernist assertions concerning the impossibility of finding any solid epistemological and/or moral ground in our world and in ourselves do not bode well for educational projects based on historical assumptions that knowledge of the world and self can serve to improve us and our physical and social worlds. Purpel and Shapiro acknowledged nevertheless that their progressive educational project must be convincing within postmodernist conditions.[30]

Purpel and Shapiro saluted postmodernist thought because of its opposition to philosophical realism's claim that we can know about complex phenomena in an objective way. Wingo defined realism as a belief in the principle of independence: the existence of a world of things and events that are not dependent on their being known. Realists believe that these phenomena are capable of being known, to some extent as they are in themselves. Moving beyond modernist realism allows us to accept the need for multiple readings, interpretations, considerations of the spiritual, embracing a sense of wonder, and acceptance of the unfinished character of our sociophysical surroundings and selves. These multiple possibilities pose threats to those whose projects depend in an important way on roughly agreed on interpretations, common ground, and the possibilities to construct solidaristic coalitions against injustices. Purpel and Shapiro believe, and/or hope, that a democratic and critical Left can and must build a superior moral vision for school and society from postmodernist uncertainties—if not chaos. One is not surprised that these authors need to logically turn to spiritual sources for their moral vision's justifications. When one abandons philosophical realism as well as viewing the epistemic subject as weak and unclear, then a step up or retreat to spiritual and/or religious justifications has been a historical strategy.

Purpel and Shapiro's educational project is explained in reaction to postmodernist problems and possibilities in the following. "Life in the United States has . . . become so painful, alienating, ethically compromised, and spiritually impoverished, that education must speak first and foremost to this human and social crisis. The crisis is pervasive and multidimensional in its effects: sometimes material, sometimes psychological and emotional, and sometimes spiritual (and often all of the above)."[31] The educational response is to construct a language, education, and politics that allows people with different needs and wants to come together—

while still respecting differences and not rank-ordering injustices and people. Out of this grim multiplicity of injustices, Purpel and Shapiro advocate education for the development of responsible, democratic, and community-oriented people. A justifiable slogan could read: the overarching moral imperative should be a compassionate, solidaristic, and participatory society. These goals lead to schooling as reconstruction. Educational Reconstructionism has not gone unopposed. Will the superior moral vision for school and society offered by Purpel and Shapiro be convincing to large segments of the student and general population?

Purpel and Shapiro's need to anchor their vision, education, and politics to something larger than their own views takes them to interesting places. They say that democracy is a necessary but insufficient part of their favored education; this is so because the goal is to heal and repair our world. The Green (or ecology) Movement shares this insistence on repair—as well as prevention. This proposed education "must touch people's spiritual and emotional lives through what have been called the feminine moral images—of wholeness, care, and responsibility. . . . The politics of radical change in these years will belong to those who can successfully articulate the postmodern—or antimodern."[32] Purpel and Shapiro associate themselves and their project with our culture's most "treasured" traditions; e.g., powerful religious texts, influential political documents, and various philosophical works. They locate themselves as heirs and participants in the historical struggle for peace, justice, love, and joy. They advise us to consider intellect, body rhythms, the soul's light, and spiritual voices. These considerations should assist us in trying to define and act upon what is good, while seeking to discern and overcome our resistance to this beneficial impulse.

It is fair to ask where this impulse to be good is grounded: in our intellect, body, soul, or spirit? This certainly takes us beyond Marx's notion of concreteness and even to a rather neoidealist position. Purpel and Shapiro concluded by positioning themselves with powerful themes from Western culture. The ones mentioned are Socrates's critical reflection: prophetic moral outrage, poetic inspiration, and the moral, religious, and sociopolitical traditions that insist on the central importance of justice, love, community, peace, and joy. They stress that hoped-for and necessary transcendence is dependent on our *willing* it. One can read this insistence on willing as a version of the kinds of volition and agency stressed in this book, yet it is possible to interpret will in a neoidealist manner. When all possibilities for solid ground and a modicum of objectivity are absent, it is not surprising that one would turn to will and transcendence.[33] Purpel and Shapiro asserted that the sacredness of life is central to their definition of democracy. This is an assertion that may not be provable to skeptics. Skeptics et al. may not think that "redemption" should be a goal of democratic liberatory education and politics. Sounding an existentialist note, Purpel and Shapiro invite us to join in the great human drama that constitutes our lives.

Our brief study of postmodernist thought with regard to social and educational considerations is concluded with an assessment that has been suggested implicitly and alluded to throughout this section. Postmodernist thought has effectively attacked foundationalism and some forms of reason. It has supported difference and marginalized people. It promises little with regard to constructing integrative democratic communities. Postmodernists have not adequately realized that their attacks on the Enlightenment and its legacy might be better directed at capitalism's tragic distortion of the progressive Enlightenment core and promise. Postmodernist attacks on the democratic Marxist project—perhaps the most effective critique and opponent of antidemocratic capitalism—does not make postmodernists reliable or effective allies for the projects and traditions championed in this book. If one views postmodernist culture as the extension of market capitalism to almost everyone and every place on earth, it is possible to understand it in reference to material and concrete realities during this capitalist period of domination, instead of as regarding this culture and history as merely a parade of ungrounded fads and occurrences.

Postmodernist thinkers argued that the current form of late, global capitalism is so large and complex—so totalistic—that it can no longer be explained. I do not agree. The educational-political challenge is to help students and others construct big-picture understandings of a very big series of seemingly unconnected pictures—a series that is not just random. Without a collective generational attempt to grasp theoretically the colossus that is capitalism, the education and society championed in this book are not likely to come to fruition. Teachers, artists, scientists, et al. must effectively learn how to represent/portray the phenomenon called capitalism so that it can be understood, opposed, and overcome—to be replaced by a moral economy, participatory democracy, social justice, respect for diversity (beyond the consumer choices characteristic of the market), and an education and society where the conditions of life allow authentic caring for one another. Perhaps the immediate task is pedagogical because any real chance of radical transformation is on hold until breakthroughs occur that will allow us to grasp once again our positioning—in class, race, and gender terms—as individual and collective actors who can and must overcome the present educational socioeconomic, and political status quos.

Once more I argue that the most important contribution made by postmodernist thinkers and practitioners to the education championed in this book has been its accentuation of *earlier forms* of respect for difference and the need for inclusion. These precursors include some multiculturalist, existentialists, and feminists. This respect for difference and inclusion has contributed to the historic progressive project to make schools more humane, relevant, and supportive for all students. In school terms, this praiseworthy project consists of "attempting to overcome oppressive teaching conditions, dehumanizing evaluation criteria, biased accountability schemes, teacher-proof standardized curricula, authoritarian administration, etc."[34] It must be stressed that emphases on difference without mention of our commonalities does not bode well for the construction of liberatory projects, as well as societies and communities in which we will need to seek out common ground and ethical compromises. The most appropriate flag for what I recommend is a mosaic, or quilt, whose distinct pieces are best understood by viewing the whole.

My evaluation of postmodernist thought (as I understand it) does not merit high marks when seen as social theory. Its contribution to helping us understand and ameliorate—if not solve—specific school problems warrants somewhat higher grades. Because schools and education are part of the larger society, analyses that are helpful to mostly intramural concerns are less relevant and/or helpful than those that attempt to address all three in a unified manner. Postmodernist thinkers' admirable insights have intellectual ancestors and contemporary counterparts who are committed to a more holistic and realizable liberatory project than they—one that is committed to transforming our schools, education *and* society.

III

The touch of green, namely recognition of the ecology movement's importance is brief. My interest in ecology—that branch of biology dealing with the relations between organisms and their environment—is as a layperson who has come to realize that the democratic project for social justice, respect for diversity, and caring leads to our relationship with the natural world. Christine Shea provided an effective bridge between postmodernist thought and ecology. She does not embrace what she calls nihilistic deconstructive postmodernism. She is sympathetic to critical poststructuralist postmodernism because it seeks to return to a human subject who is capable of ascertaining certain truths, at least for a certain community at a specific time. This form of postmodernist thought allows for resistance against oppression by those who have been marginalized. She argued that alliances can be constructed by these various groups by becoming aware of their own and other people's subjectivities and locations within contexts of oppression and possible resistance. Not everyone agrees that the poor Appalachian elderly, urban black adolescent males, Native Americans, the homeless, punk rockers, et al. who Shea writes about can achieve what she and poststructuralist postmodernists claim. Shea also writes about constructive ecological postmodernism.

The connection between some postmodernists and ecological concerns supports the logic of chapter eight. Shea argued that the ecological postmodernist paradigm follows from the late-twentieth century's crisis in ecological sustainability, one that is "unique in its range and scope, including the pollution of freshwater and marine environments; atmospheric pollution; chemical and nuclear wastes; the degradation of our croplands, forests, and grazing lands; desertification; the destruction of wilderness habitats and ecosystems; the extinction of plant and animal species; and . . . human population growth."[35] Shea's ecological, postmodernist project is built on the following commitments that serve to inform her logically related ideas for educational contexts. The first is viewing the environment as the ultimate context in which all sociopolitical and educational activities occur. Shea hopes that these activities will be progressive ones. Second, we are urged to progress beyond the "anthropocentric self," to see ourselves as part of the whole, complex ecosystems in which we live. This insistence serves to overcome the mind-body dichotomy that was discussed in chapter seven of this book. It connects with the feminist attack on gender dualisms, including the indictment that rational men can treat women and "Mother Earth" exploitatively. The third commitment is to consider nature as sacred. Shea qualifies that this sacredness is not anchored in transcendent or otherworldly guarantees but can emerge from compassionate and caring ways of relating to our natural ecosystems and cultural environments.

The fourth and last commitment is what Shea describes as "an ecological view of emancipatory pedagogical praxis." She calls for the development of "ecological intelligence" in addition to the critical intelligence supported by the critical theorists who we have encountered throughout this book. I think that it makes sense for critical theorists to strengthen their critique and praxis by taking the issues raised by ecology and Green politics seriously. Shea offers a specific curricular idea that encourages

students to inquire deeply and systematically into the "ecologically problematic" aspects of the dominant culture and society. This kind of inquiry
would surely result in a better understanding of how global capitalism has
begun to accelerate its destruction of both social and natural infrastructures on which capitalists, their agents, and all the rest of us depend.
Shea encouraged teachers to become "ecologically literate." This accomplishment is necessary in order to help students realize the importance of
ecological well-being. The many publications on ecology and education
by C.A. Bowers are worth considering in reference to Shea's commitment.

Shea thinks that metaphors are useful for understanding who we are,
what we do, and what we can become.

> The image of the classroom as a living ecological web of relationships is a favorite
> metaphor to describe the structure and functioning of the American public schools.
> This metaphor is grounded in the image of caring, sharing, and of mutual coex-
> istence; the implication here is that since we are all connected, we should all act
> cooperatively to maintain . . . our collective work environments. Here one sees
> oneself and others as part of a collective whole . . . a universal classroom, a
> part of an interconnected bioregionally based web of community alliances and
> obligations. At its core . . . the living ecological web metaphor resonates with
> the concern for the delicacy of the strands that connect us and provide us with
> sustenance—it dramatically captures the theme that we affect everything and
> everything affects us.[36]

Shea's metaphor is attractive during these times of disorganization, hyper-
individualism, selfishness, breakdown, and the seeming inability to even
conceptualize a common good—or goods. The reorganization of an increasing number of the world's population into and under global capitalism and its national and local branches is a potent threat to Shea's social
and educational, ecological, web metaphor. With regard to schools, the
web metaphor and its realization could serve to counter top-down authoritarian administrative relationships with teachers, students, and parents. If any idea and movement have a reasonable potential to unite masses
of people against the depredations caused by Frankensteinian capitalism,
they are ecological green ones.

Why is it necessary to go through postmodernist assumptions in order
to arrive at the ecologically sensitive and holistically oriented education
Shea advocates? Her response follows: "Still marginal to mainstream academic conversations, this . . . revisionary constructive postmodernism
is struggling to move us beyond the modern world's drive toward greater
mechanization economism, nationalism, consumerism, militarism, rug-
ged individualism, and patriarchy."[37]

Although the work of Murray Bookchin (the political philosopher and activist) on ecology is representative of the anarchist tradition, his anti-capitalism also gives him a touch of red—as it has been portrayed in chapter three. His focus on individual and small-group self-reliance, the local and regional, along with his deep commitment to ecological justice and survival make Bookchin compatible with some enlightened postmodernist concerns and commitments, for example, the attention to things local. His work is in keeping with feminists' attention to the local and personal. Both Bookchin and the radical feminists are also concerned with groups and totalities. Shea's constructive postmodernism is an example of analyses that is in accord with some of Bookchin's central arguments—some of which are represented in the following.

> The basic concept that humanity must dominate and exploit nature stems from the domination and exploitation of man by man. Indeed, this conception goes back earlier to a time when men began to dominate and exploit women in the patriarchal family. From that point onward, human beings were increasingly regarded as mere resources, as objects instead of subjects. The hierarchies, classes, propertied forms, and statist institutions that emerged with social domination were carried over conceptually [and actually] into humanity's relationship with nature. Nature too became increasingly regarded as a mere resource, an object, a raw material to be exploited as ruthlessly as slaves. . . . The "worldview" permeated not only the . . . [oppressors]; it became [unfortunately] the way in which slaves, serfs, industrial workers and women of all social classes began to view themselves.[38]

Bookchin continued by accusing bourgeois/capitalist societies of turning humans into objects and commodities to be exploited. Human commodities are put up for sale in various labor markets; "the natural environment is turned into a gigantic factory, the city into an immense market place; everything from a Redwood forest to a woman's body has a price. Everything is equatable in dollars-and-cents, be it a hallowed cathedral or individual honor."[39] Men and women must free themselves from commodification and domination in order to deal with the earth communally, knowledgeably, holistically, and respectfully. Bookchin warned that unless the Green Movement recognized and acted on domination in all its forms, it will fail to get at the root causes of the ecological crisis. Bookchin views ecology as critical science in a more holistic way than most other critical traditions. He claimed that ecology is also dedicated to and capable of integrative and reconstructive outcomes.

Bookchin's "social ecology" celebrates the evolutionary development of humanity as a realization of nature's potential for self-consciousness as well as this achievement's role in allowing us to exercise freedom among ourselves and in cooperation with nature. As ecologist Brian Tokar wrote: "Social ecology seeks the roots of ecological destruction in . . . capitalism and . . . [its ally] the nation-state and argues that an ecological society can emerge from forms of local political engagement that directly challenge these institutions. Social ecologists view environmental destruction as the outcome of the historical project of dominating nature."[40] Tokar informs us that social ecology seeks to construct a moral economy, a term that Bookchin borrowed from the historian E.P. Thompson when he wrote of the formation of the English working class during the early days of capitalist development in that country. In moral economies socioeconomic relationships are characterized by recognition of our interdependence and the need for caring among people and vis-à-vis the natural environment. Tokar's and Bookchin's politics seek to create a radically different kind of society, one that emerges from Green initiatives and models of living that can serve as the "cell-tissue" of a better, more just, way of living with one another on planet Earth. Their politics are based on the belief that ordinary people can and must take matters into their own hands rather than trusting unaccountable experts.

Drawing from the work of Ivan Illich, the author of *Deschooling Society* (1970) and *Tools for Conviviality* (1973), Tokar wrote that our ability to challenge the cult of the expert is crucial to resisting this "disabling" culture as well as to overcoming it and replacing it through reconstruction. The many writings by Paul Goodman serve to enlighten the reader in regard to the traditions—anarchism among them—which insist on people being responsibly autonomous, skilled, and committed to caring for the various infrastructures on which we depend for our very survival. Goodman wrote that "a priceless advantage of . . . decentralization is that it engages more minds. . . . An important hope in decentralizing science is to develop knowledgeable citizens, and provide . . . a public better able to protect itself. . . . The safety of the environment is too important to be left to scientists, even ecologists."[41] These traditions are not to be confused with the present Rightist insistence that governments be weakened so that (although not admitted by its spokespersons) capitalism can dominate our society even more than it does now.

John Foster argued that we are experiencing a deterioration of the Earth's health even though the United Nations' 1972 meeting in Stockholm officially launched the global environmental movement. He charged that "this failure to prevent the increased destruction of the biosphere can be traced mainly to the logic [and reality] of profit-oriented economic expansion in a finite world."[42] Because of the overall failure to prevent environmental destruction, Foster called for a more radical response. He granted the need for national governmental regulations of corporations as well as these governments' own more responsible policies on the environment. The richest and most industrialized countries feature both capitalist economies and formally democratic governments which does not bode well for Foster's hope for appropriate regulatory action. The capitalist imperative on formally democratic governments has generally been more powerful than the broadly conceived imperative of democracy—including one with a touch of green. Foster realizes that any successful Green politics will have to meet head on with the capitalist commodity society and its drive to cover the entire earth with goods—many of which are not biodegradable. The capitalist commodity economy and culture will have to be overcome by a moral economy based on environmental necessities. People in concrete settings who are theoretically empowered and collectively organized are necessary in order to overcome the capitalist system that blocks both socioeconomic and environmental justice. Foster gave us the following optimistic idea from the economic anthropologist Karl Polanyi's book, *The Great Transformation* (1941), in which he explained that capitalism has been characterized from the beginning by a double movement. On the one hand there was the untenable idea that an unfettered market was self-regulating, the best guarantee of the common good. On the other hand, the imposition of the market gave rise to the principle *of social protection* that sought to protect people and nature. This principle was enacted by those most harmfully affected by market outcomes. We are all affected by the destruction of our environment, natural and social, so it seems logical to think—or hope—that collective actions can be organized in answer to a "Rally Around the Environment" call. This is what the Greens, in support of the Earth (a.k.a. the "Big Blue Marble"), are attempting. Foster sounds both a green and red note as he suggests that because our historical relationships to nature are mainly through work, this activity must be conducted by workers who are democratically organized and motivated by criteria that are helpful to our own and the environment's well-being. This Marxist and Deweyan focus on the importance of labor as transformative human activity was translated into Green politics by Foster in order to ensure a broadly inclusive and collective stewardship of Earth, as opposed to the current exploitation of our planet and most of its people by capitalism's short-term gain policies.[43]

Suggested Task for the Reader
Many postmodernist thinkers have argued that because of our weaknesses as knowers (epistemic subjects) and the complexity and opaqueness of

individual/social affairs and natural phenomena, it is difficult if not impossible to construct a liberatory project. Postmodernists are especially pessimistic concerning the possibility of constructing such a project that is broad-based as well as anchored to some assurance that it is justifiable and better than other actions—or worth doing at all.

React to the above statement as a person who takes the ecological crisis seriously and wants to do something individually and/or collectively about it. What kinds of philosophical arguments would you use in order to construct a springboard for theory and praxis? How would you, as a teacher, use these arguments and assumptions as a basis for developing an appropriate philosophy of education, curriculum, and pedagogy that could help students understand the ecological crisis and the possibilities for effective Green politics?

Conclusion

I argued in the first section of this chapter that because postmodernist thought is, by definition, non- or antisystematic, the reader was advised to critically study postmodernist ideas and conditions in her/his developing intellectual frame of reference—especially in terms of philosophy. The second section featured assessments of postmodernist thought with reference to its usefulness and/or nonsupport of the theses championed in this book. The work of Rorty was featured in these assessments. Section III provided ideas and politics that characterize the ecology or Green Movement. The last section is offered as an invitation to further consider the significance and importance of the Green project—one which represents a logical extension of the book's major theses.

I argued that "back to" postmodernism is important in reference to a time before the advent of classical Greek philosophy when it was considered impossible to achieve accurate or even plausible holistic and systematic portrayals of social and natural phenomena. Although postmodernists have justifiably denounced the quest for certainty; their apparent refusal to attempt to construct comparatively accurate meanings and imperfect distinctions among better or worse does not serve our democratic socioeconomic, political, and educational project well. The postmodernist acknowledgement of and respect for differences are helpful to teachers in their relations and attitudes toward students. These attributes are also supportive of the pluribus factors in a society, but postmodernist thought is not helpful to the unum factor that is also necessary for a good society. The inability or refusal to acknowledge and support human commonalities makes postmodernist ideas less than helpful with regard to constructing liberatory, solidaristic, collective movements.

I also argued that postmodernist celebration of difference, without attempting to explain various structures in which differences and spontaneity occur, serves the capitalist project characterized by endless "new and improved" products from which to choose. Postmodernist writings suggest that no one is in charge during the last years of the twentieth century and that there is little or no possibility for linear analyses that help us understand various causalities and connections. This suggestion is odd when one can see massive daily evidence of global capitalism's attempts and success in organizing most people and places into adjuncts of the market and its sometimes-punishing outcomes.

Green thinkers and activists are convinced that their most dangerous foe is a market/corporate economy, backed by central governments, that is driven by shortsighted bottom line profit criteria. Responsible educators must allow their students to inquire into the relationships between the historic assaults on both the natural and social infrastructures on which we all depend for life itself.

Notes

1   Jean-François Lyotard's *The Postmodern Condition: A Report on Knowledge* (Minneapolis: University of Minnesota Press, 1984) is famous for interpreting postmodernism in a context of epistemological crisis.

2   For a brilliant analysis of the modernist philosophical project, see Carl L. Becker, *The Heavenly City of the Eighteenth-Century Philosophers* (New Haven: Yale University Press, 1932), passim.

3   Zygmunt Bauman, *Intimations of Postmodernity* (London and New York: Routledge, 1992), xxiv.

4   Richard A. Brosio, *A Radical Democratic Critique of Capitalist Education* (New York: Peter Lang Publishing, Inc., 1994), chapter thirteen, "The Challenge of Postmodernism to The Enlightenment and Its Democratic Legacy," and fourteen, "Postmodernism as the Cultural Skin of Late Capitalism."

5   Bauman, *Intimations of Postmodernity*, vii.

6   Zygmunt Bauman, *Life in Fragments: Essays in Postmodern Morality* (Oxford, U.K. & Cambridge, U.S.A.: Blackwell, 1995), 113–14.

7   Jon R. Snyder, "Translator's Introduction," in *The End of Modernity: Nihilism and Hermeneutics in Postmodern Culture,* Gianni Vattimo (Baltimore: The Johns Hopkins University Press, 1985), xl.

8   Bauman, *Life In Fragments*, 271.

9   Mark Lilla, "The Politics of Jacques Derrida," *The New York Review of Books* 45, no. 11 (June 25, 1998): 36. For another helpful presentation of philosophers considered by some to be postmodernists, see Kenneth Baynes, James Bohman, and Thomas McCarthy, eds., *After Philosophy: End or Transformation?* (Cambridge, Mass.: The M.I.T. Press, 1987). This work includes Derrida, Lyotard, Foucault, Richard Rorty, et al.

10 Lilla, "The Politics of Jacques Derrida," 38.

11 See, Maurizio Passerin d'Entrèves and Seyla Benhabib, eds., *Habermas and the Unfinished Project of Modernity* (Cambridge, Mass.: The M.I.T. Press, 1996) for contextual analyses of Habermas's attempt to save the best parts of the projects of the Enlightenment and modernity. The debate between Habermas and postmodernists is addressed.

12 Calvin O. Schrag, *The Resources of Rationality: A Response to the Postmodernist Challenge* (Bloomington, Ind.: Indiana University Press, 1992), 8.

13 Ibid., 32.

14 Ibid., 37.

15 Ibid., 45.

16 For a rich source of argumentation against the postmodernist attack on history, see the journal, *Monthly Review* 47, no. 3 (July-August 1995). The journal is dedicated to "In Defense of History." The first article is Ellen Meiksins Wood's "What Is The 'Postmodern' Agenda? An Introduction," pp. 1–12. The following provides the flavor of Wood's analysis. "Current theories of postmodernity . . . deny the very existence of . . . structural connections and the . . . possibility of 'causal analysis.' Structures and causes have been replaced by fragments and contingencies. There is [for postmodernists] no such thing as a social system (e.g., the capitalist system). . . . There are only many different kinds of power, oppression, identity, and 'discourse.' Not only do we have to reject the old 'grand narratives' like Enlightenment concepts of progress we have to give up any idea of intelligible historical process and causality, and with it, evidently, any idea of 'making history' " p. 5–6.

17 Schrag, *Resources of Rationality*, 10.

18 Ibid., 169.

19 Ibid., 173. For a roughly similar argument, see Richard A. Brosio, "Essay Review of Abraham Edel, *Relating Humanities and Social Thought: Science, Ideology and Value, Vol. 4*, in *Educational Studies* 22, no. 4 (Winter 1991)): 473–79. As has been argued throughout this book, the absence of certainty does not mean that everything is as good as anything else; this is because human-constructed guidelines can and have served to guard against the worst forms of subjectivism and moral relativity. The postmodernists would do well to take this historical accomplishment seriously.

20 Richard Rorty, "Trotsky and the Wild Orchids," in *Wild Orchids and Trotsky*, Mark Edmundson, ed. (New York: Penguin Books, 1993), 41–42.

21 Ibid., 43–44.

22 I argued in *A Radical Democratic Critique of Capitalist Education*, chapter twelve, that Dewey and American liberals have had the luxury to be "disinterested" in the plight of those who are sometimes referred to as the "wretched of the earth" because of the comparative freedom and economic well-being they enjoyed. My critique of Rorty's neo-pragmatist and postmodernist positions are found in chapter thirteen, section IV.

23 Carlin Romano, "Rortyism for Beginners," *The Nation* 267, no. 4 (July 27/ August 3, 1998): 30.

24 Michael Albert, "Rorty the Politico," *Z Magazine* 11, no. 10 (October, 1998): 50.

25 Ibid.

26 Ibid., 54.

27 Tony W. Johnson, *Discipleship or Pilgrimage? The Educator's Quest for Philosophy* (Albany: State University of New York Press, 1995), 92–93. There is a subsection, "Richard Rorty: You Are No John Dewey" on page 112. Supportive arguments for Johnson's position are provided by Landon E. Beyer and Daniel P. Liston, "Discourse or Moral Action? A Critique of Postmodernism," *Educational Theory* 42, no. 4 (Fall 1992): 371–93.

28 John McGowan, *Postmodernism and Its Critics* (Ithaca and London: Cornell University Press, 1991), 197. For an essay review of McGowan's book, see Richard A. Brosio, "Capitalism's Emerging World Order: The Continuing Need For Theory And Brave Action By Citizen-Educators," *Educational Theory* 43, no. 4 (Fall 1993): 467–82,

29 See Kozol's *Free Schools* (New York: Bantam Books, 1972), especially the section called, "Free Schools as a Term Meaning Too Many Different Things," and his, *The Night Is Dark and I Am Far From Home* (Boston: Houghton Mifflin Company, 1975), especially chapter nine, "Impotence."

30 David E. Purpel and Svi Shapiro, *Beyond Liberation and Excellence: Reconstructing the Public Discourse on Education* (Westport, Conn.: Bergin & Garvey, 1995), 125–27. For a sober, trenchant, and critical analysis of a politics that celebrates difference to the detriment and exclusion of a common progressive politics, see Todd Gitlin, *The Twilight of Common Dreams* (New York: Henry Holt and Company, Inc., 1995), chapter eight "The Fate of the Commons."

31 David E. Purpel and Svi Shapiro, "Beyond Liberation and Excellence: A Discourse for Education as Transformation," in *Critical Social Issues in American Education: Transformation in a Postmodernist World,* 2nd ed., Purpel and Shapiro, eds. (Mahwah, N.J.: Lawrence Erlbaum Associates, Publishers, 1998), 384.

32 Ibid., 388.

33 See my essay review of Joel Spring's *Wheels in the Head: Educational Philosophies of Authority, Freedom, and Culture from Socrates to Paulo Freire, Educational Studies* 27, no. 3 (Fall 1996): 272–282.

34 Brosio, *A Radical Democratic Critique of Capitalist Education*, 618.

35 Christine M. Shea, "Critical and Constructive Postmodernism: The Transformative Power of Holistic Education," in *Critical Social Issues in American Education*, 2nd ed., 345.

36 Ibid., 349–50.

37 Ibid., 352.

38 Murray Bookchin, *Ecology And Revolutionary Thought* (New York: Times Change Press, 1970), 52.

39 Ibid., 53.

40   Brian Tokar, *Earth For Sale* (Boston: South End Press, 1997), 188. Tokar's book examines critically—fortified by many factual details—the role of corporate greed and disregard for human and natural environments. He is unsparing in his indictment of the U.S. federal and state governments for their collaboration with corporate treatment of the environment(s) as things to be exploited for profit. Tokar calls for grassroots democratic, Green environmental movements whose activists recognize the connections among ecological and socioeconomic injustices. He is especially critical of mainstream Green politics that he claims has been coopted by the power elites in capitalist "democracies."

41   Paul Goodman, *New Reformation: Notes of a Neolithic Conservative* (New York: Random House, 1970), 19.

42   John Bellamy Foster, *The Vulnerable Planet: A Short Economic History of the Environment* (New York: Monthly Review Press, 1994), 129. For an informative issue devoted to "Hungry Profit, Agriculture, Food, and Ecology," see *Monthly Review* 50, no. 3 (July/August 1998). The introductory article to this volume includes Foster as author; he also served as one of the editors. The various contributors seek to lay bare the commodification of agriculture and of nature itself by agents of capitalism in their historic drive for profits.

43   Foster, *The Vulnerable Planet,* 142. The issue of *Radical History*, 74 (Spring 1999) is devoted to "Environmental Politics and Human Geographies"; Pamela Haag and Heidi E. Tinsman, editors, have written the following in the "Editors' Introduction." Although some Marxists have called environmentalism a "full belly politics," i.e., affordable only to those who are relatively well off; in fact, "struggles for social justice and equality are increasingly occurring through the motif of . . . environmental politics. The articles in this issue . . . explain the historical origins of 'ecology' in the early twentieth century, the intermeshed components of 'environmental racism,' and . . . 'the invention . . . of an "environmentalist" political identity.' These articles focus on the human impact of environmental change, emphasizing the extent to which geography and beliefs about the environment often shape social relations and inequities, if not . . . the very idea of the 'self'" p. 1.

Afterword

I have argued throughout these pages that the struggles for human dignity, democracy, social justice, respect for diversity, and more caring communities can be found in the philosophical, religious, socioeconomic, political, cultural, and educational history of the West. The classical Greeks viewed individuals, society, the natural world, and the heavens from the perspectives afforded by the city-state, the maritime tradition of Athens, and perhaps Mount Olympus. The ancient Hebrews' views of social and natural phenomena and spiritual things were grounded in the arid land of their region, their historical period, and a special sense of identity. Medieval Christians saw bits and pieces of their various European homes mainly from the perspectives of agricultural workers and believers whose religious leaders sought to convince them that a better afterlife was possible—if one followed religious rules. The "various Reds" in our story were grounded in the grim realities of the capitalist-driven Industrial Revolution. They too attempted to construct a liberatory theory and praxis beyond the oppression and fatigue of everyday life. This project was supposed to be realized in their lifetime—or at least that of their children's or grandchildren's.

The Deweyan progressive project was based on the liberal assumption that intelligence, especially as it was translated into action via the scientific method, could eventually empower people to use democratic government to tame capitalism and ameliorate its worst consequences—including the reproductionist schools. This project of incremental reform was based on the positionalities, perspectives, and potentials of all people who lived in the polity and socioeconomic system. Its most solid ground was the alleged power of the scientific method—broadly conceived—to solve individual, social, and educational problems. The existentialists' vantage point is from inside the thickness, complexity, and opaqueness of everyday life. This positionality does not allow big pictures. This opaqueness makes even imperfect daily survival tactics-strategy difficult to construct and enact. For Camus and some other existentialists, human contingency necessitates individual *and* solidaristic action to make it through the day in a world believed not to have been made with us in mind.

Freire's liberatory project is grounded in the materiality and discursive representations of this concreteness in "peripheral" countries such as his native Brazil. Like Marx and Dewey, Freire thinks that human intelligence and action can liberate people from various oppressions from which they suffer. His workers and students are not only the Caucasian urban dweller but also the black, brown, and indigenous people who live in rural areas and do agricultural and extractive (e.g., lumbering and mining) labor. Freirean men and women attempt to see a series of big—or bigger— pictures in order to understand and overcome class, race, and gender injustices. The spiritualists of liberation theology (and to some extent philosophy) believe that positionalities and views can also include spiritual knowledge and faith, in critical and concrete ways.

The women and African Americans discussed in the analyses of identity politics are also situated in the thickness and concreteness of everyday life. The struggles to understand their positionalities are dependent on accurate and enabling discursive portrayals. Women and African Americans have, with the help of certain allies, tried to expand the struggle for human dignity by being attentive to lived conditions *and* the part played by representations of women and blacks by Western philosophers and other keepers of the Western canons. The African-American thinkers and activists who are portrayed in chapter seven have embraced spiritual sources for their intellectual and political struggles; however, they have embraced these from *within* the discourses of "horizontal" and/or social gospel religiosity. Certain forms of "vertical," otherworldly religiosity have been criticized as either naive and/or oblivious to various forms of earthly injustices.

Postmodernists share with other thinkers in this book the sense of limitations we suffer from while attempting to make sense of our world, society, and ourselves. Postmodernists are harsh in their criticisms of thinkers, discourses, and activists who claim to be able to understand the human condition well enough in order to overcome the various oppressions and injustices in it. They condemn what they call grand narratives and all claims of epistemological certainty—especially those that promise accurate theory for liberatory action.

The Greens may have realized the significance of an unprecedented perspective. In the summer of 1969 astronauts walked on the moon; we were able to see our Earth from the perspective of what was previously called the heavens. The Big Blue Marble, as the Earth was dubbed by some after seeing the pictures of it from space, features the life-giving blue of large bodies of water. The fragility of the blue, green, and brown of our Earth home helped Greens make the case that we must care for our home and its people. The fragility of this home in a universe that appears, at this time, to be very different from Earth allows Greens to stress our commonalities even among our differences; they remind us that we are integral parts of complex ecological systems. This is neither a god's-eye view, nor one from Mount Olympus; however, it may help us rise above the pessimism of views confined so thoroughly within real or imagined opaqueness.

Perhaps those of you who are interested in the further construction of education for democratic empowerment, social justice, respect for diversity, and the possibilities for a more "caring" school and society will use some or all of the points of view described herein. You are invited to imagine and theorize about the kinds of education-schooling that are best; why they are not presently the most commonly followed practices in our schools; and what *must be done* intramurally and societally to make what is desired common practice.

Glossary

Absolutism: the principle or exercise of complete and unrestricted governmental power.

A *fortiori*: for a still stronger reason.

A *priori*: from a general law to a particular instance; valid independently of observation; existing in the mind prior to and independent of experience.

Agency: a term used to indicate human volition; ability to act in order to change society and nature.

Alienation: the effect by modernist, industrialized, urbanized, bureaucratic, and capitalist societies to make strangers of its people.

Anarchism: a political theory based on the belief that persons through voluntary cooperation and free associations can act democratically for the common good without a coercive central government and an unjust political economy.

Andro: prefix meaning male.

Anthropomorphic: ascribing human form and characteristics to nonhuman things.

Archimedean: from the ancient Greek mathematician, physicist, and inventor Archimedes who discovered specific principles of gravity, solid ground, and the lever; philosophers et al. use the term in reference to epistemological solid ground from which to alter the world via political leverage.

Bourgeois: from a French term, urban dwellers, businesspeople, and capitalists; social middle class.

Canon: a body of rules, principles, or standards accepted as universally binding in a field of study or art.

Capitalist: a person who is one of the owners and directors of large economic firms, e.g., corporations; those who direct the command heights of the economic system.

Class state: a central government that uses its power and resources mainly to support the capitalist system rather than workers.

Commodify: a term to describe and denounce capitalism's attempt to turn human beings into things, something of use value alone.

Constructivisim: a term to describe how human knowers help construct the very things they study and hope to understand; the knower is changed through the process of study and description.

Correspondence: refers to a school system's corresponding to, or mirroring, the dominant economic system.

Critical Theory: is a name for neo-Marxist thought, developed initially by the Frankfurt School, that continues, modifies, and updates Marx's claim that societies are characterized by social-class subordination and domination, specifically workers being subordinate to capitalism; Critical Theorists have come to better understand the relationships among class, race, and gender advantages and disadvantages with regard to school and society.

Cultural capital: the many advantages wealthy students have with regard to being able to do well in school.

Deus ex machina: literally, god from a machine, but refers to any artificial device used to resolve a difficult plot.

Dialectic: the practice of argumentation and analysis used in order to ascertain the relationships and causalities between the materialistic/concrete work *base* in reference to the social, political, cultural, educational practices which occur in the related *superstructure*.

Educational essentialism: a series of school practices organized around a belief that there are certain universally essential or basic things to be taught; teaching is seen as the transmission of knowledge to students who are thought to be empty vessels needing to be filled.

Empirical: inquiry guided by experimentation in reference to tangible, concrete experience; proof depends on observable consequences from the application of theory/hypothesis to the problem faced.

The Enlightenment: a philosophical movement in the eighteenth century, especially in France, based on the belief that reason should be the guide to construct better and more just institutions, including schools.

Epistemic subject: the human being as knower in reference to the conditions necessary for becoming knowledgeable.

Fallibilism: a term used to indicate certain forms of inquiry and knowing that allow the person to recognize and possibly correct errors within these forms.

False consciousness: the failure of people to recognize their relationship to power that is based on social class, race, and gender memberships; this tendency is reputed to be caused by the powers that be who obscure reasons for, and causes of, domination and subordination.

Foundationalism: a form of inquiry which claims that complex phenomena can be explained by reference to base/foundational reality and causality.

Hegemony: a term used in reference to dominant forces having loose control over subordinate people through the use of ideas, education, and propaganda which seeks to convince the governed that it is in their own best interests and that the socioeconomic, political, and educational order is natural and unchangeable.

Hermeneutic: the practice of interpreting complex writings, cultures, and societies.

Heuristic: the practice of encouraging a person to learn, discover, and understand through experimentation and problem-solving; often contrasted to didactic pedagogy characterized by the instructor telling students what they are supposed to know and be responsible for.

Historicism: a theory that history is determined by laws and recognizable causalities rather than by chance and individual human actions alone; also a search for patterns of historical evaluation that could help explain and predict historical occurrences.

Ideology: a body of ideas, doctrines, or myths that serves to guide people and social movements.

Inerrant: lack of error, especially in reference to the belief that the Bible is free from error.

Leitmotif: a recurring theme associated with particular ideas throughout a work of art or scholarship.

Metaphysics: the branch of philosophy that claims to study first principles, i.e., the nature of being (ontology); it is sometimes considered too theoretical/abstract/nonempirical to be useful for solving concrete human and natural problems.

Motivationalism: an exercise in using ideas and claims that are intended to motivate human action, although the ideas may not be fully warranted in terms of their relationship to concrete realities.

Mutatis mutandis: the necessary changes having been made.

Obscurantism: a term used by rationalists to denounce religionists who attempted to keep the masses of people unenlightened.

Operationalism: the reduction of reason and the scientific method to narrow instrumentalism, i.e., making reason and science captives to goals established from outside and by others.

Perennial philosophy: a school of thought that claims knowledge of universals and perennial truths as it draws from both Judeo-Christian beliefs and classical Greek philosophy, especially Aristotle's work; this philosophy provides scaffolding for perennialist education that relies on the so-called great books as subject matter.

Post-Kantian idealism: philosophical development in the nineteenth century that sought to overcome Kant's dichotomy in which "real" and "ideal" were separate; the attempt by Hegel, Marx, et al. to bridge the divide between the logic and reality of the capitalist economy and a hoped-for just polity.

Poststructuralism: a movement against the structuralist argument that conscious behavior was largely predetermined by impersonal objective structures; a school of thought that attempts to emphasize the contextuality and relativity of all structures rather than structuralist claims of universality; in educational terms it refers to the conviction that experience and knowledge must be filtered through language and culture, i.e., nothing can be known of experience per se because language mediates between the world and our knowledge of it.

Praxis: the translation of theory into practice.

Pro Bono Publico: for the public good.

Progressivism: a movement beginning in late-nineteenth-century America that sought to analyze and reform the worst excesses of the Industrial Revolution under capitalist direction; a call for governmental action to protect people from living by market outcomes alone; the introduction of pragmatist philosophical ideas into education, especially as a result of Dewey's work specifically aimed at school reform.

Proletariat: Marx's term for the industrial workers of late-nineteenth century who labored under the factory regime of capitalism and had only their labor to offer.

Prometheus unbound: a nineteenth-century poetic drama by Percy Shelley which can be best understood in relation to the fifth-century B.C. tragedy by the Greek playwright Aeschylus; Prometheus is punished by the gods for stealing fire from them and bringing it to human beings, then he is liberated by Hercules.

Reproduction: the process by which societal power relations and rank order are attempted to be reproduced, in part, by using schools to maintain a family's privileged position through successive generations.

Scholasticism: the system of theological and philosophical teachings that predominated in Medieval Europe based on the authority of the Catholic Church and of Aristotelian thought as it was made somewhat safe for Catholic Europe.

Skinnerian: based on the American behaviorist, psychologist B.F. Skinner who argued that free will is an illusion because we are powerfully influenced, if not determined, by our environments.

Social Darwinism: the mistaken belief that the theory of evolution explains and justifies a socioeconomic system characterized by savage competition.

Stratification: the vertical, hierarchical division of society according to social class, caste, etc.

Subaltern: a term meaning those without power, wealth, privilege, and access in society; Gramsci and other Marxists referred to workers and others who were exploited by capitalism as subaltern.

Teleology: the philosophical belief that final causes exist that move history toward these ends.

Terra firma: solid ground.

Thomism: the theological and philosophical system of the medieval thinker Thomas Aquinas; the attempted synthesis of Catholic religious faith and Greek reason in its Aristotelian form; see Aquinas's work called *Summa Theologica*.

Index

Studies in the Postmodern Theory of Education

General Editors
Joe L. Kincheloe & Shirley R. Steinberg

Counterpoints publishes the most compelling and imaginative books being written in education today. Grounded on the theoretical advances in criticalism, feminism, and postmodernism in the last two decades of the twentieth century, Counterpoints engages the meaning of these innovations in various forms of educational expression. Committed to the proposition that theoretical literature should be accessible to a variety of audiences, the series insists that its authors avoid esoteric and jargonistic languages that transform educational scholarship into an elite discourse for the initiated. Scholarly work matters only to the degree it affects consciousness and practice at multiple sites. Counterpoints' editorial policy is based on these principles and the ability of scholars to break new ground, to open new conversations, to go where educators have never gone before.

For additional information about this series or for the submission of manuscripts, please contact:

        Joe L. Kincheloe & Shirley R. Steinberg
        637 West Foster Avenue
        State College, PA 16801

To order other books in this series, please contact our Customer Service Department:

        (800) 770-LANG (within the U.S.)
        (212) 647-7706 (outside the U.S.)
        (212) 647-7707 FAX

Or browse online by series:

        www.peterlang.com